AMERICAN WOMEN
images and realities

AMERICAN WOMEN
Images and Realities

Advisory Editors
ANNETTE K. BAXTER
LEON STEIN

A Note About This Volume

Sociologist Ernest R. Groves (1878-1946) was one of the first academicians to inaugurate functional courses dealing with practical issues of applied psychology. He provided the first—and still one of the best—attempts to portray American women in a variety of historical and regional settings. The result is a series of studies depicting the changing status of women in a male-dominated society. In each case the focus is on the cultural environments which demanded compulsory accommodation by women.

THE AMERICAN WOMAN

The Feminine Side of A Masculine Civilization

BY

Ernest R. Groves

ARNO PRESS
A New York Times Company
New York • 1972

HQ
1410
.G73
1972

Reprint Edition 1972 by Arno Press Inc.

Copyright © 1942, 1944 by Emerson Books, Inc.
Reprinted by permission of Gladys H. Groves

Reprinted from a copy in The Newark Public Library

American Women: Images and Realities
ISBN for complete set: 0-405-04445-3
See last pages of this volume for titles.

Manufactured in the United States of America

- - - - - - - - - - - -

Library of Congress Cataloging in Publication Data

Groves, Ernest Rutherford, 1878-1946.
  The American woman.

   (American women: images and realities)
   Bibliography: p.
   1. Women in the United States. 2. Woman--Social
and moral questions. I. Title. II. Series.
HQ1410.G73 1972   301.41'2'0973   72-2605
ISBN 0-405-04460-7

THE
AMERICAN WOMAN

THE
AMERICAN WOMAN

The Feminine Side of A Masculine Civilization

BY

Ernest R. Groves

Author of
Preparation for Marriage, Understanding Yourself,
etc., etc.

Revised and Enlarged Edition

EMERSON BOOKS, INC.

New York: 1944

COPYRIGHT, 1942, 1944, BY
EMERSON BOOKS, INC.

REVISED AND ENLARGED EDITION

PRINTED IN THE UNITED STATES OF AMERICA
BY THE VAIL-BALLOU PRESS, INC., BINGHAMTON, N. Y.

To
Catherine Groves Peele
*And all Other American Young Women
Who with Quiet Confidence
Welcome the Testing of Modern Life*

CONTENTS

	Page
Preface	1

Chapter

I	The Cultural Background of the American Woman	5
II	The Colonial Woman	39
III	The Frontier Woman	74
IV	The Woman of the North from the Revolution to the Civil War	105
V	The Woman of the South from the Revolution to the Civil War	137
VI	The Woman of the Middle West and the Great Plains	167
VII	Woman, North and South, During and After the Civil War	201
VIII	Woman's Political and Social Advance	246
IX	Woman's Industrial and Educational Advance	288
X	The American Woman in the Twentieth Century	325
XI	The American Woman and Her Changing Status	367
XII	Near Equality with Men	401
Footnotes		425
Index		439

PREFACE

The purpose of this second edition of *The American Woman* is to bring the discussion up to date. Its writing has been a pleasure. The author's experience in writing a book is something like that of the mother who brings forth a child. There is always a background of personal relationships that does not necessarily show itself in the contents. The writing of *The American Woman* brought me more birth pains than any of my other books because of an excessive concentration on the project. This reveals how interesting I found the undertaking.

This book traces woman's advance in status in a setting of masculine dominance. It does not aim to catalogue noted women who frequently found their distinction in ways conventionally possessed by men but rather to follow the general movement that brought the average woman closer to the privileges and resources of men. Woman, if rated by the scant attention she gets in American historical writing, is the forgotten sex. This relative neglect cannot be explained by her insignificance nor can it be ascribed chiefly to the partisanship of male interpreters, although the small place given to women in our historical literature shows more clearly than anything else could how sweeping in American culture has been the superiority of the male.

While woman's functions as worker, wife, and mother have been valued, her distinctive reactions to life have often not been welcomed outside the home since, alien to the masculine scheme of things, they threatened invasion of man's prerogatives. The omission of women from American chronicles is an indictment of the civilization itself, evidence of an unbalanced appraisal of events and values, a lack of appreciation of the conserving attitudes characteristic of women from their socially assigned activities and biologically rooted interests.

PREFACE

As the American drama of life proceeds, woman gains a more prominent rôle, particularly when the stage is given a western setting. The influences that bring this about flow in two related currents. One represents an increasing encroachment upon the special privileges of men, led by aggressive, ambitious, and gifted women leaders. The other is the ongoing of more massive social changes, the momentum of a material and intellectual progress that is affecting both men and women and making their equality more natural.

This general record of the social development of American women, necessarily limited in its purpose, brings out the need of more detailed, searching discussions of specific features of her evolution. W. T. Woody, in his *History of Women's Education in the United States,* has given us one such discussion. *The History of Woman Suffrage,* edited by Susan B. Anthony and Ida Husted Harper, provides material for another which needs only, in order to gain definitive authority, the addition of our present social insight.

Many acknowledgments should be made. First of all, the Institute for Research in Social Science has made available over a period of years valuable assistance and facilities both for gathering the material of the book and for completing the manuscript. I wish especially to thank the following who in one way or another have helped me in the preparation of this book: Howard W. Odum, Director of the Institute for Research in Social Science, for encouragement and for his reading of Chapter Seven; Robert B. House, Dean of the University of North Carolina, and W. T. Couch of the University of North Carolina Press, also for reading Chapter Seven. All three of these colleagues have given me helpful suggestions but they are in no degree responsible for the content of the chapter. Ralph V. Harlow, Professor of History at the University of Syracuse, generously read the entire manuscript, and although I profited from his scholarship, he must not be regarded as having any responsibility for what I have written.

In addition I desire to record my appreciation of the help of the

PREFACE

following: Gladys H. Groves, my wife, for reading the first draft of the manuscript; Fred B. McCall, and Raymond W. Adams, of the faculty of the University of North Carolina, for information given; Georgia Faison of the Library Reference Department, Lucile Elliott of the Law Library, and Katharine Jocher of the Institute for Research in Social Science, for indispensable coöperation. I wish also to acknowledge the courtesies of Warren G. Wheeler of the Massachusetts Historical Society, Boston; Mary C. Venn, reference librarian at Oberlin College; Walter B. Briggs, acting librarian at Harvard University; Alice Lyman, librarian at the State Library of Wyoming; Estella Wolf, reference librarian at Indiana University, Harvie Branscomb, librarian at Duke University; and the editors of the *Ladies' Home Journal*.

Although credit is given in the footnotes, I also make a general recognition of my indebtedness to authors and publishers who have permitted the quotations of copyrighted material that appear in the book.

I particularly wish to acknowledge the care with which Ruth Sparks Ferriss of the staff of the Institute for Research in Social Science prepared the manuscript of the second edition for the printer.

ERNEST R. GROVES

Chapel Hill, North Carolina

CHAPTER I

THE CULTURAL BACKGROUND OF THE AMERICAN WOMAN

THE men who crossed the Atlantic and settled what became the United States were firm and confident in their intention to make the culture with which they were familiar dominant in the new land, or, in a few instances, to bring into being a different civilization but one conceived and planned in Europe. Rarely was there any understanding of the impossibility of fulfilling their designs. It was distance and the unescapable demands for new adjustments that gradually forced upon the people the building of a culture that became more and more indigenous.

There is nothing to indicate that women were more conscious than men that their migration would mean breaking away from the *mores* of the Old World, although they may have been more troubled by the prospect of trying to work out their household responsibilities in the untried wilderness. In this clinging to European attitudes and customs, which made the new undertaking an outshoot of European civilization, the first comers differed radically from those who immigrated after the Revolution. With the exception of those coming with no thought from the first of actually settling in America, the later immigrants were attracted to the United States in part that they might break away from Europe and free themselves from its irritating or limiting circumstances. They realized that they were passing from one civilization to another. Indeed, to accomplish this often was their purpose.

The English, the Dutch, the Swedish, the Spanish, and the French colonists expected to plant the culture of the land of their birth in the New World where it would flourish and become a portion of the Old Country in the New. Only the last were able to resist successfully the pressure toward change, but even they were broken off from a living, intimate contact with the historic evolution into which they were born, and were left with the task of perpetuating the cultural slice they carried over, which in time became as unlike the civilization that developed later in the motherland as it was alien at the beginning to the American wilderness.

The yeast that was to leaven American civilization was mixed and vitalized in Europe and transported, without change, to these alien shores. The men and women who brought it here, whether birds of passage possessed by the lure of covetous expectation or by the hankering for adventure, or persons committed from religious, political, or economic motives to life in the wilderness, held tenaciously to the customs, the standards, and the philosophic outlooks upon life to which they had been accustomed on the other side. Change came, but it was unsought and, as a rule, resisted. In spite of their natural effort to hold to the old and familiar, the new environment took command and gradually forced a profound reconstruction of European ways of living. This necessary readjustment in turn led to new thinking, until soon in process along the narrow coast line of North America were the beginnings of a native culture. No part of that European importation was more resistant to the new influences than the practices and the attitudes that established the status of woman. Her position was something that was so taken for granted, such a social axiom, that it was accepted by most men and women as a finality not open to question. This firmly established convention by no means assumed the insignificance of women, for it was recognized that they were indispensable in the new settlements.

Woman was the silent sex, since in man's hands were the means of social prestige and political expression, but this does not mean that her part of the burden was light nor that her contribution was considered unimportant. It was rather that the rôle that was considered proper for her kept her away from the spotlight. A long history lay behind this fact, one so interwoven with the growth of Europe that it is now difficult to disentangle the influences that operated to fix so firmly the social status of woman. Change was bound to come here as in other features of the social experience brought over from Europe, but rather more slowly than in most, because so much had contributed to the establishment of woman's position. Moreover, many of these influences were continuing and were less worked upon by the conditions of the new environment than were other aspects of the imported civilization.

The cultural ferment that was brought over from the Old Country was neither simple nor consistent. It also was a composition into which had poured influences for thousands of years, reaching back even to the pre-European civilization of Asia. To assemble all the deposits that entered into the making of this leaven would require retracing the entire evolution of culture from the birth of civilization to the English settlements in the New World. The impossibility of so exhaustive an analysis must not conceal the fact that wherever one locates the beginning in Europe of any of the causal influences that fixed the position of women in the Old World, these choices are arbitrary, since stretching from them backward are chains of events and systems of thought that brought them into being. Moreover, if it were within one's power to trace woman's history by itself through this vast stretch of time, it also would remain a partial treatment, since the experiences of women were neither independent nor distinct but organically built into the entire life of all the people, irrespective of sex.

The life of men and the life of women cannot be severed as the skilled surgeon can separate one portion of the body from its surrounding tissue. The most that can be done in seeking to trace the various factors that have established the status of women and decided their career is to draw together the most immediate of the influences of European origin and suggest their more remote genesis, in so far as they were continuing sources of contribution affecting the life of women in the civilization of the seventeenth century. Although the task in hand requires that we gather only as much of the deposit accumulated by centuries of human experience as helps us understand the background of American women, our findings are useful in their attempted interpretation, not as they are isolated but as they are related to the entire life of the people who at any time or place contributed to the composite that made up the cultural background of the colonial settlers.

It would be an anachronistic misinterpretation of this fact to go searching through the past in the attempt to establish a conspiracy against the advancement of women. It is, of course, possible to find isolated occurrences that reveal individual or organized efforts to keep women to their allotted position, but to give these much emphasis would be to distort the cultural picture. It is the *mores* rather than persons that are responsible for the retardation of women in those cases where there clearly is discrimination. For the most part, what we find are *mores* and systems of thought, natural products of the time and place, that assign women their responsibilities and, therefore, in the analysis of the modern critic, hamper the self-expression and self-determination of one sex as compared with the other. The resistance met by ambitious and aggressive women who seek freer life is not usually born of any disposition on the part of men to keep women from going forward but rather from the reluctance to accept social changes and to make the adjustments that a new order demands.

It also leads to misunderstanding to regard these clashings between persons as necessarily due to masculine opposition. The feminine protest may be great, or even greater, and the resistance to progress may chiefly come from women. On the other hand, the stubbornness may be masculine rather than feminine. It is because of these facts that nothing could be more futile than to go searching human evolution to find evidence of an ever-present conflict between men and women. The *mores* of the past, as is still true of the *mores* of the present, have given, at least so far as social opportunity is concerned, an advantage to men in comparison with women, but rarely has there been any deliberate, organized effort on the part of men to conspire against women in order to

THE CULTURAL BACKGROUND

make them socially inferior or to keep them in a state of cultural vassalage.

Another common fallacy in interpreting woman's social status has been to think of it as something definite and consistent, a situation easily described and permitting all women to be lumped together. If this were true, it would be far easier to survey the social background of American women. Instead of being permitted to follow such a wide and well-marked-out pathway one is forced to take into account every conceivable variation, as a consequence of differences due to class, religion, and politics. Even the place of habitation has to be reckoned with. In the modern world, in spite of the closeness of people who possess highly efficient means of transportation and communication, we still find differences between city and country folk. These environmental influences were all the greater before the advent of an efficient science. As an example of this, consider how the early history of Christianity reveals the significance of the Roman highways in the spreading of the new religion. It is accepted first by the cities, and the rural centers, distant from the main arteries of travel, take it over much later than the thickly settled and easily accessible parts of the Empire. Every influence, from whatever quarter, that operates upon the culture of a people may also act upon that special part which interests us—the sphere and status of women.

For our purpose, it is necessary to draw together these conditioning elements as they relate to women's culture. For convenience, these can be classified as the more distant factors coming down from Asiatic and European origin and those more immediately represented in the habits, emotions, and systems of thought possessed by the groups of people that established permanent settlement along the Atlantic coast line.

It will be misleading merely to examine the customs and the thinking of those who came to America as permanent settlers. There are also influences of more distant origin that were acting upon these people and continued to be significant even after they were out of the European environment. The most important of these were the fundamental ideas from which flowed thinking that in no small degree established the status of woman and attempted to perpetuate it. Although these underlying systems of thought deserve to be classified as philosophy, they were for the most part brought into the life of the people through religious teachings. They were not regarded as intellectual ideas but as Christian doctrine, and thus they were enforced as moral requirements by the emotions and the convictions associated with religious faith. This fact was to prove a continuous obstacle to the men and women who sought to improve woman's status. Had these notions been regarded as mere intellectual products reflecting the past and present of intellectual leadership, there would not have arisen such an emotional barrier to woman's advancement, and resistance would have lost the fierceness that came from conceiving the *status quo* of woman's life as something established by moral principles.

The thinking that functioned through Christian dogma is so laden with the contributions of the influential philosophies from early Greek thinking down, that to retrace this evolution in its fullness would require exploring the entire cultural watershed as it gave source to all the tributaries of thought that contribute to the main current. It is this latter flow that concerns us, and we are interested in it more as it enters Christianity than as an evolution of philosophy in its strictest sense. This, however, cannot be handled as if it were something fixed, a consistent system. It also has a history of change. Occasionally it has been interpreted, especially by its critics, as a final dogma without recognition that even when there is a prevailing consistency of doctrine at a definite time and place there are nearly always variations and departures from the main teaching and that always, from time to time, there are differences of emphasis as well as considerable shifting in the authoritative doctrines carried forward by the Church. The attempt to deal with the Christian teaching of any period as a consistency explains the ease with which its critics and its advocates can radically differ while they both appeal to definite facts, historically well-established.

In spite of its originality, Christianity, as it historically expressed itself, took over certain liabilities that came out of the social circumstances of the time and the character and background of those who became followers of the new religion and that influenced its teachings and its organization. One of these elements that had appeared on the stage even before the Christian way of living came to expression was asceticism, and it was doubly rooted, for it gained support from the environment as well as from individual inclination. The word *asceticism* carries two very different suggestions, one stressing the effort through a self-conscious program of life to develop high standards of spiritual experience while the other emphasizes morbid trends such as appear in extreme form in oriental fanaticism. The defenders of Christianity conceive of the ascetic expression that so soon appeared in the new faith as essentially the first while its critics are prone to select illustrations that emphasize the second type.

However wholesome the goals of any form of spiritual discipline, there is always risk, especially in those who are unbalanced through neurotic tendencies, of the effort to keep unspotted from the world taking an unsocial or a psychopathic form. Although it must be recognized that these excesses occur in the development of Christianity, the environmental encouragement that asceticism received was of Jewish origin rather than Eastern,[1] for the type of asceticism which was characteristic of Indian Holy Men was fundamentally incompatible with the Jewish teaching of ceremonial cleanliness, with its insistence upon practical moral conduct.

There was in Palestine, at the time of the birth of Christianity, a significant ascetic group, the Essenes, who illustrated what has been described as the natural religious instinct to withdraw from the world.[2] Granting there will always be controversy as to the significance of this sect at the beginning of Christianity, there is no doubt that they influenced the new faith. Although Philo tells us that this group of Jews were given their name on account of their saintliness, the etymology of the word is doubtful.[3] He describes the Essenes as pacifists who kept away from ordinary life to escape its evils, who looked upon a reverent mind as the only true sacrifice, and regarded love of God, love of virtue, and love of man as true religion. The Essenes lived in colonies and had no private home life.[4] Josephus, however, speaks of one group of Essenes who made a trial of women for three years and married them if the union was fruitful.[5] Eusebius tells us that the Essenes did not marry because they believed that association with women weakened man's character and made his spiritual life difficult. The having of children also hindered fellowship with other men.[6] It has been suggested, however, that his statements express the misogynous opinion of the writer and are therefore misleading.[7]

It is a conservative opinion that Christianity copied many features of the organization of the Essenes and their propagandistic activity,[8] and it has been shrewdly observed that the fact that *The New Testament* is entirely silent regarding them suggests that they may have had no small influence upon Christianity at the start.[9] At least in the teaching of John the Baptist, who ushered in the new faith, we have preachings very similar to those of the Essenes, and we know that the place where the reformer held forth was in the vicinity of a community of the Essenes. Although it seems probable that there were differences in the practices of Essene communities, celibacy was usually a part of their program. It was followed as a means of preserving ceremonial purity, but even so it provided a motive for conceiving woman as a tempter of the flesh, an attitude which later appeared in the teachings of some of the Church Fathers during the formative period of Christianity. It has been suggested that the Essenes were familiar with Greek thinking, especially the doctrine of the Stoics, and that the desire for self-discipline explains their sex policy,[10] but although Stoicism emphasized the need of command over one's passion, this was never interpreted in such a way as to emphasize chastity, much less continence.[11]

THE CULTURAL BACKGROUND 13

Whatever influence the Essenes may have had upon early Christian thinking and behavior, whether little or much, their teaching shows that there was among some of the Jews at the time of Jesus an ascetic trend which frowned upon the sex appeal of women. Even so, it was certainly not related to the Eastern traditions which fixed the subordination of the oriental woman. It is not in the power of the most cautious and discerning of modern scholarship to retrace history so as to charge to the Essenes their contribution, if any, to the tendency of religious philosophy through the first centuries of Christianity to conceive of women as females rather than as persons, but at least it is clear that this unorthodox sect of the Jews illustrated a prejudice brought forth from the experience of men who in their struggle for Holiness had to wrestle with sex impulses difficult to discipline.

Later we find an asceticism, born of this experience and associated with St. Paul, that more significantly contributed to the attitude which regarded woman as inferior to man. Whatever else may have influenced the teaching of St. Paul, it is evident that two notions were back of his preachments. One was the belief in the earlier period of his missionary career that the end of the world was near at hand and that the reign of the Lord, as he conceived it, was to come about in his generation. The other was his strong feeling that women should not by unorthodox conduct become an occasion for scandal and suspicion, thereby hampering the progress of the gospel. His insistence that women should accept subordination in the family and limitation in their religious service was not only in accord with the spirit of the time but also, in the effort to win converts, good judgment.

Much of this instruction to his churches, taken as isolated passages, became powerful ammunition in the hands of those who later, in spite of the complete recasting of civilization, attempted by appealing to this religious doctrine to hold women in a social status even below that given them in the first century, but, alongside these teachings of the apostle, other words of his maintained principles antagonistic to the position he himself held. His insistence upon the intrinsic value of personality was destined, with the passing of time, to become sufficient answer to the argument of those who tried to perpetuate the time-reflecting ideas of the great apostle. The situation was similar to that resulting from Paul's recognition of the slavery that existed in his day. Christianity, as it accepted woman's social inferiority and the slave type of industry, was inconsistent with its essential insistence upon the worth of the human individual, but this discordance was not uncovered until, with the passing of centuries, conventional thought had matured sufficiently to recognize this clashing of contradictory teachings.

The various places in Paul's letters where he writes regarding the need of women's observing the proprieties and avoiding temptations now sound strange to the modern ear, and, without question, they have served through the centuries as a defense of the social and religious discrimination against women, but when they are put back in the setting that called them forth, they seem less harsh. Undoubtedly it was because of the new activities assumed by leading and aggressive women in the churches, their use of the new opportunity provided by a religious faith which gave them practical means of expressing talent, that Paul spoke words of caution. It was less to hold them back than it was to restrain them from going to such lengths as would appear unseemly and react against the reputation of the churches.

In the light of what has happened through the centuries, as we look backward, the apostle's admonitions appear arrogant and loaded with masculine prejudice, but in the light of the responsibilities that burdened the leader whose task it was securely to plant Christianity in the Gentile world, they were evidences of a prudent and constructive ecclesiastical strategy. Mischief came out of them because they were torn from the situation that evoked them, but we doubly wrong the author when we attempt to use them as finalities of Christian policy.

The modern world is nearly two thousand years away from the experiences of the great missionary. His task moreover was to wel-

THE CULTURAL BACKGROUND

come women into a religious fellowship that gave them greater freedom than that which had been familiar to him or to them, while also cautioning them not to bring suspicion of the Christian way of living into the minds of the Gentiles whom they sought to convert, by unnecessarily antagonizing social customs or by starting scandals. This may seem inconsistent in view of Paul's courage as a soldier of Jesus Christ, but it is another illustration of the strange blending of prudence and defiance often found in the reformer and religious leader. As compared to many things, these problems that concerned women doubtless appeared to Paul trivial and timely, to be handled with the regard to the social conventions to be expected of one who, as an ambassador of his faith, could be all things to all men.

Another and more fundamental element in Saint Paul's teaching has been through the centuries an obstacle to the advancement of women. Here again time has abstracted from the words of the writer something quite different from the meaning of these statements of the apostle at the time they were written. His analysis of his struggle to achieve Christian living as a conflict of flesh and spirit was destined not only to encourage morbid asceticism but to debase sex, whether expressed in marriage or illicitly outside. This acted among Christians until the modern era as a continuing shadow over marriage by making it seem a necessary sop to an inherent weakness of human nature, and thus it has encouraged the conception of woman as a female rather than a person. Whatever leaning Saint Paul may have had toward asceticism, his description of his moral conflict was too profound and characteristic to be considered in the narrow way that it was interpreted by later ecclesiastical leaders.

Aside from questions of expediency which led Paul to discourage marriage on account of his expectation during the earlier years of his missionary work that the Kingdom of God would be established in his generation by the second coming of Christ, making it imprudent for the believers to start families unless driven to marriage by sex pressure, there was recognition by him of the uncompromising clashing of the old order with the new in which religion meant complete consecration to a faith that was itself morality.[12] This he dramatized as war between flesh and spirit. This striving of antagonistic impulses became a central theme in his theology but was later forced into narrower terms, thus providing a basis for sex taboo, a low conception of marriage, and an enormous amount of morbid emotional conflict such as Jerome confesses as he writes: "Now, although in my fear of hell I had consigned myself to this prison, where I had no companions but scorpions and wild beasts, I often found myself amid bevies of girls. My face was pale and my frame chilled with fasting; yet my mind was burning with desire, and the fires of lust kept bubbling up before me when my flesh was as good as dead. Helpless, I cast myself at the feet of Jesus, I watered them with my tears, I wiped them with my hair: and then I subdued my rebellious body with weeks of abstinence."[13] A great multitude of earnest, well-meaning people from this time onward, not only during Puritanism but beyond it until the present, have been led by misconstruing St. Paul's words into a wasteful and usually futile emotional conflict which indeed deserves to be called, with distinct sex meaning, the war of the flesh against the spirit.

St. Paul's interest was less in the content of the two modes of life than in the need and joy of the complete dominance of a holy life that would set the believers apart from both the Gentile and the Jew and make them a light to a lost and corrupt generation. No one would have protested more quickly than Paul any disposition to allow the sex impulse to interfere with the enthusiastic commitment to the Christian way of living, but when we consider his teachings as a whole, it is clear that he would be equally aggressive in attacking any other interest, whatever its origin, whether covetousness or ambition or vanity, that had a hampering influence upon the believer's spiritual progress. Paul's flesh and spirit came out of his vivid contrast of his present life in Christ and his earlier career. It was dualism as far as it was a contrast of experience, ending in a complete deliverance which made it possible for him to

THE CULTURAL BACKGROUND 17

exclaim: "I am crucified with Christ: nevertheless I live; yet not I, but Christ liveth in me: and the life which I now live in the flesh I live by the faith of the Son of God, who loved me, and gave himself for me."[14] It is the oneness of affection that Paul is attempting to interpret.[15]

There were social conditions in the Roman Empire of which the churches were to be made increasingly conscious that encouraged the narrower and more literal definition of the term "flesh," Paul's symbol for the temporary and the discordant as compared with the eternal and the unity of successful Christian living. As Christianity spread and grappled daily with these social influences in the great urban centers of population, the struggle for holiness assumed more and more the coloring of a sex conflict, leading to an emphasis which naturally idealized chastity and eventually celibacy.[16] Thus the words of Paul drifted away from their original meaning. This came about all the more easily because from the beginning of his gospel Paul himself recognized a distinction between a morality for the perfect follower and a morality for the lower order which nevertheless was spiritually adequate for salvation.[17]

St. Paul certainly made trouble for women of later generations when he went beyond an insistence upon the proprieties and interpolated arguments based upon the inferiority of women, as when, for example, discussing the dressing of the hair of women, he insisted: "In like manner also, that women adorn themselves in modest apparel, with shamefacedness and sobriety; not with braided hair, or gold, or pearls, or costly array."[18]

The New Testament and the Christian literature immediately following it bear testimony, as Harnack remarks,[19] of the important part that women played in the early days of Christianity through their church activities. There can be no doubt that in the circles where the new faith came, new outlook and new momentum were given to many women, a few of whom achieved permanent recognition through the documents that have come down to us. However conservative and cautious St. Paul may have been in his counsel as to church practices and domestic adjustment, there can be no gainsaying the significance of such an outburst as: "There is neither Jew nor Greek, there is neither bond nor free, there is neither male nor female: for ye are all one in Christ Jesus."[20] As an interpreter of his gospel, he provided a fundamental support for the religious equality of men and women.

Paul is also generous in acknowledging the services of women as fellow workers for Christ. In writing to the church at Philippi he declares: "And I entreat thee also, true yokefellow, help those women which laboured with me in the gospel, with Clement also, and *with* other my fellow labourers, whose names *are* in the book of life."[21] Harnack states that Paul saluted fifteen women for their work in the churches, and eighteen men.[22] Surely no stronger tribute appears in the apostle's letters than when he writes: "I commend unto you Phoebe our sister, which is a servant of the church which is at Cenchreae: That ye receive her in the Lord, as becometh saints, and that ye assist her in whatsoever business she hath need of you: for she hath been a succourer of many, and of myself also."[23]

In view of these generous words, it is reasonable to assume that the commands of Paul that women act seemly in public grew out of his feeling that many were tempted to use unwisely the new freedom and the higher religious status that Christianity had brought them. *The New Testament* discloses that the widows in the churches had an ecclesiastical significance, and Paul feels the need also of giving them admonition.[24] In the Eastern churches there early appeared a class of women who, according to Pliny's letter to Trajan, were called deaconesses. He also described an order of female ascetics or *virgines*.[25]

When one passes out of the atmosphere of *The New Testament* into that characteristic of the later ascetic literature as produced by Jerome, Tertullian, Origen, and others, it is apparent that women have lost much of their original promise with the spread and organization of Christianity, and in spite of the increasing rôle played by the doctrine of the Holy Mother. Christianity, as an incentive

THE CULTURAL BACKGROUND

for daily conduct and a succor to human needs, came close to the life of the believers during the Middle Ages largely through the meaning that Mary, the mother of Jesus, came to have. The virgin mother symbolizes, as Christian theology dominates Europe, the sympathy and humanizing trend of the early believers. Undoubtedly the influence of the pagan cults that gathered about the female divinities intruded, or at least the new took over the functioning that had gathered about the old, but it surely misconstrues what happened to regard the Holy Mother as the successor of this other worship which emphasized reproduction and fertility.

With monotheistic severity, the Jews had successfully resisted the Eastern cults about them, but at the price of remaining a separate people. Christianity had gone forth and conquered, but, as always happens in any wholesale conversion, its success in bringing an alien people under its banner exposed it to the influences of these men and women whom it took into its faith, many of them still pagan at heart, and as a consequence a complex of dogmas and practices developed through the fusion of different and even opposite reactions to life.

There can be no doubt of the need during the Middle Ages of the human appeal brought by the worship of the Virgin Mary, but its significance as an influence lifting the status of the average woman is quite a different matter. When its importance from this angle is tested by raising the question whether women escaped through it from the overshadowing of the ascetic trends of the theology of the period and the ecclesiastical masculine dominance and gained the dignity and independence that might naturally be expected to follow the elevation of Mary, the doctrine of the Virgin Mother appears to have done little to lift the social status of the average woman.[26] It is important in trying to estimate the practical consequences of this part of the doctrine of the Church to remember that Mary was a symbol not of ordinary motherhood, but that instead she was set aside by a miracle that protected her from the debasement associated with the feminine biological rôle which had evoked the pronouncements that now seem so harsh in the writings and teachings of some of the early church leaders. It was easy for the sentiment that gathered about Mary to be actually turned against the functions associated with the child-bearing of the married woman and be made a means of enhancing the virginity of those who denied themselves marriage and parenthood.

The mere fact that women lost status during the period does not demonstrate that they obtained no advantages from this human stress of the mother of Jesus. The Middle Ages, like all complex social situations, were far too variegated for so simple an interpretation. It is fairer to assert that the Mary cult did not prove powerful enough, in so far as it glorified motherhood, to nullify all the other influences that tended to suppress the value of the woman as an independent personality.

One of the strongest of the influences flowing in the opposite direction was the attitude toward women that found expression in the writings of the early church fathers. Gibbon justly summarizes when he writes: "The use of marriage was permitted only to his fallen posterity, as a necessary expedient to continue the human species, and as a restraint, however imperfect, on the natural licentiousness of desire. The hesitation of the orthodox casuists on this interesting subject betrays the perplexity of men unwilling to approve an institution which they were compelled to tolerate." [27]

Marriage was interpreted again and again as an impediment to the spiritual life. Jerome, for example, writes: "If you want to know from how many vexations a virgin is free and by how many a wife is fettered you should read Tertullian 'to a philosophic friend,' and his other treatises on virginity, the blessed Cyprian's noble volume, the writings of Pope Damasus in prose and verse, and the treatises recently written for his sister by our own Ambrose. In these he has poured forth his soul with such a flood of eloquence that he has sought out, set forth, and put in order all that bears on the praise of virgins." [28]

It was, of course, in the sexual side of marriage that the great menace was chiefly found. "The Apostle Paul tells us that when we have intercourse with our wives we cannot pray. If, then, sexual intercourse prevents what is less important—that is, prayer—how much more does it prevent what is more important—that is, the reception of the body of Christ? Peter, too, exhorts us to continence, that our 'prayers be not hindered.'" [29] Marriage cannot be eliminated, but those who accept it must recognize the lower order of their religious life. "The Church, I say, does not condemn wedlock, but subordinates it. Whether you like it or not, marriage is subordinated to virginity and widowhood. Even when marriage continues to fulfil its function, the Church does not condemn it, but only subordinates it; it does not reject it, but only regulates it. It is in your power, if you will, to mount the second step of chastity. Why are you angry if, standing on the third and lowest step, you will not make haste to go up higher?" [30]

Such an emphasis led some church members to serious moral lapses when they had insufficient will to carry out the program publicly subscribed to. "I am ashamed to say it and yet I must; high born ladies who have rejected more high born suitors cohabit with men of the lowest grade and even with slaves. Sometimes in the name of religion and under the cloak of a desire for celibacy they actually desert their husbands in favour of such paramours. You may often see a Helen following her Paris without the smallest dread of Menelaus. Such persons we see and mourn for but we cannot punish, for the multitude of sinners procures tolerance for the sin." [31]

Jerome admits that his exaltation of virginity leads to protest on the part of some, in these words:

"Some one may say, 'Do you dare detract from wedlock, which is a state blessed by God?' I do not detract from wedlock when I set virginity before it. No one compares a bad thing with a good. Wedded women may congratulate themselves that they come next to virgins. 'Be fruitful,' God says, 'and multiply, and replenish the earth.' He who desires to replenish the earth may increase and multiply if he will. But the train to which you belong is not on earth, but in heaven. The command to increase and multiply first finds fulfilment after the expulsion from paradise, after the nakedness and the fig-leaves which speak of sexual passion. Let them marry and be given in marriage who eat their bread in the sweat of their brow; whose land brings forth to them thorns and thistles, and whose crops are choked with briars. My seed produces fruit a hundredfold." [32]

Perhaps none of the Church Fathers was harsher in his interpretation of woman than Tertullian as the following illustrates.

"And do you not know that you are (each) an Eve? The sentence of God on this sex of yours lives in this age: the guilt must of necessity live too. *You* are the devil's gateway: *you* are the unsealer of that (forbidden) tree: *you* are the first deserter of that divine law: *you* are she who persuaded him whom the devil was not valiant enough to attack. *You* destroyed so easily God's image, man. On account of *your* desert—that is, death—even the Son of God had to die. And do you think about adorning yourself over and above your tunics of skins?" [33]

Origen, the most learned of the Christian leaders up to St. Augustine, was driven, in order to free himself from the temptation of woman, to castrate himself. Although this logical way of release brought widespread recoil, he had disciples who sought the same method of escape.

Granting that these passages are significant, it would be unjust to forget that other things were said that were more favorable to the status of woman. Clement of Alexandria may be cited when, for instance, he declares:

"In this perfection it is possible for man and woman equally to share." [34]

Again he speaks of the program women need to follow in order to achieve the good life.

"The wise woman, then, will first choose to persuade her husband to be her associate in what is conducive to happiness. And should that be found impracticable, let her by herself earnestly aim at virtue, gaining her husband's consent in everything, so as never to do anything against his will, with exception of what is reckoned as contributing to virtue and salvation." [35]

Thus he speaks of marriage.

"The marriage, then, that is consummated according to the Word, is sanctified, if the union be under subjection to God, and be conducted 'with a true heart, in full assurance of faith, having hearts sprinkled from an evil conscience, and the body washed with pure water, and holding the confession of hope; for He is faithful that promised.' And the happiness of marriage ought never to be estimated either by wealth or beauty, but by virtue." [36]

The main thought of the leadership seems to flow along the ascetic channel. In the following words Cyprian tries to show the virgins their advantages.

"Hold fast, O virgins! hold fast what you have begun to be; hold fast what you shall be. A great reward awaits you, a great recompense of virtue, the immense advantage of chastity. Do you wish to know what ill the virtue of continence avoids, what good it possesses? 'I will multiply,' says God to the woman, 'thy sorrows and thy groanings; and in sorrow shalt thou bring forth children; and thy desire shall be to thy husband, and he shall rule over thee.' You are free from this sentence. You do not fear the sorrows and the groans of women. You have no fear of child-bearing; nor is your husband lord over you; but your Lord and Head is Christ, after the likeness and in the place of the man; your lot and your condition is equal [to ours]. It is the word of the Lord which says, 'The children of this world beget and are begotten; but they who are counted worthy of that world, and of the resurrection from the dead, neither marry nor are given in marriage: neither shall they die any more: for they are equal to the angels of God, being the children of the resurrection.' That which we shall be, you have already begun to be. You possess already in this world the glory of the resurrection. You pass through the world without the contagion of the world; in that you continue chaste and virgins, you are equal to the angels of God. Only let your virginity remain and endure substantial and uninjured; and as it began bravely, let it persevere continuously, and not seek the ornaments of necklaces nor garments, but of conduct. Let it look towards God and heaven, and not lower the eyes raised up aloft to the lust of the flesh and of the world, or set it upon earthly things." [37]

This extract acknowledges that there were many pitfalls that rendered the virginity program difficult.

"And since we are seeking the advantage of continency, let us also avoid everything that is pernicious and hostile to it. And I will not pass over those things, which while by negligence they come into use, have made for themselves a usurped licence, contrary to modest and sober manners. Some are not ashamed to be present at marriage parties, and in that freedom of lascivious discourse to mingle in unchaste conversation, to hear what is not becoming, to say what is not lawful, to expose themselves, to be present in the midst of disgraceful words and drunken banquets, by which the ardour of lust is kindled, and the bride is animated to bear, and the bridegroom to dare lewdness. What place is there at weddings for her whose mind is not towards marriage? or what can there be pleasant or joyous in those engagements for her, where both desires and wishes are different from her own? What is learnt there—what is seen? How greatly a virgin falls short of her resolution, when she who had come there modest goes away immodest! Although she may remain a virgin in body and mind, yet in eyes, in ears, in tongue, she has diminished the virtues that she possessed." [38]

Not only were there temptations ever present, enticing to a lower level those who sought to live the superior life, but apparently, if we can trust Cyprian's observation, some went out of their way to make themselves trouble.

"But what of those who frequent promiscuous baths; who

prostitute to eyes that are curious to lust, bodies that are dedicated to chastity and modesty? They who disgracefully behold naked men, and are seen naked by men, do they not themselves afford enticement to vice, do they not solicit and invite the desires of those present to their own corruption and wrong? 'Let every one,' say you, 'look to the disposition with which he comes thither: my care is only that of refreshing and washing my poor body.' That kind of defence does not clear you, nor does it excuse the crime of lasciviousness and wantonness. Such a washing defiles; it does not purify nor cleanse the limbs, but stains them. You behold no one immodestly, but you yourself are gazed upon immodestly; you do not pollute your eyes with disgraceful delight, but in delighting others you yourself are polluted: you make a show of the bathing-place; the places where you assemble are fouler than a theatre. There all modesty is put off; together with the clothing of garments, the honour and modesty of the body is laid aside; virginity is exposed, to be pointed at and to be handled. And now, then, consider whether when you are clothed you are modest among men, when the boldness of nakedness has conduced to immodesty." [39]

The teachings of the early Church Fathers must not be torn out of their environmental context. Although we have to assume that the Christian writers revealed prejudice in their descriptions of the social conditions of the Roman Empire in their time, there is overwhelming evidence that the only fault that we can charge against them is exaggeration. Rome had conquered more of the world than it could unify and socialize. The spread of its power was too rapid for the cultural assimilation necessary for both political and social security, and it became an example of the sociological principle that disintegration always follows a too rapid introduction of new *mores*. Christianity itself added to the forces which were tending to break down the integrity of the Roman Empire. It was more than a religion; it was a new civilization in process and one which in turn assumed, as had the Empire, the burden of a heterogeneous following incorporated by organization but not thoroughly assimilated.

Low morals, licentious festivities, cruel sports, political corruption, disorganization of family life, vicious slavery, and widespread indifference to the obligations of citizenship, so characteristic of the life of the people in this period, provide the background for the asceticism and the morbid preachment of such men as St. Jerome and Tertullian.

Christianity was quickly shaping itself out of the ruin of one of the greatest of the empires, but it was not only converting, it was itself being transformed by the multitudes that became allied with it. It was soon so changed that one cannot turn from the pages of *The New Testament* to the Christian writings of the third and fourth centuries without feeling strongly that the wholesome faith and abounding love of the Apostolic Era had been superseded by an idealized asceticism.

This new turn was to give direction to the spiritual life of the Middle Ages and to pass down as a background influence upon the thinking and feeling of the early settlers of the United States. It would be untrue to the facts to insist that this notion of asceticism pervaded the life-practices of the common people of the Middle Ages. There is equal evidence of looseness so that one could argue with as good reason that licentiousness was the significant feature of sex morality. What concerns us is the effect upon the status of woman that came from building the ascetic ideal with its suspicion of the sexual impulses of human nature, whether expressed in or out of lawful marriage.[40]

The monastery was the logical result of such thinking. It was, however, more than this, and we shall miss its social value unless we keep in mind that through the centuries of the Middle Ages European society was making the transition from the Roman Empire to modern Europe and that Christianity was furnishing both the motives and the energy of this long social crisis. The monk and the nun were far from being mere products of a prevailing asceticism; they bore testimony to more than the craving for security in a period when for the average man and woman little was to be had.

The whole meaning of the monastic ideal cannot be gathered until we credit it with keeping alive the desire to practice Christianity in philanthropy and other practical undertakings. Although monasticism took over and organized the ascetic ideal, it represented no mere negative reaction of life. Had this not been, its influence would have been consistently against the emergence of woman. In spite of its aggressive suppression of impulses born of the body, leading to a definition of woman which made her the chief spiritual hazard, it also opened an opportunity to individual women to live a larger life than that ordinarily provided by marriage and domestic experience. There are, as one would expect, many illustrations in monasticism of the proneness of human nature, once it starts on a morbid turn, to go to the utmost extreme, as, for example, when it became a solemn duty of a child to dissolve his love for his parent in order that he might build a high type of spiritual life.

In spite of these morbid exaggerations, the ordinary routine of the monk and the nun was closer to the career of the modern social worker than to the type of religious devotee that we should expect the ascetic teaching to produce. The monastic movement was both a recoil from the evils of the time and an attempt to hold firmly to the other-worldness so distinctive of the Christian attitude during the first century. It was also a vocation, and it was in this aspect of monasticism that we find its chief advantage to women. It seems a harsh description of the prevailing social conditions to say that aside from marriage, which carried inherently a social inferiority for most women, there was opened to them as an alternative only the life of prostitution on the one side or that of a nun on the other.

It would be impossible in interpreting the experience of women in the Middle Ages to forget the prostitute. Her occupation may have been an ugly and challenging one, but it was on this account no less significant. Prostitution came over from the social life of the Roman Empire into the Christian era, and whatever else may be said of it, it offered attractions to a multitude of women, otherwise it would not have flourished as it did. It contributed to the current thinking that helped to maintain the inferiority of women, and it was encouraged by the prevailing asceticism, as this antagonized marriage and supported the low estimation of women.[41]

The nun, who from choice turned away from domestic experience, enjoyed social prestige. This undoubtedly was one of the appeals of the convent. It was more than a refuge in the uncertain life of the period or a mere side-stepping of the burden of the conventional housewife. It offered the only out-of-the-family career that carried social respect and provided opportunity for constructive social service. The prevalence of the nunneries attests the attraction of this calling for women and particularly for the ambitious and socially prominent women.

Granting, as one must, that the convents had their share of trouble in attempting to maintain a mode of life superior to that characteristic of the surrounding social environment, it is only partisanship that would forget their contributions to the intellectual, emotional, and moral growth of women. At the head of each nunnery was the abbess, unmarried and usually a member of an important family, exercising authority and administering responsibilities that explain why she has been described as the first professional woman developed in the Christian era. Her powers were such that even heads of royal families were known not to protest when a princess chose the career of abbess in place of marriage.[42]

The attack of the flesh was, of course, an experience that those who had enlisted under the banner of asceticism had to meet within the monastery walls as well as those less spiritually committed who struggled in the outside world.[43] The ideal Christian chastity, that is, celibacy, found its highest expression in the monastery, but it was not confined to this special type of Christian living. Gradually it became a requirement demanded of the clergy. During the eleventh century, the rule which had been formulated as early as the fourth century that those entering the sacred orders should not marry began to be strictly enforced.[44]

THE CULTURAL BACKGROUND

As the priesthood increased its elevation above the laity, pressure increased upon its members to abstain from marriage and other secular undertakings.[45] Granting that this insistence that the priest commit himself absolutely to his spiritual calling, with none of the distractions that come out of domestic obligations, had its ecclesiastical advantages, this program suggested again that the ascetic life was the religious ideal and woman, the man's greatest temptation.[46]

The inconsistencies of the period, as they had to do with Christian teaching, showed forth in the ecclesiastical regulations that attempted to deal with the practical problems of ethical control. In the code, as it had to do with monogamic marriage and infidelity, the male was given no special license releasing him from the moral demands placed upon the woman. On the other hand, we find regulations that define the sphere of woman, denying her not only ecclesiastical prerogatives given the man but also shutting her out of civic activities and making her ineligible to all civil and public offices.[47] It is, however, the social function and position of the average woman that concern us most. It would only be slight exaggeration to dismiss her with the statement that she was consigned the tasks of toil and burden-carrying as housewife and mother. Of course, as is always true in any such mass description, there were exceptions, for some women emerged from the general obscurity and maintained in greater or less degree individuality.

Men also had a hard life during this long transitional period from the break-up of the Roman Empire to the European migration to the new land of America. There was, however, a difference, and this it is that we need to keep in mind as we survey the background of American civilization. We must distinguish between the social value of woman's contribution and her social recognition. Women's activities were so thoroughly restricted to domestic responsibilities that it is easy to get the impression that she had little social function. This was not true, for her part in the drama of the Middle Ages was indispensable. It is rather that she had to keep to the background while man displayed himself.

Masculine ostentatiousness and its prestige cannot be made the measurement of social service. They demonstrate no more than the dominance of masculine *mores*. Men had command of the mediums of self-expression and social distinction. Women had small part in the constant fighting of the period. They were shut out of ecclesiastical organization, aside from the opportunity of the convent, and were denied any considerable influence in the shaping of theology that so largely determined their social position. Men, aside from their control of social distinction, also gained added importance by the fact that there was a disproportion of the sexes due to the continual fighting. Women did not escape the penalties of warfare, but their deaths were fewer than the males', even though occasionally they participated in the battle, at least during times of siege.

The fact that the woman was ordinarily shut out of soldiering had its effect upon her status, just as, even as late as our own century, the most effective argument against giving women full political equality with men was based upon the insistence that they could not discharge the military responsibilities of citizenship. All through the Middle Ages the individual man, however insignificant in other respects, was at least a pawn who had his use in time of battle.

Thus there were many influences that led to the building of the inferiority status of woman so characteristic of the Middle Ages. Feudalism had lessened the woman's property rights. Her legal subordination was well expressed by Glanvill, when he asserted that husband and wife were one person and that person was the husband.[48] The same author also reveals the prevailing attitude toward women's rights of inheritance when he asserts: "If anyone has a son and heir, and besides him a daughter or daughters, *the son succeeds to the whole;* . . . because in general it is true that a woman never takes part in an inheritance with a male, unless a special exception to this exist in some particular city by the custom of that city." [49]

The limitations and disabilities of women as compared with men

THE CULTURAL BACKGROUND

were registered in the legal system of the period and were carried forward by the English common law which in turn became the basis of our own legal principles, thus providing for a discrimination against women which in the legal field at least has not yet been entirely eliminated in all our states. As compared with the legal status women obtained in the Roman Empire, the general trend in the Middle Ages was toward legal inequality and incapacity. Principles were extracted from the *mores* of the time and hardened into the basic law providing a resistance to change that has obstructed woman's progress until our time.

This was truer in England than on the continent. There, with the passing of time, the feudal disabilities of women were gradually lightened and the doctrine, which was frozen into the English legal system, that husband and wife were one person, became obsolete. These handicaps discriminated against women all the more because of the advance England was making along other lines toward a more democratic, freer life. Feudal family law was dragged forward along with an increasing of constitutional and political liberties. It has been suggested that the explanation of this anomaly was the emphasis placed upon the idea of families as units as aristocracy grew strong, leading to the tendency to ignore women and younger sons.[50]

Women became the legal victims of the disposition of the wealthy to harden family life into a form that would resist social change. Concerning this Sir Frederick Pollock has written: "It might be a topic of curious meditation for the student of comparative jurisprudence to note how well the English land-owning families have striven, though all unconsciously, to produce in our modern society something like the image of an archaic Aryan household." [51]

This development of woman's disabilities appears to have extended from William the Conqueror to Glanvill. The Anglo-Saxons resisted the change, but without success, for as the military tenure of land increased, the powers and rights of women, who could not perform military service, decreased. Since the husband often had to perform feudal services for the *maritagium* of his wife, he was given certain rights in the *maritagium*. This illustrates how feudalism led to the lessening of the property rights of married women and widows.[52]

Chivalry was a bright spot in the drabness that characterized the life of the majority of women during the Middle Ages, especially those who kept to the conventional pathway and committed themselves to the domestic traditions. It was, however, hardly more than a colorful contrast, for it was distinctly aristocratic. It was a game open only to those of privilege and leisure, a way of escape from the ecclesiastical formalism and the feudalistic routine. It did at least challenge the morbid trends of asceticism and the theological conception of woman by its celebration of the erotic impulses of human nature. Distant as it seems, on account of its applaud of illicit love, from primitive Christianity, in its recognition of the independent personality of the woman and its acceptance of an association of men and women that approached an equality fellowship, it was closer to the spirit of early Christianity as that influenced the life of women than was the sentiment of the church of the period. It is easy, nevertheless, to exaggerate the practical consequences of this outburst of love literature and romantic codes of conduct.

The importance of the Renaissance also, as it has to do with the life of women, was rather in its prophecy than in what it immediately brought the average woman. It was a beginning in the building of the modern program, but at first its awakening came only to the favored few and even to them for the most part indirectly. The new civilization was in ferment, and naturally women began to profit from this as well as men. The old order, essentially static, was challenged, and a disorganization, both in church and politics, provided an opportunity for some women to gain for themselves better training for life and greater freedom of activity.

Protestantism and the counter reform of the Roman Catholic Church that came with it also advanced the status of woman, but less, perhaps, than one would have expected. Defiant as Luther was toward ecclesiastical celibacy, his attitude toward women was characteristically medieval. He conceived of marriage as a civil affair to be regulated by the state. It was "a temporal and worldly thing of no concern to the Church." His notion of womanhood was nothing extraordinary, and there was, as a result of his doctrine, no immediate lifting of the status of woman. The Reformation was middle-class in outlook and fundamentally, so far as it had to do with domestic experience, conservative. Woman remained socially inferior to man, and the proprieties defined childbearing and a narrow type of home-keeping as the obligation of her sex. Even in the home the male was dominant and there was little incentive for the woman of talent to seek self-expression in out-of-home activities, and very little opportunity.

Luther is representative of the other reformers. In his attitude toward women, John Knox was more backward than Luther, and, as one would expect, brutal in his preachments regarding the inherent inferiority of the woman and her subordination to man. If the Protestant leaders can be indicted for failure to carry their reforming far enough to permit women to recapture the promises of Christianity at its beginning, they cannot be accused of failure to recognize the social importance of the family. In his insistence upon the value of early education in the child's life, Luther comes nearer to modern thought, although, of course, his emphasis was to our present thinking narrowly religious. The effect of the Reformation upon the evolution of woman's status was something quite different from the pronouncements of the leaders. Luther, Calvin, Zwingli, and Knox were certainly not champions of woman's freedom, but unquestionably their assault on medievalism added considerably to the momentum essentially born of social circumstances that was to lift women to a higher status. In their acceptance of woman's inferiority, they were creatures of their time; as crusaders for greater individualism in their religion, they were contributing to the forces that were to enlarge the life of women and release them from social handicaps.

Protestantism had its economic aspect in addition to its religious significance. It was an expression of the final breakdown of the feudal system and an economic reconstruction that gave greater opportunity to the laboring and to the middle classes. In England, for example, the Reformation brought little transformation in the religious life, but with it came important changes in the political and the economic order that had continued on from the Middle Ages. The new situation made more important the economic contribution of woman's labor. By the sixteenth century in England, women, in addition to their rôle as domestic toilers, contributed to the economic support of the nation as skilled workers, even as persons who had achieved craftsmanship in the industrial arts and, in some instances, had become experienced in managerial responsibilities. Some women had been given partnerships in their husbands' businesses and others, as widows or daughters, had taken over trading enterprises that had been developed by their husbands or their fathers. Public documents of various sorts establish without the possibility of controversy the fact that there were women who were becoming experienced in all sorts of industrial, religious, and even political activities.[53]

Women were engaged as pawn-brokers, money-lenders, stationers, booksellers, contractors, and even ship-owners.[54] They were not only entering trade but were continuing the contribution in industry first started by the primitive woman, a basic social service that in fact has been rendered by ordinary women from the earliest stages of civilization continuously until now. For example, the number of women engaged in the seventeenth century in the woolen industry in England has been estimated from the ratio of three women to one man to the more radical statement of eight women to one man.[55] The silk industry, although not monopolized by women as once was true, was still chiefly a feminine industry, and it is interesting to note that the word "spinster" was originally used for spinner, bearing testimony to the importance of woman's part in the textile industry. Even agriculture, in all its forms, gave employment to women who in strength and skill proved themselves, in spite of the fact that they were commonly paid lower wages, not hampered by their sex in strenuous outdoor labor. Their

THE CULTURAL BACKGROUND

part had become so important in agriculture that it was realized from the start by the colonization companies that aside from the value of the stabilizing influence of women as wives and mothers, they were greatly needed as workers, if the new settlements were to be made permanent and profitable. The majority of the women who went to the New World did not need to cross the Atlantic to learn the discipline that comes from earning one's living by the sweat of one's brow or to prove themselves capable of entering with their husbands and brothers into the fellowship of toil. Whether they sailed from England, Holland, Spain, Sweden, Portugal, or from France, most of them were prepared, whatever their previous class experience, to share the life of hardship and productive toil that survival in the wilderness required.

Puritanism was another influence that affected the life of women. This expression of the changing religious situation, ascetic in its disposition rather than its practices, and for the most part traditional in its concept of women, through its practical consequences led her forward. Its development in England interests us, since it had a part in the founding of American civilization.

As the feudal system crumbled away, the middle class, especially those in trade or commerce, increased their power. On the whole, this change tended to lift the social status of woman. The wives of the mercantile and craftsman classes had enjoyed a degree of freedom and responsibility throughout the Middle Ages, but the breaking up of feudalism as it occurred in the fifteenth and sixteenth centuries increased this.[56] However one interprets the political efficiency of Queen Elizabeth, there cannot be question of the significance of her position as it influenced the *mores* that fixed the status of women. Her reign stimulated interest in the relation of the sexes and encouraged discussion which in itself was testimony of a changing social situation. Books dealing with the woman question were popular. The same topic was taken over by the drama and there were plays defending and criticizing the new freedom of women. The attacks that were made by various writers on the conduct of women reveal to us that individuals had broken away from the coercive routine sufficiently to bring confusion and to draw the protest of the traditionalists.

These criticisms of women's behavior are directed especially against their attention to fashion and their extravagance. Naturally these outlets of women's interests would be the first chosen, especially by the wives of men in prosperous circumstances. Whatever else might be said of this self-expression, it evidenced an enhancement of the woman as an individual and her attempt to gain prestige by dress and luxuries that would enable her to rival other women and to distinguish herself in her contacts with men. However trivial it now appears as an expression of personality, it announced the advent of a new opportunity that English Puritanism was to give women. The criticism that resisted this self-assertion of luxury-loving women came especially from writers who belonged to the aristocracy and who were opposed to the widening of the prestige of women. There were facts enough to give support to their fault-finding, but the chief motive, whether they recognized it or not in their writing, was their desire to protect the nobility from the encroachments of the commercial class. The ambition of the wives of the merchant princes offered the most vulnerable point for attack.

We are told that even demands for equality of woman with man accompanied the social changes inaugurated by the coming to power of the wealthy middle class in England. These were, of course, few but significant as forecasting a future trend. Examples are the writings of Daniel Tuvil, William Heale, and the unknown author of *Haec-Vir*.[57] In contrast with this sentiment the opposition to the enlarging freedom of women was frank and aggressive, and those hostile to the change denounced the new woman for her vices and extravagance. In spite of this, the evidence seems to be that the attitude of people in general was not unfriendly to the progress women were making.[58] This was not due to a widespread indifference as to whether or not home life was healthy, for, on the contrary, there seems to have been some interest in the idea of strengthening domestic relations by specific instruction in preparation for marriage and for motherhood. This program, as one would expect, was built upon the Bible as its basic text and represented the constructive answer to the criticisms that the luxury-loving, irresponsible woman was getting. It is easy in these times to underestimate the importance of this program for the buttressing of the family, because it seems so clearly static in character. There was no thought of preparing the woman for the freedom of life that she was to gain by sharing in the development of the American civilization on the other side of the Atlantic, but rather the thought was merely to help the middle-class women handle more successfully their household and motherhood responsibilities. It at least stressed the importance of the domestic career of the usual woman.

From another quarter also appears evidence of the changing status of woman. There began to be greater interest in the problem of divorce and a weakening of the conventional acceptance of woman's subordination to man. It is easy to exaggerate this because it stands out in contrast with the bulk of opinion which still defines woman's status in the spirit of the Middle Ages. In the literature that dealt with women and their problems this discussion of the spiritual and material rights of women at least opened up the way for the spread of the idea of their theoretical equality. It gave a slant toward contemporary social problems that enhanced the individuality of the woman and provided a way of escape from the general definition of inequality that had for so long remained an unquestioned assumption of the dominant feeling and thinking.

The trend toward a broader and freer opportunity for women that had so faintly started in the English environment was to gain impetus, without intention and for the most part without protest, as a result of the conditions that had to be met by the immigrants in the New World England could not be carried across the Atlantic. A new world forced a new order. In man's realm, politics, this was destined to appear in the most impressive and dramatic of possible expressions—a collision of the old and the new that made war inescapable. The quieter and less recognized social mutation in woman's sphere, with its ramifications and practical consequences, is beginning to seem, however, in its contrast to the trend of centuries, the most profound and the most revolutionary contribution to the modern world that has as yet come out of human experience in America.

CHAPTER II

THE COLONIAL WOMAN

BOTH economic and social pressure were behind the colonization movement of the seventeenth century. This appears in the English settlements in America, and it is with them that we are chiefly concerned in our study of the colonial woman. Feudalism was breaking up and the prevailing social conditions revealed the collision of the new and the old always characteristic of a period of transition. In some respects life was still adjusted to medieval civilization. Along other lines it was expressing the new order that had broken forth in the Renaissance. English agriculture was suffering from these changes. One of the consequences of the passing of medievalism was the development of enclosures. This new policy had reached such a point by the sixteenth century that it was in England a major social problem.[1] The small plots of land which the peasants had been cultivating, with the right of pasturage and the right to gather fuel from the woods, were being lost as land from the communal tracts was fenced in and possessed for private cultivation.

By the seventeenth century there developed considerable discontent in rural England, among both owners of small estates and tenant farmers. The first had to face the depreciation of the value of their land and decreasing rents, while the tenant suffered from lack of land, rising prices, and a feeling of economic insecurity. There was also restlessness on account of the changing social environment. From the time of the *black death* in the middle of the fourteenth century, there had been migrations into the country of persons belonging to the wealthy merchant class whose background made them unsympathetic regarding the customs of the rural people that had created "merrie England." As the enclosures pressed upon the means of livelihood of the rural folk, the new type of landowner also destroyed the gayeties and the freedom that had been so characteristic of country life in medieval England.[2]

In such a situation a considerable proportion of the population was predisposed to respond to the promise of the new opportunity offered by America in the seventeenth century. Especially was this true of the artisan and tenant classes who could, by going to the new land, become freeholders.[3] In this motivation the desire to gain for wives and children greater security and better opportunity had for the majority of the immigrants to the New World a commanding influence.[4] The appeal that was made to attract settlers to the new country by promoters of colonization always stressed the ease of acquiring land.

A large part of those who came across the Atlantic to the English settlements were rural folk who were so tied by tradition and by habit to their rural occupations that it required severe pressure to dislodge them from the motherland. They were not people easily given to migration, but when, added to their hard circumstances, there was promise of reëstablishing themselves as tillers of the soil under conditions that seemed to them ideal, they responded to the new hope and undertook the great adventure. They realized that only by a fresh start could they give to their children even as good a means of livelihood as had been handed over to them in their youth.

Discontent in England was, of course, not confined to the rural population. The cities and towns, especially those along the eastern and western coasts, also responded to the Utopian pronouncements put forth by the colonization companies. Undoubtedly a part of these urban dwellers were people who had earlier lived in the rural environment and who had never lost their love of country life. Others either were convinced that the artisan could not expect to advance in the Old Country or were of the group always to be found in urban centers who idealize rural conditions, and against the drabness of their life, with all the force of a hungry imagination, pictured the freedom, the wealth, and the prestige they could expect to achieve on the other side of the Atlantic. Among these city emigrants, also, motives of family origin contributed to the decision to break from the Old Country. Many felt themselves trapped by a poverty from which there was no way of escape either for them or their children unless they were willing to leave the land of their birth. They went forth with expectations all the richer on account of the dreary background of their life.

The women who came over did, as a rule, measurably advance their interests. If they were of good reputation, they seldom had difficulty in marrying, and with advantage. One planter states that no maid that he imported failed to find a husband within three months after starting work with him.[5]

It must be remembered that poverty was no obstacle to emigration. So great was the need of workers in Virginia that it was always possible to get transportation paid. It appears, however, that not enough took advantage of this opportunity to bring to Virginia the workers needed.[6] One of the motives that led to the colonizing of Virginia was the effort to get rid of the unemployed population of England.[7] The colony was used also to provide a method of getting rid of some who were regarded as undesirable citizens. A great many of those who were transported to Virginia after having been convicted of some offense against the law and who became servants were guilty only of political offenses and, far from being hardened criminals, were conscientious, courageous persons who had rebelled against tyranny on the part of Cromwell, King Charles II, or King James II.[8]

The pressure for workers in Virginia was so great that undoubtedly both men and women were kidnapped and transported. However, this spiriting away, as it was called, was exaggerated in the same way that white slavery was in the nineteenth century. For the most part, the worst that could be said was that promoters took advantage of the ignorance, simplicity, and readiness for adventure of the poor people, both of country and town, and induced them to seek their fortune by crossing to Virginia.[9]

It was not customary to employ white women in the field. This was true even during the period when the companies were in control. There was need of woman's labor in the household, in the dairy, and in the laundry. In addition to these necessary tasks, the making of clothing fell to the women and took a considerable part of their time. When a white servant was sent into the field to work, it was due to her failure at the household tasks or her disagreeable personality or her immoral conduct. Such an assignment was looked upon rather as a punishment than advantageous employment.[10] It was the low type white woman who was assigned work in the field and was tempted to sex relations with male Negroes. Sentiment was strong against such race mixing.[11]

There was a relatively tolerant attitude toward sex relations between female servants and male servants and even with their masters, but the general feeling was against these practices, as appears in legislation designed to discourage such conduct. In case a woman was made pregnant by her employer, she was, after her term of service, sent over to the church wardens who were authorized to add two more years and to sell her labor to some other than the man responsible. The money went to the parish to be used for the support of the child, if necessary. The woman was not allowed to continue with her employer these additional years, that there might not be the motive of obtaining her labor by making her pregnant.[12]

Toward the end of the century the law required the sheriff to arrest the woman upon learning that she had given birth to an illegitimate child and to whip her on the bare back until he drew blood. She was then turned over to her master and either had to pay him two thousand pounds of tobacco or remain with him two additional years.[13] If the illegitimate child had a Negro for its father, the mother was fined or whipped and given five additional years of service. One third of the proceeds of the sale of her services went to the informer, one third to the public treasury, and the remainder to the parish concerned.[14]

No one disputes the large part played in the establishment of the permanent settlements in the New World by women, but their contribution is usually recognized with a gracious eulogy and dismissed. This is not because of failure to realize its significance in the New World settlements but on account of its lack, from the masculine point of view, of the dramatic, a consequence of the political and social inequality of women. The dominance of masculine *mores* extends to the interpretation of events so that the raw material out of which history has to be made is saturated with masculine emphasis. The events that get recorded in the history of the period are for the most part those that have to do with man's interests and man's activities. It is only when the value of what women did is considered that we realize how distorted is the record that comes down to us.

From the survival point of view, woman's part was certainly not less than that of man, but it lacked the prestige of political and social expression. Women carried their share of burden and were equally heroic in assuming the discomforts and the hazards of the voyage across the ocean in the small and slow boats, the dangers of infectious diseases, notably the *smallpox,* and the responsibilities and hardships that accompanied the effort to establish family life in the wilderness. To these tests that were put upon woman's character must be added, in the case of many, fear of the Indian, a frontier hazard that for many years remained in the emotional background of pioneering women.

If we ask, How did settlements prosper when they were made without women? we discover the indispensableness of woman's part. For example, when with the second supply ship two white women, Mrs. Forest and Anne Buras, her maid,[15] were introduced to the Jamestown colony, we have the beginning of a stability that never could have come about if the colony had remained an exclusively male settlement. There had to be at the foundation of colonial success not only domestic life but also the contribution which was characteristically feminine. Men could make and write the history, but only as women played their part in establishing the civilization that grew up in the New World. In 1618 we find the company promoting the Virginia Settlement shipping a hundred apprentices and servants and a hundred "young and uncorrupt to make wives to the inhabitants and by that means to make the men more settled and less moveable."[16] This does not mean merely that women were needed to prevent the restlessness and discontent that were sure to undermine the settlements, but also that the work of women—their industrial as well as their domestic contribution —was required if the colony was to have any hope of permanency and prosperity.

Survival is the only adequate test of any cultural group, and it alone permits us to recover the direction of the main stream of current events in any period of civilization. Emotional upheavals, particularly of political character, and spectacular events always tempt the historian toward a relative neglect of the woman's part in the period he studies. This selective interest has led to an aristocratic registration of social happenings that has minimized the part played by the average person, who in history is apt to be the forgotten man, and even more the forgotten woman.

Experience soon demonstrated that lack of women in the Virginia colony led the men to the disposition to regard their staying as merely temporary, a hardship endured with the hope of soon gathering wealth and then returning to the mother country. At a meeting of the Immigration Society in London, in 1619, Sir Edwin Sandys stated that "though the colonists are seated there in their persons some four years, they are not settled in their minds to make it their place of rest and continuance."[17]

The first installment of women brought to Virginia, through the efforts of Sandys who realized that otherwise the settlement could not thrive, appears to have been, with two exceptions, persons of "proper character." Although they were free not to marry if they so preferred, and in any case were allowed to make their own choice as to their husbands, they soon became wives and the colony began to make substantial progress. Other English women, as reports came back of the happiness of the first group, accepted the adventure. Soon, also, husbands and wives came together from the old land to make a fresh start under the more favorable conditions in America. Married men were favored by the policy of the various colonization companies because it was realized that the woman worker was as indispensable to industry as was the wife to the emotional content of the man. Eager to establish the security that comes from domestic life, Governor Dale gave every man with a family a house with four rooms or more, without rent, and twelve acres of land.[18] For the most part the women coming to America were accustomed to hard work, many of them being experienced in English agriculture.

The Pilgrim colony, in its settlement at Plymouth, was fortunate from the first in its stress of the family basis for its community life. Indeed, the family organization was so prominent that one author has suggested that the Pilgrim leaders be studied as "house fathers" in contrast with such Puritans as Winthrop and Hooker, who were essentially men of the state.[19] The Pilgrims were fortunate also in possessing a unity built upon religious conviction, but their dominance at Plymouth must not conceal the fact that only a portion of the settlement were Separatists. In spite of the religious motive, the colony was characteristically English and established in accord with the colonial policy of the Old Country. It was backed by London merchants who had added to it artisans and laborers who were alien so far as religious sentiments were concerned. To the Crown the colony was an outpost that should prove profitable to England.

Unlike the southern colony, it did not have the economic advantage of a basic agricultural product, such as tobacco. Instead, from the beginning its survival required diversified activity. These means of support were chiefly general farming, fishing, fur trading, and lumbering. The first especially invited the participation of women, and the Pilgrim mothers were well fitted to act the part of the small farmer's wife. The men and women who made up the Plymouth church had been originally workers of the soil, although during their sojourn in Holland they had been forced to earn their living for the time being by artisanship and craftsmanship. Thus they were splendidly prepared for the hardships of a pioneering life. The non-members also came from the middle and lower classes of England. Some of them were of country origin while others came from London and Middlesex. Taken as a whole, the community ranked low in the culture of the schools, but they had the will to work and the sense of responsibility which made it possible, in their limited environment, to achieve a degree of prosperity greater than they had enjoyed on the other side, even if they failed to become as profitable as their merchant supporters had anticipated.

Most of their history was uneventful in the spectacular sense, although they had their troubles with those who, living with them, were not of their conviction. But they demonstrated, even from the days of fearful suffering during their first year, the superiority of a settlement that emphasizes the family unit over one that has to be forced through experience to stress domestic life. Later, in the Mormon settlement, in contrast with the communities made up of gold-seekers—chiefly single men or husbands who left their families behind them—we shall see the same lesson demonstrated. The Plymouth colony, as compared with that of the Puritans, has always excited an interest beyond its historic importance in size and influence. The Pilgrims were forthright in action and determined in spirit. They walked with God, but in a shadow. Their colony was destined to be eclipsed by the more significant Puritan settlement which came into being about Boston ten years after the founding of Plymouth and finally to be incorporated in it.

The Puritans pitched their civilization on a higher plane, representing the English middle class culture. They possessed familiar contact with the thinking of God and showed no reticence in announcing the Divine policy. As the Pilgrims lived their simple life in a spirit of Holiness, the more militant Puritans spread throughout the province a theological dominance and a theocratic organization perhaps excelled only by the creation of Calvin at Geneva. The Puritans were not content to live a life apart. They were aggressive. They had migrated from their motherland in protest against the autocratic policy of King Charles I and were of the same brotherhood as those who established the Commonwealth and carried the unpopular king to the scaffold.

Not only did the Puritans come to Massachusetts and then to other parts of New England in greater numbers than the Pilgrims, but from the start they were better equipped to meet the ordeals of the wilderness. In educational preparedness they stood high. They also had greater capital, a portion of them being wealthy, and, unlike the Plymouth colony, needed no support from London merchants. Instead they brought a charter establishing their status as a trading company, which they made the foundation of their colonial government. Soil, topography, and climate tended in contrast with Virginia to limit the size of their farms and to encourage their settling in towns or neighborhood groups. The plantation system in the southern states perpetuated an aristocracy, but at first this was as pronounced in the Puritan colony as in the South. From the start, however, the aristocracy of the northern states rested on a less substantial foundation. Its support was the counting house or some form of trade, and was, therefore, more open to change than that built upon large estates in the form of land passed on by inheritance. There was not, also, in the North such a wide separation of status as we find in Virginia between the planters' class and the lower type of servants. From the beginning these "poor whites" found great obstacles against their emerging from their economic inferiority. The presence of the Negro in the South also built a background that enhanced landowning classes.

In New England the diversity of industry, closer contacts of the people in village and town, and the opportunities provided by trade for the shrewd and ambitious, made class distinctions arbitrary and difficult to maintain. Naturally this difference between the sections was reflected in the life of the women, and if the southern woman was given the greater prestige, her northern sister could more easily take advantage of any opportunity to increase her personal freedom or move forward her social status. The conventional routine for women was more easily broken through where the *mores* were more fluid and democratic. This difference was, however, only one in degree, for as the original settlements developed and spread along the Atlantic Seaboard, there was, both north and south, firm conviction in regard to the essential inferiority of women as compared with men and an insistence that the female observe the proprieties and keep her place.

As we pass out of New England into New York we find, with the termination of the Dutch period, the social situation as it concerns the woman differing from the Puritan and Pilgrim chiefly in a slightly greater tolerance. Marital relations, for example, are not so harshly regulated, and offenses of sex character are punished with less severity than was true in New England. In spite of the Dutch founding, the *mores* are essentially English. During the New Netherlands era women profited from the relative freedom enjoyed by their sisters in Holland. Legally husband and wife were equals who, without an ante-nuptial contract, enjoyed a community of possession. Such contracts permitted husbands and wives to inherit separately.[20] Sometimes joint wills were made with a similar purpose. Women in New York were efficient not only in their traditional vocations, but we find them entering trade. They frequently had the authority of power of attorney in the absence of their husbands. Widows also continued the management of their husbands' estates and various kinds of business.[21]

Pennsylvania is particularly interesting on account of its cosmopolitan population. The Quaker influence was dominant and was favorable to the advancement of women, at least in comparison with conditions in the other colonies. The Friends were led by their belief in the universal inner life to hold to the idea of equality of men and women. Since men without special training were able to discover truth by intuitive experience and were permitted to express their messages, so likewise women were allowed, when the spirit moved, to speak in public.

In the central colonies elementary education was often open to girls as well as boys. In the records of New Netherlands a reference establishing this appears in 1733 in the statement that "the school children, both boys and girls, should recite" and eleven years later "about 200 scholars, boys and girls" are reported in school at Albany.[22]

From the beginning Penn had advocated free schooling for both sexes. This was carried out by legislation at the first assembly at Chester, 1682. The next year a law was passed requiring the instruction of children under twelve in reading and writing. Failure on the part of parent or guardian to teach the "sound" child was punishable by a fine of five pounds.[23] Children also were to be taught some useful trade or skill. Although the Quakers did not emphasize higher training, believing this unnecessary for their ministers, they did develop elementary education and provided it for both boys and girls. Their family life, which was exceptionally high in quality, was based upon the notion of equality of husband and wife. In accord with this, the woman did not promise to obey the husband as a part of the wedding ceremony. The Friends did not accept St. Paul's pronouncements regarding women because here, as elsewhere in their religious faith, they went back to the earlier teachings of the gospel. This attitude made it easy later for the Quaker women to enter the agitations and reform movements advocating the abolition of slavery, temperance, and the rights of women.

In addition to this liberal background of Quakerism, there were other conditions in Pennsylvania that favored the advancement of women. One of these was its geographical situation. It was the keystone state where *mores* from the north and the south, and shortly from the frontiering west, blended with those native to the colony. Moreover, the latter also were composite. If the Quakers furnished the warp, the woof came from weaving in very diverse cultural influences. One of the most important of these was the German contribution. William Penn had become acquainted with some of the leaders of the Pietistic movement in Germany, and he invited followers of this faith to join in the colonizing of Pennsylvania. In 1683 Francis Daniel Pastorius came to Philadelphia, and a few weeks later he was joined by thirteen families who established the city of Germantown. Pastorius was perhaps the most scholarly person in all the English settlements. With such leadership, German influence flowed into the cultural complex.

So many Germans came to Pennsylvania that we find Benjamin Franklin worried lest they overshadow the English. As a consequence of this feeling, the assembly voted to require the oath of allegiance of all the males over sixteen, and between 1750 and 1763 a great effort was made to teach the German children the English language by providing charity schools. These schools were for the boys, but at New Providence one was established for the girls, teaching reading and sewing.[24]

The Germans were strongly domestic and their family life functioned on a high level. Testimony to this fact comes from their low rate of illegitimacy. This we know because in their old church records they registered their unmarried mothers. Adultery was regarded as one of the greatest sins, and there was tremendous feeling against even the thought of divorce. Families were thrifty and the men and women were hard workers with great respect for industry and efficiency.[25] In these qualities women did not fall behind men, and in addition to their heavy household burdens and their work in the dairy they frequently, at the time of harvest or other special stress, went to the assistance of their husbands and brothers working in the field. The Germans established elementary education in connection with their churches, and this instruction was offered girls as well as boys. They believed that the former should be taught that they might read and understand the gospel. The more promising of these girls were given training to prepare them for teaching. They were denied theological education, since the ministry was closed to them.[26]

Another group that made an impression was that of Moravian faith. They were possessed with a strong missionary zeal but were remarkably free from any morbid trend toward asceticism. Their religious life was intense but wholesome, with strong conviction of the value of education. They believed in education for girls as well as boys and established as early as 1742, at Germantown and later at Bethlehem, instruction for girls. More than seven thousand girls attended this latter school during the first century of its existence, coming from places as distant as Nova Scotia, New England, and the southern colonies. Salem, North Carolina, was another center of Moravian influence where they also established a girls' school of high standing.

The Moravians believed that the soul was essentially feminine and the male aspect a mere temporary functioning during the earthly period. This doctrine appears not to have had any special influence on the status of woman, but undoubtedly it contributed to the interest in women's education. Marriage was interpreted spiritually, the husband being looked upon as representing Christ, the true husband of each woman. Perhaps nothing better reveals this strong religious attitude toward marriage than that their churches out-moderned most churches of the present in accepting responsibility for helping their youth in the selection of wives and husbands. Sometimes, we are told, the churches acted to help a man find a wife, even transmitting his proposal.[27] The Moravians were distinguished by their love of music, and the concerts that developed at Bethlehem attracted as visitors Franklin, Washington, and other prominent men and women of the colonies. This city became the center of the Bach cult in the United States, and it still maintains its supremacy. Salem, North Carolina, also achieved fame for its music, particularly the development of band music.

Another group that settled in Pennsylvania as a distinct religious community was the Church of the Brethren, known popularly as the Dunkers. Their first colony settled in Germantown in 1683. Pious, hard-working, severe people, they were not much interested in education, and their attitude toward women was in accord with the European conventions of the time. It has been said of the Dunkers that in 1819 they were segregating the sexes, men and women not associating except for worship or public business.[28]

Before 1720 there had been scattered migrations of the Scotch-Irish into Pennsylvania, but during the last third of the century they began to come in great numbers. This immigration into the colonies worried officials in Ireland as well as some of the prominent colonists, especially those in the ministry. Cotton Mather was one of those who had fear that their coming might be troublesome. They went to New England, New York, and North Carolina, but particularly to Pennsylvania, Delaware, and New Jersey. They met prejudice wherever they went, in part because they were erroneously supposed to be the same people as the Celtic Irish Catholics, who were not popular. They also tended to be clannish, which increased the feeling against them. They maintained strong family loyalty and held to a severe moral code. Their women were hard workers who took for granted their subordination. Divorce almost never occurred. For the most part, these Scotch-Irish Presbyterians drifted to the frontier of their period and during the first century of the history of their church in the United States they were strongest in the thinly settled portion of New England, Pennsylvania, and the Carolinas. We find them playing a prominent part when the frontier was carried over the Allegheny Mountains.

The colonial period in Pennsylvania gives in miniature that mixing of diverse cultures that has been so distinctive of the United States taken as a whole. Various national and religious groups attempted, as far as possible, to maintain unity and to protect themselves from alien influences born of contact with people of other races and different heritage. With the growth of population this separation became more difficult. Their removal from their native country also weakened with the passage of time the customs and traditions that had emphasized the differences between them. There was the beginning of that "melting pot" function which later, on a grand scale amid an even greater diversity of people, became a major undertaking of the United States.

Along with these currents and cross-currents of contacts went constant pressure of environment, for, however strong the commitment of the groups to old-country ways of living and thinking, the adjustments forced upon them by the different and compelling environment made an impression that brought people of unlike origins into some degree of fellowship and a measure of uniformity. Had this not happened, the great majority of the people could not have been welded together in opposition to the policy of the crown of Great Britain. What was true in Pennsylvania was occurring also in all of the colonies, but in none of them was there such cosmopolitan mingling, since in none had there been from the beginning such a tolerant attitude toward differences in national origin and in religious faith. In the frontier that was so soon to develop over the Appalachian Mountains this same process of assimilating and unifying people of unlike social background was to proceed, but more aggressively.

In each of the English settlements this same process of bringing into some degree of adjustment diverse social and religious backgrounds was taking place. Maryland was distinguished by its effort to develop toleration sufficient to permit those religiously widely separated, the Protestants and Roman Catholics, to live together in peace. The Carolinas, like Pennsylvania, were attracting a variegated population. There were the English, of the type that settled Virginia rather than those who went to New England, the Scotch, the Scotch-Irish, the German, the Irish, the Swiss, the Quakers, and the Huguenots. The last, on account of their nationality, met with a hostile reception at first, particularly in South Carolina, where in 1693, on account of their foreign origin, they were threatened with loss of the legal right to will their estates at death.[29] Although they had broken their ties with the motherland and were thoroughly committed to the life of their new environment, only slowly were they merged with the English population. Even at the close of the colonial period there were settlements in the Carolinas made up exclusively of Huguenots and Scotch-Highlanders.

On the eve of the American Revolution there was a large migration of Scotch people from the Highlands including the Hebrides, the Orkneys, and the Shetland Islands. Explanation of this migration is uncertain, but we know that a considerable number of people representing all the economic classes came over and settled chiefly in Nova Scotia, New York, and the Carolinas. Apparently the cause of this movement was the reorganization of land tenure somewhat similar to the enclosure acts in England. The clustering together of these people in the Carolina communities is understandable when related to the historic clashings of the Highlanders with the Lowlanders and the English.

The motive of the founding of Georgia was one that naturally emphasized the family motive. In the promotion of the colony, glowing pictures were painted of the opportunity offered in the new land for people hopelessly entangled in poverty. Its population also was a conglomeration of English, German, Lutheran, Scotch-Highlander, Swiss, Portuguese, and Jew.

The western population in comparison with old-world habits was relatively mobile. There was a considerable intercolonial migration which tended to break down the original differences between local settlements. The Puritan influence spread from Massachusetts and followed migrants as far south as New Jersey. From Pennsylvania settlers entered the western part of Virginia and the Carolinas. Those Quakers who had settled in the Plymouth colony, finding life there uncomfortable, drifted southward. Many of them eventually established themselves in the Carolinas. During the twenty years preceding the breaking out of the American Revolution, Georgia received considerable numbers of people from Virginia and the Carolinas. Meanwhile, from the seaboard communities of all thirteen colonies the frontier was drawing the restless, the discontented, and the adventurous men and women who preferred trying their fortunes in the wilderness to remaining in the more conservative and stable eastern settlements.

In spite of the hostility of Indians and the resistance of the French, the original narrow strip of English settlements was being pushed westward. This frontier conquest was swifter in the south than in the north. People from the eastern section of Georgia, North and South Carolina, and Virginia were joined by migrants, chiefly German and Scotch-Irish, who came down the valleys from western Virginia and Carolina. If we picture the English settlements by a map, giving each cultural and religious group an individual color, we have a variegated chart that by its units reveals what a cultural mixing had to take place before there could be any degree of unity. In spite of these striking differences in background and in colonizing motives, the prevailing attitudes toward women showed little variation except in the amount of emphasis given masculine dominance. Woman's status was an imported cultural pattern and represented the well-established European conventions. No cultural product brought over the seas proved more incompatible with the new social situation.

The social status of the colonial woman was so taken for granted that there was little discussion regarding it on the part of either men or women. This was true, also, on the other side of the Atlantic, but the woman question gets some consideration in the literature of England during the sixteenth and seventeenth centuries. Not until the eighteenth century, however, and then chiefly as a result of the work of Rousseau and Mary Wollstonecraft, did it receive any considerable discussion. During the preceding two centuries there had been some interest in the education of girls, and this from time to time found expression in the literature of the period. An example of this was the discussion of John Locke, *Some Thoughts Concerning Education*. This appeared in 1693, so that it was almost an eighteenth century product. He advocated the private training of girls, but more significant than his particular theory of proper education of girls was the fact that he regarded their training of such importance that he was willing to give it consideration.

In both the *Spectator* and the *Tattler* we find discussion of woman's education and, in addition, of other topics particularly interesting to women. Addison and Steele in contrast with Swift took a serious interest in women's problems and realized the growing importance of woman's contribution to culture. Daniel DeFoe, who was so often in his social thinking in advance of the other essayists of his time, was especially modern in his attitude toward women. He and Mary Astell, the author of *Serious Proposal to the Ladies* which was published in 1694, expressed their belief that women should be given opportunity for individual development. Mary Astell was credited with having been the first to suggest that schools of equal rank and purpose with those for men be established for women.[30]

Samuel Richardson in his novels revealed an attitude toward women as persons which was new and undoubtedly significant in its effect on the feeling and thinking of his women readers. His idea of man as the head of the household may have been conventional, but his portrayal of woman's character revealing the intensity of her emotional life represented a new departure and one that had social influence. The extraordinary popularity of his books shows that the complacency with which woman's inferiority had been so long accepted was coming to an end.

Mrs. Eliza Haywood, a writer of secondary rank, insisted that the faults found with women were a consequence of their wrong training for which men themselves were responsible. She also prophesied that the right educational preparation would not lessen the charm of women nor destroy their efficiency as housewives. Thus, in her modern outlook, she ranks measurably higher than her literary ability places her. All of these authors had a following in the colonies, for their writings were brought over and were popular.

Rousseau's *Émile*, although it did not appear until near the period of the American Revolution, was familiar to some of the American writers, who were influenced by it in their attitude toward the education of women. This book assumed the inferiority of woman and insisted that her training be such as to make her a useful helpmate and a capable mother. His theory, which among its other consequences was responsible for the stirring up of Mary Wollstonecraft, is revealed by the following representative expression:

> In the union of the sexes each contributes equally toward the common end, but not in the same way. Hence arises the

first assignable difference among their moral relations. One must be active and strong, the other passive and weak. One must needs have power and will, while it suffices that the other have little power of resistance.

This principle once established, it follows that woman is especially constituted to please man. If man ought to please her in turn, the necessity for it is less direct. His merit lies in his power; he pleases simply because he is strong. I grant that this is not the law of love, but it is the law of Nature, which is anterior even to love.

. . . Thus the whole education of women ought to be relative to men. To please them, to be useful to them, to make themselves loved and honored by them, to educate them when young, to care for them when grown, to counsel them, to console them, and to make life agreeable and sweet to them—these are the duties of women at all times, and what should be taught them from their infancy.[31]

Rousseau's idea of the proper function of women was close enough to the general feeling throughout the colonies to provide a characteristic generalization. He, however, attempted to support by argument the conception which in the colonies was so thoroughly embedded in the *mores* as to be rather generally accepted as a matter of course. His attempt to rationalize this long-established inferiority of women disclosed the weakness of the assumption and invited attack. Although a prophet without much honor in her period, Mary Wollstonecraft, by her forthrightness and penetration in challenging the tradition of man's dominance, gained for herself unending fame. The controversy she started belongs to a later period. The force of her onslaught was lessened in America by her reputation as a radical who believed neither in marriage nor religion.

The vocational responsibilities of women were given some attention, for we find in colonial libraries some imported books, published in the sixteenth and seventeenth centuries, discussing efficient housekeeping. They stressed the obligations of the wife, giving counsel as to how she might fulfil her religious duties and develop the domestic virtues expected of her. There were books dealing with the problems of marriage in the same spirit and from a religious background. Two other types of books dealing with marriage were to be found in colonial libraries, one light and humorous and the other satirical and coarse.[32]

Most of the little discussion that woman's status received came from books brought over from Europe. Aside from the attention given women in the theological or educational literature, we have only the speculations of Benjamin Franklin and Enos Hitchcock before 1795. The ideas regarding women that did get expression came from two sources, the sermonizing of the New England clergy and articles, few in number, that reflected European rationalism. Benjamin Franklin's two articles, reprinted in pamphlet form under the title *Reflections on Courtship and Marriage,* are an example of this European influence. This second attitude is interesting because it is the beginning of a new conception, but at the time it did not have practical importance.

In spite of theological dogma, New England women had opportunity for study and self-expression in literature equal to that offered anywhere in the colonies, and New England developed in at least as great proportion as any other section women of intellectual distinction. Mrs. Anne Hutchinson was one of the first of the New England women to achieve prominence. She, however, came to the colony rather than being developed by it. A talented and an aggressive woman, she had the qualities of mind and disposition that would to the modern catalogue her as a militant feminist. In England she had been a parishioner of Cotton Mather and admired him greatly. Once she was settled in Boston, she began to hold meetings twice a week in her own house for women, that they might discuss the sermons they listened to in the churches.

Soon her frank comments and novel opinions stirred up the entire community. She insisted that the preachers, with the exception of Mather and her brother-in-law, Wheelwright, were preaching salvation by works rather than by grace. Aside from her

THE COLONIAL WOMAN

unorthodox theology, she became a dangerous person by her insistence on the right of private judgment in religious matters. Although she had support from people of influence, including young Governor Vane, feeling became so strong against her that she was finally driven from the colony. She went first to Rhode Island, where again she got in trouble, and then to the more liberal Dutch colony, where in 1643 she and the rest of her family were murdered by Indians.

When we turn away from theory and theology to consider the practical life of women in colonial affairs, particularly in the economic field, we find women in a different situation. As has already been noted, middle-class women were in England breaking through the crust of custom and finding opportunities in trade and commerce. This was more true in the colonies and was not so confined to one economic group. In some degree all women were beginning to feel influences that, born of the new environment, were tending to enlarge and increase the opportunities of the American woman. The basic cause of this quickening of the social flow was the greater need of independent judgment and self-reliance forced upon the pioneering woman as she met her everyday responsibilities. Conditions in the wilderness, and in less degree in the better settled communities, were too new and changing to permit the following of a well-established routine.

The ever-present menace of the Indians, as it colored the background of many women in the earliest days of settlement, was a major factor, building in the woman the ability to act for herself and assume the responsibility of making decisions. There are many illustrations in this earliest pioneering period of American history of the readiness of women to handle difficult, even dangerous situations. More important than these occasions, when during the absence or incapacity of the husband she had to play her part in protecting herself and children, was the emotional atmosphere of her situation which constantly enforced the need of preparedness. Then there were the more prosaic necessities, born of isolation and limitation, that had to be met with intelligence and self-control.

For the ailing child the mother could not telephone the doctor. If a member of her family met with an accident, she was not free to call a hospital ambulance but instead had to get busy and give her own first-aid. Often she had to continue on her own skill, for there was no one that could be called in who was better qualified than herself. Even the ordinary undertakings of a diversified household economy, which carried on all the productive activities according to season that were required in the home life of the time, made demands for discrimination and foresight that could not but influence the character of women.

Under such circumstances, not only did men develop appreciation of the wife and mother as an independent person, but, what was more important, the woman learned self-sufficiency and self-confidence. Much stress has been placed upon the effect of the absence of husbands in opening up opportunity for the initiative of the wife, and rightly so, since this was another persistent influence coming from the new environment. This, however, must not be interpreted as something happening merely to those men who were prominent in business or politics. We are much impressed by the way that Mrs. John Adams and Mrs. Benjamin Franklin carried on their husbands' business and met their own household responsibilities while their spouses, on account of political responsibilities, were in Europe or in some distant city.

More important still, however, was the fact that husbands who were undistinguished in the ordinary routine of their everyday life were often absent from home. In the modern sense they may not have been a great distance, but taking into account their means of transportation, they were far enough away to require that an efficient wife be something more than a mere household drudge. In the time necessarily spent in travel, if not in the distances covered, the men of the time were, as compared with what ordinarily would have been true of them in their work in the motherland, a relatively mobile population. The taking over of responsibilities by prominent women during the absences of their husbands, on account of the prestige of these wives, had influence in the building of a tradition that women could be trusted to assume family leadership which was shared by those of lesser distinction.

Life in America for most women was certainly hard and for all exacting, but it opened up for them new opportunities, and evidence of this is the greater freedom women obtained to enter vocations that were generally regarded as belonging to men. Whether expressed in part-time or full-time activities, this wider economic competition with men was both evidence of the changing status of women and an influence in the advancing of their position. There is, of course, no necessity that women duplicate the life of men in order to prove their right to equal self-expression, but at a time when business, politics, and the professions were possessed by men because of an assumed superiority over women, the ability of the latter to break through and enter into man's own field and demonstrate their capacity to carry on was a challenge to the tradition of feminine inferiority that had so long prevailed. Women had to prove their independent personality by doing things that men were accustomed to monopolize. Nothing reveals this ascendancy of masculine *mores* more than the fact that woman, to achieve distinction in a way that brought advancement in her status, had to leave her conventional sphere of domestic activities to compete with men in trade and eventually in the professions.

It is impressive to sketch this expansion of woman's work. We have already noticed its development in Elizabethan England. The new environment quickened and widened the tendency. The greater part of the economic openings that came to women were thrust before them by circumstances, and they entered their new fields so naturally that there was little or no protest from either the men or the women with whom they associated. One of the vocations that attracted women was that of tavern-keeper. It was a more important undertaking in colonial days than at present. Conditions of transportation required the establishment of lodging places in the cities, villages, and even in the rural sections. Where they did not exist, the traveler had to depend upon the courtesy of the private household or had to shift for himself in the open air.

Not only was the demand so great that taverns were widely placed, but the business particularly appealed to widows because it could be so easily started. It required little change to turn the private home into a public tavern. At a later time, and even until now in some sections, the same sort of thing occurred when the widow or deserted wife opened up a boarding house. The colonial tavern, however, ordinarily carried greater distinction and performed a larger social service than that belonging to the woman who at a later time ran a boarding house.

There were, of course, in the colonies many women who merely continued taverns that had been established by their husbands who had died and left them the property. The full meaning of this engaging of women in tavern-keeping cannot be had unless one pictures the social functioning of these lodging places. As a rule, they were more than places where the traveler could eat and sleep. Although some of them imitated English coffee houses, the American tavern was, as a rule, a more important community establishment than these café gathering places in the Old Country. The tavern, as it developed in the colonies, can best be described, perhaps, as a sort of community club. Later it was outrivaled by the general store and by the saloon, but during the colonial period it was a popular meeting place of the people for group loafing and discussions. If it served on a lower level as a gathering place than did its ecclesiastical rival, the church, it often better represented the various classes of the community. It featured leisure, recreation, politics, and trade.

There were great differences between taverns, and some were strictly places for lodging. This narrower type was more easily taken over by the woman. It often represented a mere enlargement of the same sort of thing that she had been doing as a wife in charge of a private home. However, some so-called taverns in this pioneering period were so primitive that they hardly deserved the dignity of the term.

There were things associated with the more club-like type of inn, such as the selling of liquor, that were looked upon as work belonging to men. This, however, does not mean that there was unwillingness on the part of women to sell wine and strong drink or that there was any considerable protest against their doing this. It was rather that this part of the business of a tavern, like the taking care of horses in the stable, was regarded as naturally falling to men. There was a different feeling regarding the management of the business and the activities associated with sleeping and eating. In both these aspects of tavern-keeping, the colonies came to take for granted the ability of women to carry on.

Another type of work also associated with transportation was the keeping of a ferry. The traveler frequently had to depend upon this means of crossing bays and rivers, and it made no difference to him whether they were operated by women or by men. It was common for a widow whose husband had developed a ferrying business to carry on the undertaking. Frequently it was something easily added to housekeeping, so that the mother could care for her children while maintaining her means of economic support.

Women also were engaged in agriculture. It appears to be true that in all the colonies they were permitted to own land on the same terms as men. This in itself was no small matter in advancing their status. Although widows most commonly remarried, feeling the need of a man to take care of their farm or plantation, there were women, both north and south, who after the death of their husbands continued to cultivate the land that they had inherited. The large plantation was, of course, found in the South and to a less extent in the Middle States. The New England farm tended to be small, requiring less managerial skill than was necessary to maintain the southern plantations. Instead of taking charge of the labors of others on a large single-crop scale, after the southern fashion, especially after the development of slavery, the New England farm woman had to be equal to the doing of many things as she earned her living in the more diversified farming of the north.

Mrs. Elizabeth Digges of York County appears to have been the wealthiest of the women owning plantations in seventeenth century Virginia. Her slaves numbered one hundred and eight, and the inventory of her estate in 1699 shows that she had one of the best furnished homes of the period. Inheriting her large plantation from her husband, at one time governor of Virginia, she managed it herself. Eighteenth century Virginia newspaper advertising revealed how frequently women were engaged in agriculture. We find them offering land and farm products for sale, houses for rent, and, in the South, making numerous references to their slave property. They have Negroes for sale or to lease. They also announce rewards for the return of runaway slaves.[33]

Eliza Lucas was one of the women in agriculture that achieved distinction. She was the daughter of a British army officer who, finding that the station to which he had been sent in the West Indies was not a healthful climate for his delicate wife, brought his family to South Carolina in 1737 or 1738. Colonel Lucas was forced to leave the plantation and rejoin the army. He left his seventeen-year-old daughter, Eliza, in charge. He appears to have been exceptionally modern in his idea of the proper sphere of woman. As a result Eliza received better training for the meeting of her managerial responsibilities than was common among the women of her time and place.

Her father interested her in seed culture and sent her, for experimental purposes, seed and plants. Among the former were those of the indigo, a plant which required skilled cultivation. In spite of the failure of her first year's crop, probably on account of the hostility of the overseer her father had sent over to help her get started, she finally succeeded in harvesting the plant. In 1744 she replanted all the seed she had raised the previous year and soon was able to supply her neighbors, many of them Huguenots familiar with the cultivation of indigo, with seed adapted to the climate. The result was that England began to import indigo from the colony in preference to getting it from French sources, and until the Revolution it was one of the chief crops of South Carolina. Soil such as that found on St. Helena's Island was especially adapted to the growing of indigo, and the product there was of such high order that the cultivation of the plant continued even after the Revolution and the passing of the bounty that England had paid to encourage the development of an adequate supply of dye material within the Empire. Although this indigo experiment was the most successful of her ventures, Miss Lucas had other interests which she tried to work out, including the planting of a grove of fig trees and one of oak trees.

Eliza Lucas, when she was twenty-two, married Colonel Charles Pinckney and went to live on his estate about five miles from Charles Town. She continued her interest in agriculture and on her father's plantation, which she still supervised, experimented with the silkworm. Although the mother of three children, she found time to experiment also with the growing of hemp and flax. Her silk did not turn out so well as her indigo, but she was able to produce enough of the raw material for the weaving of cloth sufficient for three gowns. She was interested also in the art of weaving cotton and wool, and her instruction in these industries worked out successfully. In 1758, on the death of her husband, she was left to manage a vast estate scattered through the colony. In spite of innumerable difficulties, because of her unusual ability she was able to make the estate profitable.

Good seed was one of the great needs of the agriculturists, both north and south, and many women storekeepers supplied their customers with imported seed. Apparently Hannah Dubre was the first to raise her own seed and offer it on the market. In the *Pennsylvania Gazette*, in the fall of 1753, she inserted the following: "To be sold by Hannah Dubre, living in the Northern Liberties, next plantation to Capt Peal's, within two miles of Philadelphia, . . . All sorts of seeds either wholesale or retail, at very reasonable rates." [34] Several times every autumn, and occasionally in the spring, for the next fifteen years this advertisement appeared.

On the southern plantation it was common for the wife of an overseer to be assigned the task of managing the dairy and the poultry yard. Another position frequently filled by women on the plantations was that of housekeeper. This, however, was so near the ordinary domestic tasks of the housewife that it cannot be regarded as an illustration of woman's breaking into the economic domain conventionally belonging to man.

Women engaged in trade throughout the colonies, and their entrance upon this type of vocation, as was generally true in agriculture, came about usually through the death or absence of the husband. Often, however, they began as co-laborers with their husbands. Some women, themselves, started in business. This might come about in the effort to add to the earnings of the husband or, upon his death, the woman might prefer to start something new rather than continue in his occupation. The most common of the trades that women entered was that of the retail shopkeeper. Newspaper advertising before the Revolutionary War demonstrates that there were many women keepers of retail shops who sought to attract patronage through the newspapers, although, as one would expect, women were more conservative in using this form of publicity than were men. The following is a representative insertion:

Mrs. Mary Pelham, (formerly the widow Copley, on the Long Wharf, tobacconist,) is removed into Lindell's Row against the Quaker's Meeting House, near the upper end of King Street, Boston, where she continues to sell the best Virginia tobacco, Cut, Pigtail, and spun of all sorts, by Wholesale or Retail, at the cheapest Rates.[35]

Peter Faneuil, at Boston, furnished many New England women with imported goods for their retail shops, amounting sometimes to thousands of dollars in value. Besides engaging in general store business, women were in millinery, dry goods, gown-making, and even in tailoring. Between 1760 and 1775, no less than thirty-six women keepers of millinery or dry goods shops advertised in the papers of Charles Town, and we are told that at least thirteen such women advertised in the *Virginia Gazette*.[36] Women were also in such occupations as laundering, dyeing, starching, and the like. Undoubtedly trade careers made to some women more than mere economic appeal. Zest for selling, for competition, and even the gambling impulse turned them to enterprises that were considered man's rather than woman's normal sphere. An example of the third motive was the entering of New England women of the coast towns in a venture "when a ship set sail with a cargo."

Men as well as women found it easier to enter a trade than a profession. The latter, however, had an almost unsurmountable obstacle when they felt any leaning toward a profession, since it was almost impossible for them to get the necessary training. This was true in the field of law and, except for the Quakers, in the field of theology. As medicine developed into a science, women were also denied preparation for the doctor's profession. In the earlier period, when much of what we would now call medical service consisted of the concoction of various herbs and the carrying out of what now we would consider the work of the nurse, women had a freer opportunity than they did later. The gate to these basic professions of the lawyer, the minister, and the doctor was shut to women not on account of proven incapacity but by *mores* that forbade the woman any opportunity to show her ability.

One field now included in medicine was exclusively possessed by women in the earlier period of English settlements, and that was obstetrics. This was so firmly established by custom that it was only gradually that the physician supplanted the midwife. Even yet in some sections and classes we find in the United States a preference for the midwife rather than the physician. This is especially true among the rural Negroes in the South. The possibility of this vocation as a form of social service for women is splendidly demonstrated by the work carried on by Negro midwives on St. Helena's Island.[37]

Of all the professions, schoolteaching was the one most open to women. The first mention we have, at least in southern records, of a woman teaching school, is of a Mrs. Peacock. She seems to have had charge of a small school in Rappahannock County, Virginia. Women were tutors, school mistresses, and proprietors of private schools. Frequently they carried on this kind of work as a part-time occupation. Popular education was provided by the English and the Dutch almost from the beginning of their settlements. The first school in New Amsterdam started in 1633. As early as 1647 Massachusetts passed a law requiring the establishment of schools. Every town of fifty families was required to maintain a common or elementary school, and every town of a hundred families, a Latin school.[38] In the same colony, between 1660 and 1672, among the other regulations that strengthened community life, we find a requirement that the families "endeavor to teach . . . their children and apprentices so much learning as may enable them perfectly to read the English tongue and knowledge of the capital laws." [39]

Although we are not certain that in the early period there were more women teachers in the elementary schools than men, it is clear that their number gradually increased. The Latin schools which gave preparation for college were monopolized by men. By 1680 the records show that there were many women teaching in the elementary grades. It must be remembered that at this time there was no prejudice against a married woman teaching. Instead, we frequently find the husband and wife working together in the giving of instruction. For example, John Dommett, advertising in the *American Mercury* of Philadelphia, on March 19, 1730, his curricula and fitness, adds this postscript. "N. B. His Wife also Teaches Reading, Knitting, and all Sorts of Needle Work, very cheap." [40]

Women in the colonial period also became journalists, their entrance usually coming about through the absence or death of husbands who had developed newspapers. Women were beginning to show their interest in literary expression, which was so soon to become the freest professional opportunity open to women. The journal of Madam Knight was one of the most sprightly of those produced during the period, whether written by a New England man or woman, but unfortunately it was not published until more than a century later.

Mrs. Joseph Rowlandson was the wife of the first settled minister of Lancaster, Massachusetts. During King Philip's War, while her husband was absent from home, she and her three children were taken captives by the Indians. Less than a year later she was ransomed. She wrote an account of her experiences, which was published in both Boston and London. Although this record cannot claim literary value, it is an impressive account of her experience and especially valuable for the light it throws upon the ways of the Indians. It had a wide reading and was deservedly popular. Mrs. Simon Bradstreet was another woman who had in some degree a literary career. Coming over from England with her husband and her father in 1630, after having married at sixteen, she became the mother of eight children. Although her husband, years after her death, achieved the distinction of being governor of the colony, her life at Andover, Massachusetts, was that of the ordinary, over-worked pioneering wife and mother. She is credited with having been the first American poet. In any case she was one of the first to write in verse, but for her own delight rather than for publication. Her poems were eventually published by her brother-in-law in England, without her knowledge. This book contains an exclamation revealing the conventional attitude toward women writers in the colonial period.

"I am obnoxious to each carping tongue
Who says my hand a needle better fits,
A poet's pen all scorn I should thus wrong;
For such despite they cast on female wits,
If what I do prove well, it won't advance—
They'll say it's stolen, or else it was by chance." [41]

The keeping of diaries was nearly as common among women as among men, and although this sort of writing brought no distinction to women, it at least attested their interest in the events that came under their observation and their unwillingness, in spite of the demands of their strenuous life, to be so engrossed in their multitudinous domestic tasks as not to have any degree of intellectual outlet.

Of all the unpleasant happenings of colonial history, nothing is so revolting to the modern mind as the records of the persecution of witches. Although the belief in diabolical possession flared up in all the colonies except New York, where the social maturity of the people, due to Dutch influence, withstood the superstition, it was only among the Puritans that the effort to discover and punish witches took violent, epidemic form. The record of Pennsylvania is nearly as clean as that of New York. We have evidence that the notion lingered there, but it was so incompatible with the Quaker spirit that it made no headway and never came to malignant expression.

In New England the craze flamed in two distinct periods—from 1647 to 1663 and later from 1688 to 1693. The first outbreak appears to have been an offshoot of the same sort of frenzy as obsessed the followers of Cromwell during the English civil war period. If, as seems probable, its revival in the second period was due to the ambition of the clergy to regain prestige, its consequences were exactly opposite their desire. Witches were sought out, tortured, tried, and hanged. During the sixteen years of the first period there were eight hangings in Connecticut and six in Massachusetts. The climax of the superstition appeared at Salem, Massachusetts, in 1692, when one hundred and fifty persons were accused and imprisoned and twenty executed after having been horribly tortured.

The final reaction of the people against this mob-mindedness was symbolized by the confession of Samuel Sewall, who publicly acknowledged his irrational behavior and asked forgiveness. In the end the clergy weakened their hold upon the people by their part in the crusade, and their support of the persecution of the Baptists and the Quakers. It is not strange that the historians think of this wild outbreak of social passion as the chief blemish of Puritan culture. When, however, it is related to its fundamental primitive origin, the recoil that followed the persecutions has a greater meaning, an optimistic slant of significance in the evolution of American women.

This reaction marks the end in American sentiment of one of the oldest, most persistent and consequential of the social handicaps of women. The belief in witchcraft is not utterly dead, because we have seen in our own decade its reappearance in isolated, ignorant communities, but the superstition was shaken from the hold

THE COLONIAL WOMAN

that it always had possessed over common thinking. We can find the meaning of this only by digging deeper into the superstition and finding its source in some common notions regarding women in primitive society.

Of all the taboos among preliterate folk, none is stronger or more widely diffused than that revealing primitive man's fear of woman.[42] She was regarded as the possessor of special magic endowment, and although she was sought, since she was both desirable and indispensable, she was also regarded with suspicion, in part because of her very attractiveness. Men attempted to get protection from her menacing powers by heavily weighing down her life with social regulations. There were particular times when women were supremely dangerous. One of these was the menstrual period. There were also individual women who were thought to possess more than ordinary gifts of magic.

This dualistic attitude toward women, both seeking and fleeing her, persisted into the historic era in spite of the advance of man during his European evolution. Even with the spread of Christianity we find these two opposite attitudes toward women continuing. The tendency, however, as man slowly matured socially, was to restrict the possession of magic to a special group of women. Their power was black magic and its origin an alliance with Satan.

Naturally the kind of women from whom men recoiled, especially when in any way they were peculiar, came to be thought of as witches. We now know that often these unfortunate women were afflicted with some malady of neurological origin which led them to attract attention by strange behavior. This odd or irritating conduct was interpreted as evidence that they had sold out to the devil, and any unusual occurrence in a community was blamed upon them. The favor of such persons, more commonly women than men, was sought and their enmity feared. Thus gathered about the conception of the witch man's dualistic attitude toward women. The predominant feeling was that of fear, and it was this that became mob passion as the drive against witches was revived in the Puritan era both in America and England.

As was natural, the old, the repellent, and the mentally and nervously abnormal women were chosen as victims. The witch craze of New England has a terminal significance that alone justifies its discussion in the evolution of American women. There are students of human nature [43] who emphasize the inevitableness of sex antagonism between men and women because of their mutual dependency, but the anachronistic outburst of the persecution of witches at Salem brought a social revulsion that at least changed the form and, undoubtedly, also the force of this fundamental conflict due to sexual differences. The helpless victims of mass superstition through their sacrifice brought an end to one of the oldest and most cruel of the social exploitations of women.

Soon, to curb the ever advancing status of women, a new doctrine of woman's inherent physiological inferiority appeared, taking the place of the fear-driven taboo that throughout the primitive and early historic periods of human society had attempted to prevent woman from using the dangerous magic with which it was supposed they were endowed. Instead of petering out, the ancient dualism died in a bloody outburst that brought in return a correspondingly strong revulsion against both the idea of female magic and its theological derivative, the responsibility of Eve for the sinfulness of man. Undoubtedly, in some small degree at least, this reaction against witch hanging added momentum to the influences that were bringing increasing social opportunities to women in America.

No brief summary of the cultural setting provided by the Atlantic strip of colonies can do more than suggest the opportunity it offered women to achieve in North America an original social status. The forces released by our modern machine-supported civilization were destined to affect increasingly the life of women everywhere, but in our country, quickened by a new and favorable environment, they have at last in these days carried women near to full equality with men. So far as the relationship of the sexes is concerned, this seems to be the goal of trends that appeared early in American life. If so, it must prove more than the end of a drift characteristic of our social experience. It must also become the supreme testing of the biologic and social soundness of a new order in the man-woman association.

In climate, physical resources, racial stock, inventive genius, political freedom, educational opportunity, and religious incentive, a great American experiment was given favorable circumstances for its growth and trial.

CHAPTER III

THE FRONTIER WOMAN

Life Beyond the Appalachian Mountains
Through Jackson's Administration

THE colonial settlements, once they were securely planted, became a frontier with the Atlantic Ocean separating it from its European base. The immigrants from the Old World had hardly established themselves along the narrow strip of coast before some of them felt the attraction of the undeveloped territory stretching westward. As the coast and tidewater communities grew and extended, absorbing their one-time western fringe, and the whole area became a continuous well-settled portion, a new frontier pressed westward.

Once the pioneers broke through the Appalachian Mountains, this second frontier began to develop features distinguishable from those of the older section on the eastern slope and became self-conscious of its distinction at least as much as were the colonists at first in their relations with the motherland. The first frontier was made up of people engaged in fur-trading, farming, cattle-raising, mining, and fishing. As the frontier moved on, the fisherman was left behind and the advance was led by the fur or leather trader. The latter's way of livelihood required a wilderness into which civilization had at least only faintly penetrated. As the westward drift of population gathered momentum, the fur-trader was forced great distances forward throughout the section we now describe as the Middle West.

The fur-trader was no excursionist who, with the cultural traits of the seaboard communities, went into the wilderness to trade

THE FRONTIER WOMAN

and then to return to the older section. Whatever his place of birth, he belonged to the frontier environment. Sometimes for trading or other purposes he returned to the older area, but it was never to him homeland. This reveals how rapidly the original European stock was being Americanized, for what was true of the fur-trader was only in lesser extent true of the frontiersman, whatever his occupation. The American wilderness had produced a type of person who was thoroughly divorced from European traditions and even alien to much that was characteristic of the feeling and thinking of settlers on the eastern slope.

Although the fur-trader was no ambassador of colonial culture, he did break open the way for the spread of the white man's policy through the western territory. Upon him fell the task of contact with the Indian, and his aggression, whether peaceful or warlike, drove the Indian from the land and opened the gateway for the coming of the frontier farmer who followed closely the footsteps of the fur-trader. It was the rapid way in which this second type of invader followed the first that made English culture dominant over the greater part of the North American continent. This westward migration of farmers, as it penetrated the wilderness, decreed that a substantial and native culture should develop west of the Allegheny Mountains and provide opportunity for women to break away from the traditions of European origin more rapidly than was possible in the area of the first settlements. There was no departure from the conventions, leading to changes in the institution of marriage or the form of family life. The conventions related to the first, however, were somewhat adapted to the peculiar conditions of the environment, and although family life cannot be described by a generalization that makes it a single type, its spirit and its activities revealed the influence of the pioneering ways of living.

The one striking fact in this cultural reconstruction was the faintness of contact with Europe. Even those who came straight from England, Ireland, and Scotland to their homes in the frontier were engulfed in the same indigenous life into which those arriving from the older sections of the colonies were submerged. The new culture was to be something not so much broken from the old as reshaped and transfused by reaction to an original experience, enforced by the stern necessities of a different environment. Women shared in this transformation, and this measurably advanced their progress.

The difference in outlook between the coastline communities and the frontier appeared early, especially in Virginia where the distances between the two were greater than in New England. As early as 1676, when the older settlements of Virginia accepted the plan of protecting themselves from the Indians by chains of forts, their scheme met with little support along the frontier, since the people there were unwilling to accept security if it came from being fenced in. The coastal towns sought stability and looked eastward to the old country for their source of culture. Those who already had their eyes to the west were in a different mood. They were not caught by the vision of an original civilization but merely sought opportunity to live the kind of life that attracted them and to improve their economic conditions. The motives that led them into the wilderness were mixed, but primarily these two were most prominent: the eagerness to get rid of situations in the older communities which they did not like, and the desire to acquire cheap land.

In the first decade of Puritanism in New England we see groups detaching themselves from the eastern settlement and, led often by the minister of the flock, going farther into the wilderness. Dissatisfactions with those in political or theological control and the feeling that they were being overtaxed gave impetus to their migration. Thomas Hooker, for example, led his congregation from Cambridge, Massachusetts, to Hartford, Connecticut. Sometimes newcomers from England, finding themselves out of sympathy with conditions in the towns of their first settlements, or finding opportunity less promising than they expected, went forth to the newer regions of which they heard only glowing accounts.

In New England, on account of limited territory, the frontier was soon destined to be swallowed up, undistinguished because its culture had neither the time nor space to take on permanent original traits. This was not true of the western part of Virginia and the Carolinas. Along this southern strip appeared the first intimations of the native civilization which, in Kentucky, Tennessee, and Ohio, was soon to take root. A similar situation to that which so early developed in Virginia was later to show itself in the North as small farmers, dissatisfied with their unprofitable soil or irritated by the narrowness of the prevailing Puritanism, moved out of New England into Western New York and even Ohio.

Thus early we see the tendency for the restless and radical to move away and leave the more conservative people within New England, those who desired to maintain the social situation as it was. President Timothy Dwight of Yale, speaking of the migrants of his time, declares them smitten of the "Ohio fever," a discontented lot, victims of "a consuming fire which made of them potential revolutionists."[1] Once the barrier was broken and the New Englanders poured into the New West, a considerable population was removed from the territory where they had been born. In 1830 about one-third of the population of the United States were living east of the Appalachian Mountains and the frontier people had come to have the balance of political power.[2]

A great part of the European emigration that entered the colonies in the eighteenth century finally settled on the frontier. The Germans, for example, chiefly landed in Philadelphia, but, attracted by cheap land, they went into the West where, knowing the value of the soil to be found there, they established themselves in the thickest forest. They cleared their plots of land and sought through hard work to gain economic security. They were especially drawn to the rapidly growing section west of the southern colonies.

Although they came largely in family groups, they were noted for their strong individualism. Another foreign group that usually disembarked at Pennsylvania were the Scotch-Irish. They also drifted into the frontier where they became a barrier against the Indians much welcomed by the Quakers. Intensely Calvinistic, they stood strongly for personal liberty. Both the Germans and the Scotch-Irish easily became at home in the backwoods and adopted the prevailing spirit with its emphasis on free competition, its doctrine of equal rights, and its idealizing of the notion of the self-made man. They were people who felt themselves capable of meeting local problems of government, who had little sympathy with legal technicalities, and who never hesitated by extralegal associations to deal sharply and effectually with any lawless individual or group requiring social discipline. The frontier settlers were not homogeneous in background but they shared a common reaction to life in their independence, self-reliance, and readiness to accept direct methods of dealing with the Indian, the criminal, and the unpopular administrative official. They were more quickly fused in the unity of common passion than were the peoples in the older seacoast settlements. It was easy for them later to unite under the leadership of their idol, Andrew Jackson.

Kentucky was especially inviting to those seeking the frontier, because it was to the Indians a territory given over to hunting, and although the Indians resented the coming of the whites, they were less aggressively hostile than when their sections farther north and farther south, where they had established residence, were invaded. The attractiveness of Kentucky appears when we realize that in twenty years it took equal rank with states that had been founded 150 years earlier. This remarkable growth reveals more than the economic advantages offered. It also shows how many people there were who preferred the wilderness with its cheap land, freedom, and rough-and-ready practices over the more conservative and less plastic life of the older communities. The free atmosphere, the buoyancy, and the fluidity of customs all had their drawing power to a certain type, whether a native of America or a recent European emigrant.

All these characteristics of the environment had meaning for the woman as well as for the man. The wife of a frontiersman was no servile follower who, contrary to her inclination, was pushed into an alien environment. If she belonged, as she usually did, she was as much committed as the male. If she found herself, through Indian warfare, disease or accident, a widow, she usually did not turn back from the wilderness, seeking security in some thickly settled section of one of the colonies or later of a state, but instead she usually accepted a second husband and carried on as a pioneering woman.

She also felt the atmosphere of freedom with its stress on independence, its fear of stereotyped or arbitrary governmental practices. In teaching her children she emphasized not only the ideal of the self-made man but also of the self-reliant woman. Her domestic responsibilities did not lead her to imitate men in their practices, but in her outlook upon life and her emotional temper she was as much a product of the pervasive environment as was the man. Her hardships and lack of opportunity might forbid her showing the new feminine disposition in fullness, but her children or her children's children were to carry to clear expression the tendency that gave the frontier woman her distinction.

It is difficult for us in these days to visualize the isolation, the feeling of distance, and the difficulty of communication that made the pioneering family in Kentucky seem so far away and detached from the kinspeople back in Pennsylvania, Virginia, or the Carolinas, from whom years previously the husband and wife had gone forth to accept the life of the wilderness. One of the burdens of the frontier settlers was this uncertainty of communication. Letters had to be carried by someone coming into or going out from their neighborhood. It was customary to make public the time and place when individuals planned to start a journey to an eastern town or city or to return to the frontier. At best, mails passed slowly. It took a long time for letters to reach their destination and to receive an answer in return. Daughters could not seek counsel of their mothers when perplexed or when face to face with some family crisis. Self-reliance was a necessity. Even neighbors were likely to be too far away to be sought for assistance except in matters of great seriousness. In such an environment it was difficult for the woman not to grow up emotionally.

A brief reference already has been made to the rapid growth of Kentucky. The population of about 75,000 in 1790 had ten years later become almost 225,000. The tremendous inflowing of people which so rapidly brought under settlement the entire Mississippi Valley was one of the most extraordinary of modern migrations. At the beginning of the American Revolution it is estimated that not more than five thousand people were to be found in this area outside the city of New Orleans. By 1790 there were about 110,000 white people, and in another decade, 377,000. The national census of 1830 reported the population growth as follows: Kentucky 687,000 inhabitants, Tennessee 681,000, Ohio 937,000, Indiana 348,000, and Illinois 157,000.

In four decades the frontier west of the mountains had come to have more people than the original colonies had acquired with the assistance of government and commercial organizations during an entire century.

The development of Kentucky is representative. Although separated from the older settlements by three hundred miles of wilderness, in the ten years from 1790 to 1800 it had come to have nearly as many people as the state of Connecticut, more than half of that of Massachusetts, and a third of the population of Pennsylvania.[3] There was another distinguishing feature connected with the growth of the western territory. It was an extremely mobile population. Not only the fur and leather traders and the wood choppers, but even those who meant to settle permanently on the land kept moving, many of them with almost the ease of confirmed nomads. Some were restless wherever they settled, wishing to go still farther west. Others wandered about attempting to find the place that promised to satisfy their heart's desire before they took firm roots.

Their faces turned westward, even though many of them at times, especially the women, must have had moments when imagination and memory flew in the other direction. A portion of them, notably those entering the territory before the Revolutionary War, were confirmed Separatists, more than willing to sever ties in the colonial communities where they had formerly lived. They were seekers of a new and different civilization and felt their distance from the majority of the descendants of those who earlier had left Europe and had planted the colonial settlements.

Some were discontented, some were bitter, and some merely sought greater economic opportunity and a freer type of life. Whatever their reaction to the older communities, rarely did they wish to bring into being in the wilderness a duplication of the civilization from which they had broken. This disposition explains how it came about that the people west of the Alleghenies made to American culture their original and dominant contribution. Their traits revealed more than the influence of a frontier environment. As a matter of fact, this disappeared under the influx of permanent settlers with remarkable rapidity. It was rather the working together of an environment and social disposition that accounts for the distinction that the midwest culture achieved. Undoubtedly a large proportion of the settlers, especially during the latter part of the period discussed, were essentially easterners who reluctantly left their old homes in order to better themselves economically. These were not the men and women who set the cultural pattern but, going into the west to better themselves, they were by impulse naturally responsive to the characteristics built by those who had earlier established the frontier communities.

There is an emotional revealment in Daniel Boone's description of thousands of families leaving their peaceful habitations "to wander through the wilderness of America in quest of the country of Kentucky." Few of them recognized that they were enticed by that star of empire that through the centuries has so steadily led civilization westward. Rarely were they conscious of any ambition to establish social or political dominance. In this they differed from many of the leaders of the colonial settlements. Most of those who poured into the western wilderness were individualists, even though they commonly came as members of family units. They wanted a fresh start, plenty of room, and great freedom. To these motives frequently were added love of adventure, of hunting, and in some, it must be confessed, love of Indian fighting.

The pioneering coloring did not take the same shade as it appeared in the motivation of women, for they naturally leaned toward the conserving purposes matured by their domestic experiences and accepted rather than welcomed such hazards as, for example, came from the colliding interests of the white and the Indian. There must have been many family tragedies in cases where women could not make the transition required by the new situation and feel at home in the wilderness. It was the other type of woman, who was a pioneer at heart, into whose hands was given the torch of empire similar to that carried by her mate.

Those who entered and possessed the wilderness came as individuals or as family units. They did not, as a rule, settle, as had so often happened in early colonial history, by groups. Rarely did they deliberately seek solitude. They felt self-sufficient and, although they enjoyed having neighbors, they usually did not care to have them very near. Probably they were motivated as much by the desire to be free to expand as by the desire to be rid of close contacts. However, it matters not what led the individual families to scatter through the wilderness rather than to cluster together in compact communities, the result was an isolation that encouraged self-reliance and independence. This disposition can easily be exaggerated and undoubtedly one is tempted toward its over-emphasis, but, even when this impulse is restrained, the fact remains that life in the wilderness did much to create that intense individualism which has been so characteristic of American life.

The frontier stands in contrast with the colonies and later states only in that the environmental pressure which tended to encourage this life-reaction was greater in the West than in the East. Always, however, one must keep in mind that there was no barrier in the development of the *mores* which walled off the two sections from one another. Interaction was continuous and influences flowed back and forth between the two groups so that the distinction was in the one's possessing a quality more or less rather than in either one's having what the other lacked.

No trend was more unmistakable on the American frontier than that toward a democratic attitude. The traditions brought over from Europe were clearly aristocratic. Even New England with its town-meeting government attempted to perpetuate class distinctions, and this disposition appeared in politics and in the church as well as in social contacts in the more narrow sense. There were influences in the colonies, particularly in New England, that operated against an autocratic culture. These were resisted by the leadership, including the clergy. The trend was the exact opposite in the Trans-Appalachian frontier. Men and women were expected to stand on their own and not attempt to boost themselves by the records of their ancestors. They could not force recognition by rehearsal of family history. It was not enough to belong to families of wealth or distinction. The individual must prove himself. Unless he had the character to support his claim, expressions of family pride or vanity appeared ridiculous.

There was more than an indifference to eastern ways. On the part of many who went into the frontier there was a positive antagonism. They wanted to be rid of traditions that had irritated them back in the old settlements. It would be misinterpretation to insist that the frontiersmen maintained social equality. It is rather that they refused to accept artificial or vicarious distinctions. It was obvious that there were genuine differences between people and there was a disposition to credit individuals with their superior merits, but the basis for determining character traits rested upon personal behavior. The methods for giving or denying prestige were distinctly frontier measurements. The Westerners were willing to follow leadership, but only as it was supported by qualities that they approved and admired. Their democracy showed itself in their inclination to give, as far as possible, equal opportunity for advancement, but once the character of an individual became clear, his position in the community was rather firmly fixed. This democratic trend not only influenced women but favored them, because it encouraged the habit of judging an individual by his personal traits, that is, according to his possession of the virtues that the frontier emphasized, and such a turn of mind weakened the traditions that supported masculine dominance and sex discrimination.

Circumstances frequently operated to force even the earliest of the backwoodsmen who invaded Kentucky and Ohio to join together in a degree of coöperative self-protection. An example of this was the forming of caravans by those making passage through the wilderness that stretched between the older communities from which they started and the territory of their destination. Nor were they always free to scatter, once they were in the territory they had chosen for settlement. The dangers from the Indians were such that often the individuals had to keep near the central fort if they were not actually enclosed within it. Just as soon, however, as the pressure that came from the menace of the Indian lessened, the tendency to spread out and preserve independence generally showed itself. This impulse was not a product of deliberation built upon a self-conscious philosophy of life but rather a characteristic inclination of most of the individuals who as hunters, traders, and farmers entered the wilderness. It was also a trend encouraged by an environment providing such a quantity of cheap, or even free land, to be had by merely squatting upon it.

The *mores* reflecting the independent life of the backwoodsman and the frontier settler were all the more substantial because they were the natural outflowing of a type of personality and an encouraging environment. There was another bond besides protection from the Indians that drew the people, in spite of independence and diversity, into a degree of unity—their suspicion of the East, particularly of land speculators and politicians. From the first there was a determination to keep from coming under the control of eastern capitalists and statesmen, an attitude that has continued until the present, as appears in the midwesterner's personification of Wall Street and also in the habit of both political parties in the nomination of their presidential candidates of taking this feeling into account.

Whatever its promises, the frontier offered no easy life, and few there were who entered the wilderness without realizing how stern and continuous must be their struggle for survival. From the moment they sought to cut out a space for habitation by muscle and axe, they were engaged in a contest that demanded every quality of an efficient, healthy body and a vigorous, determined mind. Was there ever offered a better opening for the right type of person? Never was there less hope for the easy-going, lazy, inefficient, and the unhealthy. Men and women had to be hardy as well as courageous and industrious. There was strong incentive, except for the hunter and trader content with a roaming life, for the establishment of a family not only for its economic advantages but also for its efficiency. Even the hunter and the trader were usually family men who had left their people in the safer, better settled sections merely because, like the modern commercial traveler, it was impossible for them to have their wives and children with them as they carried on their means of livelihood.

It is most misleading to draw the picture of the frontier's men or women in such a way as to give them a common likeness. The records that have come down to us show that individualism expressed itself through great differences, but there were, according to the testimony of travelers, qualities of character that were common to the people. They tended to be straightforward, democratic, free from artificiality, and independent. They were apt also to be rough in speech and manners and over-ready to react to a supposed insult.[4] In spite of their familiarity with toil, hardship, and, all too often, tragedy, they met life heartily and with confidence.

If a multitude of native Americans went into the wilderness because of dissatisfaction with conditions in the older communities, it was also true that many inhabitants of the older region were delighted to be rid of people who seemed to them a potential hazard. The conservative easterner distrusted the West as certainly as the pioneer was suspicious of the leadership and the policies of the colonists on the other side of the mountains. This skepticism regarding the character of the pioneers was forcefully expressed by the learned, Puritan-minded president of Yale, Timothy Dwight, who said: "They are not fit to live in regular society. They are too idle; too talkative; too passionate; too prodigal, and too shiftless to acquire either property or character." [5] Even though this is an unbalanced as well as an unsympathetic interpretation, it does caution against the exaggerating of pioneering excellency.

As a matter of fact, along with the type of person that has been described there were many undesirables that for one reason or another fled into the wilderness. For some the new territory served, as did the frontier of the Far West later, as a place of refuge for men in trouble with the law back home. Others, although not criminals, were ne'er-do-wells to whom the West seemed to be an opportunity to rid themselves of poverty and misfortune, a transformation of circumstances that the neutral-minded observer realized could only come by a miraculous change of character. It is, therefore, misleading to interpret the frontier as a gathering place of the social cream from the older section of colonial America and later the United States. It was rather that the unsettled region attracted a type, an individual that was destined in the process of time to make a distinctive contribution to the cultural life of the country. The frontier developed something distinctive and indispensable, but it did not monopolize the social virtues.

The culture of the West could never have stamped itself on American civilization as it did had there not been an interaction between the two sections, each influencing the other. One of the characteristics of American *mores,* encouraged by pioneering conditions from the earliest colonial days to the final settlement of the Far West, can perhaps be best described as the disposition of local groups to take into their own hands the functions that in a mature and well-disciplined community are delegated as a matter of course to the police and to the courts. This trend toward a peculiar expression of lawlessness has been from the beginning until now a persisting flaw in American character, a product chiefly of rural isolation and pioneering individualism.

The most radical and tragic out-coming of this, lynch law, is distinctly an American evil and reveals the readiness so characteristic of the pioneers to turn to direct action in dealing with unconventional, unpopular, and criminal behavior. This unwillingness to make proper use of the courts and this proneness for social passion to become mob spirit have been charged to the influence of the Scotch-Irish who in the earliest days of the frontier introduced practices of their homeland in the effort to deal with vice and crime,[6] but the American tendency to evoke lynch law, which still disgraces us, is too characteristic, too persistent, and too spontaneous to be explained as essentially a European importation. It seems rather to offer for some an opportunity to express sadistic impulses and to enjoy excitements and satisfactions that were experienced by a portion of the early settlers in their war with the Indians.

Undoubtedly there is another feature of this unfortunate American weakness which the frontier encouraged. The suspicion of eastern authority, the excessive confidence in local direct action, led to an impatience and at times to a distrust of legal routine similar to the Puritan jealousy of the magistrate. The combination of pioneering individualism and rural monotony not only led to the putting of judges into legal strait-jackets but accounts for the emotional satisfactions found by a minority in expressions of lynch law.[7] The more the judges were tied by precedent and by professional conventions, the more excuse those who were determined to try and to execute alleged offenders found for their mob spirit. Unfortunate as has been this trait throughout American history, its significance is greatest as evidence of an emotional immaturity which the social situation of frontier life fostered and which has been so stubborn and glaring as to make Americans notorious everywhere for an individualism quick to withstand regulation and authority, whatever its source.

The willingness, even eagerness, of the frontier people to turn to direct action was a characteristic expression of their individualism. Undoubtedly the tar-and-feathering or lynching perpetrations gave outlet also to a craving for combativeness somewhat as did their fighting with the Indians, the French, and later the English. This lawlessness was more than a break of monotony that possessed a peculiar fascination. It permitted struggle on the social level that necessarily had strong appeal for men and women attempting to conquer the wilderness. Even when constituted authority was permitted to deal with offenders according to the law, there was still the disposition to regard the trial as a contest, and this attitude has had a profound effect upon our legal practices.

The sessions of the court—like the funeral, the wedding, and the church services, one of the few opportunities for social gatherings—drew people who came to witness the battle of wits and who entered into a trial, especially when it was criminal rather than civil, with the same spirit with which the average American now goes to the football game or the prize fight. Spectators gathered at the courthouse to enjoy a battle royal. Many of them on the slightest provocation found greater satisfaction in joining with others in deciding outside of court procedure the guilt and punishment of someone who had come under the ban of public opinion. There is plenty of evidence also that the pioneer was influenced in his attitude toward the law by his localism and jealousy of external and distant authority. The settlers wanted law and order but they preferred to keep its administration in their own hands. This, of course, explains the trend of judicial practices toward making the judge a mere umpire, a result that is making it impossible for the court at present to function effectively under the conditions of modern life.

The struggle, unescapable in the frontier, and which colored all the life of the people, influenced women as much as men, but the conventions somewhat determined a different expression of this for women than for men. It is in the religious life of the frontier that the women reveal in their most characteristic reactions their sense of struggle. This deserves detailed interpretation in any history of the American woman's religious experience, but in passing we need to recognize that women uncovered their emotional repercussions to their wilderness life in a less militant and dramatic form by personifying their experience through religious symbolism. This is just the turn one would expect, taking into account the narrower and more coercive conventions that restricted women's recoil from their ever-constant sense of struggle. Unquestionably it also constituted one of the roots of woman's readiness later to enter the crusades and reforms. Men and women cannot be subjected to such a pattern of behavior as the frontier in America encouraged and perpetuated without generating emotions that carry over into other relationships than those constituting the bulk of their everyday routine.

It was natural also in a society so strongly emphasizing individualism, economic self-sufficiency, and local independence for the idea of success to become personified in the self-made man. Here there was a decided break in the aristocratic emphasis on the family found both north and south in the older settlements. The man, and later the woman, who typified to the frontiersman and his descendants the acme of success, was he or she who, with only opportunity for struggle, forged ahead and achieved distinction. How greatly this notion has been entrenched in the thinking of all Americans, and especially those of the great Middle West and the Far West, appears when we consider how greatly it has influenced politics, especially presidential campaigns. The westerner has had a fellow feeling for the man who has made his way and too frequently a suspicion of anyone in politics who has inherited wealth. The break in this tradition came with the career of Theodore Roosevelt who from experience and temporary residence in the Northwest seemed in accord with pioneering standards in spite of the fact that he had inherited wealth and had been subjected in his education to eastern culture.

The self-made man in politics demonstrates the great distance between the temper of the American West, the creation of the frontier, and the feeling and thinking revealed by English political practices. The English constituency conventionally takes pride in accepting the leadership in parliament of some representative of an old and prominent family. Abraham Lincoln, on the contrary, is a perfect example of the kind of career that the pioneering man and woman appreciated and coveted. In this respect Lincoln has long ceased to be a creature of flesh and blood but instead has become the personification of the emotional fulfillment of cravings, both conscious and unconscious, of a great people. He has achieved folk deification, but this never could have come to him merely on merit. It was needful also that there should be the sharp contrast of an humble beginning and later greatness. Unless he had been self-made, he could never have become the perfect representation of western spirit, and, because of this, internationally the symbol of America.

In a less expansive way than was true of man, the frontier woman also had opportunity to become self-made. She could not hope to reach the heights of power or distinction or influence that were open goals for men, but she could arrive at a reputation, at least locally, for knowing how to handle herself and her circumstances and thus gain respect and even admiration. Poverty or birth in a family of ne'er-do-wells did not determine her position in the community. In the long run her character as an individual tended to decide her standing. If she had the push to free herself from hard circumstances, she was given credit for her initiative. Unlike her brother, however, her stage was small and gave her little room to show either talent or ambition. She could accomplish most by attracting the attention of a man who had the impulse to make much of himself and joining forces with him. The frontier woman, so far as this opportunity for advancement through personal effort was concerned, was different from her sister living in the older and better-settled communities only in that she had greater freedom from the traditions and conventions that hampered and lessened the ambitions of women in both sections.

Aside from their own career, pioneering women were influenced by the idealization of the self-made man in their attitude as mothers. They could vicariously extend their ambitions through the life of their children in a way that they had no thought of doing for themselves. We know how the Jewish women came to hope, many of them, about the time of the birth of Jesus, that they might bring to the chosen people the much-desired Messiah. In a similar fashion, the American woman was incited by the social atmosphere of the frontier to hope great things for her children, especially for her sons. This did not become a self-conscious, dominant expectation in the mind of the average woman any more than was the high ambition of the exceptional Jewish woman shared by all the mothers of Palestine.

The pioneering mother could be depended upon to give practical direction to her desire to advance the possibilities of her children. Naturally she sought an ally in the schools. The emphasis upon education was, of course, confined to no section of the developing United States, although there was a widespread interest in education almost from the beginning of colonial history. As this attitude swept into the Middle West, carried by the pioneers, it gained momentum, at least in its insistence upon a democratic program reaching from the most elementary school through the university. New England was thoroughly committed to the program of democratic elementary education, and men and women from this section who settled in the frontier were particularly zealous in their demands for school privileges for their children, but they carried their idea farther than did their contemporaries in the older communities. As the settlements matured in the well-settled Middle West, people insisted that the state provide, at public expense, opportunities for higher education similar to those of elementary and secondary education. Turner tells us that the state universities, although advocated by men of

New England origin, reached down into the ranks of the common people in a way that was not true of the eastern institutions of higher learning.[8]

The new departure was as deeply rooted in the feeling of women as of men; perhaps more so. It was merely carrying into practice the notion that the hard-working, ambitious, talented person had the right to claim the assistance of the community and the state in his effort toward self-achievement. This interest of the pioneering woman, as well as of the man, appears in the development of coeducation in both college and university. Radical as this was from the viewpoint of eastern educational theory and practices, it seemed to those who had descended from the pioneers or who had absorbed the culture of the section a most natural and logical expression of educational democracy.

As has been frequently observed by students of social experience, there is no division of labor with accompanying specialization so common and so natural as that built upon the distinction of sex. Starting with the obvious need of recognizing the biological responsibilities associated with childbearing and child care, the *mores,* as they develop and spread, artificially separate the activities of men and women until the privileges and obligations of the two sexes are chiefly determined by social customs and these in a great measure become arbitrary. Since the *mores,* as a rule, have responded most to the reactions of men, the cleavage between the two sexes as it has appeared in social experience has hampered woman as compared with man while the incapacity, so largely forced upon her, has been charged to the inherent weaknesses and deficiencies of the human female.

Whenever there has come about so great a social crisis as to weaken and confuse the *mores* and to require reconstruction, the precision of the former cleavage between the activities of men and the activities of women has been broken down. This happened in the readjustments that survival required as the Europeans crossed the Atlantic and became permanent settlers in America. As this took place women profited and advanced their status. The same thing happened again but with more fundamental consequences as men and women went into the frontier and for a second time established pioneering life in the American wilderness. The *mores* that had carried on in America, with some exceptions, an inflexible division of labor of men and women, in spite of the short intervening time between the two cultures, were more distant from the frontier way of living than were English customs from the first settlers. Women and men in the newest parts of the New World came closer together in a fellowship of labor than was possible in the Old World. This resulted from women joining with men rather than the reverse, since they could do the same things that men had been accustomed to doing and their help was urgently required. More significant than the occasional aid given by women when Indians attacked or when some other urgent demand arose for extraordinary assistance was the fact that so much that had, through specialization, been turned over to men was now given to women. Just as structure in the growth of the body responds to function and attempts to adapt itself to the processes, so the theory and the *mores* that registered social practices were reshaped by the larger and the freer life of women on the American frontier.

The hunter who was the vanguard of those who poured into the new frontier from the older settlement lived in a way that suggested a revival of primitive life in the early stages of agriculture. As the men fought, the women and children carried on the necessary industries of a self-supporting family, including the cultivation of the soil. The resemblance is, however, superficial, for both the man and the woman were heirs of a vast accumulation of human knowledge as they maintained their simple life. They were breaking down, or, perhaps better, had broken away from, the conventions that had so precisely defined the life of men and the life of women, but, as the process of rebuilding social habits proceeded, the greater heritage of the pioneering woman as compared with her primitive predecessors appeared in the *mores* as they reflected the greater richness of the later woman's life. Strenuous as was her existence, affording little opportunity for leisure and forcing her to prove herself a near-equal to man, because of the significance of her rôle as an industrial partner, it was nevertheless true that whatever freedom she acquired through the process would be expressed in the use of resources gathered through the centuries of social evolution. The frontier released her from handicaps arbitrarily imposed by social habit and permitted her, once she was given release from the traditions and customs that were mere vestiges of past experience, to include in her self-expression the advantages available for the widening and enriching of her life as well as for that of man.

The people who invaded the frontier naturally fall into two types—the hunter and the farmer. The first required a considerable area, thinly settled, to carry on his livelihood. In the North he tended to specialize in furs and in the South in skins which he turned into leather. Occasionally he was a man without family ties. More often he supported a family stationed back in the more thickly settled region. The majority of the hunters were, however, men who maintained a family life in the wilderness adapted to the needs of their vocation. The wife accepted a temporary and limited type of home-making, with a household economy adjusted to the migratory habits of her husband. As soon as the pressure of population began to decrease the game, it became necessary for the family to move to new quarters. Some of the hunters had Indian wives. These women were well prepared, from tribal experience, to accept the limited home-life associated with their husbands' moving about.

The second type of pioneer provided the main source of frontier culture. He went into the wilderness seeking land for cultivation. Usually he was a family man. Indeed, both he and his wife were as a rule strongly domestic. In spite of hard circumstances, no family has ever been more knit together, both emotionally and industrially. The farmer settled on the land, and as his circumstances improved, his house became more comfortable and at-

THE FRONTIER WOMAN

tractive and his wife's life easier. Sometimes, however, he, like the hunter, had the nomadic impulse and easily pulled up stakes once he got the idea that he would do better somewhere else. Frequently he exhausted the soil so quickly that it was for his advantage to move on. The drift was always farther to the west.

There were many families, especially at the beginning of the settlements across the Appalachian Mountains, that maintained a mixture of the hunting and the farming method of livelihood. Such, for example, was that of David Crockett, and in his autobiography he has given us one of the most vivid and revealing pictures of the frontier home. One of the interesting features of this type of family life was the ease with which the young couple could start their housekeeping. Land was cheap; often to be had by merely clearing and using it. Household furnishings were few and of the most simple character—usually homemade. Health, pluck, and loyalty were the resources that the frontier lovers needed safely to start their marriage, and with these they had sufficiency. Crockett brings this out characteristically, and his description faithfully represents common experience.

I remained a few days at my father's, and then went back to my new father-in-law's; where, to my surprise, I found my old Irish mother in the finest humour in the world.

She gave us two likely cows and calves, which though it was a small marriage-portion, was still better than I had expected, and indeed, it was about all I ever got. I rented a small farm and cabin, and went to work; but I had much trouble to find out a plan to get anything to put in my house. At this time, my good friend the Quaker came forward to my assistance, and gave me an order to a store for fifteen dollars' worth of such things as my little wife might choose. With this, we fixed up pretty grand, as we thought, and allowed to get on very well. My wife had a good wheel, and knowed exactly how to use it. She was also a good weaver, as most of the Irish are, whether men or women; and being very industrious with her wheel, she had, in little or no time, a fine web of cloth, ready to make up; and she was good at that too, and at almost any thing else that a woman could do.

We worked on for some years, renting ground, and paying high rent, until I found it wan't the thing it was cracked up to be; and that I couldn't make a fortune at it just at all. So I concluded to quit it, and cut out for some new country. In this time we had two sons, and I found I was better at increasing my family than my fortune. It was therefore the more necessary that I should hunt some better place to get along; and as I knowed I would have to move at some time, I thought it was better to do it before my family got too large, that I might have less to carry.

The Duck and Elk river country was just beginning to settle, and I determined to try that. I had now one old horse, and a couple of two year old colts. They were both broke to the halter, and my father-in-law proposed, that, if I went, he would go with me, and take one horse to help me move. So we all fixed up, and I packed my two colts with as many of my things as they could bear; and away we went across the mountains. We got on well enough, and arrived safely in Lincoln county, on the head of the Mulberry fork of Elk river. I found this a very rich country, and so new, that game, of different sorts, was very plenty. It was here that I began to distinguish myself as a hunter, and to lay the foundation for all my future greatness; but mighty little did I know of what sort it was going to be. Of deer and smaller game I killed an abundance; but the bear had been much hunted in those parts before, and were not so plenty as I could have wished. I lived here in the years 1809 and '10, to the best of my recollection, and then I moved to Franklin county, and settled on Bean creek, where I remained till after the close of the last war.[9]

When we inspect more closely the kind of life lived by the pioneering woman, we find need of imagining what it meant to live amid constant danger from the Indians. Even though the

Indian tribes were at a great distance, one could never be sure that some marauding group would not unexpectedly attack. Much of the time there existed a truce between the whites and the Indians, but never during this period on the frontier was there genuine peace which gave any measure of security. Neither group trusted the other. Individuals on both sides were constantly starting trouble. The drunken whites or the drunken Indians quickly gave vent to the suspicions, hatred, and even love of killing which were so ingrained in many of both parties. They were representative of two uncompromising cultures in conflict, and conditions that made for warfare were ever present. The Indian menace was a shadow from which pioneering women seldom escaped. They had to accept it as a hazard of life, as, for example, seventeenth century colonies had been obliged to accept smallpox.

The Indian danger was felt by men also, but with a difference. As the women usually had to face the menace with a spirit of endurance, the men reacted more aggressively, and, it must be confessed, with much satisfaction in the case of many of those who went early into the western wilderness. In Crockett's autobiography we find a typical expression of the impulse of the man as compared with that of the woman.

The Creek Indians had commenced their open hostilities by a most bloody butchery at Fort Mimms. There had been no war among us for so long, that but few, who were not too old to bear arms, knew any thing about the business. I, for one, had often thought about war, and had often heard it described; and I did verily believe in my own mind, that I couldn't fight in that way at all; but my after experience convinced me that this was all a notion. For when I heard of the mischief which was done at the fort, I instantly felt like going, and I had none of the dread of dying that I expected to feel. In a few days a general meeting of the militia was called for the purpose of raising volunteers; and when the day arrived for that meeting, my wife, who had heard me say I meant to go to the war, began to beg me not to turn out. She said she was a stranger in the parts where we lived, had no connexions living near her, and that she and our little children would be left in a lonesome and unhappy situation if I went away. It was mighty hard to go against such arguments as these; but my countrymen had been murdered, and I knew that the next thing would be, that the Indians would be scalping the women and the children all about there, if we didn't put a stop to it. I reasoned the case with her as well as I could, and told her, that if every man would wait till his wife got willing for him to go to war, there would be no fighting done, until we would all be killed in our own houses; that I was as able to go as any man in the world; and that I believed it was a duty I owed to my country. Whether she was satisfied with this reasoning or not, she did not tell me; but seeing I was bent on it, all she did was to cry a little, and turn about to her work. The truth is, my dander was up, and nothing but war could bring it right again.[10]

Later we find the same thirst for military adventures coming to the surface and bringing from the wife unsuccessful protests.

Soon after this, an army was to be raised to go to Pensacola, and I determined to go again with them, for I wanted a small taste of British fighting, and I supposed they would be there. Here again the entreaties of my wife were thrown in the way of going, but all in vain; for I always had a way of just going ahead, at whatever I had a mind to.[11]

Women, however, were not always mere passive sufferers. When circumstances required, they too could handle the rifle and join with their husbands, or, in the absence of the latter, become their substitutes, defending their children with skill and courage. In one Indian war which broke out in the Northwest in 1790, we find a hundred women joining St. Clair's army, preferring to share the hardships and dangers of the campaign to being left behind, open to the risks of homes exposed to Indian raiders. St. Clair, an obtuse and stubborn Scotchman, unfamiliar with Indian tactics, in the fall of the next year was suddenly attacked near the site of the present city of Terre Haute. As soon as the war whoop of the savages was heard, the women took their places, side by side with the men, and we are told that most of them died in battle.[12] Many times when the scattered families of a community had gathered for defense within the stockade, women took part in the defense as a matter of course. For example, in 1777, when Logan's Fort on the Wilderness Road was attacked by a hundred Indians, the women moulded bullets for the rifles of the men,[13] thus doing their part in what proved a successful defense.

During one of the ever-recurring Indian conflicts on the frontier during the last third of the eighteenth century, an attack was made on a household of two men, a woman, and children. The latter at play in the yard called out that Indians were coming. One of the white men rushed to the door but was instantly shot. An Indian got into the house and was struggling with the remaining white man, who tried in vain to grasp a weapon, meanwhile shouting to the woman, Mrs. Bozarth, to give him a knife. Instead she grasped an ax and killed the Indian instantly. Another Indian burst in and shot the white man who had not yet had time to get anything with which to defend himself. Again the woman swung her ax, and for a second time an Indian fell to the floor dead. She then was able to close the door. Finally the Indians gave up trying to get into the house and left, Mrs. Bozarth being the only survivor, for her children had already been killed and scalped.

Such revelations of women's courage are impressive, but it was not in these rare events that the pioneering housewife and mother proved the quality of her character. It was the wear and tear of a relatively primitive, hard, and exacting way of living that best portrayed her pluck and resourcefulness. Possibly not in a lifetime would circumstances throw her into the situation that required that she battle and kill, but there was always for many of these pioneering women the possibility of such an occurrence. Willingness to carry on, with clear eyes as to the possible peril, provided a testing of character much as did the domestic routine. She just had to depend upon herself and was always set to meet any challenge, whether it came from the Indians, epidemics, scarcity of water or food supply, or accident. She, too, was an individualist, resourceful and quick to resent any curtailing of her independence. Her life did not bring her military or political opportunities such as those through which the men found self-expression, but within the range of her life, her experience was similar to that of her husband.

Frontier life rested upon a domestic economy. Even the dress of men and women revealed the influence of their environment rather than the tradition of eastern communities. The men to a great degree dressed like the Indians. The women's dresses were made by their own hands at the loom, woven with a fabric of flax and wool. Much use was made of deerskin. Kitchen utensils, even table dishes, were fashioned out of wood. As families became more prosperous, household equipment was improved and increased. Wooden dishes were replaced by pewter, crockery being too easily broken. Nearly every household had its own loom, and each family made the moccasins and shoes that were required. The food was simple and cooked at the fireplace. The common saying that the good mother proved herself by teaching her child at an early period not to crawl into the fireplace throws light upon both the meagerness of household equipment and the multitudinous duties that had to be met by the efficient housewife.

In 1816, Indiana, at that time one of the farthest outposts of American civilization, contained within its territory 2,512 looms and 2,700 spinning wheels, nearly all used by women in their private cabins to make cloth from wool that had often been sheared by the housewife and from flax gathered by herself. Anna Howard Shaw, in her vivid picture, *The Story Of A Pioneer,* shows the spirit of coöperation that made possible family survival. Her father, having established a claim in the Michigan woods, left his son James to maintain it while he returned as a wage earner to Lawrence, Massachusetts. The son was joined some months later by the mother, two sisters, a boy of eight, and Anna herself, then a girl of twelve. The mother was sickly. The father had had time merely to clear space enough to establish the walls of the cabin. The family was a hundred miles from the nearest railroad, forty from the nearest post office, and there were no neighbors save the Indians for six miles. Although this referred to a later period, it was typical of pioneering experience.

None of the family had had experience in pioneering. A family counsel was called and each member of the family undertook to do his part to establish security and comfort. First, the cabin had to be finished. Lumber was obtained for floor, windows, and doors from a sawmill nine miles away. Soon James took sick and had to go east for an operation, where he remained. The family, consisting of the mother, three young girls, and an eight-year-old boy had to carry on. The mother, who was incapacitated by an affliction that made it impossible for her to stand upright without the aid of a chair, took over the sewing. The two older sisters did the house work. James, before his departure, had, with the aid of the two younger children, cleared land for the raising of potatoes and corn. The seeds were planted by chopping the soil with an ax, and, on account of the fertility of the soil, grew splendidly. Anna and her young brother gathered quantities of wild gooseberries, raspberries, and plums. They also caught fish, by the means of a snare made from wires taken from a hoop skirt and stuck on the end of a pole, the girl frightening the fish and the boy catching them in the wire loop as they swam to discover the meaning of the disturbance.

The first winter the family lived chiefly on corn meal, but even so, they were more fortunate than one of their neighbors who had only coarse, yellow turnips until the coming of spring when they had leeks. Anna tells how she and her younger brother, one day when James happened to be away from home, were terrified by coming across five Indians who were making for the cabin. They hurried home and prepared the mother who greeted the unexpected guests with apparent assurance and fed them and later let them take away as gifts such things about the cabin as they made clear by signs they wanted. A few months later the same group of savages returned, bringing an abundant supply of venison and cranberries. Another experience occurred when, fortunately, James was at home. This time there were seven of the Indians and they had with them several jugs of whiskey. They were soon intoxicated and lay about the fire. One by one members of the family slipped up into the attic carrying all the weapons with them. Finally James himself climbed up, leaving the Indians in a stupor. Then the ladder was drawn up. Before this retreat the Indians had amused themselves by making signs of scalping the older sister. It was a long sleepless night, but the family knew that they were safe unless the Indians should take it into their heads later to burn down the cabin. Morning came and the savages withdrew, but without attempting to harm any of the thoroughly frightened family. This brief summary is a representative picture of the resourcefulness, the ingenuity, and the courage that had to be accepted as a matter of fact by those who attempted the pioneer's life.

Out of such a setting it was inevitable that women should gather the spirit of confidence and independence and gain from their male relatives an appreciation and trust through their sharing in fellowship the character-testing struggles and dangers. The theory and assumption of masculine superiority melted as with common effort both men and women were welded together by their ordeals of fire. The woman who participated in nearly all the basic means of livelihood, even in the perils, demonstrated her personality with a certainty that no one was inclined to gainsay. This maturing of woman, these opportunities of self-expression, led to no upheaval, no theorizing as to the rights and position of women as compared with men, but it laid the basis for a more equal relationship of the sexes, and what happened in the vocation experience was to be carried presently onward to logical consequences that were bound to upset the social scheme that had so long maintained women's social inferiority.

The courtship code and the marriage *mores* tended toward the same results. Young people courted early and married young. The surplus of men over women enhanced the value of the latter. Marriage was expected, and for the woman at least there was little else for her except the spinster's career in some other person's household. It was a serious handicap to the man, unless he was content to be a migratory hunter, not to marry. The death of the mate was to either husband or wife a tremendous economic misfortune, in addition to the sense of personal loss. Marriage was literally an investment, for the single man or woman found it almost impossible to become established in the frontier. Public opinion strongly enforced the economic pressure and turned the young man and woman early toward a home of their own. The same conditions had prevailed in the colony, but both the men and the women had been less independent, less free in their courtship and in their choice of a mate, on account of the lingering in the *mores* of influences of European origin, especially those maintaining the authority of the parent. The frontier life encouraged the impulses of independence on the part of youth. Often precociously matured, the young people resented interference from any quarter, once their thought seriously turned toward the finding of a mate. They could not only claim independence, but, with the wilderness open before them, demanding from them for success only strength, health, and skill, they could maintain it.

Conditions of life made any degree of chaperonage almost impossible. It was most natural for young men to escort young women to their homes from any sort of entertainment or public festival. To insist upon the presence of an older adult appeared not only arbitrary but silly. Moreover, the unsecluded girl was accustomed to taking care of herself and had no need under ordinary circumstances for such protection. She had been brought up to assume self-responsibility, and freedom was given her as a matter of course. It would, however, be misleading to interpret this attitude as merely due to environmental conditions. In the earliest days of the New England settlement we have a situation at least resembling that of the later frontier. There, however, we find greater resistance to the freedom of youth and more willingness on their part to accept restriction and parental control. Although the frontier situation favored everywhere the freedom young people enjoyed, there was also working toward this end a social atmosphere which came forth from the civilization as a whole rather than merely from the distances, isolation, and the difficulties of adult supervision. Youth also was sensitive to the forces that were developing the characteristics that we find in older men and women on the American frontier.

As now, surrounded by the comforts of modern life, we look backward on the pioneering woman, her life seems hard and narrow. We also feel its insecurity. These reactions do not appear to have been common among the women who actually went through the experiences. One traveler, who had seen many families crowding their way into the wilderness, assures us that among the "many hundreds of these moving caravans" he scarcely ever saw an unhappy or anxious face.[14]

CHAPTER IV

THE WOMAN OF THE NORTH FROM THE REVOLUTION TO THE CIVIL WAR

THE cultural break between the English settlements in America and the motherland, which led to the Revolutionary War and finally to the birth of the United States of America, was gradual and progressive. It was a mass movement which came to expression in every class and in all sections of the country. Nowhere, as it spread, was there any distinction of sex. It drew the sympathy of women just as it did that of men, and once the war came, women, according to their opportunity, supported it as fervently as did the men. The fighting, of course, took place on the masculine stage, and this naturally has led to the minimizing of the part women played in the conflict. Here and there individual women took over for the moment the male rôle and won patriotic immortality by some spectacular deed of cunning, suffering, or bravery.

In history, written from the masculine viewpoint, even with aristocratic emphasis, these few women, who under unusual circumstances distinguished themselves, have been made representative of the patriotism of their sex. It is, however, to the ordinary contributions of average women that we need to look to find the really significant part played by American women in the culminating struggle between the English government and the colonies. Women substituted for absent husbands and sons, suffered the fears associated with the absence of loved ones who went forth to battle, endured the privations of social disorganization and often of the ruin imposed by the invading enemy, and furnished what they could from their own labor to succor the army in the field or those suffering from disease or wounds. In short, women carried on in this war just as they have in every American conflict, accepting their share of the burden according to the conventions. They suffered equally but differently, and because of this latter fact were pushed into the background by the historians' interpretations.

The prominence given to political leadership, military strategy, and occurrences on the battlefield must not hide the fact that the break with England was essentially domestic, a reaction of homes which were rarely divided in their allegiance. All families were not of one mind, for the Tories were too many and too sincere to be ignored; but usually, whichever turn the colonial individual family took, the attitude of the wife and mother was as strong as that of husband and son. The war passion of the women was, of course, likely to be strongest in those sections that had severely suffered by the actual presence of British forces. In the Revolution, as was later true in the Civil War, in strength of bitterness and hostility there were women who were more intense than were their husbands and sons who had engaged in battle with the enemy. What was true during the war also showed itself in the preliminary tension which drove the two sections of the English empire irresistibly toward war. Once their passions were aroused, groups of women did not hesitate to take direct action, as appears in the following portion of one of Abigail Adams's letters to her husband John.

[July 31, 1777] I have nothing new to entertain you with, unless it be an account of a new set of nobility, which has lately taken the lead in Boston. You must know that there is a great scarcity of sugar and coffee, articles which the female part of the State is very loath to give up, especially whilst they consider the scarcity occasioned by the merchants having secreted a large quantity. There had been much rout and noise in the town for several weeks. Some stores had been opened by a number of people, and the coffee and sugar carried into the market and dealt out by pounds. It was

THE WOMAN OF THE NORTH 107

rumored that an eminent, wealthy, stingy merchant (who is a bachelor) had a hogshead of coffee in his store, which he refused to sell to the committee under six shillings per pound. A number of females, some say a hundred, some say more, assembled with a cart and trucks, marched down to the warehouse, and demanded the keys, which he refused to deliver. Upon which one of them seized him by his neck, and tossed him into the cart. Upon his finding no quarter, he delivered the keys, when they tipped up the cart and discharged him; then opened the warehouse, hoisted out the coffee themselves, put it into the trucks, and drove off.

It was reported that he had personal chastisement among them; but this, I believe, was not true. A large concourse of men stood amazed, silent spectators of the whole transaction. . . .[1]

In a later letter Mrs. Adams, discussing what was to her most grievous, expressed the sentiment of the less articulate members of her sex when she wrote:

[December 23, 1782] If I had known, sir, that Mr. Adams could have effected what he has done, I would not only have submitted to the absence I have endured, painful as it has been, but I would not have opposed it, even though three years more should be added to the number (which Heaven avert!) I feel a pleasure in being able to sacrifice my selfish passions to the general good, and in imitating the example which has taught me to consider myself and family but as the small dust of the balance, when compared with the great community.[2]

In the reconstruction that followed after the Revolutionary War and brought into being the new government with its constitution, women as compared with men were not prominent, but this also easily leads one to forget the importance of the influence of women in the building of the new nation. They, like most men of the time, kept away from the stage where the leaders discussed, debated, and compromised, but these commanding personages were merely the architects of a new culture which was being built by average men and average women. The new government drew its strength from family support and not from an exclusive male allegiance.

Although, on account of its commitment to masculine dominance, the eighteenth century in its historic interpretations could not avoid stressing and exaggerating the male aspects of its events, the war of the Revolution was another illustration among the great happenings of civilization of the fact that no mass movement can be exclusively supported by one sex. It was also true that the new social order had consequences that were bound to change the life of women as well as that of men. In the spirit that led to the war, in the Declaration of Independence that became its symbol, and in the Constitution which attempted to build a workable program, there were implications that concerned women that only time could draw to the surface.

As in all revolutions, the leaders proceeded with the conviction that certain changes could be made while a large area of life would remain as they were accustomed to having it. The rôle of women fell in this second category, and only a few like Abigail Adams caught a glimpse of the disturbing effects that eventually the political changes would have on the status and practices of women.

Naturally this shift, which can perhaps best be described as a shrinking in the territory of masculine predominance, appeared first and clearest in the West where the conditions of life of both men and women encouraged its expression. This, of course, does not mean that the woman of the East, as she encountered the traditions of subordination, played no part in the social reconstruction that followed the war. It was rather that her influence had to be expressed in accord with the conventions and exerted to a considerable degree indirectly. This, however, need not be interpreted as meaning that her service was ineffective, but rather that it had to enter action through the medium of men who were given credit when, as legislators, administrators, publicists, or scholars, they made some practical contribution to the social order. This influence of women chiefly appeared in society and especially at the capitol, where women of thoughtfulness and charm came into familiar contact with men of prominence. This is illustrated by the opportunity that came to the wife of the President of the United States or the hostess of the White House, chosen by the unmarried chief magistrate.

The serious, clever, and ambitious woman, who had entrée to the most exclusive society of her time, played a rôle in the social and the political events that we are likely to underestimate because of the way by which she had to bring about her accomplishments. It was, however, inevitable that some women, particularly those who felt the social grievances of their sex, should not be satisfied by this indirect method of social manipulation. Especially was this true because those who felt most the handicaps and injustices resulting from woman's social and political status were usually women who neither by birth nor marriage moved in the most distinguished society. Intrigue and second-hand methods of exerting influence through masculine leadership were denied to them. But even if it had been otherwise, they would not long have been content, for they were strong characters who under any circumstances would have coveted direct action.

Dolly Madison may be used as a representative of the other sort of woman. She had the gift as well as the inclination to make good use of her social position, and we know that her husband found her a political as well as a domestic helpmate. During the first third of the century, society, in the narrow sense of the term, was the most effective outlet for women who coveted a degree of power. The form their ambitions took neither challenged the traditions nor provoked situations which led to sex antagonism. The male whose designs were blocked or hampered by the maneuvering of some attractive and strategic woman could not rid himself of her opposition by an appeal to the masculine prerogatives, because she was acting within the code. The best he could do was to find a female ally of his own.

In spite of the spectacular character of the acts of patriotism of women who for the moment played the masculine rôle during the war, or the effectiveness of clever, ambitious women maneuvering in society, along neither of these lines must we look to trace the main stream of woman's progress during the period. Nor shall we find this in the agitation for women's rights already near at hand. Significant and impressive as these movements are, they reveal fundamental changes that had already occurred in the life of women, creating the appetite for greater advancement as well as showing the direction that woman's progress was to take.

The momentum that was carrying woman's status forward came chiefly from her changing social experience, a product of environmental conditions in the United States, especially in the frontier. It leads to deception, however, to think that influences grew up west of the Alleghenies and poured forth gradually dissolving the traditions of the more conservative and thickly settled communities of the eastern slope. The environmental conditions that were making the conventional status of woman more and more out of accord with the life she was actually living were in both the East and the West. It was rather that the more newly-settled region was less custom-bound, thus giving women a larger opportunity to take advantage of the changing circumstances. We must not look merely to the life of women to detect these changes, for much that was occurring in her experience was a reflex of the advance that was occurring all along the line in American culture.

The individual women of social prominence who were using their opportunities for leadership and the women who later organized to achieve a political and legal equality with men were out on the skirmish line, but the main army that followed after was of more massive strength. Humanity again was on the march. The customs and ideals that took for granted woman's inferiority and the necessity of male predominance were growing more and more out of accord with the kind of life that both men and women were living. The changing civilization, when looked at from the viewpoint of its concern for women, became a period of transition which reached its culmination in the events of the First World War and the Second.

As we now look back upon the period of our interest in this chapter, we feel the temptation to see the advance of women as a gradual evolution, but only from a long-distance survey can it be so described. There is also the danger, always present in social generalizations, of conceiving of the movement as consistent. As a matter of fact, the United States showed great variation as its culture expressed or affected the life of women and great differences as to sections, classes, religious groups, and educational and family environments. In the determining of social attitudes the western section had the leadership. Vocational changes, as the result of the rapid development of industry, were moving in the Northeast more rapidly toward modern life.

The South was holding more firmly to tradition, but it was distinguished by great variation in classes. In many respects the women of the aristocracy were enjoying in the Southeast the greatest prestige ever achieved under the code of masculine dominance. In all sections there is need of recognizing the differences between the city and the rural populations. In spite of these differences, the influences of social origin that were undermining the foundation upon which masculine dominance rested were, in greater or less degree, at work everywhere.

One important fact we, as we look backward, must keep in mind. Civilization as it had to do with women was not only in transition, it was moving with great rapidity. This was characteristic of American life in all its aspects and was one of the things in the New World that impressed the European visitor. Material conquest of the continent was going on at a most rapid pace, and this was forcing a similar social tempo. Captain Marryat pictures this vividly as he writes of the improvement—"so rapid, indeed, that those who would describe America now would have to correct all in the short space of ten years; for ten years in America is almost equal to a century in the old continent. Now, you may pass through a wild forest, where the elk browses and the panther howls. In ten years, that very forest, with its denizens, will, most likely, have disappeared, and in their place you will find towns with thousands of inhabitants; with arts, manufactures, and machinery, all in full activity."[3]

One illustration of the changing life of the American people was the excess of women over men, as revealed by the census of 1860, in eight of the older eastern states: Connecticut, Maryland, Massachusetts, New Hampshire, New Jersey, Rhode Island, New York, and North Carolina.[4] Taking the population as a whole, there were 730,000 more men than women.[5] In California there were 67,000 more males than females, and in Illinois the excess was 92,000, but in Massachusetts the sex ratio was reversed, with a female predominance of 37,600.[6] In the area of the eight states named, there were 74,360 more women than men. Taking the United States as a whole, at the time of the eighth census, the ratio of the number of males to that of the females was very nearly 104 to 100 for the native white population. Among the foreign-born the ratio was 117 to 100. Ten years previously it had been 124 to 100.[7]

No one would discount the practical influence that the excess of males over females had had from the days of the first settlement. The following table describes the situation as it existed from 1820 to the Eighth Census.

TABLE I [8]

Year	Males	Females	Excess of Males
1820	4,898,127	4,740,004	158,123
1830	6,529,696	6,336,324	193,372
1840	8,688,532	8,380,921	307,611
1850	11,837,661	11,354,215	483,446

The law of supply and demand clearly operated to the social gain of women while they were fewer in number than men. During the period when the great majority of American people were rural and for the most part farmers, the males who sought to make a living on the land were in desperate need of marriage, for without a helpmate success was difficult, and when there were more men than women, the latter not only had a good chance to marry, if they wanted to, but also a prestige born of the social situation. As the frontier wave pushed westward, with it went these advantages that came to women in communities so predominantly male.

There was a small proportion of the men who went into the wilderness who married Indian women or who lived with them temporarily, and often this appeared expedient for the trapper and especially for the trader with the Indians. On the whole, however, here there was a decided difference between those who settled in South America and the men who founded and developed the United States. A much larger proportion of males in the southern hemisphere were willing to mix race or blood. Even those white men in North America who had no aversion to sex relations with the aborigines did, as a rule, recoil from the thought of marrying them. In any case the white woman had a status distinctly different from the Indian squaw.

The twelfth census, which revealed the changing ratio of the sexes in the older sections, also disclosed an industrial trend which was to have profound influence upon the life of American women. Fortunately, as the frontier situation passed in the East, there came from a different quarter an increase of opportunity for women. Machine industry, which had a slow development on this side of the Atlantic, was now proceeding at a rapid pace and began to offer the unmarried woman in the industrial communities of the Northeast the means of independent livelihood. If the West offered the best chances for matrimony, the East was creating the rival which in our own time is giving marriage such sharp competition.

At the beginning of the era covered by this chapter, nearly all the people in the North, the South, and the West were gaining their living either from a self-supporting farm or from some business indirectly connected with it. The self-sufficiency of the New England farmer, for example, was indeed surprising. He gathered by his own labors an abundant and varied diet. About the only things he used that he could not himself provide from his own soil were salt, tea, coffee, molasses, and rum. There was the same self-sufficiency in regard to clothing as in regard to food. Early in the nineteenth century Gallatin wrote as follows concerning this household source of textiles.

"But by far the greater part of the goods made of those materials (cotton, flax, and wool) are manufactured in private families, mostly for their own use, and partly for sale. They consist principally of coarse cloth, flannel, cotton stuffs and stripes of every description, linen, and mixtures of wool with flax or cotton. The information received from every State and from more than sixty different places, concurs in establishing the fact of an extraordinary increase, during the last two years, and in rendering it probable that about two-thirds of the clothing, including hosiery, and of the house and table linen, worn and used by the inhabitants of the United States, who do not reside in cities, is the product of family manufactures." [9]

A consequence of this self-sufficiency of the New England farmer was a low standard of living. There was no opportunity for specialization, and even the professional man had to interrupt his law or his medical practice to carry on the agricultural enterprises on which he had to depend for part of his support. The farmer, to a very great extent, had to be his own mechanic, as from time to time he did the best he could as mason, carpenter, wheelwright, and general Jack-of-all-trades. The consequence was that agriculture itself, as compared with that of England in the same period, was backward and inefficient. Hours of labor were long and the toil, broken by little leisure, arduous. Industry and thrift were two of the virtues most applauded and most practiced.

The standard of living, although relatively low as compared with that of rural people in the same section in our time, was superior in comforts and in resources to that commonly found on the frontier or among the laboring classes of Great Britain. This fact, with the love of sweeping generalizations, is the explanation of the glowing accounts we find of farm life in New England in the reports of travelers, of whom Timothy Dwight is a good example. The following is one of his descriptions of conditions of life in rural New England:

"The means of comfortable living, are in New-England so abundant, and so easily obtained, as to be within the reach of every man who has health, industry, common honesty, and common sense. Labour commands such a price, that every labourer of this character may earn from one hundred and twenty-five to two hundred and fifty dollars a year. Hence every one may within a moderate period purchase himself a farm of considerable extent in the recent settlements, and a small one in those which are older. Even those, who are somewhat below the common level in these attributes, may, and do, acquire small houses, and gardens, where they usually live comfortably." [10]

After discussing in detail the diet of the people, which gives the suggestion of abundance, and their recreation, he continues as follows regarding the ambition of the people and their opportunity for advancement.

". . . No man here begins life with the expectation of being a mere labourer. All intend to possess, and almost all actually possess, a comfortable degree of property, and independence. The ascent to better circumstances, and higher stations, is always open; and there are very few, who do not attempt to rise. He, who is discontented with his present condition, is at perfect liberty to quit it for another, more agreeable to his wishes; and a great multitude actually quit their original poverty and insignificance, for wealth and reputation. No disadvantages result to the community from this source; the benefits, derived from it, are very numerous, and everywhere visible." [11]

One of the influences that discouraged careful tilling of the soil in the Northeast was the abundance of land on the frontier. When virgin land could be had so easily and so cheaply, there was little motive to husband rather than to exploit the soil. The influence of land speculation worked in the same way, giving the migratory farmer disinclination to develop a long-time agricultural policy. As soon, also, as improved methods of transportation—first the canals and then the railroads—gave the West access to the eastern market, the farmers of New England and the Middle States had to meet a competition that checked any considerable lifting of the scale of living of the rural people of the East.

It is important to keep in mind how subservient women were in their economic status, since their support came ordinarily through the earnings of their mates. In spite of the fact that there were, as we have seen, from colonial days openings in commerce and in the types of industry existing at the time, for the exceptional women who maintained economic independence, the vast majority of women found in housewifery or through helping some other woman to carry on her household tasks, or in a less but increasing opportunity to teach, their only means of livelihood. Even in the latter the young woman who sought a position ordinarily found herself confronted with a school board made up of men. In whatever direction she turned, the woman of the period who attempted self-support was met by an economic control in the hands of men.

The life of the average woman of the period, like that of the average man, was hard. The greater part of the manufacturing processes carried on by the family was regarded as the proper task of women. In addition to caring for their homes, day by day, by cooking, house cleaning, and other labors included in general housekeeping, the wife was chiefly responsible for making the clothing of the family, the soap, and other materials that had to be provided by home-manufacturing, and for the preparation of food preserved for winter consumption. Taking into account the amount of muscular energy they had to expend, their meager

THE WOMAN OF THE NORTH

household equipment and resources, and the size of the families of the period, it is clear that most women in maintaining their homes had to over-drain their strength. In addition, however, there was the care of children, the nursing of the sick, the labor associated with community enterprises such as weddings, funerals, house-raisings, and with childbirth, that one unescapable burden, not shared by the man, which made such demands on woman's biologic vitality, both physiological and nervous, and with which nothing among the hardships of man could be compared.

Both birth rates and death rates were high and the women, whose ordinary household duties forced them to work to their limit, grew old quickly and broke early from too frequent pregnancies. Here as elsewhere social practices reflected masculine dominance, and the lot of women who again and again, with no spacing, were called upon to deliver life, however much regretted and how often undesired, was accepted as one of the necessary misfortunes belonging to the female.

As the factory system grew during the period and immigration increased, the rural economy which maintained a self-sufficient household gradually turned to a type of farming that largely depended upon the sale of farm products in towns and cities. Land was still cheap and labor relatively scarce and costly. This situation led to the development of agricultural machinery, very gradual at first, designed to increase the output per man. The evolution of the plow from the wood instruments of the colonial period to one of cast iron and of movable parts was perhaps the most important of these inventions. The mowing and reaping machine followed, supplementing the efficiency of the rapidly improving plow.

Improvements that lightened housework came more slowly. A common explanation of this has been the lack of inventiveness among women. Even if we had the evidence to demonstrate innate differences in this special field of imagination, following sex lines, we would still need to recognize another cause of the slower coming of household devices. The masculine dominance of the period extended to the family pocketbook, and that usually meant a greater willingness to spend for machinery that was expected to increase production and profits than for mechanical aids that would help the housewife in doing work of which the man ordinarily did not have first-hand knowledge. This economic situation naturally turned the attention of the inventive genius toward machinery needed in industry and on the farm.

There was another fact that later in the Northeast hampered the woman in her housekeeping as compared with the man in his farming. The woman had to carry on her toil under conditions determined by the character of the farmhouse. In this construction not much thought was given to conveniences that would lighten household tasks. Architecture tended to follow the pattern set in the colonial period, and both men and women lacked the critical attitude toward the architectural conventions that would have stimulated the building of better adapted houses. To a very great extent in the Northeast the farmhouses were handed down generation after generation, and the woman had to conform to the situation as she found it.

As the birth rate decreased, many of the houses were too large, especially as the scale of living of the well-to-do women tended to increase the general standards of housekeeping for ambitious, conscientious housewives. Even when the eastern woman began to profit from the inventions that did help her, there was a large leakage of energy as she added certain conventions to her household schedule instead of increasing her leisure. The woman of the Middle West was more fortunate. In the frontier period it was necessary to build simple, compact, and relatively small houses. By the time farm owners were in a position to expand, there was greater response to influences that were tending to modernize housekeeping, but it is easy to exaggerate the differences in the architectural history of the two sections. Both east and west there was a relative retardation in the use of inventions within the home as compared with what was happening in industry and on the farm.

THE WOMAN OF THE NORTH

The changes in woman's life and status that were taking place in the northeastern section came from the development that was taking place in industry more than from what was happening on the farm. The first third of this period was one of transition, household manufacturing gradually giving way to the factory system. The industrial revolution which so rapidly went forward in England during the last third of the eighteenth century and the first two decades of the nineteenth century led eventually to a similar development in North America, particularly in the northeastern states.

The ruralism of the United States and the English attempt to maintain a monopoly by forbidding the exporting of machinery and the emigration of workers familiar with the new inventions retarded the coming of the factory system on this side. On the other hand, there were organizations and political leaders, among whom Hamilton was conspicuous, committed to the doing of everything possible to encourage factory manufacturing in the United States. From 1790 to 1830 there was a rapid evolution of the factory system in America. It was not, however, a consistent sweeping aside of household and small shop production and the coming of the large mill, but a transition during which many different types of manufacturing coexisted. Goods produced by households, by individual craftsmen, and by small shops and mills competed with the output of factories, but they were gradually supplanted.

The transference from household to factory production was most rapid in the field of the textiles. Except in isolated hamlets, spinning and weaving in New England and the Middle States went out of the homes into factories before 1830. We can distinguish four stages in the process: when the household was self-sufficient and independent; when it was supplemented by the factory; when it received material prepared at the factory; and, finally, when the factory was independent and dominant.[12] In the local industrial community and in each line of manufacturing, taking the country as a whole, there was much overlapping.

Women had long predominated in the household production of textiles, and it was natural that they followed the industry as it went out of the home into the factory. It is interesting to find that in the town of Leicester, Massachusetts, in 1814, when one of the clothiers of the town began to employ men to work on hand looms in the weaving of woolen cloth, there was local criticism, it being felt that men were doing women's work in the same way that later there was feeling against male milliners and dressmakers.[13] There were, however, other influences than social conventions that were encouraging the working of women and children in the factories. One was the abundance of the labor supply and the other the scale of wages.

As early as 1790 Massachusetts, Rhode Island, and Connecticut reported an excess of females.[14] In these three states, where there were many women eager to respond to a new opportunity for employment, the textile industry developed most rapidly. In 1810 the Secretary of the Treasury, in his official report to Congress, stated that at the end of the preceding year out of the sixty-two cotton mills in operation throughout the United States, eighteen were in Rhode Island and ten in Massachusetts. At the close of the War of 1812, which had greatly stimulated the factory production of woolens, Connecticut had twenty-five factories, the largest number of any state.[15]

Women had, of course, been employed in the textile industry prior to the time of the establishment of the factory system. The United Company of Philadelphia for Promoting American Manufactures is said, before the coming of the machine, to have employed as many as four hundred women. Most of these appear to have done their work at their own homes. This enterprise, established in 1775 in Philadelphia, and apparently the first joint stock manufacturing company in the United States, at one time advertised for women workers as follows: to "employ every good spinner that can apply, however remote from the factory, and, as many women in the country may supply themselves with the materials there and may have leisure to spin in considerable quantities, they are hereby informed that ready money will be given at the factory, up Market Street, for any parcel, either great or small, of hemp, flax, or woolen yarn. The managers return their thanks to all those industrious women who are now employed in spinning for the factory." [16]

Although machine industry in the factories gradually took over the bulk of the production of textiles, a remnant of women was left who carried on various phases of the manufacturing in their own homes. This was true also in other industries. An example of this was a Boston Card Factory that employed not less than twelve hundred people, chiefly women and children, who at their own homes inserted by hand the wire teeth, which were shaped and cut by machinery, into the leather support of the cards used for combing wool and cotton. The farming out to women in their homes of certain sorts of work as a side-line of some manufacturing processes continued throughout the nineteenth century and to a less degree still lingers. In the author's youth, a considerable number of housewives in a small New England industrial community received barrels of baseballs, all finished at the factory except for the sewing on of covers, which had to be done by hand. This final work the women did in their homes as they had time and inclination, being paid according to the quantity and the grade of the balls they sewed.

The general trend of the machine industry as it opened up new opportunity for wage-earning women was unmistakable. The factory system was promoted and defended not only by business men and political leaders but even by philanthropists as a means of giving employment to women and children who otherwise would remain idle with no means of self-support. Looking backward we are too apt to interpret this argument as the insincere rationalizing of profit-seekers, but the fact remains that it was also the point of view of benevolent and public-spirited men of the time.

The shift of population from the rural sections of New England to manufacturing towns, as a consequence of the development of industries in Fall River, New Bedford, Manchester, Lowell, and

Lawrence, demonstrates that there were many women who were eager to respond to the new vocational opening provided by the development of factories. The advice, "Go West, young man," was more than an editorial admonition. It was to a multitude of ambitious men a compelling social suggestion that met with enough response to influence the population of the New England and the Middle Atlantic states. The influence of this western drift, added to the development of machine industry in the towns and cities, would have resulted in a more troublesome excess of females over males in the rural sections had it not been for the new means of livelihood that opened to women in the industrial centers.

The changes in population in Sandwich, New Hampshire, a rural community at the foothills of the White Mountains, is an illustration of what happened. As a consequence of the two migration movements over a hundred years, the population drift in this community was as follows:

TABLE II [17]
Population, Sandwich, New Hampshire

Year	Population
1810	2,232
1820	2,368
1830	2,743
1840	2,625
1850	2,577
1860	2,227
1870	1,854
1880	1,701
1890	1,303
1900	1,077
1910	928

To what extent the factories influenced the excess of females over males in New England cannot be known with certainty, since that difference existed from the first census, but at least it is clear that the surplus women invited the development of factories in the area as did the abundant water power. The sex ratio of females in New England appears in the following table.

TABLE III [18]

Dates	Proportion of Females to 100 Males
1790	100.82
1800	100.48
1810	100.87
1820	103.01
1830	102.46
1840	101.34
1850	100.87

The new factory enterprises were defended on the ground that they offered work to women and children and made use of few men who were fitted to enter agriculture. It was argued that the mills permitted a part of the population that had not been contributing greatly to national wealth—the women and children—to become profitable producers. There were those who insisted that the scarcity of male workers and the high cost of labor made it impossible for the United States to become an industrial nation, but the answer to this was the large number of women and children actually at work and for wages considerably lower than those that would have had to be paid men. As proof of this, there were in Massachusetts in 1850 nearly twice as many women as men employed in the manufacturing of shoes, but their total monthly earnings were slightly less than one-half of that received by the men.[19]

There can be no doubt that to a great many parents who had unmarried daughters, and to these young women themselves, the opportunity to go to a neighboring town or city and find work in the mills seemed, and in fact was, a decided economic advantage. Of course, the employees were native Americans and the young women who left their rural homes to enter cotton and woolen mills, shoe factories, and other machine industries, suffered no loss of prestige and, as a rule, no drop in living conditions. They were also no less likely to marry than if they stayed at home. Indeed, often there appeared to be better promise of matrimony if they left their small rural community and went to industrial centers. The really significant aspect of the industrial evolution, as it influenced women, was its gift of a degree of economic independence which, in spite of the insecurity and hardships, long hours, and low wages, without destroying the hope of marrying, gave women another choice for survival than becoming a wife or an unattached female in either her parents' or some other's household.

The influx of women looking for work in such places as Lowell and Waltham was so great that they could not all find living quarters, and the mill owners were obliged to establish boarding houses. Buildings were constructed to house and feed the women workers. The mill owners sought capable women of character to take charge of these company-owned and -managed boarding houses and took pride in the character of the accommodations they offered. These establishments were given a publicity that was not only an additional enticement to rural parents to let their daughters leave home and to the latter to break away, but also was so widespread as to attract the attention of foreign visitors. For example, Charles Dickens tells us that the reason he gives a chapter in his *American Notes* to his visit in Lowell is that he had been left with such a vivid memory of his experiences there. If his account of Lowell seems too glowing, suggesting that he was guided through the establishments, let it be remembered that he was looking at things from the background of conditions in England. This is his description of the boarding houses.

"They reside in various boarding-houses near at hand. The owners of the mills are particularly careful to allow no persons to enter upon the possession of these houses, whose characters have not undergone the most searching and thorough inquiry. Any complaint that is made against them, by the boarders, or by any one else, is fully investigated; and if good ground of complaint be shown to exist against them, they are removed, and their occupation is handed over to some more deserving person."[20]

The Reverend William Scoresby, who published in 1845 his impression of the New England factory system, became so enthusiastic for the boarding house program that he attempted to introduce it at Bradford but failed, because, he said, the English girls were too accustomed to the regulating of their own affairs and resented supervision.[21] Harriet Martineau criticized severely and for nearly an entire chapter the conventional boarding houses that were so common everywhere at that time in America. She contents herself, however, with saying concerning conditions she found on her visit to the Waltham mills, "most of the girls lived in the houses provided by the corporation which accommodate from six to eighteen." Evidently there was nothing in the mill-type of boarding house to stir strong condemnation.

The corporations were not content merely to regulate the boarding house regime, but they also had rules regarding the personal behavior of the workers. This appears to have been accepted by the New England operatives more or less as a matter of course, although occasionally there was protest from some workers' organization or from individuals. It is interesting to raise the question whether similar regulations could have been successfully imposed on the young women on the western side of the Alleghenies. Prohibition of any employment in the mills of a woman of immoral reputation seems to have been strictly enforced. Although the owners appeared sincerely anxious to protect the welfare of their women workers, as well as to maintain conditions that would invite the coming of the right sort of employees, these paternalistic attitudes proved in the long run incompatible with the growing independence of women, and the system prospered only in the earlier period of industrial transition.

Another feature of the mill town that impressed visitors was the educational and recreational opportunity offered the women workers. At Lowell on the lyceum platform we find such lecturers appearing as Emerson, Edward Everett, and John Quincy Adams. It is said also that of their audiences at least two-thirds were mill women. Lending libraries, debating clubs, and various church and female organizations were maintained. There was also a considerable literary interest, and Charles Dickens testifies that he carried away "four hundred good solid pages," which he read from beginning to end, of original articles written by the female workers, which had been published in the *Lowell Offering,* a periodical which they supported. There were other magazines that served as a literary medium of women who were or had been mill operatives.

Lucy Larcom, who achieved later a national reputation as a writer, discovered her talent while working in one of the mills of Lowell. She has recorded this aspect of the life of women factory workers in an article, showing that there was a considerable output.[22] This writing is significant chiefly, perhaps, in revealing the type of persons who sought work in the mills. Clearly of the middle class, many of them were efficient and ambitious. It is no exaggeration to say that they went to Lowell, New Bedford, Waltham, Manchester, and other mill towns with purposes and from backgrounds suggesting in our own time the girl graduate of the high school who enters the normal school or the state university with the hope of advancing her economic interests, finding a mate, and spending with profit her time before marriage.

Teaching was another occupation that attracted women by offering them the means of self-support. Many of the mill operatives had been or later became teachers. At one time a hundred and fifty women who had previously been teachers were employed by the Merrimack corporation. The superintendent who gave this information also stated that the average earnings of these ex-teachers had been 17¾ per cent more than the average wages of women employed by the mills.[23]

The factory system in the Middle Atlantic States, and especially in Rhode Island, developed in sharp contrast to the sort of situation found at Lowell and Waltham. In this other type of the textile industry, mill owners and managers assumed no responsibility for the conditions of their workers. Their program was similar to that which had already developed in England. They had no company boarding houses, no set of regulations, and furnished no encouragement for self-improvement. Their policy was to employ families, including children as young as they could be put to work. In the first cotton mill, started by Samuel Slater at Pawtucket, Rhode Island, it is said that the workers consisted of seven boys and two girls between the ages of seven and twelve years.[24]

The *laissez faire* policy was not, however, confined to the Atlantic States and Rhode Island. An agent of one of the largest mills of Fall River made this answer to the question whether his company assumed any responsibility for the physical, intellectual, and moral welfare of the workers. "We never do. As for myself, I regard my work-people just as I regard my machinery. So long as they can do my work for what I choose to pay them, I keep them, getting out of them all I can. What they do or how they fare outside my walls I don't know, nor do I consider it my business to know. They must look out for themselves as I do for myself. When my machines get old and useless, I reject them and get new, and these people are part of my machinery."[25]

The native factory population was extremely mobile in the early period of machine industry. It is said that the New England girls who entered cotton mills on the average did not remain more than a year. This rapid turnover was used as an argument defending the long hours of labor. It was said that the young women did not remain long enough to be hurt.

Although it was true, as Lucy Larcom asserted later, that the great majority of the girls working in such mills as those at Lowell had no literary taste or other cultural impulses but merely worked as they had in their rural households, they did represent a high type of New England rural character, and as fast as immigration brought workers who would accept lower standards of living, they left the mills and a more permanent and less demanding working class took their places. The Irish, and in less degree the English, the German, and the French-Canadians accepted positions that were less inviting than other opportunities that were rapidly opening up to the native women. This spread of industrial opportunity drew the latter away from the textile factories, where their wages were low and where there was less demand for skill than, for example, in the machine processes associated with the making of shoes. But in this connection it must be remembered that the textile mills were not only the first to attract a considerable population of women wage earners but also that the development of these industries stimulated others and established the social convention that approved women's working outside their homes.

Thus the textile mills opened the door to an opportunity for women which rapidly increased as one occupation after another provided the means for an independent, self-supporting wage-career for women. Women had gained an entrance into the economic experience that had so long been reserved for men, but they were not to find their passage easy, although, for their ultimate escape from masculine dominance, it was sufficient that they had broken through.

While the entrance of native New England young women into the textile machine industry enlarged woman's vocational opportunity, both directly and indirectly, it did not mean that these industrial pioneers escaped the long hours of toil which were the lot of those living and working at home. The working schedule of the mills was similar to that found on the farms. Even at Lowell we find children not older than ten working from fourteen to fifteen hours daily. There the mills started at five o'clock in the morning and continued until seven in the evening, with one-half hour given to breakfast and to dinner. Sometimes, when there was need of rushing, the mill kept open until nine or ten o'clock at night, and sometimes work started at four in the morning.[26]

In 1832, in New England, the length of the working day in the mills varied from twelve to fifteen hours, most of them having a schedule of thirteen hours. A committee of the Massachusetts Legislature, investigating labor conditions of children, reported in 1825 that the working period appeared to be from twelve to thirteen hours daily except on the Sabbath. The factory bells rang early enough to awaken the women and children in time for them to be at the mill when work started. At Lowell, in 1846, the bell rang at four-thirty, and the employees were disciplined if they were not at work at five. At Paterson, New Jersey, women and children had to be at work at four-thirty, and it is said that this regulation was enforced by the use of the cowhide.[27] Although the mill schedule was undoubtedly more exacting and fatiguing, on account of the monotony and continuity of the work as compared with the changing, intermittent labor in the household, so far as the early rising and long day were concerned, the situation was not unlike that in the homes from which the women workers had come. This fact not only reveals the low scale of economic productivity on the New England farms but also the impossibility of the women mill workers' making any considerable or serious attempts to advance in culture. They literally seldom had the energy.

The wages of both women and children were low, but today they sound lower than they actually were in comparison with the earnings in other lines of occupation. For example, in 1828, one investigator estimated that there were at least twelve thousand women working in the sweat shops of the clothing industry in Baltimore, Philadelphia, New York, and Boston, who did not earn by constant employment more than $1.25 a week. The average wage paid in the Massachusetts cotton mills in 1831 was said to be $2.25 per week, and in Newark, N. J., $1.90. Miss Abbott has reported from an old copy of a record book preserved by the Waltham cotton mills a complete payroll. In the Carding Department we find three women receiving $1.50 per week, the lowest wage; twenty-four, $2.25, the most common earnings; and one receiving $3.66. In the Spinning Department the corresponding record was: three women received $2.00; twenty, $2.25; and one, $4.00. Among the weavers, there were three earning $1.75; twenty-nine, $2.25; and one, $3.92. One hundred and twenty-six of the weavers were women and four were men. Two of the men received $12.00 a week, and the other two received $6.60.[28] It is hard now to realize that such a wage scale among those who first went into the textile mills tended to raise women's earnings generally. A great majority of these women workers in the mills could not fully support themselves but had to depend upon some assistance from their families. Some, especially in the Lowell mills, achieved complete economic independence. This need of family help was true, of course, in the other occupations at the time open to women.[29]

The mill experience also stimulated the economic aggressiveness of American women. This is all the more remarkable in view of the limited opportunity the women of the time had to work for wages. In spite of the narrowness of the field open to them, we find in 1836 the women at the Lowell mills striking because of an increase in the price of board of 24 cents a week, one-half of which the girl was to pay and the other half to be taken by the mill from her earnings and turned over to the housekeeper. Twenty-five hundred women struck. Although the effort failed, it drew the attention and sympathy of the men who met at the next annual convention of the National Trade Union.[30]

In Paterson, New Jersey, in 1828, a strike occurred which originated among the children. In Dover, New Hampshire, in 1834, a strike was called at the threat of a reduction of wages, in which the girls took a prominent part. Although women workers tended, as one would expect from the conventions of the time, to be more docile and less free than male workers, their discontent, even if to little purpose, was expressed from time to time during the early period of the industrial transition, the formative period of the

American Labor Movement. Their mobility, their interest in marriage as a career, their obligations when they became mothers, and their lack of experience, as well as their social and political inferiority, and, on account of the social conventions, their lesser freedom, proved then as now a handicap in any concerted movement.

Their feelings of insecurity and unjust treatment occasionally flared up, showing that at least they were conscious of their unequal situation and had the impulse to better their conditions. So far as the mill industry was concerned, women were indeed the weaker sex and the more easily preyed upon by the exploitation of the time. This, however, was no new situation brought about by machine industry. It was true on the farms and in the earlier textile manufacturing in homes which preceded the coming of machines. The development of the mills meant at first merely changing the form of woman's labor. The conditions under which she worked were already established. Women constituted a cheaper class of workers than men. Therefore, the mill owners absorbed them in their industries to the fullest extent possible.

Taking women out of the household was the innovation. The conservatives viewed this with a critical attitude and their dire prophecies were many. They were right in insisting that something was happening that was bound to have unforeseen social consequences. The crust of prejudice and custom, upon which rested woman's economic inferiority, was being penetrated by a new force—economic independence—which at first gave no inkling that it was friendly to the advancement of woman's welfare.

The attempt of the more socially-minded mill owners to regulate and supervise the conduct of their female employees was only in the most narrow sense motivated by ideas of public welfare. The effort came rather from the realization that people generally were suspicious of the new type of work offered women and that a steady and adequate labor supply would be difficult to obtain if it were not generally felt by parents of the Northeast that the environment and habits of the working girls were safeguarded. There was a feeling among the farming population that factory conditions encouraged loose morals. It was because of this that there was in the thinking of the most conscientious employers a prudential regard for the well-being of their workers.

The mill owners had no interest in such matters as the effect of long hours on the physical health of the women, the nervous results of tension, or the other risks of modern industry that are now regarded seriously by an efficient management, but, aside from those who held to the *laissez faire* doctrine, they did feel responsibility for the morals of their young women. This, when sifted, largely meant that the latter were religious in the sense that they regularly attended church and that they were sexually virtuous.

Not only on account of the strength of the impulse involved, but also because of the prevailing social situation, moral pressure and moral laxness surged about the sex code. So far as men were concerned, the double standard, although ideally frowned upon, in practice was largely taken for granted. There was considerable prostitution, and the houses, generally more or less segregated, were in large towns so well known as to be familiar even to boys. In spite of the various expressions of sex laxity, the prevailing attitude toward this problem of human conduct was that of prudery and taboo. Sex was seldom openly acknowledged except in sensational preachments against immorality. Nevertheless, it was not given even the restraint that in these days of greater liberality good taste insists upon. For example, we find a freedom in the newspaper advertisements of the period that would now shock the most sophisticated reader. The inconsistencies of the past in social attitudes are always clear as we look backward, but certainly this incongruity of both suppression and exploitation of sex at the same moment is to us difficult to understand.

Much was made of the distinction between the good and the evil woman, the pure and the impure. The latter was not treated with the severity of the early Puritan era, but she was a social outlaw without rights, while, on the contrary, the woman of virtue was supposed to have the respect and protection of any man, whether a relative or stranger.

Naturally the men who decided the policy of the rapidly advancing industry of machine production were sensitive to a public opinion that insisted upon the social protection of the young, virtuous woman worker. Mill owners were interested merely in advancing their industrial program, but it was expedient and, of course, to many of them also in accord with their wishes to prove themselves careful of the moral welfare of the women who flocked from their rural homes to the manufacturing centers. Commitment to material advancement was dominant, and the effort to build a prosperous business subordinated all other interests.

The protection of women and children was merely incidental. Indeed, the concentration on production, trade, and wealth, seemed to Harriet Martineau the one obstruction to woman's gaining social justice in the United States more rapidly than elsewhere. Feeling this, she was much less impressed than Dickens and others with the benevolent, paternalistic policy at places like Lowell and Waltham. Her reaction led her to write:

"If it were not for the external prosperity of the country, the injured half of its society would probably obtain justice sooner than in any country of Europe. But the prosperity of America is a circumstance unfavourable to its women. It will be long before they are put to the proof as to what they are capable of thinking and doing: a proof to which hundreds, perhaps thousands of Englishwomen have been put by adversity, and the result of which is a remarkable improvement in their social condition, even within the space of ten years." [31]

The large place given the boarding house in the guardianship program of the mill owners was more in accord with the habits of the times than it now seems. As early as Harriet Martineau's visit to the United States, in 1834, the boarding house had become such a characteristic aspect of American life in the Northeast as not only to attract her attention but to convince her of its unwholesomeness. This, in part, was her appraisal.

"It is a circumstance very unfavourable to the character of some American women, that boarding-house life has been rendered compulsory by the scarcity of labour,—the difficulty of obtaining domestic service. The more I saw of boarding-house life, the worse I thought of it; though I saw none but the best. Indeed, the degrees of merit in such establishments weigh little in the consideration of the evil of their existence at all. In the best it is something to be secure of respectable company, of a good table, a well-mannered and courteous hostess, and comfort in the private apartments: but the mischiefs of the system throw all these objects into the back-ground." [32]

Undoubtedly the author was right in ascribing both economic and parasitic motives to the vogue of the boarding house in America. It is true also that the Americans of this time and in this section had grown very distant from their English ancestry. The tenacious love of privacy of the one stood in vivid contrast with the gregarious tendencies of the other, and this fact made a strong impression on English visitors. Lyell, writing ten years after Harriet Martineau, expresses his dislike also for the boarding house scheme of things.

"As we intended to pass nearly two months in Boston, we determined to look out for private lodgings, such as might be met with in every large town in England, but which we found it almost impossible to procure here. It does not answer to keep houses, or even suites of apartments to let in a city where house-rent is so dear, and well-trained servants so difficult to hire, even at high wages. In this country, moreover, the mass of the people seem to set less value on the privilege of living in private than we English do. Not only strangers and bachelors, but whole families, reside in boarding-houses, usually kept by a widow who has known better days, and is a good manager, and can teach and discipline servants.

"During a former tour, we had found it irksome to submit to the rules of a boarding-house for any length of time; to take every meal at a public table, where you are expected to play the agreeable to companions often uncongenial, and brought together on no principle of selection; to join them in the drawing-room a short time before dinner; to call on them in their rooms, and to listen to gossip and complaints about the petty quarrels which so often arise among fellow-boarders, as in a ship during a long voyage." [33]

Captain Marryat, who several times shows his irritation at the American's disregard and dislike of solitude, declares:

"The Americans are as gregarious as school-boys, and think it an incivility to leave you by yourself. Everything is done in crowds, and among a crowd. They even prefer a double bed to a single one, and I have often had the offer to sleep with me made out of real kindness. You must go 'east of sun-rise' (or west of sun-set) if you would have solitude." [34]

The large place given the boarding house in the Waltham and the Lowell schemes was less paternalistic than it now seems, and nothing was more natural for the mill owners who felt any degree of responsibility for the care of their young women workers or who felt the expediency of protecting against possible criticism, than to concentrate upon the boarding house as the basis for their program. It was not out of accord with common practices to impose regulations. The mill management merely took over what happened to be a distinctive social institution in the period and adapted it to the circumstances of the mill town.

It was only for a brief time that the native young American girls from rural communities furnished the bulk of the mill workers. By 1842 foreign immigration had become such a source of help for the mill executives to draw upon that it attracted attention in Fall River. The exodus of the native American workers began from that city and from Rhode Island. By 1860 the mill workers were mostly English and Irish. In Massachusetts and New Hampshire, where the non-family type of employment was more common, the replacement did not start quite so soon. By 1873, however, the mills throughout the area were largely manned by persons of foreign birth, chiefly English, Irish, Scotch, and French-Canadian.

The significance, therefore, of this entrance of native young women into a new vocation and a semi-independent means of livelihood must be found in the effect of this experience as it implanted in the *mores* a more liberal attitude toward women working outside the family and in the stimulus it gave them to invade vocations that had been for so long almost the complete possession of men. So far as development of industry was concerned, the going of the native young women into the mills suggested a brief visitation of no lasting significance. Looked at, however, as something that loosened long-established traditions, it appears as having added measurably to the influences that were making ready for the entrance of the new American type of modern woman.

CHAPTER V

THE WOMAN OF THE SOUTH FROM THE REVOLUTION TO THE CIVIL WAR

In the growth of the United States from the War of the Revolution up to the time of the breaking out of the Civil War, no section was so distinctively set apart from the country as the group of states that were known as the South. It was chiefly rural, but it had little in common with the farming areas of either the North or the West. Its fundamental differences came from a peculiarity of soil and climate, but built upon these was a culture which grew increasingly unlike that developing in the other sections.

So variegated and complex an evolution as civilization never comes from the operation of a single, independent cause. Avoiding this overstatement, it is, however, not too much to say that in the Northeast the commanding influence that accounted for much of the social development characteristic of the section was the machine. In the West it was the ambition to own land and to establish the reputation best expressed in the term, self-made. In the South it was slavery, and this had in the culture of the section a direct, clear dominance not true of its rivals north and west.

At the opening of the period, in prestige, political power, wealth, and cultural standards the South could justly be described as the most favored portion of the United States. Its misfortune, which in time was destined to bring it tragic consequences, came from the development of a type of agriculture that demanded cheap, unskilled, muscular labor, an adequate supply of which it seemed could be had only by the maintenance of African slavery. At the beginning of the period this century-old method of production was taken as a matter of course in the North just as it was in the South, but it was the calamitous fate of the latter that as the economic and humanitarian trends in the North and the West, and in most parts of the civilized world, led to the disappearance of the slave system and strong feeling against it, southern culture became more and more dependent upon it. This situation was the result of the dominance of cotton in the agriculture of the southern states.

During the colonial period the cultivation of cotton had been insignificant. Tobacco was the important crop. It also was tied up with the slave method of production, but neither it nor the cultivation of rice, another rival, created such a demand for slave labor as did cotton. During the Revolutionary War the blockade of the English fleet, closing the source of the supply of textiles and of the raw material which the colonies had imported, led to an attempt to find a substitute for the latter in cotton and its cultivation was extended. The artificial situation of the war, with the signing of peace, came to an end, and there would have been no lasting consequence of this effort to develop a new source for textile manufacturers had it not been that the invention of machines for the spinning and weaving of cloth opened up a new use of cotton. Even so, there was little incentive for the growing of cotton, because it was so expensive to separate the seed and the fibers of the boll of cotton. When Eli Whitney, in 1793, produced his mechanical contrivance, permitting a much more rapid and less expensive method of carrying on this separation, everything was set for a tremendous development of cotton production in the South.

The Whitney invention made it possible to harvest short-fiber cotton with profit. This not only opened a great part of the Southeast to cotton production but also made it possible for its cultivation to be extended in the Southwest where the virgin soil was especially inviting. After the Revolutionary War, some Georgia planters experimented with the long-fiber cotton, the seed of which they had got from the Bahama Islands. They found that they could produce an even better grade of cotton, but it was possible to grow the plant only in the lowlands along the eastern coast. This zone was from twenty to thirty miles wide and extended from the Santee River on the north down to the Florida Everglades.[1]

As a result of the invention of the cotton gin, the growing of the short-fiber cotton soon became the chief industry of the South and the supply of a large portion of the raw material needed for the development of the northern textile industry. This in turn provided a market for the greater part of western agricultural products. Thus the chief agricultural crop of the South supported in large measure the prosperity of the Northeast and indirectly that of the West and the Northwest. It also fed the cotton industry of Europe, especially that of England and Scotland. With this immense international demand, and as many as four hundred thousand square miles of land upon which cotton could be successfully grown, the economic security of the South seemed impregnable, but the edifice rested on the foundation of slave labor, and the machine industry that the cotton planter helped to make possible was bringing into being forces that would in time undermine the support upon which southern civilization rested.

The passing of slavery was inevitable; indeed, it then seemed not far away in view of the growing sentiment against it in the South at the very time that Whitney's gin made it almost overnight seem indispensable to the existing southern culture. This invention, however, as we now see, gave it merely a respite, for the influences that were bound to force its passing were already in operation. Unfortunately, the moment they had gone far enough to release a portion of the eastern and western population from the traditional acceptance of African slavery, impatient feeling rushed ahead of the slow-moving but invincible economic pressure, born of the spirit and circumstances of machine industry, and created a moral issue.

Stephen A. Douglas seems to have been one of the few who realized the positive determination concealed in the *laissez faire* attitude toward slavery, foreseeing that economic conditions would not only restrict it to a limited area of the nation but eventually crush it. As so often happens in the ongoing of civilization, agitation against slavery was anticipatory, an attempt precociously to hurry what the fateful forces, given time enough, were sure to bring, but with the least possible disturbance.

In no section of the United States was the career of women more dependent upon that of men than in the southern states. Because of this, as we survey woman's life in the South in this period, we are apt to see it in the shadow of an approaching final collapse of southern culture. This is distinctly unfair. In so far as this approach spoils a just appraisal of the experiences of southern women in this period, it must be resisted.

The cleavage between the North and the South was gradual, and until the later years of the stretch from 1830 to 1860 few there were who caught a glimpse of the coming collision. As now we look backward, the southern states seem the tragic victims of an inevitable social and economic evolution. They were enticed by economic influences to build their cultural life on a foundation that in time was destined to be swept aside. Their prosperity, substantial though it seemed, was linked to a system of production that was soon to be socially out of season. Replacement was forced upon them in the most exhausting and demoralizing of all possible ways, futile struggle, and they were left with an alien population, a backward people, many of them only yesterday plucked from savagery, and land which then, as now, encouraged cotton cultivation, the agricultural crop that was perhaps the most exploiting of the soil, demanding cheap labor and resisting, as compared with the grain growing of the West, the use of machinery.

The life of southern women appears in a family setting. This is, of course, largely true both North and West, but the woman's dependency on the status of her father and her husband is more pronounced south of the Mason and Dixon line than elsewhere. As a consequence, it is impossible to give the career of southern women any satisfactory generalization. The section is characterized by conditions of life that range over greater differences than in the North or West, from the lowest level of slavery on the one

THE WOMAN OF THE SOUTH

side to the highest aristocracy on the other. Although the plight of the Negroes stands by itself, it definitely shadows the whites, and not merely those who are on the economic level closest to the slave. It is this variability of cultural conditions that has led to such contrasting pictures as we have been given of the Old South.

Many of the unfavorable pictures of southern life that have come down to us were the reactions of travelers. As we read them we must keep in mind that the writers are usually Europeans or people from the North who were prejudiced against slavery and also unfamiliar with rural travel in the United States. The South was like the West in having its population scattered over a large territory, but there were three features that led the visitor to paint his descriptions of the people in darker colors than those of the frontier. He was less prepared to accept the hardships he encountered in going through the South than those met in the West, because in the latter case he underwrote them from the first, realizing the newness of the settlement.

The discomforts associated with travel in the South also left more vivid impressions, because those who came as strangers did not realize that a large proportion of the most exacting clientele of the region depended upon private hospitality, thus lessening the income and lowering the standards of hotels that had to look to the general public for support.

Then, also, the difficulties due to bad highways and lack of bridges, about which the travelers so frequently complained, were due to characteristics of soil and rivers and the high cost of road maintenance that had to be met by a rural population already suffering from their alliance with an anachronistic system of production. Even today in the South, when roads are unpaved, it is very difficult to keep them in the condition that may be had with a very little effort in New England where gravel is so abundant and flowing water is accustomed to accept its confining banks. The heavy rainfall in the South, which at times was suggestive of the tropics, the type of soil that so quickly eroded or became thick, sticky mud, the long stretches of lowland so easily flooded, which often made travel unpleasant and depressing, and even dangerous, became the background of the observer's reactions. As an example of this we have Charles Dickens's description of coach travel in Virginia, or Harriet Martineau's picture of country life in the South.[2] The former wrote:

Our road lay almost wholly through dense pine-forests; and the constant succession of these trees, with scarcely any other variety, made the way gloomy and monotonous. The road itself was the worst we had ever yet travelled over, it being formed apparently by the mere removal of the requisite number of trees to open a path through the forest, and then left without any kind of labour being employed, either to make the road solid in the first instance, or to keep it in repair. We were, accordingly, sometimes half up to the axletree in loose sand, sometimes still deeper immersed in a running brook, or soft swamp, and occasionally so shaken and tossed from seat to roof, and side to side, from the pitching and rolling of the coach, that it seemed to me the motion was more violent and excessive than that of the smallest vessel in the heaviest sea. We were all, in short, bruised and beaten by the blows we received from these sudden jolts and pitchings, so as to suffer severely; and this, added to the pinching cold, made our journey extremely disagreeable.

On the basis of the statements of travelers, it is quite possible to draw up a general indictment of southern culture, leaving out the area under French influence, and this has been done by some modern interpreters who accept these criticisms from visitors in the South as just appraisals of the conditions characteristic of the section.[3]

In sharpest contrast are descriptions of a part of southern life on an entirely different level and with another setting. Much of this was closed to those who wrote romantically of the South,[4] as it was to those who, like Harriet Martineau, had at the beginning a strong bias toward the abolitionists' program.[5]

The North was predominantly industrial and commercial. Its characteristic atmosphere was that to which most of the European and northern travelers into the South had become adjusted. Without much consciousness of the fact, the type of life with which they were familiar constituted for them the proper standards, and naturally the rural south, with a culture fundamentally colored by slavery, appeared peculiar and unfit, toward which they could not but be critical. This does not mean that they did not respond to the charm and beauty of the South. They all recognized its beauty. Even Harriet Martineau pays tribute to these qualities. There was, however, a fundamental and preconceived antagonism that made them better interpreters of the flaws of the South than discoverers of its excellencies.

Although there was a great number of non-slave owners among the white people of the South, the system supported the culture of the section and indirectly affected the life of every one, at least after the coming of the cotton gin. In this regional development, the planter, with his wide acreage and many slaves, was dominant. His prestige and his influence far excelled that of the mill owner in the North who was in a similar way the leading representative of its distinctive culture. The manufacturers in the Northeast had to force themselves into a social prestige that had long been possessed by politicians and by those who had achieved distinction in the professions or as publicists. In the South the great plantation owner from the first assumed both political and social leadership, and, as slavery became more entrenched, his position became the more secure. Politics, for example, was usually one aspect of the planter's interest; indeed, the position of the large landowner in the South suggests that of the English squire in the eighteenth century. The planter's ascendancy showed itself in the church, in education, and in society in the narrow sense, as well as in affairs of government. In this prestige the planter carried his wife with him.

If in this period there had come about the development of an economic rival such as would have resulted had a diversified manufacturing system started in the South, as it did in the North, the sway of the planter would have met competition. Then the clashing of two different types of culture would have occurred in the region itself rather than between the North and the South, and the latter might have escaped the suffering that came from being forced to assume nearly all the burden of replacing a productive system that, although functioning in the South, was national in origin and in instigation.

From a different angle, had the industry of the North developed exclusively along the line of cotton mills, there would have been an alliance of mill owner and planter, which, though it might have delayed the shedding of the slavery system in the South, would have permitted in the end its replacement, as in other parts of America in the century, without the passion and the economic disturbance of a great war. This would have proved as advantageous to the Negro as to the white, for his social status rested on *mores*-sanctions and could not be changed by the mere signing of a legal document or without the passing of time. The War and its aftermath delayed the advance of the Negro into citizenship in spite of emancipation. The same system that gave the planter's wife eminence committed her to its support, and eventually not only demanded from her supreme sacrifices but also hampered her orderly progress during the cultural changes of the nineteenth century.

Although the American planter of the South suggests the English squire as far as influence is concerned, there is no parallel between their vocational functioning. The planter was considerably more than just a large farmer. His plantation was a community in itself. Whether he cultivated cotton, tobacco, rice, or sugar, he had to carry on many activities in addition to the raising of the crops.

The plantation endeavored to be self-supporting, as had the colonial farm in New England or that on the frontier in the West, but on a scale so much greater that it was necessary to have

THE WOMAN OF THE SOUTH 145

considerable specialization. It is a rare visitor who at Mount Vernon does not catch a glimpse of the range of the interests that had to be met by George Washington as he supervised his estate. The plantation meant not only farming on a great scale but the carrying on of considerable business. In addition to these financial obligations, the white children on the plantation had to be furnished education, hospitality had to be maintained, and the colored men, women, and children not only supervised but cared for in almost every detail, a responsibility which both self-interest and economics enforced.

The task of the planter's wife was in proportion to that of her husband's. Her career was nothing like that of the wife of the wealthy mill owner in the North with whom she can in social opportunity and prestige be compared. The benevolence of the Northerner could be, and generally was, expressed impersonally in gifts and at a later period through organizations that attempted to meet the needs of the mill workers and advance their general welfare. The wife of the planter had to maintain intimate relations with the workers on her husband's farm. Illnesses, childbirths, deaths, marriages, and even quarrels and jealousies had to be attended to. More demanding than these happenings was the constant necessity for enforcing discipline, supervising the ignorant, careless, and indifferent workers, and maintaining an atmosphere conducive to contentment.

If it be true, as has been said, that the Negro slave before the Civil War enjoyed the only economic security that has yet been achieved in the United States, the women of the plantations themselves accepted as their share at least half of the responsibilities that made this possible. Indeed, the wife, more than the husband, was likely to have calls made upon her judgment, her patience, and her insight that were costly to nerves and to emotions. Upon her fell that most exacting of all tasks—the leading of dependents into an alien and more mature culture. Such a tutelage did not fall exclusively upon the women of the South, but they had the greater responsibility for the more constructive influences, and the rapid progress of the Negro race in America, both during slavery and since, proves that it was given a good start.

There were consequences that grew out of the experiences of these wives of slave owners that must have recognition in any attempt to interpret the cultural significance of the women of the South. As the women-heads of the plantation families attempted to meet their responsibilities, they were forced to realize the fact of inequality as surely as western life tended to stress upon frontier women the principle of equality. Each of these contrasting notions is rooted in human experience. What these southern women had driven into their thinking, through constant contact with the poor whites and Negroes on their very different levels of culture, was the conviction that to ignore existing inequalities between human beings leads to exploitation as certainly as when advantage is taken by the superior of another's weakness or ignorance, the fundamental sources of inferiority.

Whether these differences between persons at any time and place come from an inferiority of biological inheritance or from unfavorable circumstances of environmental origin matters not for the moment. If such variations between people exist, they must be taken into account in any sound social policy. No lesson of history is clearer than that it is difficult for those who have power and opportunity to accept their position and act with sympathy and justice toward those less fortunately situated. In supreme degree this exacting test of character was forced upon the southern women in their daily association with their Negro servants, and there is proof that they met the challenge successfully. In no other way can one explain the attitude of most Negroes toward the white women of the plantations during the Civil War when the latters' husbands and sons were away fighting.

Great differences between people, whether due to inheritance or accident, are always uncomfortable facts, but in civilization, from its beginning, the social practices have recognized their existence. Southern women cannot be indicted as out of accord with the

American theory of equality because they acted in the belief that this phase of individuality had to be reckoned with. In spite of the Declaration of Independence, with its statement that all men were created equal, an aristocratic code flourished along the entire Atlantic Seaboard, dating from the earliest settlements, that was so taken as a matter of course that it was not even recognized as inconsistent with this political pronouncement. When a constitution was drawn for the new government, the implications of the existing American *mores* were built into the document, and had it not been so, the document would have failed of ratification both North and South. Slavery tended to perpetuate, strengthen, and extend these original social patterns of America and to resist the influences coming chiefly from the West, rooted in the ideals of a practical democracy and symbolized by the notion of the self-made man.

The continuous and intimate contact of leaders of thought and fashion with the Negroes, especially the field workers who made up the base line from which gradations of poverty and wealth were measured, unconsciously and irresistibly led to a realistic, even fatalistic, acceptance of differences in standards of living. This prevailing social philosophy discouraged ambition even among the whites born into poverty or low middle-class standards and all but paralyzed the hopes of Negroes. Perhaps what was more important, it nourished in the well-to-do the disposition of non-interference. The aristocracy did not fail in practical benevolence, but its good will was chiefly expressed in personal relationships. The philosophy of life did not stimulate organizations designed for the self-improvement of the poor and underprivileged. This attitude was well expressed by the author of an early publication who has several times recorded this sentiment: "—and the great majority of planters with whom I conversed, lament an evil which cannot be cured by immediate emancipation—which seems almost to baffle the hopes of futurity—and which, while it appears as a stain on the lustre of their freedom, seems almost beyond the reach of a remedy." [6]

Again we have a situation similar to that characteristic of rural England in the eighteenth century. There was a fine sense of the obligations of practical charity on the part of the better type of people, particularly women, but it was largely confined to the giving of material aid. It would be most untrue to say that there was no inclination on the part of social leaders to rescue talented and promising youth born into a family by tradition shiftless and poverty-stricken, but the customary reaction, as compared with the West or even the North, was to assume that the family drift would continue.

Since the slavery system was undoubtedly growing more uneconomic even for the plantation owners, its indirect influence on people on the lower levels, particularly poor whites, was such as to encourage a poverty that victimized the family rather than expressed its innate traits. The loss that this must have meant to southern communities where the slave system dominated is suggested by such careers as that of Andrew Johnson's, and the success of the few men who were strong and fortunate enough to escape from their family status.

There can be no understanding of the conditions of the Negroes in the South during the period unless one realizes how seriously and how practically the plantation mistresses accepted the burdens that the slave system put upon them. Naturally these women were most sensitive to the claims made by those who as house servants came in constant contact with the family. This does not mean that there was indifference to the sick or aged field worker but rather that there was naturally greater supervision and sympathy for the Negroes who were so often about. There was automatically a selection of the more attractive and more capable Negroes for household service, and this operated also to direct the attention of the white women to the workers at the house. Buckingham was impressed by this fact and writes: "Here, too, as elsewhere, there is a great difference between the condition of the field-slaves on the plantations, and the domestic slaves about the houses of respectable families. These last are as well fed and as well clad as the free domestic servants of many countries of Europe, though far inferior to those of England; . . . In the domestic service of most private establishments here, there are often more slaves than are necessary for the labour required of them, many being kept for state, or ostentation; and as the coachman, footman, lady's maid, butler, cook, and other household servants, are continually passing before the eyes of the master and mistress, as well as their visitors and guests, they are almost sure of being well clad and kindly treated, because the sight of dirty and miserable-looking attendants would be painful to those by whom they are surrounded, as well as to themselves." [7]

The ordinary routine of the planter's wife was such as necessarily to include a great amount of services, which, in the North, would have been thought of as charity. We have heard so much of the festivities associated with the aristocratic life of the South that it is hard to appreciate the responsibilities that fell upon the wife of the planter. A classic description of this side of southern life comes to us from the *Life of Leonidas Polk*.

The life of the mistress in those patriarchal days was not one of ease. As soon as the breakfast was over and the day's supplies distributed, the many guests of the house were left for a while to their own devices while she made the rounds of the quarters,—that is, the village containing the cabins of the field negroes. The sick were visited, and the proper food and medicine for them were set apart. Then the nurse-house, where the little children were cared for by the elder women, was inspected. Daily those who could walk were brought out for exercise as far as the back door of the "big house," as they termed the master's residence, and there the mistress gave each a biscuit, and sometimes with a word of kindly admonition. Then she bestowed a general superintendence upon the room where the regular seamstresses and the delicate women cut out and made the clothing which was always prepared in advance for plantation use. Later in the morning Mrs. Polk went into the school-room, where her children were at work under their governence. With swift fingers she plied her knitting-needles while she sat listening to the instruction given them. Often a quick, pungent remark from her added something never to be forgotten to the day's quota of knowledge. She kept up a voluminous correspondence, which would have overtaxed a less systematic woman. She had no patience with those who find in their pleasant engagements a pretext for neglecting the small, sweet courtesies of life. The young people about her who were inclined to defer paying visits and replying to letters knew they would hear her rebuke, "What! You have not leisure or wisdom to make and to keep friends?" Her afternoons were given up to receiving and making visits, always a heavy demand upon one's time in a country neighborhood.[8]

Undoubtedly the loyalty that the Negro in general showed to "his missus" during the dark days of the Civil War was chiefly his reaction to the customary ministrations of the white women. It was just not possible on the well-conducted plantation for the owner to have the impersonal relationships that were found between employer and employee in the northern mills. Self-interest and human sympathy not only prompted regard for the claims of dependents, whose only security was the disposition of their owners, but were enforced by a public opinion that reacted against neglect and indifference. The spectacular evils of plantation life that the abolitionists made use of as ammunition for their attacks were commonly the faults of the overseer and usually unknown to the owner and especially to his wife. In the same way, exceptional exploitation of women and children in the mills of the North came from the overseer who took advantage of his position.

In its social structure and general trend the North was as committed at the beginning to an aristocracy as was the South. This appeared in education, religion, and politics. The town form of government, with its local town meeting, provided a medium for democracy, but it did not forbid an aristocratic leadership in politics.

The difference between the North and the South appeared with the ongoing of time; in the slave states the original aristocratic structure of society continued, while in the North there were too many conflicting sources of prestige for anything to persist comparable with the influence of the first families of Virginia. This does not mean that southern society was arrested and had no evolution but rather that its development proceeded with a consistency that preserved its original traits. It stands in contrast with the West rather than with the North, for although the latter had its aristocracy submerged by rapid industrial change and social complexity, it never achieved the militant, self-conscious democracy that grew up west of the Alleghenies. The spirit of the West appears in the career of Abraham Lincoln and even more in the deification of his life. In a similar way, but with opposite motives, the South finds in the life of Robert E. Lee the ideal of its aristocratic outlook.

The social philosophy of the West has so predominated and so permeated, at least in theory and sentiment, all quarters of the country, in part as the result of the outcome of the Civil War, that American thinking has never frankly faced the difficulties of maintaining genuine democratic culture or the advantages associated with an aristocratic structure of society. Nevertheless, one of the clearest lessons of social evolution is the fact that the impulses that defeat democracy are stubborn and hard to handle, while, on the other hand, in any free society, aristocracy sooner or later becomes in some form the basis of prestige.

Our interest in the southern structure is confined to the significance it had for the life of women. The feminine pattern south of the Mason and Dixon line had its appeal, for it possessed the advantages that a well-established, socially-accepted aristocracy always has. Without assuming that they represent a biological peculiarity native to one sex as compared with the other, since there are environmental conditions that are sufficiently explanatory, it is clear that the conservatory inclinations of women stand on the whole in contrast with the aggressive and predatory traits of men.

Undoubtedly a multitude of modern women who appear competitive and ambitious, if they could be released from the prevailing American reaction to life, would prefer a well-settled status and escape from struggle or even from rivalry. It was this placement, this security from dislodgment, that came to the wealthy and prominent southern women as a distinctive trait of slave-state culture as compared with what was true elsewhere. It is interesting to find an English observer glimpsing the meaning of this as he writes:

> The principal causes of this difference from the coldness, formality, and reserve of the north, is, no doubt, partly to be attributed to climate, partly to the different style of living, and a great deal to the circumstance, that as all persons of moderate fortunes live here upon a footing of equality with the wealthiest, there is not that straining after distinction, and the practice of various arts to obtain it, which prevail in cities where the aristocracy is composed of three or four grades, or castes, each anxious to outrival and overtop the other, which begets uneasiness, jealousy, suspicion, and an extraordinary degree of fastidiousness as to the acquaintances formed, the parties visited, and the guests entertained. The graceful ease and quiet elegance of the southern families, make their visitors feel that they are in the society of well-bred and recognized gentlemen and ladies; while in the north, the doubt and ambiguity as to relative rank and position, and the overstrained efforts to be thought genteel, make the stranger feel that he is in the presence of persons new to the sphere of polished society, and labouring under an excessive anxiety about the opinion of others, which makes them a burthen to themselves.[9]

This stratification did not affect merely the well-to-do women. It created a social atmosphere that permeated all classes. A woman, whatever her social position, had the advantages of a well-determined rôle. If poverty limited her opportunities and brought her a daily burden of hardship, it also released her from any obligation to go beyond her station and imitate those who were more fortunate. She had little incentive to progress but she was saved from the discontent and loss of self-respect that is so likely to come to those who in a fluid society feel themselves underprivileged. Let him who insists that such a reaction to life is contrary to human impulses ponder the meaning, for example, of the strength and long persistency of the caste system of India.[10]

The meaning of the southern woman's experience and the value of her contribution in the building of a program for women have been obscured by the flux of modern civilization and its rapid changes during the last century and a half. An age when women struggle with emotional insecurity is ill-prepared to appreciate a situation exactly its opposite. Moreover, there has been a disposition to regard aristocracy as it flourished in the South as an outgrowth of the slavery system. Although fostered by slaveholding, the aristocratic culture was not dependent upon it and eventually suffered from being linked with an economic organization increasingly out of accord with the industrial development of the modern world. There were many influences that gave strength to the prevailing southern social culture. Cities are notoriously hostile to an aristocracy and the South remained rural. Immigration tends toward class unsettlement, at least if the newcomers have an open passage, as they so largely did in the North and the West, to the gathering of wealth or the holding of public office. The South attracted a very small proportion of the European immigrants that came to the United States during the period covered by this chapter.

The great range of economic differences between the various classes of the South, especially the fact that the Negroes on the lowest level were blocked from moving upward, encouraged a stratification. The South, however, was able to maintain a thoroughgoing aristocracy chiefly because it was able to carry to maturity the earliest American patterns. These in the beginning had been brought from England. Never departed from, these first traditions became the foundation-principles of the native civilization as it developed. The West, on the other hand, was a social upstart, a spontaneous and haphazard blending of people and environment. It had broken from the seaboard conventions and was making a fresh start. The North also was in the throes of innovation, because in it was occurring the development of the machine industry, which, with all its indirect consequences, was bringing into being the modern world.

American sentiment has so antagonized recognition of aristocracy, except in the South, that the term has become almost a synonym for parasitic exploitation. No well-secured, socially-approved aristocracy has deserved this interpretation, and such a description was not true of the society of the South.

The wife of the planter, on account of the nature of her husband's wealth, ordinarily had placed upon her an exacting task, as we have seen, and rarely had anything like the freedom enjoyed by the wife of a man of wealth in other sections. In addition to this sharing of the managerial obligations that necessarily came to the conscientious owner of slaves, there was the wider type of responsibility which has always been assumed by an aristocracy which has achieved social approval and has not been resisted as something alien and exploiting.

The traditions of both the English and the southern aristocracy enforced a keen sense of public service. Granting that in the latter the self-interest of the dominant group was emphasized, this does not mean that there was a conscious attempt to substitute class advantage for public welfare but rather that it was felt that the interests of the ruling classes and of the rest of the people were essentially the same. That this was the feeling also of the large majority of those who did not belong to the wealthy families is not to be denied, for otherwise the leadership that moved toward separation from the northern states would have been repudiated.

There was no desire on the part of southern women to hold public office, but, in accord with the conventions that fixed the feminine rôle, they responded as did their husbands to the social responsibilities that belonged to them as members of the aristocracy. They were women leaders in their community from whom all sorts of public service were expected. Much of this was expressed through personal relationships and responsibilities associated with religious or social fellowship.

The rôle of the southern woman was clearly defined and in accord not only with the prevailing masculine dominance but with a family system that was in spirit patriarchal. It is in this fixity of the woman's life in the South that we find what is most significant in her career for light upon our present modern feminine problem. There is no evidence of a general discontent, although undoubtedly there were southern women who under other circumstances would have acted outside the conventions that determined what was proper for them.

In the South we find not only the division of labor between the sexes but a separation of social experience. This habit of maintaining a man's world and a woman's world appears to have evoked no impressive protest from either individual women or men. To say that they had to accept what they found is to forget that the *mores* sooner or later reflect the reactions of people as individuals. It would have been strange if there had not been women, at least in the early portion of their life, who chafed against the proprieties that so definitely held them to their prescribed sphere of life; but, on the other hand, the general acquiescence suggests that most women found satisfaction in such an assignment to domestic responsibilities. It would seem from this reaction of southern women that the modern program must eventually provide free choice between two opposite careers for women, to be decided by type of personality and individual preference rather than from the mere fact of their being females.

Even without assuming any innate differences between the sexes, the interests of women, clustering about their biological function as childbearers, tend toward establishing traits of personality that harmonize with domestic experience. If this were the only sort of influence that determined the growing character of the girl and the career of the woman, the division between the sexes could be made clear-cut and the status of the female would become fixed and stable. This cannot be at present, because woman responds also to an environmental pressure as a result of her freedom to enter vocations formerly dominated by men. In American culture this second type of social conditioning comes from three sources: an independent spirit which especially flourished in the frontier; the new and larger opportunities given women for the earning of a living, as a result of the development of machine industry; and those miscellaneous and less easily-defined conditions that constitute the modernism of our present civilization.

In the cultural period before the Civil War, this second stream of social pressure was beginning to disturb the moorings of women who by training had been prepared for a firm anchorage. The South was so resistant to the new order that there the conventional rôle of women remained secure. The modern woman, at least in the middle class, still shows in a multitude of individual experiences the conflict that comes from being attracted in two opposite directions. It is the opinion of many observers, and it is surely what one would expect, that a considerable proportion of women who would find themselves in the dilemma commonly stated as family versus career, would, if not pressed upon by social suggestion, prefer concentrating upon home and family and would do it without any thought of the need of defense, and without the feeling of inferiority that we find in some American women who choose the domestic rôle.

The historic background of the southern woman is such that it provides the most responsive and approving environment for those who from training or impulse turn toward the family career. In the period of our study there was a difference in the social patterns set before women of the various classes, but there was one definite, social exaction put upon women in every gradation of economic circumstances, the acceptance of the domestic career. The prestige establishing this, which swept through all classes, had its source in the idealization of the female rôle on the upper level. It was well described by the wife of Ex-President John Tyler in an article first printed in the *Richmond Enquirer*. Thus she pictures the southern woman:

> ... Her circle is, literally and emphatically, that of her family; and such she is content that it shall be. Within that circle her influence is felt over the relations of life, as wife, mother, mistress—and as she discharges the duty of one or all of these relations, so is she respected or otherwise. To cast a doubt upon her fidelity in any one of them, is to excite against her the odium of the community, and, in a great measure, to dethrone her from her high position. She knows nothing of political conventions, or conventions of any other sort than such as are held under suitable pastors of the Church, and are wholly directed to the advancement of the Christian religion. Such is emphatically the case with the women of the Southern States. Do you wish to see them, you must visit their homes. Do you desire to ascertain the nature of their employments, you must enter their family circle, and, believe me, good sisters of England, you would find in their Christian deportment, and perfect amiability of manners, enough, at once, to inspire you with the most exalted respect and esteem. You might find no splendid vestments of dress, no glittering diamonds, no aristocratic displays. No, the vestments they wear are those of meekness and charity, their diamonds are gems of the heart, and their splendor the neatness and order and contentment which everywhere greets the eye; and that neatness, that order, and that contentment is in nothing more observable than in the well-clothed and happy domestics who welcome your arrival, and heap upon you every comfort during your sojourn under the roofs of their masters.

You will see then how utterly impossible it would be to expect the women of the United States to assemble in convention, either in person or by proxy, in order to frame an answer to your address. Nay, I must, moreover, in all frankness, declare to you, that the women of the South, especially, have not received your address in the kindest spirit. They regard it as entirely incompatible with all confidence in, or consideration for them, to invoke the imposition of the women of what are called the free States, in a matter with which they have no more to do than have yourselves, and whose interference in the question can produce no other effect than to excite disturbance and agitation and ill-will, and, possibly in the end, a total annihilation of kind feeling between geographical sections. It is the province of the women of the Southern States to preside over the domestic economy of the estates and plantations of their husbands—it is emphatically their province to visit the sick, and attend to the comfort of all the laborers upon such estates; and it is felt to be but a poor compliment to the women of the South, to suppose it necessary to introduce other superintendence than their own over the condition of their dependents and servants.[11]

There were many influences that worked together to build in the South the strong family life which was a distinguishing feature of the section. The rural situation, the relative isolation of households, the plantation unit of production, each contributed its part, but the clearness and strength of the *mores* that fixed the activities and the status of women counted most. The family had an important recreational function in the North and especially in the West, but nowhere was it so dominant as in the South. The church also emphasized the family. Church attendance was so common that it was looked upon as one of the proprieties. The Bible was the most read book and often, among the poor, the only one the family possessed. It was used to interpret and enforce family obligations. Among the Scotch-Irish the family altar flourished. More significant than any of these expressions of the familial support of religion was the constant enforcement of family ties, family responsibilities, and family ideals through the teachings and preaching of the churches.

Although family relationships tended to be strong and demanding, as was true throughout rural America at the time, and domestic virtues were exalted, there was, as is so apt to happen when two groups widely separated in culture and economic circumstances are thrown together, an antagonistic element that led to inconsistency in sex standards. Odum has vividly portrayed this and the distress it brought to the men and women who realized its social consequences in the following:

The old Major, following his inclination to philosophize by linking institutions with morality, was wont to raise some questions about the consistency of the old southern emphasis upon the family and the sanctity of the home. Here, he would urge, sometimes sadly and sometimes half bitterly, was a great society with the family as its central unit, and with the glory of the home the glory of its culture, with the sanctity of its womanhood the measure of its purity. And yet in two larger ways the culture of the old institutional South set standards in violation of fundamentals of home and family unity. There was, in the first place, the extra-familial relationships of the master of the big house with the women slaves in violation of all codes of chivalry towards his own family and the utter lack of respect for the personalities of Negroes. For this sort of thing Uncle John had less than no respect and towards its standards came as near profanity as ever his religious conscience would allow; while the old Major himself found it hard to defend even after the manner of southern logic.

In still another way the southern pattern contributed to the disintegration of the Negro family. Husbands and wives among the slaves were sold to go into different parts of the country, sons and daughters were taken from family settings and distributed wherever the buyer might decide. There was here also, then, another striking case of unreality, so much so that many of the Southerners never even saw the rank inconsistency of their high morality for the purity of the women and the family in theory and their low morality in the practice of the opposite.[12]

The size and importance of the family unit in the South encouraged the patriarchal organization which was more developed in that section than elsewhere. It has become a proverb in modern life that no house is large enough to contain two families, even though they are related by blood. This incompatibility is a creation of the prevailing modern spirit with its emphasis upon individualism. Among the rural folk, before the Civil War, there were a multitude of American families, made up of kinspeople in various relationships, who lived together in harmony. This was possible because the family had a head with final authority. It was customary for this power of making familial decisions to be exercised by one male member, but, as a rule, a great part of the household management was left to his wife, and in this sphere she was given full control. This explains why there was not the clashing that is so likely to occur when parents and married children live together in these days. There was no feeling against her deciding things among those who had to accept subordination, because such was the common practice in large families. There was also less difference between generations and therefore less reason for conflict than in our time, when the rapid flow of culture so easily leads to differences between those who are older and those who are younger.

The culture of the section stressed domesticity in all its phases. Young people became interested in courtship early. The older girl was carefully chaperoned, but this did not mean that she was denied opportunity to meet men. On the contrary, she had much social life. This, of course, was particularly true in the higher classes. The unmarried woman, however, was supervised more than was customary in the North and particularly in the West. At adolescence romantic love became the commanding interest, at least for the young women. Flirtation was common and both sexes were proficient in the arts of courtship. It has been suggested by some interpreters that women made much of their courtship days because their life after marriage was so exacting. Doubtless in many instances, as the later experience was contrasted with that of the earlier, it did appear that there had been a fading away of zest, but it is assuming too much to suppose that this was often anticipated. The impulses of later adolescence sufficiently explain young people using to the utmost any opportunities for comradeship and courtship that the conventions provided.

The southern girl was fortunate, especially in the higher classes, in being born into a situation that gave her the privilege of concentrating upon the interests that were most seasonable. She did not need to think of preparing for a career that would bring her permanent or temporary self-support. Her chief motive was to find a mate and get married, and this was not only the way to happiness but the only satisfactory basis for her economic security. Care must be taken, however, not to stress the attention given to flirtation and wooing as something distinctive of the South, since the same interest in love-making was characteristic of the North and West. Yet the South stands alone in the type of conventions that grew up to protect the young woman who was being courted. This code of proprieties, it must also be confessed, had the additional purpose of giving the family opportunity to influence the marriage of their children.

An aristocracy by impulse safeguards itself by the seriousness with which it scrutinizes the alliances brought by marriage. This was especially true in the South. It was not only youth who had their thoughts turned toward courtship and weddings, but also parents kept in mind the need of bringing about wise marriages as they educated their children and exercised their control of recreation and festivities. Sometimes this interest on the part of parents went so far as to be a coercion from which a son or daughter attempted to escape by running away and getting married. It is said that Greensboro, North Carolina, became a Gretna Green for Virginians who entered upon clandestine matches.[13]

One of the consequences of the seriousness with which southern parents guarded and influenced the marriage of their children was the tying together of widely scattered individual families through a feeling of common loyalty. This brought about a super-family organization which wielded both social and political power, which De Leon describes as follows: "And these great family connections ramified into a meshed and interwoven consanguinity that held the interest of neighborhoods, and through them of all the Dominion, bound to common aspirations and to common interest. The unification of newer and less directly descended states has been a political or material advance; that of the Mother Virginia has been, time out of mind, one of pride and hereditament." [14] In Boston and in Philadelphia we find a similar regard for marriage alliances among members of prominent and wealthy families, as is illustrated by the Phillips, the Adams, and the Quincys in New England, but never did this become as marked as in the southern aristocracy.

It was natural that the wedding was made the supreme social event. The stress placed upon it tended to encourage and elevate courtship and indirectly to help parents who were trying to guide their children into wise marriages. The young woman was apt to look forward to it as the supreme happening of her life, and as a result she was not easily enticed toward a secret marriage nor even one that her father and mother could not enthusiastically celebrate. This influence was none the less effective because it was unconscious, as a rule, in the mind of both parents and child.

Young people married early and became parents early. Although it is hard to believe that grandmothers were frequently found in North Carolina at only twenty-seven years of age, it is true that even girls of the higher classes sometimes married as young as thirteen.[15] This tendency to marry early was not peculiar to the South. It had been from the first characteristic of colonial and pioneering conditions.

As educational opportunities opened to women, and business and industry, by offering them economic self-support, began to compete with matrimony, this feature of American life became less marked among the natives, particularly in the cities. Nevertheless, omitting the Negroes, who have always married early in the rural south, Ogburn found in 1920 the East, South-Central group of states—Kentucky, Tennessee, Alabama, and Mississippi—ranking first in the percentage of native parents who between fifteen and twenty-four years of age were married, while the West, South-Central states—Arkansas, Louisiana, Oklahoma, and Texas—ranked second, and the South-Atlantic states—Delaware, Maryland, the District of Columbia, Virginia, West Virginia, North Carolina, South Carolina, Georgia, and Florida—ranked third.[16] Although this is chiefly due to the influence of contemporary conditions, it is not altogether unrelated to traditions that have been maintained from the earliest days.

Thus we find that these same three groups of states also have the highest record for early marriages in the urban centers, but not in the same order. The West, South-Central and the East, South-Central change places. The South-Atlantic still remain third.[17]

A high birth rate is expected with early marriage. The large fecundity of native Americans was a striking phenomenon during the period, and this was true in the South as it was in the other rural sections of the United States. Growth of population was universally favored. Children were desired by some, unquestionably, on account of their economic asset, and the *mores* at every point supported the large family. It is doubtless true, as F. A. Walker stated, that no population ever showed greater reproductive vigor than the native American stock prior to the Civil War.[18] The southern people at this time, both white and colored, appear to have been largely free of syphilis, and this was another condition propitious for a rapid increase of population. Later the disease was spread through the South during the war and particularly affected the Negro birth rate unfavorably, since many years were to pass before science developed any effective method of attacking the malady.

As was to be expected, a price was paid for this growth of population, and again it was the woman who chiefly bore the cost. European observers were impressed by the swiftness with which the American women grew old. This was not merely because of their many and frequent pregnancies but that, in addition to the necessity of meeting this strain on the body, most of them also had to overwork. Moreover, the great majority of them lacked any adequate prenatal preparation for childbirth, and this showed itself in later ill health and premature decay. In the South the women on the higher economic level had the best care that was then procurable, and they did not suffer so much from frequently bringing children into the world as did most American women. Interest in any sort of birth control was rare indeed. Even if contraceptives had been provided at this time by science, the mere suggestion of their use would have been shocking to the southern people, irrespective of sex or class.

The great unity of sentiment among the southern people after secession is apt to make us forget how diverse a population they were. There were great differences in classes, in soil, in climate, in crops, in religious and family traditions, in cultural background and opportunity, and in prosperity. Neither the North nor the West had such contrast in social conditions, and only the latter rivaled the South in the variety of its physical features. Even so short a distance as that from Charleston, with its famed distinctions, to the communities across the Georgia border brought in sharp contrast speech, manners, and ways of living. The plantation has so richly colored the romantic and traditional South that the great divergence of multitudes of men and women from this standard of living is easily obscured. The poor whites were at the greatest distance from the aristocracy, and it is easy to forget that they must appear in any true picture of southern conditions prior to the War. In both these groups, those on the lowest and on the highest economic planes of living, there were gradations still easier to ignore in descriptions of the slavery-supported civilization.

There was one idea so common among southerners that it explained why they and people of the other sections regarded those living in the states that later seceded, irrespective of their great differences, as one people. Belief in state's rights was so axiomatic and universal that the individuals who thought differently, like General George Thomas, who remained in the Federal army after his native Virginia left the Union, were so rare that they may be thought of as individuals in the South but not of it. The support given slavery was nothing like as strong as the Southerner's insistence on the sovereignty of the state. Concerning it women had the same feeling as men. This doctrine was, of course, not original with the South, although perhaps from the first it had meant more to the people south of the Mason and Dixon line than to those of the North. About it rallied the entire variegated southern culture, including slavery, its peculiar trait.

The South perpetuated the sentiment of state supremacy so evident at the time of the forming of the Union. The rest of the country more and more departed from it and put in its place a superior loyalty to the nation. Toward the end of the period, as the feeling and the thinking flowing forth from such opposite sources met in the minor collisions that forecast the tragedy soon to be, we find the women of the South alienated in allegiance, in sympathy, in life outlook, from what was characteristic of their sex north and west. More and more they drew together, ever becoming more convinced that the people of the North were conspiring to destroy their civilization.[19] We therefore find no difference in the reactions of men and women as the two parts of the nation come closer to their inevitable clashing. This does not mean that all southern women were alike in their conviction that war was bound to come or in their feeling toward its coming. There were great variations among which the influence of age, temperament, imagination, and circumstances counted heavily, just as was true of the men.

As the War drew very near it would perhaps be unfair to distinguish the enthusiasm of most of the women for the on-coming conflict, especially those who were younger, in comparison with that of men of the same age and class, but certainly the responses of the women to the crisis stimulated men and made them more confident of victory. The average northern woman, as later she was drawn into the conflict, had neither such fervor nor such readiness to accept the verdict of a war that came to her rather as a duty than as a crusade. The temper of the women of the South as the War grew more certain shows how thoroughly and characteristically southern they were and this in turn explained the seriousness of the shock that came later with the ending of the War, the period of reconstruction, and the deep, long-lasting consequences which both experiences brought them.

CHAPTER VI

THE WOMAN OF THE MIDDLE WEST AND THE GREAT PLAINS

DURING the period, from Jackson's administration to the Civil War, the frontier continued its movement westward until it finally reached the Pacific Ocean, while the ever-expanding zone of the stable rural settlements followed more slowly after. The new territory taken over by the aggressive pioneers blended, as it became more thickly populated, with the older Ohio and Kentucky occupation, making a vast empire of people with similar interests and background from the Allegheny Mountains to the Pacific Coast. There were, at the time of our interest, especially in the region of the Rocky Mountains and the Western Desert, great stretches where there were few or no permanent inhabitants. The West comprised not only a natural division of relatively homogeneous people but a territory vast in size and representing in resources a domain of wealth never excelled.

In spite of the common characteristics of the western people, there was a cultural difference that soon began to make its cleavage, and because of their different attitude toward slavery, the West and the Northwest at one point of increasing importance were distinguishable from the Southwest. This, of course, does not mean that there was anywhere a consistency of attitude, since especially in the Middle West both points of view regarding slavery were strongly held, as appeared, for example, in the Lincoln-Douglas debates in the contrast of sentiment evoked by the two speakers in northern and in southern Illinois. The slave culture of the Southeast spread into the Southwest and into the southern part of the middle section, but in the latter it was so diluted that it was chiefly a defense of the slavery system rather than a duplication of the southern planter's civilization. The Southwest was increasingly marked off from "the free territory." It finally became distinct in spite of the fact that both sections came from a frontier basis.

The original impetus of the earlier frontier as it developed west of the Alleghenies continued. It permeated the life of the New West. It maintained its stress of the same fundamental traits as characterized the former period, but these were, of course, influenced by the passage of time which furnished a new and different setting. As transportation developed, especially railroads, and as the stream of mechanical inventions, so soon to be a flood, started, western life not only reflected these changes, even when they occurred chiefly in the thickly settled portions of the East, but in addition East and West were bound together in a more effective way than was true in the earlier stages of western settlement.

There was another fact that changed the complexion of the rapidly developing culture of the entire territory, particularly north of the Ohio to the Canadian border, and stretching westward to the Rockies. Whereas at the beginning there were offered refuge and opportunity for the overflow of discontented peoples of the East, as the great Midwestern Empire became open to the permanent settlement of men and women committed to western culture, the area developed first the decision of balance between the Old South and the Old North as they grew farther apart, and then later became dominant, at least along political lines, over the older states of the Union. The influence of the West also appeared profoundly in all aspects of the economic problems of the East. Thus, at last, the West not only provided opportunity for American sentiment and routine to develop free from European culture and to a less extent from that of the eastern states, but also permitted a flow of culture backward into the older territory.

The woman's movement in its various aspects was thus doubly rooted, once it appeared in clear form. It found a part of its vitality in the industrial conditions of machine culture of the Northeast and another in the spirit of life in the New West. Naturally, as it began to make its conquest, it met with greater opposition in the East where masculine conventions had been firmly planted at the time of the original settlement and most especially in the Southeast where they had been protected and encouraged by an almost feudal-spirited rural civilization.

Emotional attack and recoil appeared in greatest strength in the Northeast where agitation struck strongly against well-established practices. More rapid headway was made in the spread of woman's rights in the West because there the battle, on account of the general feeling and practices, was in part already won. There it was necessary only to crystallize and mature conventional sentiment in order to enlarge politically, socially, and educationally the life of women. This does not mean, however, that there were no obstacles to overcome or that all westerners, men or women, welcomed the innovations and demands first put forward by the more aggressive women and their male advocates.

Although any narrow theory of economic determinism must be avoided in interpreting the setting the West gave to the advancement of woman's status, the advantages of the resources of the section must be recognized. Had it not been for the great amount and the varied character of the natural wealth of the western territory, there would have been no magnet for the attracting of people both from the East and from Europe in sufficient numbers to make possible a native culture, nor would there have been economic support for the freer life of women.

Once the whites broke into the wilderness, they discovered that the region was one of the most favored spots of the earth's surface. The vast territory enticed first the pioneers and then the settlers with substantial promise. No part of the United States, indeed no portion of the world at the time, had more to offer. Its soil had greater fertility, as it was found on the prairie plains, than any other American territory or any part of Europe except some land bordering the Black Sea.[1] Not only had the soil been lavishly enriched by ancient glacier deposits, giving it a guaranteed productivity superior to that of other sections, but there were also vast accumulations of copper and iron ore stored away in such abundance as to appear inexhaustible. Awaiting later utilization were enormous stores of gas and oil. The depth of the soil, except in the Far West, was reinforced by abundant moisture.

The Great Lakes, the Mississippi and the Ohio Rivers and their tributaries furnished from the beginning of the white occupation of the regions means for the transportation of raw materials to the older Eastern markets and to a lesser degree to those of Europe. The territory offered no serious obstacles to the spread of railways, when they appeared, and these arteries of commerce advanced rapidly over the prairie and plains, once they broke through the eastern range of mountains. Nowhere had nature ever provided a more favorable theater for a new act in human culture.

The incoming settler had a choice of the richly grassed prairie land or the uncut forests where the axe had to have precedence over the plow. In northern Michigan, Wisconsin, and Minnesota a dense growth of white pine prevailed with a scattering of the deciduous trees that dominated the other timbered sections.

It was absence of trees that constituted the most impressive feature of the western spread of this inland empire, The Great Plains. From the ninety-eighth meridian to the foothills of the Rockies an enormous expanse of territory was broken off from the rest of the section by geologic and climatic differences. It was comparatively level and treeless, lacked adequate rainfall, and was victimized by the periodic sweep of great winds of high velocity. In the summer these rapid-moving currents of air passed over the land with an ocean-like speed and strength, but laden with death rather than life. Vegetation died quickly under the fierce attack of the heat. The farmer could only helplessly watch his hope of harvest disappear as his crops were destroyed by the terrific blasts. The dark green cornfields were sometimes utterly ruined in so short a time as a two-day period.[2]

The human organism was by no means exempt. The winds brought, as the body reacted to its environmental punishment, nervousness and irritability along with the more obvious torture of burning eyes, raw throat, and cracking lips. The European or the Easterner who attempted settlement in the Great Plains had no inkling of the changes necessary in his culture habits for successful adaptation in this new and alien environment. Survival demanded resourcefulness as well as ability to endure. It is well to remember that at this time the section was without the irrigation and other applications of modern science which in our day have made much of it a veritable Eden.

Between 1830 and the Civil War the Great West not only grew greatly in size and in population, as compared with the frontier of the earlier period, but it also changed in its composition. The latter appeared in the demands for governmental help in developing inland improvements for the purpose of bringing the crops of the section to eastern and European markets. As people poured into the region and settlement went on at an unprecedented rate, a feeling of prosperity followed which, herd-inflated, turned into an orgy of economic optimism and speculation.

The West cried out for better communications. The older and wealthier states responded in competition for trade and prestige. The Federal Government had been held back from such undertakings by the strict constitutionalists, but nothing blocked the States. New York State led off with the Erie Canal. Ohio, Indiana, Illinois, and even Missouri had no hesitation in creating an enormous capital debt by issues of bonds for roads, bridges, canals, and finally railroads. Reaction, once it set in, was swift and complete, and the collapse left the people prostrated.

Besides the abiding hate of banks and mortgages left by this experience in the minds of the people, there were two consequences that eventually had significance for the progress of women. One was the stimulus that this improved travel and land-craze was to migrations from New England and New York by way of the Erie Canal and the Great Lakes. A flood of people from these states poured into southern Michigan and Wisconsin and northern Illinois and the northern and central portions of Indiana. Many of the inhabitants of Pennsylvania and Ohio also responded to the western promise and its easier accessibility. As a result, people with non-slavery sentiments began to dominate the area.

However disastrous this use of public credit had proved, it gave the people a conception of the proper functions of a state that carried far beyond any narrow, *laissez-faire* doctrine. It was not a great step to pass from the idea of subsidizing railroads to that of founding, by means of public taxation, a university open to all qualified candidates irrespective of sex. Those who came with Puritan heritage brought strong convictions regarding the need of educational opportunity. This, of course, does not mean that the western migrant reëstablished New England on the prairie and in the forest. In the first place, those who left New England and New York were the more restless and less satisfied, who by their departure gave evidence of their desire for change. They also were operated upon by the environment, and their settlements were by no means mere offshoots of eastern civilization. They were, however, committed to the idea of education. Even though they were men of action, they coveted for their children better opportunities than had been open to them during childhood in the section of their birth. Undoubtedly the women, as a rule, were even more ambitious that their children should have the best educational advantages possible. The newcomers sought economic advancement, but not without far-away purposes, among which was advancement through education.

Previous to this opening up of better methods of transportation, the South had in greater proportion contributed to the growth of western population, but not from the planter's class. These southern migrants were less familiar than those coming from the Northeast with the democratic program of educational facilities. Disciplined by aristocratic *mores,* they were restless for land and for economic opportunity. They were not so appreciative of the significance of their previous cultural discrimination and therefore not so quick to seek better educational opportunity.

Another considerable influence came from the settling of Germans. More than half a million entered the West in the period between 1830 and 1850. In their thrift and educational ambitions they shared characteristics of the New Englanders. These German folk who went into the West from 1815 to 1852, besides their desire to advance economically, were eager to escape from the political and class restrictions against which they had chafed in the Old World. Some of them were political refugees and men of rich but independent intellectual achievement who felt the pull of democratic ideals. A few dreamers among them sought to establish centers of German culture, some even having the hope that they might build a German state, using the German language, in the West—a second but liberal fatherland. The great majority, however, concentrated upon the task of improving their financial status, but they were by disposition not averse, once the challenge came, to the development of popular education on a state-wide basis.

It is clear that the majority of those who went into the West as settlers carried with them an extraordinarily strong individualism. They were the kind of people who asked only opportunity to make the most of themselves and who felt that given this they would make headway. They were free from the extravagant schemes of quickly gaining wealth and returning to the old environment from which they had come, such as gave energy to a portion of the seaboard settlers in colonial days. Unlike these adventurers, they sought merely the means of working their way, and the wealth they sought was for the most part land.

Individualistic by disposition, the environment into which they went encouraged still more this, their fundamental social reaction. With the exception of a few selected groups, they were in no degree socialistic. Therefore one might have assumed that they of all persons would be the last to challenge the prevailing political notion that the best government is one that interferes as little as possible with the citizens. The forces, however, that encouraged this individualism also led toward a democratic society. There were no traditions built upon artificial class differences. Each man was expected to prove his own worth. Individualism, it was soon realized, would be nothing but an oddity, a mere boastful, emotional assertion, unless the economic system could be made such as to provide free and equal opportunity for all. This meant that a functioning democracy had to be realized or the great purpose of western settlement must fail.

Out of their economic struggle, particularly their dependency upon eastern markets, came the feeling that a genuine social democracy could not be maintained unless it became a public policy supported by governmental forces. It was natural for this belief to give birth to the conviction that it was the business of the state to open up channels of trade and to legislate to protect western agriculture from eastern exploitation. By such processes of feeling and thinking individualism, with no sense of inconsistency, turned to the government as the one effective organization in the securing of democratic ideals.

Embedded in this thinking, where time was soon to bring it to expression, was another motive for recourse to the state for aid—the necessity of opening up a democratic opportunity for education—and this was the second consequence of the bond programs of the states that was to affect in the West the status of woman. As soon as there was a widespread grasp of the value of equal opportunity for education at all the intellectual levels, the state university became an indispensable ally of the legislative program, promoting and protecting a practical democracy.

The people of the region, once they committed themselves to the popularizing of educational resources, were not content to abort their program on either the elementary or the secondary level. They were in no mood to accept the intellectual aristocracy with which eastern people, north and south, had for so long been familiar. For the state to provide educational facilities that would in actual practice keep open the avenue to training and culture according to the individual's desire, industry, and capacity, seemed to them not only a proper function for the state but an essential responsibility in the maintaining of a democratic society.

Another ideal of western democracy began to appear as the public program of equal opportunity for education matured. A genuine democracy must not in its educational policies discriminate between the sexes. This connection was even a greater departure from eastern conventions than the idea of a state-supported university. The idea of giving women the same educational opportunity as men, and at the same institutions, was too modern an advance for many to take until in their thinking they had broken more from eastern and continental practices, but it was not alien to western sentiment, and almost from the first it was supported by forward-looking men as well as women. This program, once it came, was not to be confined to state-supported institutions, and so it came about that coeducation at the highest as well as the lowest levels became an essential trait of the life and thought of the western people.

With such an origin, it was inevitable that the instruction offered in higher institutions of learning tended not only to be democratic but to take over new cultural responsibilities as a natural function of a university belonging to and serving the people. Undoubtedly, as Lester F. Ward, the eminent American sociologist, has said, this social program of a complete public school educational system, culminating in a state university, was not only the most effective step that democracy had taken for its own security, but also the supreme achievement of a socialized policy.[3]

The conservative way of extending the education of women before the Civil War was by the founding of separate institutions for them. Some of the pioneers in this development were Catherine Beecher at Hartford, Connecticut and Cincinnati, Ohio, Emma Willard at Middlebury, Vermont and Waterford and Troy, New York, and Zilpah P. Grant and Mary Lyon at Derry, New Hampshire and Ipswich, Massachusetts, and the latter at Mount Holyoke, Massachusetts. The coeducational program, providing training for men and women together, was so radical and so out of accord with the thinking and the feeling even of most educated people at the time, that it is interesting to see how naturally the new idea came into being at Oberlin. In planning the Oberlin community the need of giving women training was taken as a matter of course, and there seems not to have been any realization of the significance of the departure that led to the giving of this instruction. The first catalogue the college issued lists the various sub-divisions, classes attended also by women, including the female department among the rest. Reference is made also to the female seminary which pupils at any age above eight years might enter for one term only.

There seems to be evidence that there were some interested in Oberlin who feared bad effects from the new policy and that there was a movement under foot to separate the male and female departments, doing away with their common classes, and that if it had not been for the financial crash of 1873, which prevented an endowment of the institution that had been expected, this division would have been made. In the catalogue of 1835 we find the following:

> Young ladies of good minds, unblemished morals, and respectable attainments are received into this department and placed under the superintendence of a judicious lady whose duty it is to correct their habits and mould the female character. They board at the public table and perform the labor of the steward's department, together with the washing, ironing, and much of the sewing for the students. They attend recitations with young gentlemen in all the departments. Their rooms are entirely separate from those of the other sex, and no calls or visits in their respective apartments are at all permitted.[4]

In so cautious a way coeducation started, but the innovation expressed a changing attitude toward women and their education which in two more decades was to become widely recognized and increasingly supported. It is clear that the Oberlin founders held no new or special views "of the rights or the sphere of women,"[5] but nevertheless a break had been made in educational conventions and one that was soon to prove a decided advantage to American women.

Coeducation was not only in harmony with the spirit of much of western thinking, it was also a logical development of public elementary and secondary educational systems. Although girls were excluded from elementary education at first in New England, by 1790 we find Boston permitting girls to have the same opportunity as boys. This was a practice in New Amsterdam from the beginning. The dames' schools of the Middle Atlantic and the Southern states generally took in girls as well as boys. Among the Quakers it was common practice to allow girls to attend the same schools as boys. As the idea of free public education developed, it was natural to open up the same elementary opportunity for girls as for boys.

In the West particularly, as the secondary school grew out of the public elementary school, the same attitude was expressed regarding the right of girls to have access to this higher type of education. The next step was to provide college education for girls. The western people had no firmly built traditions that held them from taking the next step and offering women as well as men educational opportunities on the highest level. There was also the motive of economy to encourage the giving of these facilities at coeducational colleges and universities. There was, however, enough of eastern habits and standards clinging to western people from the older sections to hamper and delay this development of woman's higher education in the Middle West.

As the West developed, evidences appeared that it was to determine the political and greatly influence the social evolution of the United States. One of these was its rapid growth of population. This has already been noted during the earlier period of the western settlement. The trend continued from 1830 to the Civil War. For example, the state of Illinois from 1830 to 1840 had a growth of population greater than that of the entire South Atlantic states during the same time. Perhaps a more impressive comparison is between the population increase of the entire Atlantic Coast region with that of the Mississippi Valley during the same ten years. The gain in the latter was nearly twice that of the older section. Ohio, unsettled wilderness in 1790, fifty years later had nearly as many people as Pennsylvania and twice as many as Massachusetts.

The increase of population in the western area was all the more significant politically because it was so scattered as to permit, through the assignment of two senators to each state, a great and rapidly increasing power in the higher chamber of Congress. We are told, for example, that before the War of 1812 the senatorial distribution was six senators from the Mississippi Valley, ten from New England, ten from the Middle States, and eight from the South. By 1840 the Mississippi Valley section had acquired twenty-two senators, twice as many as the total number from the New England and the Middle States and almost three times as many as from the entire South. This same section by 1840 also had acquired the balance of power in the House of Representatives, and it was becoming clear that in the struggle between northern and southern cultures, ever growing more intense, the region west of the Alleghenies was destined to decide which should survive.[6]

Even though during the first decade of the period the Middle West was already establishing its dominance politically and socially, its ever advancing frontier gave promise of a still greater spread of settlement and accompanying power. During the second decade people were pouring into Oregon, the new northwest territory, and Texas, the new southwest. The fur traders and the missionaries had pushed their way into what was known as Oregon, a Pacific Coast strip west of the Rockies, north of 42° and south of 54° 40′. To the American immigrant Oregon meant a valley running southward from the Columbia river approximately to the northern boundary of present-day California.

The routes west from Missouri had been found and charted by Lewis and Clark and by John Fremont, who was assisted in his exploring by Kit Carson, the famous scout. The distance from Missouri to the Oregon country was somewhat more than two thousand miles. For the slow-moving caravan the journey through heavily forested areas, over deserts and mountains, was tedious, full of hardships, and always potentially dangerous.

Beginning in 1842 in a small way, the immigrant parties that took this trying, hazardous trail gradually increased. The population influx was artificially stimulated by the fact that the territory was jointly claimed by Great Britain and the United States. The feeling among the people of the latter that as much as possible of the Northwest should be annexed by this country led to more rapid settlement than otherwise would have occurred. The unfriendly attitude of the Mexican governors of California toward American immigrants, and lack of interest in that portion, added all the more to the northwest flow of population.

When the dispute of the two nations was finally arbitrated and the northern boundary made the forty-ninth meridian, with the exception of Vancouver Island which became British, the occupation of Oregon had reached a point justifying making it a territory, and in March, 1849, its first governor took office. Oregon thus became in the Northwest the American outpost, and from it to the thickly settled areas of the Middle West was a vast territory which was to be another and the last frontier in the growth of the United States.

A similar extension occurred in the Southwest. The first incentive toward an American encroachment resulted from the colonizing of a group of Americans in Texas under grants from the Mexican government. In time came the independence of Texas, its recognition by the United States government, the resulting war between Mexico and its northern neighbor, and finally the gain by the United States of a new frontier including California, Arizona, and New Mexico. A great portion of this territory was similar to that stretching between the Oregon settlement and Missouri—mountain, desert, and plain—but the discovery of gold in California became a tremendous drawing power in bringing from the distant East and the nearer West hordes of people, many of whom became permanent settlers.

Gold was the magnet, but once the people were drawn into the Pacific Coast territory, they discovered eventually a greater wealth, and one not to be exhausted, in the fertility, the climate, and the contact with the markets of the Orient. Between the Pacific Coast settlement and the fringe of the more thickly populated Middle

West there stretched a final frontier occupied by a people untouched by eastern tradition, thoroughly sympathetic with the cultural traits that had been nurtured in the early West and matured in the later West, who were by impulse prepared to advance the social and political equality of women.

In a movement so complex as that of the American evolution of the status of woman, and one so characteristically expressing pressure, the product of the contemporary social trends, it would be misleading to credit the frontier environment with more than the encouraging of the advance of women toward a near-equality with men, the hastening of a social change in process in all sections, and the expressing of it in its most radical and spectacular form. It was not strange, however, that the fundamental sex discrimination, the denial of suffrage to women, was first swept aside in such states as Wyoming in 1869 and in Utah in 1870, where woman suffrage was inaugurated while they were still territories, in Colorado in 1893, and in Idaho in 1896. To explain this as an expediency in the effort to attract women into the territory where there were more men than women conceals the fact that there was a public opinion willing to take the step, conscious in some degree of the consequences that such a radical change in public policy would have.

It is as necessary in interpreting this woman suffrage trend to be careful not to read out meaning as not to read it in. At least the program would never have been conceived by any sizable group of men as a possible appeal to woman's immigration during earlier periods of frontier history. There was certainly a degree of social sensitiveness to the demands that were being made in the eastern section by a small, much advanced, and very aggressive group of women.

There can be no controversy regarding the mixture of motives that led Wyoming, while still a territory, in 1869 to grant suffrage to women. The passage of the legislation that so radically broke from many centuries of social custom came about from attempts at political expediency, from the willingness to make what was assumed to be a mere political gesture, from the wish of some of the Democrats who controlled both Houses to embarrass the Republican governor who was expected to veto the measure, but also from sincere determination to advance the status of woman. William H. Bright, author of the Woman Suffrage Bill, undoubtedly used all these arguments and in addition was given votes by some who thought the whole matter a joke. But these various explanations as to how the law passed, in comparison with the more fundamental social willingness of at least an intelligent leadership to recognize and accept an advanced status for women appear occasions rather than causes of the legislation.

They reveal how at the moment the bill happened to get made into law, but much more significant than this political maneuvering is the fact that the governor finally did sign the bill and the subsequent legislature did not repeal it, and that it was in accord with laws already passed and with others that followed. One of these was a change of the common law principles regarding the property rights of women, which reversed the long entrenched practices of English speaking people and gave the wife the same treatment under the statutes for distributions as the husband. Perhaps more significant still in showing the trend toward greater equality of women was their gaining the right to serve as jurors.

It was not to be expected that these radical departures should come without protest, criticism, and deliberate attack, but they persisted and exerted immediately social influences that could not be gainsaid. The entrenchment of this political and legal progress through public support proves that more was behind the passage of the first legislation establishing woman suffrage than appears in the reasons that led many of the politicians to vote for the law. The fundamental interest of Bright appears to have been based upon a conviction that the giving of suffrage to women was just, a belief that was rooted in his appreciation of his wife and of her sympathy with the idea of woman suffrage.[7]

Mr. Bright, at the age of 25 years, had been elected to the Council, later the Senate, of the first Wyoming Territorial Legislature, from South Pass City, Sweetwater county, now a ghost city but then a flourishing mining town of some 6,000 inhabitants. Mr. Bright had been a colonel in the army of the Confederacy and had come to Wyoming from the state of Virginia. Undoubtedly he was influenced in his attitude toward woman suffrage by his feeling that a nation that gave the suffrage to ignorant, recently-emancipated slaves had no excuse for denying the same rights to intelligent women like his wife and his friend, Esther Morris, merely on account of their sex.

Mrs. Morris, who had come into the territory from Peru, Illinois, was a neighbor and intimate friend of the Brights. She had heard Susan B. Anthony make an appeal for suffrage for women and had been converted to the cause. It is said that in the cabin of the Brights the two families often talked over the subject, and Bright came to have the same feeling regarding suffrage as the two women whom he greatly admired. At the first Territorial Legislature he was elected speaker of the Council. He soon introduced his bill for woman suffrage, which read as follows:

> An Act of Grant to the Women of Wyoming Territory the Right of Suffrage and to Hold Office.
>
> Be it enacted by the Council and the House of Representatives of the Territory of Wyoming:
>
> Sec. 1. That every woman of the age of eighteen years, residing in this Territory, may, at any election to be holden under the laws thereof, cast her vote, and her right to the elective laws of the territory, as those of electors.
>
> Sec. 2. This act shall take effect and be in force from and after its passage.[8]

What he wrote finally became the law, with a change in the age qualification from eighteen to twenty-one. There appears to have been no difficulty in getting it passed through the higher chamber, six members voting for it, two against it, one being absent. The bill then went to the House of Representatives where it had a stormy passage. There was bitter opposition to it on the part of some of the members, led by Ben Sheeks, who also was elected from South Pass City. Again and again at various times when the bill

THE WOMAN OF THE MIDDLE WEST

was considered, he maneuvered in the effort to defeat it, postpone it, or by amendments to make it unworkable. Eventually the bill reached a final vote on the question of its passage and became law with seven voting for it, four against it, and one being absent.

It was generally felt that Governor John A. Campbell would veto the measure, but instead he signed it. After listening to both the friends and the enemies of the bill, he seems to have made his decision on the grounds that the right of women to vote or hold office in Wyoming was a rational and logical sequence to some of the laws which had been passed by this same legislature—laws giving widows guardianship of their minor children, giving women the right to acquire and possess property, and giving equal compensation to both sexes when they had equal qualifications to teach. In 1919 Mrs. Campbell, the wife of the former governor, made the following statement as to why her husband signed the bill.

> The spirit of justice to women and their intelligence influenced Governor Campbell to sign the bill. It was that exactly and nothing else. . . . Governor Campbell carefully considered and weighed the importance of the measure and with a full conviction of its justice and possible good for all future time gave it his approval. It was the deed of an intensely upright and enlightened judgment.
> His veto message when the repeal was attempted, states explicitly the principles by which he was guided and which positively refute any other reason which those attacking the law have since brought forward.
> I am glad to say this to the women of Wyoming in their heyday of victory for the cause, a result which to me clearly vindicates Governor Campbell's action in the matter.
> So I clasp hands with you across the distance which separates us and joined by my daughter thank you for the opportunity which has been given me for greeting and good wishes.
>
> Very sincerely,
> Isabella W. Campbell [9]

In 1919 the only member of the Legislature then living was Ben

Sheeks, the young unsuccessful opponent of the bill. He was then a Superior Judge in the state of Washington, and in the following letter he stated the attitude he had come to take toward woman suffrage.

>Montesano, Washington
>October 14, 1919
>
>Wise as I thought myself fifty years ago I am willing to admit that I have learned some things since.
>
>I have advocated and voted for woman's suffrage, and have no doubt of the wisdom and justice of my later action, whatever the good women of Wyoming may think of my former conduct.
>
>Yours truly,
>Ben Sheeks [10]

There was, of course, no influence coming from frontier women's organizations to account for this innovation in suffrage policy. The battlefield was in the Northeast. It was there that woman had the greatest need of self-protection through the right to vote, and it was there that social resistance clashed most strongly with the efforts of those who were leading the crusade. The South had only hearsay knowledge of the controversy, since there women had neither motive nor desire to assume through suffrage the responsibilities of political life. The Midwest was more responsive but at the same time it did not have the industrial development that did so much to make evident to women the danger of their non-voting status.

Each of the successive frontiers from the colonial period down had afforded an opening to the more progressive trend in woman's status. Thus the first colonial environment had multiplied opportunities for women to enter into small businesses because of the death or absence of their husbands. When the last frontier came on the stage, woman's right to vote had become, as looking backward we now see it, the next logical step in the American woman's advancement of status. The Oregon territory, the mountain states, the Great Plains area offered favorable environment for the rapid

THE WOMAN OF THE MIDDLE WEST

coming of a social trend which was bound to make headway slowly in the Northeast and in the Southeast not at all.

It is not reasonable to charge this favorable disposition merely to distance or to time. The people of the Far West were indeed a long way from the original seaboard settlements. There also had been more than a century of cultural history which made possible in the new territory a social outlook more consistent with the trends of the period than could develop in the region where the original tradition of European occupation persisted in diluted form. Granting the significance of these facts, there is another that must have recognition.

Both the plain and the mountain area presented a different pioneering problem than that met by the first settlers who landed on the Atlantic seaboard or by their descendants who later pressed into the western wilderness. To a considerable degree the first, according to our common figure of speech, had to conquer the wilderness. The last frontiersmen to survive had to reconstruct the environment which they found, and they still in these present days wrestle with their task. This experience taught them the necessity of departure from routine, a lesson enforced by the new type of farming adapted to the peculiarities of soil, lack of moisture, and great distances from markets. The settlers were prepared through struggle, hardship, and adaptability to meet with native friendliness, even eager hope, suggestions of social change and experiments not only in political and industrial affairs but even within the fundamental human relationship of man and woman. No group could accept the innovation of woman suffrage without being conscious that it was a decided break in the conventions that had shaped the masculine and the feminine rôles in the United States.

Undoubtedly there was a fundamental recoil on the part of many women when they entered the Great Plains. This psychological reaction became a considerable barrier blocking family immigration into the area. It is reasonable to assume that multitudes of women, as Webb has suggested, balked at leaving the timbered regions and entering the forbidding, even oppressive, shelterless stretches, and that often the family that had intended to enter this last frontier went elsewhere.[11] This reaction of women gave a peculiarity to the Great Plains region of which, undoubtedly, the men became conscious, and one that made them eager to offer the women any inducement that would make the country more inviting to them. Other American frontiers, however they may have at first suffered from the predominance of men over women, had no persistent, inherent obstacle as the settlements developed that repelled women. Indeed, the women followed the men as the country was opened up more rapidly than one might have thought possible. This was due in part to the great amount of family migration into the Midwest territory.

The Great Plains and the mountains were, however, in an essential sense man's country, repellent to women not only because of its newness or its scattering of settlements, but because it was unfamiliar, a land in sharpest contrast to the country of their childhood and youth, a region that seemed oppressive, extravagant, and withering to the American women who, however pioneering and adventurous in spirit, were not nomads in disposition or experience. Desert land, even treeless sections, appeared alien to them, a country to traverse rather than to settle. Thus in the westward movement the American woman migrant came finally to something new and unexpected. It was not merely that she herself hesitated to try the family fortune in territory that seemed so uninviting, but as an actual or prospective mother she felt unwilling to gamble domestic values in what seemed an unfavorable environment. Certainly this was not the feeling of all women. Families did go into the territory, even single women, but the general drift was clearly toward settlement in the more familiar country which still provided opportunity for newcomers who desired to settle on cheap land with hope of advancing their status.

Those women who found themselves at home in the Great Plains and the mountains were closer to the type of men who liked the country than to the women who recoiled from it. It would be an exaggeration to declare that these women were masculine in their disposition, but undoubtedly they shared the feeling of men who became captives to the physical and psychic qualities of the Great West. Even a scattering of women so akin to masculine attitudes would tend to reverse the argument that was beginning to center about woman suffrage. The question would not be, Why should such women be permitted to vote? but rather, On what basis is it reasonable to deny suffrage to them? Of course, the notion of masculine dominance and the traditions that assigned women to the home prevailed in the territory and the habit life of the white settlers. It was, however, more rapidly and more easily dissolved than similar ideas in other sections. The break with other kinds of conventions prepared the way for change at this particular point.

The inclination toward radical experiments, so characteristic of the people of the section, even to the present, most naturally prepared for the suffrage innovation. The conditions of life tended to emphasize the value of the individual, whether man or woman. This led to the looking upon women not as persons possessing conventional qualities expected of the female but as personalities aside from any sex characteristic. It grew increasingly difficult for men to conceive of women as inferior and to discriminate against them politically, educationally, or in any other way.

The American woman in every frontier period had been characteristically self-reliant and self-expressive. This had brought her increasingly prestige and opportunity, taking her farther and farther away from the social disabilities of the original continental traditions, but nowhere had she gone farther or with less protest from men in her trend toward full social equality than in this territory of the Far West so markedly separated from the rest of the country. The land did not bring her advancement but it provided conditions that encouraged her progress.

It is interesting to see how effectively the Great Plains acted as a barricade against the midwestern influx. For example, we are told that from 1820 to 1850 this migration reached its highest point. At the beginning of the period immigration had advanced to the great bend of the Missouri river, and thirty years later it had made a well-settled area only in a straight line north and south of this point.[12] Although the Indian occupation of the territory farther west had some influence in stopping the spread of people across the Missouri, undoubtedly the forbidding character of the land, its strangeness to those unfamiliar with desert and mountain, chiefly discouraged people from entering the country for settlement.

There was, however, during the period of our study an artificial incentive that brought settlers into Kansas. There was the increasing tension between the North and South on account of slavery, which rapidly was becoming a moral issue both north and south of the Mason and Dixon line. Missouri had already become committed to the slave system. Nebraska, on account of climatic conditions, was clearly bound to be free territory. Kansas, between the two, could be either an extension of northern or of southern culture, according to the predominance of settlers from the free or the slave states.

Stephen A. Douglas, by supporting Lewis Cass for nomination for president by the Democratic party, revealed at least as early as 1848 [13] his support of the doctrine of Popular Sovereignty. Later in his attempt to postpone conflict and compromise the sectional differences by his Kansas-Nebraska bill, leaving the people free to make their decision for or against slavery, he brought the issue to the forefront of politics. His interest was chiefly in getting a western railroad through to the Pacific Coast. His attitude toward slavery was one of *laissez faire,* since he believed, as would now appear, that time and patience rather than agitation or moral crusade would solve the northern and southern differences. Contrary to his purposes, his interest in developing the Kansas-Nebraska area brought to a new intensity the fundamental passion of northern versus southern sentiment. As a consequence, Kansas was settled largely by people straight from the eastern coast, particularly from New England. These persons came in the spirit of a moral crusade, determined to save Kansas from the southern grasp. Frequently they came not as individuals but as companies of persons having the financial backing of eastern societies organized to keep Kansas free from slavery.

This led to a considerable family migration and carried many women who otherwise might not have willingly settled in the region as permanent settlers. Effort was made by southern leaders to induce slave owners to push into Kansas, but without success. Their reluctance discloses the truth in Douglas's contention that in the long run climate and physical conditions rather than law would prove effective in preventing the spread of slavery into the Great Plains region.

The successful settlement of Utah by the Mormons illustrates the motives which brought people into the West, and which appealed as much to women as to men. The Latter Day Saints, determined to find a haven where, untroubled by Gentile interference, they might live their religious faith and social philosophy in accord with the dictates of their own conscience, went far into the most frontier section of the Far West. They were the largest and most successful of the many social groups who had in common only the desire to find some place where, without outside interference, they could maintain their own peculiar community or commonwealth.

It is easy to forget how many of these idealistic or self-contained organizations settled somewhere in the West because only there had they hope of being let alone in their undertaking. In these enterprises we find no holding back on the part of the women, even where, as was true of the Mormons, their venture meant going far from the life with which they had been familiar and accepting a struggle for survival in the most forbidding of environments. The peculiar doctrine of plural marriage of this particular group was so obnoxious to conventional American sentiment that there has been little appreciation of the courage and sincerity revealed in their long, slow trek from Missouri westward—hardly less than that shown by the Pilgrim fathers—their social stability, and their practical agricultural efficiency. History also has given scant recognition to the fact that the Utah colony attracted women from the older West, from the East, and from far-away Europe.

The West, particularly its more thinly settled fringes, attracted idealistic groups since it was the most promising of all the territory then open to immigration, not only because of its cheap, fertile land, but on account of its offering of isolation. These settlements, made by people held together by emotional commitment to a distinctive life-philosophy, did not directly influence either the thinking or the practices of western people as a whole to any great extent, since they were by their own choice usually separatists, through fear of contact with the non-believers. But indirectly they did emphasize a feature of the frontier, social independence, which rightly seemed characteristic of midwestern and farwestern Americans. The settlements of these various peculiar groups helped spread a notion of freedom and opportunity which in its sweep even made an impression on idealistic individuals and discontented classes in Europe.

There is no definite, consistent influence that came out of these idealistic, self-contained communities, so far as the status of woman is concerned. She did profit in the end from the spirit of tolerance, so far as western people achieved this in their relation to peculiar social groups, and from the disposition to accept experiments along social lines, which at least was encouraged by the founding of these various communistic communities numbering several hundred and including hundreds of thousands of persons.

One of these was the Harmonists, a German group under the leadership of George Rapp. They settled in Economy, Pennsylvania, in 1824, but later moved to Harmony, Indiana. In 1825 their property was bought by Robert Owen for his communistic adventure and was rechristened New Harmony. The Zoarites, financed by English Quakers, established themselves at Zoar, Ohio. A Swedish group, led by Eric Janson, established themselves at Bishop Hill, Illinois, in 1848. The Huterian brethren, a Mennonite body of Germans, maintaining existence from the sixteenth century, first settled in North Dakota in 1874. Another German group, founded by Dr. Keil, and holding all things in common, established a community at Bethel, Missouri, in 1844 and later, in 1852, at Aurora, Oregon.

Although the community organized by Robert Owen lasted a mere two years, it was the most talked about and influential of the non-religious, communistic settlements and contributed significantly to the culture development during the early period of the Midwest. Its founder's radical theory of marriage was the very antithesis of the common trend toward asceticism which appeared in the teaching of many of the groups, excepting of course, the Mormons.

This distrust of the marital state, aside from that of the Shakers of eastern origin, appears strongest perhaps in the Amana Society, the Community of True Inspiration. This group, one of the most interesting and distinctive of all the idealistic organizations that settled in the West, brings out in high relief the appeal the wilderness had for European brotherhoods as the propitious place to establish an ideal society. To Christian Metz, the leader of this Amana crusade, was revealed as early as 1826 through "a hidden prophecy" the will of the Lord that a migration be made to America. Thus came the command:

> I proceed in mysterious ways, says thy God, and My foot is seldom seen openly. I found My dwelling in the depths and My path leads through great waters. I prepare for Me a place in the wilderness and establish for Me a dwelling, where there was none.[14]

Later came an even clearer message from the Lord reading as follows:

> Your goal and your way shall lead towards the west to the land which still is open to you and your faith. I am with you and shall lead you over the sea. Hold Me, call upon Me through your prayer when the storm or temptation arises. . . . Four may then prepare themselves.[15]

This German congregation settled first in western New York on land that they bought from the Seneca Indians. They prospered but felt the pull of the distant frontier, and in 1854, twelve years after the founding of their American settlement, Brother Christian Metz began to reflect the will of the Lord that they move farther westward. Later that year they finally received this plain command: "You shall direct your eyes toward a distant goal in the West to find and obtain there a start and entrance for a settlement."[16] After considerable searching, first in Kansas and later in Iowa, they established themselves during the summer of 1855 on a favorable site north of the Iowa river.

Marriage was not denied to the members of this community but it was interpreted as a spiritual risk, a falling from grace, while the single life had "bestowed upon it a special promise and a great mercy."[17] When young people married they were temporarily reduced to the lowest spiritual rank, from which they were expected to climb upward, and this same marking down followed the birth of each child.[18] It is interesting to notice that in spite of this the native impulses of the people toward domestic independence led them to maintain separate homes inconsistent with their communistic organization. This recognition of the needs of family experience contributed considerably to the content of the people and the success of their undertaking. As one would expect, taking into account their German origin, custom enforced masculine dominance and proclaimed the man as head of the family.

If one turns to the experience of these various brotherhoods expecting to find in their influence something directly affecting the advancement of woman's status, disappointment surely follows. Although radical in many respects, these organizations were generally conservative, even ascetic, in their attitude toward the relation of the sexes. Owen's teaching at New Harmony is an exception.

The advanced position of Indiana in legislation regarding marriage and divorce was in part due to the influence of the Owens, father and son, and also to the spirit of liberality that gathered about their experiment at New Harmony. Robert Dale Owen summarizes his contribution as a member of the Indiana Legislature in the following statement:

As to my action in the Indiana Legislature: I was a member of that body during the sessions of 1836–'7, and '8, and in 1851, but I have not the materials here that would enable me to give particulars. In a general way I had the State law so altered that a married woman owned and had the right to manage her own property, both real and personal; and I had the law of descents so changed that a widow, instead of dower, which is a mere tenancy or life interest, now has, in all cases, an *absolute* fee in one-third of her husband's estate; if only one child, then a half; and if no children, I think two-thirds. I also had an additional clause added to the divorce law, making two years' habitual drunkenness imperative cause for divorce.

I took no action in regard to suffrage while in the Legislature. In those days it would have been utterly unavailing.[19]

Nothing perhaps so reveals the modern outlook of this pioneer in the advancement of woman's rights as the marriage contract that he and his wife, Mary Jane Robinson, shared. Their union was closer to the experience of today than to the conventions of 1832.

New York, Tuesday, April 12, 1832.

This afternoon I enter into a matrimonial engagement with Mary Jane Robinson, a young person whose opinions on all important subjects, whose mode of thinking and feeling, coincide more intimately with my own than do those of any other individual with whom I am acquainted. . . . We have selected the simplest ceremony which the laws of this State recognize. . . . This ceremony involves not the necessity of making promises regarding that over which we have no control, the state of human affections in the distant future, nor of repeating forms which we deem offensive, inasmuch as they outrage the principles of human liberty and equality, by conferring rights and imposing duties unequally on the sexes. The ceremony consists of a simply written contract in which we agree to take each other as husband and wife according to the laws of the State of New York, our signatures being attested by those friends who are present.

Of the unjust rights which in virtue of this ceremony an iniquitous law tacitly gives me over the person and property of another, I can not legally, but I can morally divest myself. And I hereby distinctly and emphatically declare that I consider myself, and earnestly desire to be considered by others, as utterly divested, now and during the rest of my life, of any such rights, the barbarous relics of a feudal, despotic system, soon destined, in the onward course of improvement, to be wholly swept away; and the existence of which is a tacit insult to the good sense and good feeling of this comparatively civilized age.

Robert Dale Owen [20]

I concur in this sentiment,
Mary Jane Robinson

Indiana claims to have organized the first state woman's rights society, and tradition reports that rather than let his wife attend its meetings, a man of prominence in Indianapolis locked her within the house, although he did not himself feel that he was doing an unseemly thing in attending a public meeting of this organization.[21]

It is interesting to glimpse an indirect influence of New Harmony tradition in the acceptance of the first woman student at the University of Indiana. Sarah Parke Morrison, of the class of 1869, entered the university twenty years after her brother, although she was two years older than he. The inspiration of her ambition appears to have been a speech that she heard Robert Dale Owen make in the State Senate at Indianapolis on woman's rights. He was a friend of the family and in sympathy with her father's interest in public education. One day her father, who was president of the Board of Trustees of the State University, suggested that she apply for admission. The time had come, he said, when he thought it might be possible for a woman to get permission to matriculate. This is her statement as to how she came to enter the University.

About three days before starting my father said the Board might wish to ask me some questions and I had better go with him. I went accordingly, but heard nothing until, I believe, Commencement day noon. Dr. Richard Owen, brother of Robert Dale Owen, and a professor, came into Mrs. Wylie's parlor where I was, and said my father was detained a few minutes by some business of the Board but had commissioned him to bear me the news that my appeal had been read and the law examined, and finding no impediment the Board had declared the doors of the University open to young women upon the same terms as to young men.[22]

Not only did Owen himself, through his announcement of radical doctrines regarding marriage, that had some part in wrecking his experiment, reveal his distance from the existing *mores,* but among the number of able people [23] that he brought to his colony were some that were far in advance of conventional American thinking in their belief regarding the rights of women. Among these was the aggressive social reformer, Frances Wright, who appears to have the credit, while at New Harmony, of being the first woman in the United States to demand political equality for her sex.

The liberal attitude at New Harmony, the bringing together of so many distinguished scholars as to make the Indiana village for a time the scientific mecca of at least the entire western territory, the consistently progressive and effective influence of Owen's son, Robert Dale, were influences working together that tended to advance the status of woman. There was, however, no such direct contribution from the other organizations scattered from Ohio to the Texas frontier in the Southwest and to that of Dakota in the North, but there was an indirect contribution from the mere fact that these different types of radical departures from ordinary social life sought the West. This gave it a distinction and advertisement that impressed the more radical and liberal thinking people throughout western Europe.

Thus was added to the economic appeal of great stretches of cheap land and the romance of the West the spread of the idea that the American frontier offered a haven for socially frustrated and restless peoples everywhere. The situation in Germany and the Scandinavian nations was such that this conception of the West as a place of freedom led many men and women in these countries to the decision to leave the fatherland for America.

The influx of Germans, Norwegians, and Swedes into the western territory meant that the frontier, as it filled up, contained a large number of political and social radicals, who, having broken from one set of traditions, were more ready to accept a new alignment of the man-woman relationship. This disposition might not appear at first because, although radical in many respects, the immigrants were too saturated with the European atmosphere of masculine dominance to welcome quickly a change in woman's status. The foundation of this break had been laid, although covered up in the thinking of those who sought the West to break away from limitations and regimentation that had become in the countries of their birth intolerable.

The emotional trend of many of these people, so far as it had to do with the change of woman's status, appeared more clearly in the second generation of these Germanic and Scandinavian stocks. The Scandinavians enjoyed too democratic an experience to have the political unrest of the Germans, but they did feel a discontent, chiefly of economic origin, and in lesser degree a dissatisfaction with the aristocratic, hierarchical characteristics in the Scandinavian state churches. The Germans who came to America from 1815 to 1862 reflected a political and intellectual restlessness in addition to their desire to find in the new land better economic opportunities.[24]

As one appraises the indirect influence of the idealistic communities that settled in the Great West, the question naturally arises, Would it have been possible for the Oneida Community to have continued their most remarkable and revealing experiment in eugenics if they had left the hostile East and sought refuge, as did the Mormons, in the distant frontier? Possibly their successful financial operations so depended upon near markets that there could be no thought of going West; possibly Noyes had become convinced that at most such a migration could give them only a brief respite from outside attacks. It may be that he himself had grown to feel that there were inherent obstacles that made adherence to the Oneida sex program unwise. Now, however, since we are beginning to appreciate the eugenic value of this social experiment, it is interesting to speculate whether this community, had they followed the courageous policy of the Mormons, would have been able to carry on for a longer time the nearest approach we have to directed human breeding.

The characteristic family of the West revealed clearly its self-unity. Its patterns were essentially those that had appeared in each frontier development of the American settlement. There were in the Far West, as had been true in the preceding frontier period, a large number of men who were either unmarried or who had left their families behind in some more thickly settled community. The discovery of gold on the Pacific Coast artificially exaggerated this tendency in California and the mountain states. We are told that in the early days of San Francisco a woman on the street attracted attention, and a child even more so.

The family culture of the entire West reflected both the virtues and the vices of a strongly-knit, narrow but democratically-inclined type of family experience. Along with the independence we find also intolerance, lack of social discipline, and the spasmodic breaking out of the spirit of lawlessness. In contrast with the spirit of distrust of government we have the impulse, appearing again and again in times of stress or grievances, to force by political pressure solutions popular at the moment. The Populist Party movement is a typical illustration of this disposition to seek government aid in time of trouble.

The Western Frontier gave the character of the individual some sharp testing. The ordeal put upon the wives was emotionally more severe than that which fell upon their mates; at least it required a more patient, quiet courage, and undoubtedly it meant more continuous strain. There was the breaking of former family ties, a feeling of isolation which tended to encourage melancholia and constant fear, especially where there was danger of Indian attacks or where dangerous wild animals prevailed. The terrors of imagination, especially in the absence of husbands who of necessity frequently had to go long distances, had to be faced as well as the realities. In addition was the feeling of helplessness in times of emergency. A multitude of sensitive women were put on the rack of loneliness and fear during the latter days of confinement, even though they hoped for a degree of temporary help from some neighboring woman at the actual time of childbirth.

The West unmade as certainly as it made women. Some deserve to be called Mothers of the West, the fountainhead of a superb stock. Others broke under the tension, losing their attractive feminine traits and their efficient domestic habits. It was this latter type of woman that was portrayed realistically, and certainly with sympathy, by Caroline Matilda Kirkland in her book *A New Home, Who Will Follow*. Its description was too faithful to the conditions of the typical Michigan frontier village to be pleasing to those who insisted that all western experiences appear in the bright colors of a socially-optimistic daydreamer. Her book is a good antidote for those who refuse to recognize that the western democracy was at times a leveling down rather than an equality sought by lifting up those on lower levels.

The possibility of illness rested always as a black cloud on the horizon of the imagination. Probably no dread was more wearing in the life of the mother of children than the possibility of a sick child that could not receive adequate medical service. In the period discussed in this chapter there was a dearth of good doctors, especially in the Far West; that is, the Great Plains, the mountain mining settlements, and the Pacific territory over the mountains. It was natural that the better type of doctor preferred to stay east where his income was more secure and the practice of medicine easier. In the West there were great distances to be covered over the worst of roads, and many families who were too poor to add much to the doctor's meager income but who had to have medical attention.

The western frontier was not so healthful as perhaps one would expect from the outdoor life of the people. Accidents were frequent from the men's hunting, cutting timber, and from time to time the fighting of Indians. Epidemics came into the region from the more settled sections, particularly scarlet fever. In certain lowlands, as had been true in Ohio, there was a considerable amount of ague and fever, which now we realize were transmitted by mosquitoes. Recourse in illness often had to be to the few simple remedies which each family stored away for emergency. Drugs were commonly used that are seldom administered in these days. Even surgery occasionally had to be carried on with crude household utensils such as kitchen knives or a meat saw.[25]

Many women brought to the frontier, although they had vague forebodings, no clear notions of what awaited them. Their introduction to the crude and meager home-life of the wilderness often shocked them and sometimes so deeply that they never recovered. Anna H. Shaw relates an experience that was typical of what happened to many women. Her mother, when she arrived at the spot in the Michigan woods chosen by her husband for the new home, felt the contrast with what she had known so terrifically that her daughter says it seemed almost as if the woman died emotionally.

> It was late in the afternoon when we drove up to the opening that was its front entrance, and I shall never forget the look my mother turned upon the place. Without a word she crossed its threshold, and, standing very still, looked slowly around her. Then something within her seemed to give way, and she sank upon the ground. She could not realize even then, I think, that this was really the place father had prepared for us, that here he expected us to live. When she finally took it in she buried her face in her hands, and in that way she sat for hours without moving or speaking. For the first time in her life she had forgotten us; and we, for our part, dared not speak to her. We stood around her in a frightened group, talking to one another in whispers. Our little world had crumbled under our feet. Never before had we seen our mother give way to despair.

... She seemed to have died and to have returned to us from the grave, and I am sure she felt that she had done so. From that moment she took up again the burden of her life, a burden she did not lay down until she passed away; but her face never lost the deep lines those first hours of her pioneer life had cut upon it.[26]

Now that we understand, through recent endocrine knowledge, how profoundly the emotions affect the organism, we have the explanation of the rapid way in which some women, as they tried without bitterness and with courage to face their ordeal and do their part in establishing the frontier home, grew prematurely old, became sick, or even died. Everything depended upon the temperament of the woman and the severity of the struggle put upon her.

The Great Plains area became the last frontier in the growth of American civilization. This meant that its women not only encountered the hardships, the limitations, and the hazards that had always accompanied isolation and pioneering life but at a time when relatively they were heavier and more soul-searching than during earlier periods. The advancing standards of life through the application of science in the well settled areas made life on the last frontier seem more distant from the resources and the comforts enjoyed in the thickly-inhabited communities.

This contrast undoubtedly had a selective influence, discouraging some women, and therefore the families to which they belonged, from trying their fortunes in this western territory. On the other hand, the Far West had for others all the greater appeal. Its spaciousness, its physical features, its plains, deserts, and mountains, its atmosphere of newness, freedom, and promise, not only led many women to accompany their husbands in the adventure of new settlement, in the typical American pioneering spirit, but even induced some women to take advantage of the homestead laws and assume the responsibilities of developing their own grants of land. Women's resourcefulness certainly has never accepted sharper testing than this and for such persons customs and traditions maintaining social inferiority were incongruous.

CHAPTER VII

WOMAN, NORTH AND SOUTH, DURING AND AFTER THE CIVIL WAR

AFTER 1850, as American civilization developed, there was increasing expression of that fundamental division between the North and the South that allowed no compromise. The schism that resulted from the two opposite cultural trends had appeared early, but not at first did it foreshadow the rupture that was and, in its long-reaching consequences, that is the chief tragedy of our history. In the late fifties, the forces that were sweeping the people toward conflict were as swift in current as waters nearing the Niagara chasm, but few there were, North or South, who realized the maelstrom near at hand or the wreckage it would leave. At bottom, the incompatibility of the two cultures rested on economic differences, but the separation was wide at every point where comparison could be made between the feeling, the thinking, the habits, in short, the entire social substance of the two increasingly distinct types of American people.

Unhappily, their clashing during the decade more and more became emotional and moral, and the peaceful adjustment of their divergence grew correspondingly hopeless. Looking backward, it now seems as if there ought to have been a political leadership sensitive enough to have apprehended what was happening and sagacious enough to have provided time with its opportunity to reunite northern and southern cultures without recourse to the surgery of a great war. This retrospective optimism commits the fallacy of leaving out of account the moral turn the contention had taken which led irresistibly to that final collision, war, which so often has settled uncompromising differences between civilizations.

The only opportunity to save the two groups of American people from the costly, cruel struggle of war was before their differences in political leadership had crystallized into moral form, and naturally at that time few foresaw the disaster so near at hand. Now, when it is certain that inexorable social trends, given time enough, would have eliminated the chief cause of their conflict, it seems strange that men in high places could not have foreseen what was happening and brought about the necessary truce. We forget that when time begins to work against any social practice or condition, the scrimmage line of its attack is likely to be taken over by the agitator and the moralist. Thus in human experience, the natural, gradual reconstruction that could be made by impersonal, objective, temporary changes, is aborted by the impatient dogmatists and power-craving reformists and passion-stirring God's anointed. The moral crusade brings its counterattack and just, intelligent settlement soon becomes impossible. The moralist rushes in to force immediate, spectacular changes, and soon the ongoing human evolution, which is beginning to transform some particular tradition or culture trait through the benevolent reshaping that results from new conditions of living, new experiences, and eventually new thinking, is changed into a life and death struggle of opposing groups. This is what happened in the American conflict that fundamentally grew out of the institution of slavery.

The agitator and the moralist never can be made to realize the temporary aspects of social good and evil. As soon as any practice begins to show itself out of season, there is recognition neither of the value of its previous functioning nor of the certainty of its passing. Those who defend the old order realize the first fact but from many motives are blinded to the second. Two moral groups, each convinced of the rightness of its sympathies, force the issue and draw into their conflict the greater number of people, differently minded, who, unhurried by passionate agitation, would find some compromise of their differences, at least for the moment, and through motives of expediency finally arrive at a settlement without the losses that any decision through warfare necessarily brings.

Southern aristocracy, which in its earlier period after the formation of the Union had given a quality of leadership indispensable to the security of a democratic state, rested upon a support that time was bound to undermine. It was tied up with human slavery, and during the nineteenth century this means of production rapidly became an anachronism, an institution so contrary to the spirit of the time that nothing could prevent its passing. All life in the South was colored by influences from the plantation, which was committed to slavery so completely that without it there seemed no way by which it could exist. The aristocracy became feudal-spirited through its alliance with slavery and more and more withdrew within itself, thus protecting its existence as changing conditions made the facing of social reality increasingly difficult. It attempted to maintain throughout the South a self-sufficient culture needing only economic relations with non-slavery peoples and, by preference, with European markets where its agricultural products were so indispensable that financial interest lessened the expression of hostility to a slave-supported culture.

The South had protected itself to a great degree from the cultural interference of the people in other sections by its political dominance. It had achieved and maintained political leadership by the quality and the force of its representatives, but as the modern drift set more and more strongly against slavery, it used its power as a means of defense, and, when the Middle West grew in population and political influence, the southern leaders began to feel insecure as they struggled against the ever-increasing predominance of the non-slave-holding population, especially since they exaggerated the significance of the northern Abolitionist movement. Meanwhile the attack on slavery grew greater and more violent, and becoming more sensitive to the falseness of such interpretations of it as culminated in *Uncle Tom's Cabin* they failed to realize either the strength or the fundamental source of the pressure against their system. However unjust, this attack of the crusader who was often basically neurotic and therefore extreme was nevertheless an announcement to the South of the fact that modern life was demolishing slavery as a means of production and that there was need, if southern culture was to persist, of finding some substitute for it. It was a great national misfortune that on account of the influence of crops and soil, slavery, which of course was introduced both North and South, flourished only in the latter region. If it could have persisted, even in less degree, in the North, although there would have been clashing and disturbance, the agitation would not have taken a sectional form and undoubtedly there would have been a replacement of free labor for slave labor without the disaster of war.

Southern people had, and not without reason, great confidence in their ability to repel any invasion of their sovereign rights in case of war, a calamity which the majority of those who had become convinced that the secession of the South from the rest of the Union was necessary did not anticipate. Southern culture, however, was in the peculiar predicament that this very effort to defend itself by an appeal to arms would certainly destroy it. Such a struggle would level the defenses that had preserved the southern culture, because the skill of strategy and battle courage had to be enforced by a modernized army and industry, both antagonistic to the feudal-spirited civilization that made slavery possible. Even if, in the last days of the Confederacy, slavery had been surrendered in the effort to repel the invader [1] and the South had won its cause, it would have found after the end of the struggle that its characteristic culture had received a death blow from which there was no hope of recovery.

The wreckage of the aristocracy had tragic consequences that were much greater than otherwise they would have been, because of the relative impotency of the middle class in the South. The plantation and its satellite industries had tended to create only two classes among the whites. This two-fold classification was not complete, but there was no strongly-established, politically-influential middle class that could share the shock of disaster at the end of the Civil War. This fact made it easier for the northern agitator in his pre-war crusade to stir up feeling against the southern system, because there was no basis of sympathy or understanding between the middle class that dominated the North and the aristocracy that controlled the South. Western people were even more alien to an aristocratic system, since their social conditions were still so fluid that it was difficult to draw any line to distinguish classes. Some families were wealthy and some were poor, but circumstances were too changeable for any hard and fast distinctions to be maintained. The prosperous family of today may have been in a near yesterday hard struggling pioneers. Democratic trends were too vigorous to allow any attempt at stratification.

Aside from the fact that the southern aristocrat was also a large slave owner in nearly all instances, his social status was a source of antipathy and a cause of misunderstanding among the powerful middle class people of the North and the great mass of democratically-inclined people of the West. Slavery to these outsiders, who rarely knew anything at all at first hand about southern conditions, was always seen in a setting of great wealth and interpreted as a one-way exploitation. Never was there any fair recognition of the obligations and the definite responsibilities that the reputable slave-owner had to accept. If there had been any realization in the North of the two-way functioning of the slave system as it characteristically operated, the agitator would never have had such a chance to inflame passion. Certainly, outside the South, there was little appreciation of the difficult task slavery put upon the planter's wife.

In any attempt to understand the effect of the Civil War upon southern women, it is necessary to start with the wife of the plantation owner. She symbolizes the feminine rôle in southern society and in the most dramatic portrayal possible reveals as sweeping a social cataclysm, resulting from the War, as has ever happened in the western world. Throughout the United States at that time, with few exceptions, the status of individual women was determined not only by the prevailing convention reflecting male dominance but also by the position and disposition of individual fathers and husbands. In no section of the United States was this as true as in the South. Few women could escape this placement. Neither wealth nor poverty liberated them. Even if they were financially independent and entirely free from any man's supervision, which was in itself difficult, there were still strong, definite, thoroughly-supported codes which were too entangling to give any woman, whatever her station, any considerable degree of independence. As a consequence, the destiny of the woman of the South was inseparable from that of man's, and the war that crushed him in the end came even more heavily upon her.

It would be most misleading to think of the planter's wife as merely a woman of wealth. This gives a suggestion of freedom from responsibility, of easy-going leisure, which was certainly not characteristic of the life of these southern women. It is only as we realize that they were, in spite of their wealth, mistresses of plantations that we get the slightest glimpse of the deeper meaning of their career. The Southeast was predominantly rural, and its chief crop was cotton. This generally meant that the man who had wealth also administered a plantation and was dependent upon slave labor for the carrying on of his enterprise.

Any absentee policy was hazardous in the extreme. Although there was on every sizable plantation an overseer, an intermediary of the system, which was not only a real need but also a requirement of the aristocratic code, this did not take away the indispensability of the personal supervision of the owner himself. He could have his vacation, his trips to the coast, to the mountains, or to the North, especially during the dull periods of his yearly cycle, but if he stayed away at crucial seasons, his pocketbook soon suffered. He was bound to the plantation by his slave system. It is this that explains in part the centralizing of sport, entertainment, and the gayety about the plantation so characteristic of pre-war southern society.

If the planter was tied to the plantation, his wife was even more bound to it than he. There were no seasonal breaks in the responsibilities that necessarily fell to her as the mistress of a great plantation. To her came the task of taking care of the human, the domestic, personal problems that were inevitable in the bringing together of the colored workers—men, women, and children. The responsibilities came to her because she was the mistress, and they could not be delegated for any length of time to another. She alone was the woman-head and the final authority.

Even when she possessed great wealth, the planter's wife was unlike her sister of means North and West. The wife of the northern mill owner rarely had any personal obligation to the workers in her husband's factory. From benevolent purposes she might take some interest in their welfare, but she did not have the everyday task of supervision, of management, nor the need of responding at any time to emergencies such as those of birth, death, and illness, which at any moment of day or night might intrude upon the leisure of the plantation mistress. As we read the diaries of these plantation women, we wonder how they could carry the burdens they married into when they became "the Missus." [2] It also amazes us, looking backward, that they could make the quick transformation most of them appear successfully to have accomplished from an irresponsible, romantic youth, with its gayeties, flirtations, balls, and usual freedom from household responsibilities, to the detailed, never-ending, versatile routine that followed immediately upon the wife's coming to the plantation to live. The same code that protected her before her marriage put upon her soon after the wedding the largest and most exacting of domestic programs. The mill owner's responsibilities may not have crossed the threshold of his worker's home, but on the plantation the entire life of ignorant slaves was in the hands of the plantation owner and his wife, and her task commonly carried her into the most intimate experiences of her child-like subjects. Self-interest and the code, thoroughly supported by public opinion, meant that she could not shirk her responsibilities without her husband losing money and she and her family losing face.

Northern people had no appreciation of this side of the planter's wife. Harriet Beecher Stowe realized it and did her best to make it vivid, but her more spectacular pictures assaulting the slave system concealed from most readers her recognition of the obligation the system brought to the planter's wife. For example, there was no understanding by one who had not visited the South of how much patience and kindliness were necessary on the part of the woman head of the plantation in the carrying on of its everyday routine. Few northerners or westerners had any idea of such a relationship between the immature slave and the planter's wife as is pictured to us by Mrs. Smedes.

. . . Her motherliness extended over the whole plantation. She had a special eye and care for any neglected or unfortunate or ill-treated negro child, and would contrive to have such cases near her. One deformed, sickly girl, who was of no value in any sense, she took to the Pass one summer for the benefit of the sea-bathing. In the Burleigh household of servants there was usually some young negro so hopelessly dull that her own mother would not try to teach her to sew or to do other useful things. Under the sheltering wing of the mistress this girl would be patiently taught to do many things. Sophia was aware that this was not the way to have her household ordered in the best style. She was quite indifferent to the public opinion that required only fine-looking, thoroughly trained servants about the establishment of a gentleman. Many of her servants were intelligent, and filled their departments well, and the dull one was screened by being kept in the nursery and about her. The objects of her patience and kindness were devoted to her and proud of her favor. In many instances they became much better instructed than would have been thought possible by one less conscientious and full of faith than herself.[3]

In no section of the country was the division between the rôle of the wife and the rôle of the husband as clear-cut as in the South. A great part of the life of the man was entirely apart from that of his wife. If she knew of it at all, she knew of it indirectly through what he said or in some more roundabout way. Politics, which generally attracted him seriously, offered no place for her. If she were interested, it was because through his career she found satisfaction. There were no incentives for her attempting to break in, and had it been her wish, she would have found no opening. The same was true in a large measure of his financial undertakings apart from those that affected her directly because they were part of the domestic economy. The moment we compare her completely conventionalized career, from birth to death, with the freer, equality-inclined social practices of the married woman in the Far West, we see how distinct at this point these two sectional cultures were. The cultural trend of one was toward fixing the woman within a wide domestic circle, the fellowship of families; that of the other, toward drawing her out into the man's world as a fellow worker. The western woman may not have had a great interest in politics and may have felt no stirring of gregarious ambitions that were manlike and not to be satisfied with family experience, but in spite of this she was getting preparation to claim more out-of-the-family opportunity, once the stress of severe economic struggle passed.

An impressive part of the code that both honored and limited the woman of the South was the chivalry that was shown her. This came from complex feelings. It was protection, appreciation, and unquestionably also compensation.[4] As is true of all conventional sentiment, it had an element of play-acting. It also had the motive of enhancing the qualities of the well-bred woman by separating her from the mere femaleness of the poor-white or colored women. The double code of sex ethics always tends toward this distinction of two types of women, in accordance with what the psychiatrists recognize as efforts at compensation, but especially did miscegenation, to the degree that it was associated with the slave system, tend toward an attitude that lifted the white woman of virtue away from all possible likeness to the colored female. To accomplish this, the southern lady had to be interpreted as more than a woman just as certainly as the slave must be made to seem less than a woman.

This same mechanism of compensation appeared in the North in the attempt to separate the prostitute and the moral woman, but as the difference between the two was not felt to be so great as that between the aristocratic white woman and the female Negro, it likewise never went so far in expressing distinction. In the West the half-breed woman and the Indian squaw illustrated the same principle.

It would, however, be a one-sided analysis of the chivalry of the South that contented itself with the motivations discussed. Perhaps more than anything else the southern conventions reflected the prestige-emphasis of aristocracy. Since man dominated, it was natural that he should have exalted through sentiment the type of woman his culture created. It marked her off from other women through her elevation, and in lifting her he not only satisfied his desire to idealize but he also added to his own prestige. Of course, nobody supposes that these were conscious motives, except as they were expressed in personal ambition and relationship, but what was true of each southern gentleman became characteristic of all and was crystallized into a social code.

It was natural in a society where the rôle of women was so definitely drawn and masculine dominance so secure, for compensatory sentiment to glorify the virtues of the woman and to place her upon a pedestal. The situation at the time encouraged this disposition in the southern *mores*. The elevation of the southern woman tended to distinguish her, certainly in the minds of southern people, from her northern sister who did not enjoy such a measure of chivalrous attention. Thus the southern woman was given a distinction, something in which both the men and the women of the upper classes felt pride. In so far as outside criticism of the slave system penetrated southern consciousness, one of the defenses was emphasis upon the excellencies achieved south of the Mason and Dixon line, and among these was the superior position of women. This tended both to maintain chivalry and also to shut off from the life of the women the influences coming out of modern life that in other sections were either bringing or preparing to bring a greater equality of the sexes. Naturally it was rare to find among young women any protest against the idealization, the homage, and the practice of social courtesies characteristically carried on by men.

Although with this system went a definition of status after marriage often in sharp contrast with the spirit of courtship days, the older woman appears not to have made emotional protest against this change of circumstances but to have accepted, as a matter of course, her adult responsibilities. Chivalry included her as certainly as her daughter and undoubtedly pleased her as well as having meaning to her as reminiscence of her premarriage flirtation days.

Although southern women, as a rule, left to the men the management of public affairs and took interest in politics only indirectly through the careers of husbands and sons, they were not the less tied up with the civilization of which they were a part. They had the same belief in southern rights, the same theories of the sovereignty of the state, the same confidence in the destiny of their culture, as the men.

The rapid happenings that ended in the secession of the southeastern states, including Texas, and finally the War, had the same meaning for the women as for the men and affected them in the same way. Their commitment to their native state, which led them to hold firmly to the doctrine of state's rights, which certainly was held without difference of section at the time that the United States came into being, led them to resent any sort of federal interference as an invasion of their political and moral rights exactly as in the case of the men. They commonly had the same notion that the North ought to let them withdraw from the Union and that there was no substantial northern sentiment that would seek to challenge secession with test of arms.

Once the War broke, their mood was the same as that of the men. It would be quickly over; the superiority of the South would make attempts at invasion futile, a feeling that was strengthened by the defeat of the Federal troops in the first great battle of the War—Bull Run, as it was known in northern literature, or Manassas, as in southern. This enlistment of the sentiment of women does not mean that there was not among a great multitude of them a recoil against the idea of war, and a greater anticipation of what it might mean. It was inevitable that the mothers and wives, who viewed the contest from a distance and who saw their loved ones go away from their home to the battlefield, without the relief that activity in any adventure, however dangerous, gives, should feel the hazards of warfare more keenly than did most of the men. The effect of the War upon women North and South was to bring them immediately into the contest. They responded to the emotional appeal as did the men, but with this difference; the rôle offered them, in accord with the conventions, was chiefly sacrificial and vicarious. They welcomed, however, at the start such opportunities as were offered them to support their husbands and sons in the field, and their sympathy led them increasingly to the undertaking of unfamiliar services.

Rather soon it appeared that the southern women were destined to a closer contact with the realities of the struggle and were most rapidly to move away from former habits of life and in greater numbers to engage actively in war work. Like the women folks in the North and the West, at the beginning their interest found its chief expression in giving the soldiers a good send-off when they started for the army and in preparing kits for their pleasure and comfort once they joined the distant troops. The following gives a vivid picture of these early days in the South before the women of the upper classes had been wrenched by the War from peace traditions:

"We girls worked very hard, as we thought, giving concerts, tableaux, &c., by which to raise money with which to purchase for these boxes. I can see even now the bevy of bright-eyed, red-lipped, white-handed girls, flitting hither and thither in their dainty dresses and bright ribbons. What a lovely picture they made tripping, or kneeling by the huge boxes, packing parcels marked for 'Captain,' or 'Lieutenant,' or 'Private,' so and so. I smile with a sadness akin to pain as I recall the contents of those first boxes, the proceeds of what we call labor! Wine and jellies, mammoth cakes and confections, dainty toilet appurtenances, china and majolica shaving cups, inlaid dressing cases, perfumery, &c. There were bursts of silvery laughter and little shrieks of delight as we found one more place where something could be stored. There were books, too, small blue and gold bound volumes of the poets, interlined with pencil, and holding between the leaves a cluster of blue-eyed violets, purple pansies, or a geranium leaf, clasping on its green heart a rosy oleander." [5]

War soon ceased to be a romance, and women were quickly made familiar with its grimness. Introduction came first through direct contact on the part of women in Virginia and Tennessee, but even the first battles in these states sent sick, wounded, and mutilated men to the villages and cities of the deeper South. As an example of the quick change from a mirth-loving, pleasure-seeking, war-adventuring city to one of determination, sadness, and sacrifice, we have the experiences of Richmond after the Battle of Seven Pines.[6] The young girls and older women who had thrust food and fruit upon the outgoing soldiers as they marched to battle a little later ministered in their homes to wounded and dying soldiers who had to be cared for outside the over-crowded hospitals. In addition to opening their own homes, the women also became nurses at the hospitals, thus assuming a task that they carried on throughout the War, a burden ever increasing, ever becoming more nerve-racking for women frustrated by lack of facilities to ease suffering and to help bring back the convalescent to health.

If one wishes to feel in some measure the practical adaptation to circumstances of these women, their physical and emotional hardihood, in carrying on in that most soul-tearing of all ministration—when one cannot lessen pain and help recovery on account of lack of resources—a glimpse at the hospital life at Ringgold, Georgia, will suffice. These hospitals were established in the fall of 1862 to take care not only of the wounded but those suffering from typhoid fever, pneumonia, dysentery, and scurvy, as a result of the exposure and privations associated with Bragg's retreat from Kentucky. On one of the most bitter days of the winter word came that preparation must be made for two hundred sick men who would arrive that same night.

There was not an empty bed in either of the two hospitals. Attempt was made to get permission to open the one church of the community and turn it into a hospital. Although the request was denied, there was nothing else to be done, so the church was taken over. Fires were made in the two stoves the building afforded, pews were taken out, and since there was no way of getting beds or even making them, all the available ticks were filled with straw and spread on the floor. When these gave out the straw was scattered over the floor, as when one stables horses. When the pillows gave out the backs of the pews were made into supports against which knapsacks could be piled up slant-wise to rest the heads of the men. They arrived, all sick and some dying. Some could just totter; others were on stretchers. They had thrown away their clothes and were suffering from the bitter cold. The description of this experience gives us an understanding of the kind of service rendered by women workers in the Confederate hospitals.

. . . Not one in twenty had saved even a haversack, many having discarded coats and jackets. One man had gained possession of an india-rubber overcoat, which, excepting his underclothing, was his only garment. Barefooted,—their feet were swollen frightfully, and seamed with fissures so large that one might lay a finger in them. These were dreadfully inflamed, and bled at the slightest touch; others were suppurating. The feet of some presented a shining, inflamed surface which seemed ready to burst at any moment. Their hands were just as bad, covered with chilblains and sores. Many were tortured with wounds which had at first seemed slight, but by neglect and exposure had become sources of exquisite torture. The gleaming eyes, matted hair and beard hanging about their cadaverous faces, gave to these men a wild, ghastly look utterly indescribable. As they came in, many sunk exhausted upon the pallets, some falling at once into a deep sleep, from which it was impossible to arouse them, others able only to assume a sitting posture on account of the racking, rattling cough which, when reclining, threatened to suffocate them. Few would stop to be undressed: food and rest were all they craved. Those who crowded to the stoves soon began to suffer from their frozen feet and hands, and even ran out into the snow to ease their pain. The surgeons worked faithfully, and the whole force was in requisition. But, alas! alas! death also was busy among these unfortunates. The very first man I essayed to feed died in my arms, two others during the night. The poor wounded feet I tried to handle so tenderly bled at every touch. The warmth of the room, while it sent some into a sound sleep which seemed death's counterpart, caused terrible agony to others, who groaned and screamed. It seemed to me just as if these men, having previously kept up with heroic fortitude under trials almost too great for human endurance, had, as soon as the terrible tension was lessened, utterly succumbed, forgetting all but the horrible pain that racked them.[7]

We have become so accustomed to women serving as nurses in war that we are likely to forget what a break this rapid extension of hospitalization meant in the life of women both North and South. Hospitals had begun to appear during the decade preceding the Civil War in the larger cities. It helps us to realize how few women were trained in any professional sense for nursing before the War to know that, in spite of the influence of the conflict in stimulating the growth of hospitals and accustoming people to the need of them, there were, as late as 1873, only 149 hospitals in the entire United States, and more than a third of these cared only for insane patients.[8]

Both North and South a greater number of women were engaged in occupations supporting the War than in any philanthropic or relief activity. This employment of women in war industries had greater meaning in the South than in the North. In the former section manufacturing was already well established, and, as we have previously noticed, many women were engaged in textile manufacturing and the like. In the Confederate states the development of industries on the scale required by war activities meant something new, for only a small number of the women in that section had had previous experience with this type of work. To some extent, particularly at the beginning of the War, machines were imported from Europe and skilled mechanics to take charge of them. For the most part the Confederacy had to depend upon its own ingenuity and to create almost at once, from meager resources, factories for the making of ammunition, harnesses, rifles, shoes, and the other necessities without which the War could not be carried on.

There certainly was a new order in the South when it could be said that the streets of Richmond at the dinner period were thronged with women going to or returning from factories engaged in the manufacturing of clothes, cartridges, and other war necessities.[9]

Although factories came into being quickly and offered many women an important part in the prosecution of the War, the home industries that were carried on were even more indispensable, and few women there were who had no part in this work, so utterly foreign to the pre-war experiences of most of them, but without which there would have been no hope of the South surviving. For example, one of them writes from Alabama as follows:

> We not only had to furnish clothes for our own immediate soldiers, but there were others belonging to the company whose friends were entirely out of reach, and we clothed them to the end. The clothing for the negroes was a heavy item, and all supplies of that kind were cut off, and we could only give them what was made at home. On every plantation, and almost in every house, were heard the constant hum of the wheels and click of the looms. The soldiers' clothes were a constant care. As soon as one suit was sent another was made, for they often lost their clothing, and it had to be ready to send at a moment's notice.
>
> We wore homespun dresses, which were really very pretty. At a little distance they looked like gingham, and we were very proud of our work. We dyed them very prettily, and were more anxious to learn a new process of dyeing than we ever had been to learn a new stitch in crochet or worsted work. We knitted all the undershirts the soldiers wore, also socks and gloves, be-

sides those required at home. We often knitted until midnight, after all the day's work was done, and ladies knitted as they rode in their carriages. Indeed, we were very busy, and in the constant employment found our greatest comfort. I heard one woman say: 'I never go to bed until I am too tired and worn out to think.'

And through all the trials, and trouble, and work, the love of the South kept us up. We never would listen to the thought that we might fail. We fully realized what defeat meant, and dreaded it so much that we were willing to risk our all rather than submit to it. We had the hardest lot. The men were moving about—to-day a fight, or looking forward to one, the constant excitement keeping them up; and even when not on duty the camp seldom failed to provide amusement. We at home had to sit still and wait.

Now in those last two years all our medicines were exhausted, and we had to go to the woods for bark, and roots and herbs. We made quinine of dogwood and poplar, boiled to a strong decoction, and then to paste. We had to do the work of a chemist, without his laboratory. We made our own mustard and opium and castor oil. This last, with all the refining that we were capable of, was a terrible dose, and only used in extreme cases.[10]

All through the South women learned to make substitutes for things once so cheap that little thought was given to them. For example, thorns were made to take the place of pins, and persimmon, peach, and gourd seeds had holes bored in them and were then used for buttons. Here is a list of house-made dyes.

For yellow, sassafras; for drab, kalmia or dwarf laurel; for slate color in cotton and blue-black, in wool or linen, willow bark; for chocolate brown, red oak bark; for lead color, white oak bark; for dyeing cotton a dun color, sweet gum bark; for dyeing wool lead color, the seeds of guinea corn.[11]

The following extract gives some idea of the quickness with which women leaders turned from the life of an aristocrat, served constantly by slaves chosen for the task, to acceptance of the hard manual labor the War needed of them.

Were these the same people—these haggard, wrinkled women, bowed with care and trouble, sorrow and unusual toil? These tame, pale, tearless girls, from whose soft flesh the witching dimples had long since departed, or were drawn down into furrows—were they the same school girls of 1861? These women who, with coarse, lean and brown hands, sadly and mechanically were stowing away into boxes, (not large ones,) meat, bread, cabbage, dried fruit, soda, syrup, homemade shoes and coarse home knit socks, garments of osnaburg and homespun, home-woven clothing of every description—these women with scant, faded cotton gowns and coarse leather shoes—these women who silently and apathetically packed the boxes, looking into them with the intense and sorrowful gaze that one casts into the grave—were these, I say, could these be the same airy-robed, white-fingered women, so like flowers, who, months and months ago, (it appeared an eternity) packed away, 'mid laughter and song, smile and jest those *articles de luxe* for the boys at the front?

Before the close of the conflict I knew women to walk twenty miles for a half bushel of coarse, musty meal with which to feed their starving little ones, and leave the impress of their feet in blood on the stones of the wayside ere they reached home again. When there, the meal was cooked and ravenously eaten, though there was not even salt to be eaten with it. Yet these women did not complain, but wrote cheerful letters to their husbands and sons, if they were yet living, bidding them to do their duty and hold the last trench.[12]

One of the problems that proved most troublesome for the generals high in command, often explaining their defeat or the incompleteness of their victory, was the great number of men who left the army for short periods, often at critical moments, in order to help their women folks whom they had come to know were in desperate situations. This was especially true of the last year of the

War, in spite of the fact that the women tried to hide from their men their home circumstances. Some understanding of their suffering, their nearness at times to actual starvation, reached fathers and sons in the armies and accounted for the departures that were catalogued as desertions.

The effort which women put forth to keep alive the spirit of their former life and to maintain cheerfulness and courage was seen in the starvation parties which became so popular. Balls were held without refreshments of any kind, and soldiers on furlough were refreshed by gayeties that hid by common consent any underlying sadness or despondency. As the soldiers covered up as much as they could of their own suffering, so, when they visited their homes for rest or convalescence, their mothers, sisters, friends, and sweethearts concealed their own sufferings, as far as possible, with the same spirit.[13]

The significance of woman's activities, which took every form necessary for the carrying on of the economic life of the section and the maintenance of the troops in the field, and of the spirit with which she made her contribution, lies in its contrast with her life before the War. She jumped from the pedestal where she had been placed by popular sentiment and accepted any task of hardship and responsibility as a matter of course. Although her work took unfamiliar expression, often of a sort that would have been unimaginable in the pre-war days, she had had a practical training as mistress of the plantation that is apt to be forgotten, or at least minimized, by those who think of her as she appeared in her social gayeties. Her sewing, dyeing, planting, reaping, clothes-making, and the like, have meaning when they are placed against her former background. Not only was she demonstrating a quick, effective adaptability, most unexpected, in trying circumstances; she was also in the process of transferring from one type of life to another. There were southern Joan of Arcs, who imitated masculine rôles and, like Belle Boyd, played an important part in the military history of the South. We must, however, turn to the average woman who busied herself with ordinary tasks, if we wish to see the new women of the South in the making. War and its aftermath were destined not only to change them from what they once had been but also to make them the most distinctive grouping of women in our history, most self-contained, most bound together by a subtle, ever-vital emotion rooted in memories.

It is easy now to see how the circumstances of the War severed, except in fond recollections, the southern women from their past, while at the same time considerably preventing them from sharing the development of woman's life that was so apparent during the next decade outside the southern states. Military strategy, as the situation determined it, forced upon the North the invasion of the South in an attempt at victory and gave the South the task of driving the enemy from its soil. This meant that under any circumstance southern women would have had closer contact with the War than those of the North. The meaning of this becomes clear when we contrast the experiences of French and Belgian women in World War I with those of the German, the English, or the American. Terrible as is warfare at a distance, since it means to the womenfolk the sending out of their dear ones, perhaps never to return, it is nothing like the stark realities that come to women whose homes are within the battle area.

Even had the Confederacy maintained its cause successfully, there would necessarily have come, from the personal sufferings of the women in the war territory, to southern women a profounder scarring than to northern women; but the turn the invasion took, especially in the last two years of the War, enormously added to the depth of women's feeling. This destruction of property, the cruel waste of even the means of livelihood, and the terrorizing, have come to be symbolized by Sherman and his march. It was a form of attack upon the South utterly unlike the policy, for example, of McClellan during his all but successful attempt to capture Richmond in the early period of the War. It was a program that attempted utterly to prostrate the South and end the War, influenced no doubt by the recognition that the northern people were growing weary of the contest, or at least that the Administration so thought.

No one questions the strategy that led Sherman to cut into the deep South and destroy the sources of food, ammunition, and other war supplies that were supporting the Confederate armies. The final crumbling of Lee's army came certainly as much from its ever-dwindling supplies as from the constant pressure of Federal troops. Sherman's strategy did much to end the fighting, but it did more to prolong its bitterness by transforming a physical and political secession into a spiritual and timeless alienation. The conflict ceased on the battlefields but it lived on in the hearts and minds of southern women. The prayer, "Let us have peace!" was as futile as Lee's entreaty that the women of the South do nothing to keep alive the War.[14]

If it be true that Americans have perpetuated the memory of the internal strife of this period,[15] the chief explanation of this must be found in the South and in the memories transmitted to their children by the women who suffered. Allowing for the exaggerations on the part of southern women, the shocks of disappointment, the rationalizations that always appear to soften defeat, the fact still remains that in the effort to end the War by completely demoralizing the portions of the South he invaded, Sherman assumed a policy, whether in its details authorized by Federal chief command or not matters little, that was sure to delay and make difficult reunion.

There were, of course, different strategies involved in the invasion of the South by Federal troops and the going into the northern territory by the Confederates. With the exception of minor cavalry raids in the latter case, the purpose, especially on the part of Lee, was to inspire sympathizers with the South, particularly those of Maryland, to commit themselves to the cause of the Confederacy. Apparently Stonewall Jackson, at least at times, believed that the Confederates should go far enough into the enemy country to strike at the Union vitals, but this was not the notion of either Lee or Davis, who were influenced by their hope of European recognition. As a consequence, their military strategy could not include any program of devastation. We can imagine a different situation which would have meant penetration by Confederate troops into the industrial and commercial centers of the North, and the burning of supplies and factories, which would have been fully justified as war measures. What we cannot believe is that under any condition Lee would have committed what happened along the march of Sherman's army in the deep South. The latter's military strategy was overshadowed by what seemed to be a campaign directed against women and children.

It was this needless addition to the ruin that always accompanies an invading army that registered so deeply in the consciousness of southern women. They could not forget, not because of bitterness, not even from hatred, but through recollections of suffering that seemed inflicted in the spirit of vengeance. Sherman went victoriously northward but left behind him little children crying from hunger and terror, an enemy that even time could not conquer. Their mothers, helpless for the moment, never forgot nor forgave. Their experiences gathered an everness that allowed no fading. This they handed on to their own daughters, until it seemed as if through female descent the struggle of the states was destined to become in the South socially immortal.

National loyalty, unstinted in its willingness to sacrifice in three subsequent wars, helped southern women to extract bitterness from these war memories, but it could not dislodge the revulsion still the heritage of southern-born women. Sherman has been sentenced, defeated in purpose, to march unceasingly northward!

If one points to the shorter memory of French, Belgian, and other European women who suffered from World War I, there is need to consider who were the victims in the South, and how. Many of them had been people of wealth and superior culture, accustomed to leadership. It was natural, as they won back their position, that they should use their prestige to crystallize southern feeling into a stubborn barrier against everything originating among the people held responsible for their war misfortunes. Also the how has significance. It was not a long-distance, impersonal assault but a face-to-face meeting between family members on the one hand and individual soldiers on the other. This gave a sense of maliciousness, a basis for specific accountability, that heightened all the burning, robbing, devastating that occurred as northern troops penetrated the deep South. It was difficult in World War I to particularize the responsibilities of the suffering. This meant shorter memories among the women who endured the war experiences. Moreover, a greater amount of destruction came from the military operations themselves, the havoc of high explosives, an essential part of modern warfare.

There were bands of lawless deserters who belonged to neither army and who took advantage of the anarchy, political and social disorganization in great stretches of territory, that were more feared by the women of the South than even Sherman's soldiers. A considerable part of the atrocities that occurred must be charged to them. One southern woman writes:

But the Federal soldiers I did not fear at all, as I did the "Jayhawkers." They were composed of roving bands from both armies, united for the purpose of plunder—calling themselves Confederates usually, but feared by friend and foe alike.[16]

Indirectly these happenings were added to the recoil against the North in the emotions of southern women. They were consequences of the demoralization that followed the invading armies. This menace increased during the closing year of the War. Even among the regular troops there were occasional expressions of the chaos associated with the breaking up of the Confederacy. In *The War-Time Journal of a Georgia Girl,* Eliza Frances Andrews gives us an example of this in the riot of a Texas regiment as, joined by disorderly elements among the soldiers and citizens, it plundered the Commissary Department. Negroes and children joined in the mob, and the provost guard refused to interfere. They were too good soldiers to fire on their comrades.[17] Such happenings in the last phase of the War gave many women not only a first-hand knowledge of the meaning of war but also of its worst of all consequences, social anarchy.

The full shock of the ruin that came upon the South was not felt until the War came to an end. Up to that moment, even though everything went badly, the women kept their hope, but with the final collapse forbidding realities had to be faced. Never had a proud people felt greater shock. One question forced itself into consciousness. Was this the end of the fighting, the starving, the going naked and cold, the surrendering to death of children, husbands, friends, and fathers? [18] One woman closed the diary that she had been keeping through the War with two short sentences, laconic and pathetic.

May 4.—General Johnston surrendered on the 26th of April.

"My native land, good-night!" [19]

Overnight they lost their South and found themselves in Gethsemane. Crucifixion was near at hand! Stunned as they were by poverty, helplessness, and tragedy, it was fortunate that they had no glimpse of the greater ordeal so near.

Under the most advantageous circumstances, including freedom from passion and bitterness, the orderly emancipation and resettlement of the colored slaves of the South would have challenged to its utmost the political, economic, and legal leadership of both North and South. The treatment, immediately following the end of the conflict, of the slaves freed as a war measure, and the extending to them of suffrage, reveals a political incompetency in meeting a great social crisis that is, fortunately, unparalleled in our history. Lincoln, we have reason to believe, would have done better had he lived, but it would have been even for him a forthright struggle and one that would have prevented the deification that followed his assassination.

A most delicate situation, requiring an extraordinary sense of justice, constructive purposes as well as sympathy, had become a vested interest of an oligarchy of politicians representing mixed motives, personal revenge, love of power, and sadistic impulses. A program of long-time consequences that needed to be handled by large-minded, practical, forward-looking men and women representing both North and South, was in the control of politicians of opposite traits, who expected to keep themselves in power by maintaining the southern states as their political preserves, a vote-giving rotten-borough, perpetuated by subservient Negro suffrage. The upper and lower strata of society were to be reversed by legislative edict. The program absolutely failed, but the prostrated South had thrown upon it what has been rightly described as "a grotesque parody of government, a hideous orgy of anarchy, violence, unrestrained corruption, undisguised, ostentatious, insulting robbery such as the world had scarcely ever seen."[20] The neurotic Sumner[21] and the vindictive Stevens reveled in their unexpected power. Their sentiment was perpetuated by an oligarchy which, until broken by the courage of Rutherford B. Hayes, has been charged with menacing the American system of government in a way that has not been true of any other political combination in our history.[22]

The woman of southern culture was made over into the new woman, the transmitter of southern isolation. The men, in order to survive economically, had to make adjustment in some degree to the existing circumstances, however discouraging and oppressive. The women were freer to fall back upon their life of feeling, and this they did to a costly extent as affecting their interests and those of other women from whom they were alienated by emotion that flowed forth from the past.

To poverty, helplessness, and grief was added humiliation. To realize this in full measure, one must turn from the Reconstruction program as conceived at Washington and see it in operation.

There were Federal officers, tactful and sympathetic, who did their best to carry out a policy which they quickly recognized was certain to fail and one that they found increasingly distasteful. Then there was the other type who reveled in power, free to express primitive impulses that under ordinary circumstances have to be curbed and concealed. In the critical days, when southern sentiment was taking the shape that would dominate for many years to come, a most delicate problem of social readjustment, built in ignorance of conditions and influenced by personal animosity, fell into the hands of this second type as well as the first. They exploited to the utmost the opportunities such a situation provided, especially when they used to enforce their authority Negro troops who had just cast aside the discipline of slavery and had not yet acquired that which comes from the experiences of freedom. To the southern women it seemed a continuation of the War with a one-sided attack.

It is not strange that we find in their diaries exclamations that the horrors of the fake-peace were greater than those of the preceding War. It is necessary, in order to understand why they recoiled from everything connected with the North, to consider some of the happenings that did much to crystallize unformed feeling into a definite, aggressive, continuing sentiment. The following incident undoubtedly was exceptional, but it was just such spectacular exaggerations that became in the common mind representative of Yankee rule.

. . . If the Yankees cashier Wild, it will give me more respect for them than I ever thought it possible to feel. He is the most atrocious villain extant. Before bringing the Chenaults to town, he went into the country to their home, and tortured all the men till Mr. Nish Chenault fainted three times under the operation. Then he shut up the two ladies, Mrs. Chenault and Sallie, in a room, to be searched by a negro woman, with a Yankee officer standing outside the door to make sure that it was thoroughly done. When the ladies had stripped to their last garment, they stopped and objected to undressing any further, but were compelled to drop it to the waist. . . . Disappointed at not finding any other plunder, the Yankees took their watches and family jewelry, and $150 in gold that Mr. Chenault had saved through the war. I have this from Mrs. Reese, who got it from Sallie Chenault herself, after they were released. After searching the ladies, they kept them in the woods all day, while they searched and plundered the house. Miss Chenault says she doesn't suppose there was much left in the house worth having, when the Yankees and negroes had gone through it. I believe all the ladies have now been released by Col. Drayton, except Mrs. Nish Chenault, who is detained on a charge of assault and battery for slapping one of her negro women who was insolent to her! How are the tables turned! This robbery business furnishes a good exposition of Yankee character.[23]

Perhaps even the War did less to detach southern women from the contemporary movements of their sex in the North and West than the disheartening days that started soon after the assassination of Lincoln and continued into Hayes's administration. They were separated by memories from the women seeking reforms along the entire front of woman's contact with life, a cleavage resistant both to personal interests and to the spirit of the time. They were emotionally isolated. The temperance and suffrage women leaders of the North and West had most of them taken an active part in anti-slavery agitation before the War. This was sufficient to alienate the sympathies of prominent women in the South, but this was only an added barrier to the fellowship of the two groups of women. The War and its aftermath were sufficient to fence in the southern woman and to make her almost by instinct contrary-minded whenever she gave any attention to the demands put forth by the aggressive women leaders of other sections of the United States.

It is easy to see the losses that came to southern women from this policy of separateness, this retreat to the past, this flowing of energy into a persisting revolt against memories which bitterness had made timeless. Woman's advance elsewhere also suffered. The southern woman had had an active part in a culture that even more than that of New England had wrestled with the problems of social maturity. Until its energy had been turned aside in the effort to protect slavery as an institution, it had made the dominant contribution in the evolution of American society. In comparison with it western civilization was adolescent. This attracted the hopeful who sought new beginnings and established the democracy of expectation, the program of giving each individual the testing of a fresh opportunity. It had the spirit of a new country, with the advantages and the problems that come from the pioneering stage of society.

This type of culture carries the cause of its own passing. If it has the energy to develop, its embryonic life must eventually become itself a mature civilization. Then it comes face to face with profounder problems than the ones that affect those who in a spirit of youth draw their sentiment from what they anticipate rather than from what they have. The southern woman had experience with the obligations of a leadership that was responsible rather than buoyant. Her contributions along every line of woman's advance not only would have helped to give balance in the agitations that concerned her sex but also to prepare women and men for the testing of approaching social maturity. Now, as we face facts distasteful to American tradition and wrestle with the problems that follow the passing of the frontier, we have need of what was lost in the evolution of American women after the Civil War because of the self-isolation of southern leadership.

The fundamental incitement in American history up to the World War had been conquest of physical environment. This effort to subdue the land not only attracted those from older civilizations who felt the pull of the new opportunity but also increasingly enforced the break between the culture that was matured on one side of the Atlantic and the other that was in process through its relatively fresh start in the New World. This incentive, however vital and aggressive, brings through its own successes loss of momentum. Even though the extraordinary development of modern science has given this conquest a new turn and extended its period, the passing of the era dominated by the task of outer control of nature grows more and more apparent.

Attention now, by pressure of events, is driven toward that inner control of human nature that must become a possession of the people themselves rather than an efficiency in manipulating their environment. This is the unescapable problem that always appears with social maturity, and in spite of all the handicaps of southern people, they are still more prepared to deal with it than the people of any other section.

New England and the Middle States might be equally matured, were it not true that they have had successive waves of immigration, bringing people who have had to make a fresh start and therefore, in some degree, have prevented the people of these sections from reaching the social experience achieved in the South. There the presence of Negroes, wrenched from their own culture, forced to imitate that of the white, offered no competition to the prevailing civilization, forced no reshaping, but on the contrary strengthened the disposition of southern people to preserve their social dominance. If this has meant trouble for the South, keeping it from using the resources of social change, it nevertheless has given preparation for meeting the sorts of problems that sooner or later replace those related to the conquest of environment.

The southern woman shared in the advantages of this maturity, and since the questions that concern the relation of the sexes were rapidly passing from adolescent to more mature adjustment, as the events of the next decade reveal, there was need, for the best development of the movements that attempted to establish and conserve women's rights, of just such influences as southern women from their personal experiences and outlook upon life were prepared to give. It is interesting to notice that one of the few contributions that southern women have made nationally has been the Congress of Parents and Teachers, which in its constructive purposes reveals the spirit of southern leadership as compared with the agitative motives of some of the northern organizations of women.

The prestige of leaders among the southern women had a rural background while that of the North, for the most part, was rooted in urban life. The concentration of social dominance among city dwellers aggravates the stresses that accompany the transition from youthful to mature cultural adjustment. Reaction to this unbalancing of the prestige centers appeared in the suspicion of Eastern, urban domination among the peoples of the Western and Great Plains areas. An influential, rural-minded woman's leadership, representing the South, might not only have provided an antidote for this distrust but also have added an attitude of mind greatly needed in the woman's movement. The shut-in policy of southern women made such a contribution impossible, and we still suffer its loss.

The aloofness of southern sentiment to the woman's movement is best revealed by the history of the adoption of the Nineteenth Amendment of the Constitution. At the time this became the law of the land, the legislatures of ten states had failed to ratify it. Of these all but one, Delaware, were southern states. They were: Virginia, Maryland, North Carolina, South Carolina, Georgia, Alabama, Louisiana, Mississippi, and Florida. This attitude of southern states was all the more impressive because the administration at Washington was Democratic, and President Woodrow Wilson, as party leader, made known to prominent politicians in the various states his desire to have the legislatures accept the amendment. Eagerness for its adoption, in the interest of party expediency, was also shown by state officials. There were also many prominent southern women who were most earnest in attempting to get their states to ratify, but the general sentiment of their sex expressed lack of interest or opposition.

Tennessee ratified, but not without a long, bitter contest. Before the amendment was finally adopted, no southern state had given woman full suffrage. Kentucky and Tennessee had legislated presidential suffrage, and Arkansas and Texas had allowed women to vote in the Primary, but not until 1917. There were, of course, many different reasons for this unwillingness of the southern states to declare for woman suffrage, but basically it was detachment from the influences that were changing the status of woman in the rest of the country, a sectional reaction reflected by the opposition or indifference to suffrage on the part of a large, if not the greater, portion of southern women.

The War affected northern women as profoundly as it did southern women, but differently. Its significance for them was not in its shock, its dislodging of social routine, but in the greater opportunity it brought. Its effect was more complex because it became allied with the social trends of the period, and appears as much in what it started as in what it accomplished. Its immediate results were similar to those that appeared in the South, with the important difference that the fighting was on distant territory. The War greatly stimulated northern industries. These not only flourished during the War period but at its end were left better prepared to meet competition than before. Then there were the more subtle influences that came from this industrial expansion because woman in the North was quick to use the advantages that these consequences of war conditions gave her. She both advanced her status and gathered incentive to demand still greater opportunity.

Her immediate war services were similar to those carried on by southern women. On April 15, 1861, the very day that President Lincoln issued his call for volunteers, women in Bridgeport, Connecticut, and Charlestown, Massachusetts, organized a Soldiers' Aid Society for the purpose of assisting the troops. So rapidly did similar societies come into being throughout the North that ten days later the Woman's Central Association of Relief was organized in New York City to coördinate the local associations. Later this became a subsidiary of the Sanitary Commission, which had branches in the large cities almost always managed by women. This Sanitary Commission itself was the result of a petition to the Administration from a committee of the Woman's Central Association of Relief. They asked for the appointment of "a scientific board, to be commissioned with ample powers for visiting all camps and hospitals, advising, recommending, and, if need be, enforcing the best-known and most approved sanitary regulations in the army." [24]

During the War the Woman's Central Association of Relief and other similar aid societies expended over fifty millions of dollars, which they had collected for the soldiers' needs. This money came through gifts from the women themselves, or through their efforts, and also from fairs held in the cities chiefly that yielded more than five million dollars. There was, of course, especially in the earlier period of the War, waste and misdirection in the attempts to serve the soldiers as a consequence of lack of experience and faulty organization. Material shipped for the soldiers swamped the railroads already taxed with the transporting of troops and necessary war materials to the front.

Nursing was carried on by women in the North just as it was in the South. The Federal Government was fortunate in its choice of a superintendent of female nurses. Early in 1861 the Secretary of War chose for this position Dorothea Dix, a selection which was approved by the entire North, since there was no other American woman who had so demonstrated her fitness for such a responsibility. Her work for the prisoners and insane before the War throughout the United States had given her preëminence in practical philanthropy.

She started for Washington soon after the first of Lincoln's volunteers reached the Capitol and began nursing some of the Massachusetts soldiers who had been injured by the mob at Baltimore as they passed through the city for Washington. Miss Dix quickly organized a nursing service, personally appointing all the women regularly employed in the hospitals except some of the hospital matrons. She did her best to weed out unsuitable women, but as always happens in American war services, some got in that should have stayed out and some were refused that afterward in other activities proved their fitness. Miss Dix was known best as an administrator. She inspected Federal hospitals far and near and proved her fellowship in such work with her great English predecessor, Florence Nightingale. Her career and her organization did much to impress American people with the aptitude of women for nursing, and as a result nursing became one of the first professions chiefly possessed by women. In a decade after the War women's nursing was beginning to take on a professional status. As early as 1862 a school for the training of nurses was started at Roxbury, Massachusetts, in connection with the Woman's and

Children's Hospital organized by the woman medical pioneer, Dr. Marie Zakrzewska.[25]

The women nurses met with hostility from many of the surgeons in the Federal army who were opposed to their employment. Undoubtedly some of the doctors did their best to discourage this war work of women. Here is testimony as to the difficulties of the nurses in some of the hospitals at the beginning of the War.

Some of the bravest women I have ever known, were among this first company of army nurses. They saw at once the position of affairs, the attitude assumed by the surgeons, and the wall against which they were expected to break and scatter; and they set themselves to work to undermine the whole thing. None of them were strong minded. Some of them were women of the truest refinement and culture; and day after day they quietly and patiently worked, doing by orders of the surgeons, things which not one of those gentlemen would have dared ask of a woman, whose male relative stood able and ready to defend her and report him. I have seen small white hands scrubbing floors, washing windows, and performing all menial offices. I have known women, delicately cared for at home, half fed in hospitals, hard worked day and night and given, when sleep must be had, a wretched closet, just large enough for a camp bed to stand in.[26]

It is only fair to say that the value of the women soon became convincing, and opposition to the new social departure gradually disappeared.

There was great need of the services of women and of the organization that rapidly developed under the leadership of Dorothea Dix. For example, in November, 1861, a Wisconsin soldier writes as follows:

As yet we have done little fighting, but have lost a large number of men. They are dying daily in the camps and hospitals, from pneumonia, dysentery, and camp diseases, caused by severe colds, exposure, and lack of proper food when ill. ... For two days and nights there was a very severe storm, to which we were exposed all the time, wearing shoddy uniforms and protected only by shoddy blankets, and the result was a frightful sickness.

Our hospitals are so bad that the men fight against being sent to them. . . . I really believe, they are more comfortable and better cared for in camp with their comrades, than in hospitals. The food is the same in both places, and the medical treatment the same, if there is any. In the hospital the sick men lie on rotten straw; in the camp we provide clean hemlock or pine boughs, with the stems cut out, or husks when we can jerk them from a secesh cornfield.

We need beds and bedding, hospital clothing and sick diet, proper medicines, surgical instruments, and good nurses—and then a decent building or a good hospital tent for the accommodation of the sick. I suppose we shall have them, when the Government can get around to it, and in the meantime we try to be patient.[27]

The women nurses were not content with doing hospital service in the cities of northern localities to which wounded troops were transported for treatment. They also served in the field hospitals and ministered to the soldiers as they fell in battle. One of the first women who broke the barrier and obtained permission to serve the soldiers in hospitals behind the battle line was Clara Barton. At the battle of Antietam she followed a train of artillery of Burnside's corps and established a first-aid hospital in a barn right behind the fighting troops. The operating tables were ranged on the wide piazza of the nearby house. As night fell the surgeon in charge of a thousand men, dangerously wounded, lying about found that there was only one small piece of candle for illumination and that soon his work would have to stop on account of darkness. Then Miss Barton came forward with an emergency supply of thirty lanterns and an abundance of candles, having learned from previous experience that it was impossible to depend upon the coming up to the battle line of the necessary hospital supplies.[28]

There was another kind of work that was organized and carried on by northern women. In the South a similar service was provided for the soldiers by the hospitality in accord with southern custom that led individual families to receive and care for the soldiers who were starting homeward. The United States Sanitary Commission and the Western Sanitary Commission met this problem of Federal troops by establishing soldiers' homes at Washington, Cincinnati, Chicago, St. Louis, and other northern cities. These received disabled men, furnishing food, shelter, and medical attendance, and assisted them in their transportation homeward.

The homes were managed by a woman matron who had under her female assistants. Sometimes opportunity was provided for the staying of the mothers, wives, and daughters of wounded soldiers who needed attention before they were strong or well enough to travel. In addition soldiers' lodges were established, providing temporary stopping places for soldiers going to or returning from the front. These were managed by women as were the soldiers' homes. Then there were in the West homes for refugees—families northern in their sympathy—who had been driven from southern or border states or who in the conflict had been reduced to poverty. Besides the women nurses there were visitors who went to the hospitals, just as did southern women, to cheer the courage of the soldiers and to bring them refreshments, to write letters for them; in short, to substitute for their relatives and friends who were too far away to give them help.

The care of families made destitute, or at least reduced to hard circumstances because the male members had gone to the War, was another line of philanthropy in which northern women were active. Frequently this suffering was due to the irregularity of the government and even the state in paying wages to the soldiers. Families received help from wealthy men, sometimes this being promised at the time of enlistment. In one year Philadelphia distributed $600,000 for soldiers' aid, having at one time 9,000 beneficiaries that were getting help from the city. A considerable part of the bounty money received by many of the soldiers when they entered the army, at least a half of such payment, went to the families of the soldiers. Counties, states, and cities distributed assistance from public funds in addition to money gathered through gifts. One of the results was the increase of local taxation and the piling up of debts. For example, Vermont, Rhode Island, and Connecticut, which had no debts at the beginning of the War, were left with debts of $16,000,000, while that of New York State increased during the same period $15,000,000.[29] The distribution of this public and private relief was largely handled by women.

Although the North did not suffer the destitution that came to the South from the blockade, the penetration of the invading enemy, and the general breakdown of economic life, each of which grew more oppressive as the War continued, it did have its economic troubles. Hard times were felt during the first year of the War especially, and later there was the burden of high prices. Not only did some soldiers' families need help at the beginning, but all through the conflict. Especially was this true of families who had lost their chief means of support through the death of husband or son. There were local philanthropic organizations just as there were national. Both of these were largely supported and managed by women. Undoubtedly these activities had an attraction for women in addition to the opportunity they offered to express patriotism and social sympathy. Some of this interest was akin to that which in our own time leads women into professional social work. Certainly the Civil War stimulated the development of organized charities and in the North, as in the case of nursing, this development gradually opened up a new occupation for women. The American Social Science Association, the first organization in America attempting on a large scale to deal with problems of charities and correction, was formed in 1865. It was the forerunner of the National Conference of Charities and Correction, which in 1917 became the National Conference of Social Work.[30]

The rapid expression of interest along the lines of organized charities after 1870 reveals the incentive which came from experiences during the Civil War. This movement was retarded in the South by the more pressing problems of reconstruction and the reëstablishment of economic life, aid taking on for the most part the more personal form of friendly assistance, in accord with the habit of the rural South.

The effect of northern experience with dependency appeared not only in the interest leading toward the development of private charitable organizations, some of which, of course, had started before the War, but also in the organization of public welfare activities. For example, we have the coming of the State Board in Massachusetts in 1863 and in Ohio and New York in 1867. Illinois, North Carolina, Pennsylvania, and Rhode Island organized the same type of work in 1869; Wisconsin and Michigan, in 1871; and Kansas and Connecticut, in 1873.[31]

The Civil War also stimulated woman's professional ambition along another line where the barrier to her progress was to prove exceedingly stubborn. Before the War a few women had sought medical training. One of these was Emily Blackwell, who tried to enter ten medical schools without success before she was, in 1852, allowed instruction in the Rush Medical School in Chicago one year. The next year she was permitted to matriculate at the Medical School of Western Reserve University, where she graduated in 1854. She helped, with her sister Elizabeth, to organize the Woman's Central Association of Relief, April 29, 1861. Elizabeth Blackwell even more dramatically had pushed her way through tradition and had been graduated from the Medical School at Geneva, New York, later taken over by Syracuse University. Elizabeth helped Dorothea Dix, Dr. Mary Walker, and Clara Barton organize nursing in the northern army during the War. The two Blackwell sisters and other women who had received medical training organized the Ladies' Sanitary Commission for the purpose of furnishing supplies and nurses for the northern armies.[32]

Dr. Mary E. Walker, who graduated from the Medical School at Syracuse in 1865, did most to familiarize American people with the idea of the woman as a practicing physician. Not at all masculine in appearance, she chose to wear man's garb, and although this attracted attention, her skill and service were such that it was accepted, first at Rome, New York, where she was practicing before the War, and later while she was connected with the army. She demonstrated her professional competency as a field surgeon in the second corps of the Army of the Potomac, and as early as 1863 effort was made to get the War Department to commission her, at first without success, since the army regulations did not authorize the employment of women as surgeons. Later she was commissioned lieutenant and assistant surgeon, and thus had the distinction of being the first woman ever to serve on the staff of an American army during war. During the War she was captured and served imprisonment at Richmond. She and Dr. Elizabeth Blackwell, working with Dorothea Dix, did most to organize the nursing service of the northern armies.[33]

When Dr. Walker retired to private life, she continued her choice of men's clothes. After the War she became interested in woman suffrage, and her reputation and attire made it possible for her to draw a sizable audience wherever she spoke.

The innovations that the War brought in woman's experiences in the North are impressive, and because of this there is a tendency, looking backward, to overestimate their importance. Significant as these new openings were, the more massive consequences of the War, as it affected the advancement of women, must be found in the changes that came to the great multitude of average women. From this angle the War made its chief contribution in enhancing the value of women, in turning over to them a large part of the productive activities. The conflict greatly stimulated the already increasing use of machinery in agriculture. There was a great expansion in the manufacturing of mowers and reapers, and their use released a great many men, especially in the West, for fighting. Even so, there was great need of women workers, some at times of emergency and others in full-time employment.

Women, with the help of older children, managed sizable farms from New York to Kansas.[34] A missionary writing from Iowa says that he saw more women than men driving teams on the roads and working in the fields.[35] The number of women doing work on the farms increased as the War continued. The following gives Mary E. Livermore's description of what she saw during her visit to Wisconsin and Iowa in 1863.

As we dashed along the railway, let our course lead in whatever direction it might, it took us through what seemed a continuous wheat field. The yellow grain was waving everywhere; and two-horse reapers were cutting it down in a fashion that would have astonished Eastern farmers. . . . Women were in the field everywhere, driving the reapers, binding and shocking, and loading grain, until then an unusual sight. At first it displeased me, and I turned away in aversion. By-and-bye I observed how skilfully they drove the horses round and round the wheat field, diminishing more and more its periphery at every circuit, the glittering blades of the reaper cutting wide swathes with a rapid, clicking sound that was pleasant to hear. Then I saw, that where they followed the reapers, binding and shocking, although they did not keep up with the men, their work was done with more precision and nicety, and their sheaves had an artistic finish that those lacked made by men. So I said to myself, "They are worthy women and deserve praise; their husbands are probably too poor to hire help, and like the helpmeets God designed them to be, they have girt themselves to this work—and they are doing it superbly. Good wives! Good women!" [36]

This work was, of course, only in its form or amount different from what many women had done in the same section in earlier pioneering days. Nevertheless, the value during the national crisis of the contribution of these women who farmed, along with that which came from women in textiles and other manufacturing, made an impression which registered in what may best be called social consciousness, that conventional thinking and feeling which more than anything else defined the status of woman.

When the War broke out, it is estimated that women workers were performing one quarter of the manufacturing of the country.[37] Cotton, paper, and woolen mills, and factories making shoes and rubbers, were at that time heavily dependent upon women. The scarcity of men, as a result of the conflict, the desire to get the work done as cheaply as possible, and the increasing use of labor-saving machinery all worked together to give more industrial employment to women. The greed of contractors, the apparent lack of interest in woman's welfare on the part of the government, and the competition of women against one another for work, explain the low wages. Perhaps the women most exploited of all were seamstresses hired by the government to make army clothing or by contractors who were authorized to supply the troops.

In spite of the increasing cost of living, women along certain lines had no advance in wages, and in some there was an actual decrease.[38] Native American women preferred, nevertheless, to keep their pride in such occupations rather than to enter domestic service in competition with Irish immigrants and Negroes. They were repelled from the factories, as these lowered their standards for employment and took in more and more of the immigrant women who applied for jobs.

The professions also opened more widely to women as the result of the War. Many women replaced men as teachers in the schools. Teaching had been the first profession outside the home which women could enter. From colonial days it had offered the means of livelihood to some women. The War necessarily led to the increase of employment of women teachers, but even so, there was discrimination in the wages paid women as compared with men. For some years even before the breaking out of conflict, women teachers had been supplanting men in the lower grades of the cities. This tendency, as men went into the army, spread into the smaller towns and villages. For example, in Illinois, in 1860, there were 8,223 men and 6,485 women employed as teachers. In 1865 this proportion had changed to 6,170 men and 10,843 women. It is interesting to see how much more men were paid than women. For example, in Massachusetts, in 1860, men received $47.71, and in 1865, $59.53, while the change in women's wages was from $19.95 to $24.36. In Illinois the advance was from $28.82 to $38.89 for men and from

$18.80 to $24.89 for women. These wage scales illustrate the tendency both East and West.[39]

Clerical work was another line of occupation that was affected by the War for the advantage of women. A great many of these women were employed at Washington in government departments. Not only did they replace men who might be soldiers, but it was said that they were both cheaper and more efficient employees.

Since the profession of medicine was firmly organized and conservative in its notions regarding the proper relation of the sexes, the increase of women doctors, in spite of almost insurmountable obstacles, reveals the changing status of woman which was favored by war conditions. It has been estimated that in the North, by 1864, there were from 250 to 300 women doctors of medicine, all graduates of medical schools. There were at least five medical institutions that permitted women to receive instruction. This is an impressive number when one takes into account the strong prejudice against women entering the medical profession, a bias strong enough to lead the Pennsylvania State Medical Society and the Philadelphia County Medical Society to refuse their members the right to consult with women physicians.[40]

The influence of the War must not be interpreted so much as a breaking down of the barriers that hampered woman's advancement in industry and in the professions as the enhancing of the tendency to increase woman's opportunities and to give her greater equality with men, resulting chiefly from the industrial and educational changes that were operating before the War and that would have, in any case, increased her sphere of activity. The War gave greater momentum to trends already under way. Women were moving toward an economic independence of men and, as a consequence, toward greater equality. Advancement had already gone far enough to call forth reformers who in their demands were far ahead of the thinking or even the wishing of their fellow women. In 1863 the *Progressive Manual* lists twenty-three women, headed by Susan B. Anthony, who were crusading for women's rights, also the names of seventy-six women who were showing their break from the conventions limiting the freedom of women by wearing habitually short skirts, according to what was beginning to be called "the American custom." [41]

There would have been a still greater demand for the employment of women but for two other changes also taking place. One was the invention and improvement of labor-saving machines, leading to greater production with less workers, and the other, the influx of immigrants. President Lincoln had recommended to Congress legislation to encourage immigration to the United States, and in 1864 a law was enacted for this purpose, including the authorizing of a Commissioner of Immigration, to be appointed by the President and to serve under the Department of the Treasury.

The War broke in upon the routine that had conventionally fixed the activities of women and introduced them to new experiences which necessarily changed their attitude toward life, making them along all lines more aggressive. One of the results of this was the momentum that the various sorts of war experiences gave to the organization of women's societies and the greater activity of women in philanthropic activities and in societies attempting to carry out various sorts of reforms. So marked was this tendency that the Woman's Club Movement is dated as having started in 1866.[42] This was due to the rapid extension of interest generated by the War, but preceding this there had been, especially in the North, organization that prepared the way for the Woman's Club Movement.

There were consequences of the War that directly affected the rôle of women in American society, although only indirectly related to feminine experience. One was the deaths and incapacities caused by the War that necessarily removed numbers of potential husbands, leaving many women without marriage opportunity. This was particularly significant in the South. In the North, male immigration lessened, especially in the lower economic classes, this effect of the War. There was, of course, an inevitable decrease of reproduction during the War period. Besides this drop in the birth rate, there was disorganization in family life because of the death of fathers of children, and also, in less degree, on account of their absence during the War period.

The consequences of the War on mating would have been much more serious if it had not been for an excess of males in 1860 and the coming to America during the decade of 1860-1870 of approximately 450,000 more men than women.[43] What cannot be measured is the loss in the quality of the population due to the death of young men who were carriers of superior germ plasm. The women who might have married them, if they mated at all, often had to choose men of lesser biologic vitality.[44] It is not improbable that the South has suffered in its development since the Civil War as much from the dysgenic effect it had on population as from the replacement of slavery by free labor, the property loss during the conflict, and the general disorganization of the Reconstruction period.

Another effect of the War that has been given less attention than it deserves was the spreading of venereal infection. It is said that there was little of either disease among the colored people of the South before the Civil War. For six decades both syphilis and gonorrhea have prevailed in the South among Negroes more than in any other part of the United States, with the possible exception of certain Indian groups. The following description, not overdrawn, reveals how this infection was given its distribution.

> The mass of letters found upon [the Yankee] slain, and about their captured camps, disclosed a shocking prevalence of prurient and licentious thought, both in their armies and at home. And our unfortunate servants seduced away by their armies, usually found . . . that lust for the African women was a far more prevalent motive, than their pretended humanity, for their liberating zeal. Such was the monstrous abuse to which these poor creatures were subjected, that decent slave fathers often hid their daughters in the woods, from their pretended liberators, as from beasts of prey.[45]

It was not, however, merely the colored people who suffered from the vice which had fungus-growth during the War, as a consequence of the breaking down of habits, the anonymity, the loneliness, and the stimulus of passion of the soldier's life. The force of temptation which led to this cannot be realized until one brings to mind how young the majority of the troops, North and South, were.

One of the indirect results of the spread of venereal infection was the growth of opposition on the part of women to the double standard and finally their crusade against prostitution.

The increase of interest in woman suffrage was one of the most important of the influences that the War had on women leaders in the North. The giving of the right to vote to Negroes enormously added to the feeling of discrimination felt by prominent women who were antagonized by the policy that denied them political status. The demand for woman's political equality had been gradually gathering strength, but after the War it grew rapidly and became assertive. The agitator led the way, but the mass-strength of this insistence upon the rights of women came from changing economic and social conditions more and more and from recognition of the handicap to women from society's discrimination between the sexes.

The placing of the word "male" in the Fourteenth Amendment brought forth bitter resentment from such leaders as Elizabeth Cady Stanton and Susan B. Anthony. Giving the vote to the Negro, so recently a slave, and denying it to women seemed to these suffrage leaders more than social injustice—an attitude that was nothing less than an insult. On the other hand, southern opponents of woman suffrage were made the more antagonistic, claiming that giving women the right to vote would mean allowing a great number of illiterate colored women to cast their ballots. Since the southern states had found means of protecting themselves from a similar multitude of Negro male voters, this ground of opposition, which so often appeared in Congressional debates, seems to have been an argument rather than a motive.

Northern politicians, on the other hand, were reluctant to support woman suffrage because they felt that the voting of women would be disturbing and, from a party viewpoint, inexpedient. In contrast, the commitment of the male Negro voter to the dominant political party, the Republican, was a decided advantage. The agitation for woman's rights, given momentum by woman's war experiences and the giving of the ballot to Negro men, was soon to force both men and women to attend to a great national issue.

CHAPTER VIII

WOMAN'S POLITICAL AND SOCIAL ADVANCE

From the colonial days onward immigration had been a constant influence, making it difficult for American culture to crystallize. The southeastern states were least affected, the northeastern, the most. For more than a century this coming in of peoples who had been nurtured in European traditions largely contributed to the economic development of the country and to the fluidity characteristic of American feeling and thinking. This quality was only a relative distinction that grew vivid when comparison was made with European conditions. Any sizable social group is intolerant of discord in social standards and sentiments by which habit life is antagonized. The strength of this human inclination toward the routine appears clearly in the mushroom towns that sprang up in California in the early days of gold mining. In spite of the great diversity of background, disposition, and motives, a common need led toward group-supported tradition as a basis for law and order.

Although, therefore, the flux of American culture can easily be overstressed, it was nevertheless a feature of our developing civilization and one that included change and one that had meaning for women as well as men. In the period from the Civil War to the World War there were two sources from which flowed influences that hampered crystallization and both of them directly affected the experiences of women. One of these was European immigration, the other, invention. Until 1896 immigration, including as it did peoples chiefly from the United Kingdom, Germany, Scandinavia, and Switzerland, tended toward a relative plasticity of culture. After that a shift in the predominant type of immigration meant the coming to the United States in great numbers of people from southern and eastern Europe, chiefly from Italy, Austria, Hungary, and Russia, who were largely unskilled rural peasants from a social heritage much more distant from the American background than had been true of those who had come from western Europe.

The consequence was a diluting of American culture with the isolation of groups of Europeans that tried to maintain their habit life while reaping benefits from the economic and political opportunities in the new land. From this to a considerable extent during the period a cleavage appears, the native American on the one side and the alien on the other. This, of course, is true only as a mass generalization. Individuals from Italy and Russia entered quickly the prevailing social life, just as the individual Englishman, German, and Scandinavian in the previous epoch of immigration had stood aloof. The cultural picture, as seen on a large scale, unmistakably reveals a division, a situation that was new.

The long-existing cleavage in the South between the white and the colored population was, as a result of the confusion of emancipation, the breakdown of the Confederacy, and the bitterness due to the reconstruction program, more intense and self-conscious than ever it had been before. The new ambitions, the agitations, the advance of status appearing in the North and West, belong to the group of women that possessed the native traditions. The other group of women also advanced their status in the proportion that their families responded to the new conditions of American life, but their progress came through imitation, from using opportunities that the other line of advance had made possible. The capture of new territory, the pushing forward of woman's rights as a new achievement, came from the energy, the courage, and the avariciousness of women who were on the native side of the cleavage.

We have already noticed how the rural young women of the middle class in New England withdrew from the mills in the preceding period of industry as European immigration crowded into the factories. This trend of withdrawal before the competition of immigrant groups continued, becoming stronger as those women, whatever their origin, who had assimilated American standards felt the competition of the other type of women accustomed to lower standards of life and closer to the feelings and customs of eastern and southern Europe than to those of the United States. The dominant group of women did not at first feel the drag of this cleavage situation, but the fact grew more impressive as woman's outlook grew clearer and wider.

Self-interest as well as benevolent impulse led women leaders to work for a cultural integration. The Settlement Movement was one of the first attempts to make both groups of women mutually appreciative of the other's values and thereby hasten the amalgamation of American women. The influx was too great for the organizing influences to catch up with the forces that made for separation. The result was a gradual change of American sentiment regarding immigration.

Except during the periods of depression, approximately 500,000 immigrants yearly entered the country from 1880 onward. During the last three decades of the nineteenth century the total number of those coming here, according to immigration records, was 11,746,000, a greater number than had entered during the preceding fifty years.[1] In the early years of the new century there was a still greater incoming. In 1907 immigration reached its highest figure, 1,285,349. The year before the outbreak of the World War, the number entering was 1,218,480.[2] The problems created by this stream of culture flowing from Europe and diluting our own took a form that attracted increasing attention. The first evidence of the approaching reversal of American sentiment regarding immigration was the Federal Government's taking control of immigrant regulations in 1882.

Aside from the disorganization resulting from a vast multitude of persons coming into America with alien backgrounds, especially in the great cities, there were specific ills in the realm of marriage and the family that were charged up to immigration. Dike, a foremost student of family problems, in his report as corresponding secretary of the National Divorce Reform League in 1887, writes:

> The uncertain marital relations of some immigrants from countries where illicit unions take the place of lawful marriage to a serious extent, and where illegitimate births for the whole country are from eight and ten to almost fifteen per cent of the whole number of births . . . and where in certain localities and among certain classes, especially servants, who are a large part of the emigrants, unchastity must exist among a very large proportion.[3]

Social problems originated from the fact that the new type of immigration was less a family form than had been true of the first type of immigration. The proportion of males to females was greater.

Immigration furnished a considerable percentage of those entering prostitution and a still greater proportion of those directing the business of procuring girls and managing houses of prostitution. It was stated in a report of the Immigration Commission on the importation and harboring of women for immoral purposes that persons in the business of prostitution had representatives abroad who selected and forwarded women to various cities. The Committee on Interstate and Foreign Commerce, in a report made to the Sixty-First Congress, submitted evidence on the operation of a syndicate which brought to America women assigned to prostitution and which had headquarters and distributing centers in at least eight cities.[4]

The most noticeable effect of the new immigration as it affected the life of women appeared in the field of industrial competition. The newcomers either accepted or were driven to a lower scale of living than that to which the native women in the same occupations were accustomed. Many of the newcomers would save money on incomes that to the Americans were not sufficient for survival. They had come here filled with hope of moving out of poverty and eventually of gaining wealth, and, disciplined by hard circumstances on the other side, they were prepared to make the best of meager opportunity. As one woman competitor expressed it, "but they're different from us. They eat what the rest of us throw away, and there's no work they won't do." [5]

The eastern and southern Europeans tended to herd together in the cities in nationality groups. Although it cannot be charged to them that they created the American slums, it is true that they helped perpetuate this urban evil. They became victims of corrupt machine politics, brought down the value of real estate where they congregated, and by their sharp competition drove the native women and the immigrants from western Europe out of the trades and businesses into which they flocked. A good illustration of this appears in the invasion of the clothing industry by Russian Jews, beginning somewhat before 1880. The newcomers were chiefly males, and as they increased the native women were forced out of the industry. This shift was chiefly in the large cities where the Russian Jews had settled in great numbers. In the smaller towns the clothing industry showed a larger proportion of women workers who in such localities were free from the competition of the Jewish workers. This advantage did not, however, remove the menace of sales competition between the two types of manufacturing plants.

Investigators of the sweating system were so impressed by the dominance of the Jewish immigrants that they came to feel that the sweating industry was a characteristic of this national group and that the Jewish workers preferred filth to cleanliness and the sweat shop to the well ordered factory.[6] As a matter of fact, the sweating had preceded the coming of these people to the United States, and later they were in great measure crowded out by Italians, who in turn had no choice but to enter an industry attractive only to those who were forced to accept the lowest scale of wages.

A by-product resulting from the evils connected with the immigration problem was the enlisting of the interest of leading women who were attracted to the cruelties and dangers of economic exploitation by the magnitude and impressiveness of the problem. The situation brought a challenge to which thoughtful women responded. A large part of the program of the settlements as they came into being was concerned with the needs of immigrants. Attacks were made upon the evils arising from the conditions of immigrants in the United States, through publicizing the facts, that tended to awaken and socialize public opinion through legislation directed at the elimination or the control of the worst features of sweat shops—overcrowding, unsanitary conditions, and rotten politics.

Women were not content with expressions of sympathy but sought practical means of relieving the situation and in the process were matured in their social thinking. Most of them also were made to realize the importance of giving suffrage to women. It seemed desirable as a means of making effective the attempts at reforms largely promoted by women and also to give to a different group of women the opportunity to use the ballot for their self-protection.

If comparison can safely be made between the two sexes, it would seem as if it were fair to say that the women leaders were more sensitive to social exploitation and more ready to direct their reforming efforts toward improvement than were men in public life. Time also seems to have proved that they were right in their emphasis upon the necessity of suffrage. Because no miracle has resulted from their gaining the right to vote, we are apt to discount the effect of their political equality upon party leadership and eventually upon legislation. Of course, it is fair to remember that these leading women represented a small part of their sex in America, but they cut the channel for the serious thinking of their followers and invaded the complacency of many men, and the fashion in which they tackled the evils that had come to be taken largely as a matter of course soon gave a start to programs of reform along many lines.

For example, Mrs. Florence Kelley, who early had joined the residents of Hull House, Chicago, becoming concerned with the sweating system in that city, suggested that the Illinois State Board of Labor investigate and discover the facts. The head of the Bureau accepted her suggestion and appointed her to make the study. The report, when finished, was transmitted to the state legislature and a special committee was appointed to survey the situation and make recommendations. The result of this appeared in the drawing up of a bill designed to regulate the sanitary conditions of sweat shops and to fix fourteen as the age at which a child might be employed.

In order to get this first labor law of the state of Illinois passed, it was necessary for the women interested to agitate, and this they did by addressing small groups in open meetings over a period of three months. The trade unions, church organizations, social clubs, and similar groups were led to support the proposed legislation, and it was finally passed. Jane Addams tells us that the residents at Hull House had in connection with this legislation their first experience at lobbying. She insisted on certain prominent Chicago women accompanying settlement folks who, with trade union representatives, worked at the State Capitol for the passage of their bill. Although she was reluctant, as she tells us, to undertake lobbying, leaders of women throughout the United States soon accepted this effort to exert pressure on legislative bodies as a solemn task of public service and became skilled in the process. Always, however, their influence was weakened by the fact that they were without votes.

The opponents of woman suffrage frequently pointed out the opportunity of indirect influence women enjoyed, maintaining that this was so effective that it should satisfy. Leading women were however taught by experience, as again and again they appeared before some legislative committee to support forward-looking legislation, that their lack of suffrage tremendously handicapped them. This explains the fact that women of practical experience in public affairs were apt to be strong for woman suffrage.

No one familiar with society life at our Capitol City from the inauguration of George Washington would underestimate the influence women had exerted to help or hinder political measures, but their effort had had to be sublimated so as to seem within the proprieties. Once the taboo was broken that had made it improper for women openly and directly to advocate political legislation, the time had come when women could unhesitatingly, in open fashion, work for bills they desired passed and against those that seemed bad. In spite of their handicap as non-voters, in most of the states they soon found that they wielded a power little suspected and one that the professional politician feared. Their lobbying, including efforts for the national suffrage bill, became good schooling, teaching them as nothing else could the need of women actively participating as human beings rather than as females in the social and political movements of the time. This conviction, as it spread among women, led to a deliberate effort to free American culture from masculine dominance, thus hastening the process of reshaping which impersonal spontaneous influences were bringing about.

For the most part, these political maneuverings were stimulated and directed by a group of women representing an aristocracy of social maturity. There were enterprises that offered schooling for other types of women. One of these was the Woman's Club. Its contribution came chiefly through the opportunity it brought the women in local communities. The Woman's Club Movement, as we think of it now, started the year after the closing of the Civil War. It resulted from the need women felt of expressing a side of their life that reflected their extension of interest and activities.

It is rarely true in social history that a new movement comes into being full grown, and this was true of the Woman's Club organization. It is easy to find running through the entire history of the United States from the days of Anne Hutchinson the tendency of women to get together and to organize their interests. Before the Civil War, however, most of these groups of women were organized to carry on some definite type of activity. For example, the Female Association in New York City, organized about 1795, was an attempt to promote the education of girls on the Lancastrian plan. It was incorporated in 1813. Many of these organizations were interested in missionary activities. They were so common as to be represented in nearly every female seminary. Even when their function centered about the support of missions, their programs reflected the growing interests of the educated group of women and were suggestive of the kind of club that came after the War.

It is easy to see that one of the influences leading to the rapid development of clubs that took place was the void created in the lives of many women by the ending of the philanthropic and professional services that had come to them from the conflict. More significant however was the growth in the life-outlook of women as a result of their educational progress and the loosening of the restrictions that had been imposed by the social code.

Not only was there a rapid widening of interest and a reshaping of values, but as a consequence of women entering in so great a degree into the world of affairs, especially since they were, unlike men, not accustomed to its traditional routine, they felt the need of drawing together for self-support. Although they had never been absolutely shut out of the political and social life of the nation, they were for the first time introduced to it as active partners with men, and the more true this was, the more they took, as do newcomers in any business, an unconventional attitude toward what they found. It was just this that the practical politicians feared, as did students of public affairs without self-interest who regarded this political inexperience of women as socially dangerous. Women, sensitive to their separation from the routine dominated by men and sensing the suspicion and skepticism of men, were drawn together, rallying around philanthropy, reform, and the intellectual interests that had captivated them in seminary and college.

The founding of the Sorosis Club of New York City illustrates this feeling on the part of women that their new interests and activities seemed to many men an intrusion liable to upset the social order. Mrs. Croly, becoming angry when she found herself shut out of the dinner that the press was giving Charles Dickens on his visit to New York City, merely because of her sex, set about building an organization that would reflect the prestige of the intellectual and professional women of the United States.

Alice Cary, much against her wish, was made the president of the new organization. In the announcement of its purpose in her first and only address, she said that the organization should function to bring women deeper and broader ideas, to encourage them to think for themselves, and to get their opinions at first hand. She went on to say: "We have also proposed to open out new avenues of employment to women, to make them less dependent and less burdensome, to lift them out of unwomanly self-distrust, disqualifying diffidence, into womanly self-respect and self-knowledge; to teach each one to make all work honorable by doing the share that falls to her, or that she may work out to herself agreeably to her own special aptitude, cheerfully and faithfully. . . ." [7]

In the earlier period of their growth the women's clubs tended toward an emphasis of professional and cultural interests. The artistic and the literary side of culture had great attention. Later more stress was put upon reform, particularly along lines of educational activities.

The New England Women's Club started in 1868. Julia Ward Howe, famed for her "Battle Hymn of the Republic," of the New England intellectual aristocracy, was one of the founders. This organization was active in reforms. Edward Everett Hale paid tribute to its activities. "When I want anything in Boston remedied," he said, "I go down to the New England Women's Club." [8]

Although the Woman's Club Movement was without parallel in the direction it took and the widespread community appeal it made, its beginning without doubt was influenced by organizations among the intellectual élite in the larger cities. Many of these organizations were open to both men and women. We find Julia Ward Howe asserting that the Boston Radical Club of which she was a member was one of the most important social developments in the last quarter of the nineteenth century. This apparently started in the fall of 1867, preceding by one year the New England Women's Club which she was to help form.[9]

Among other things the Woman's Club provided an outlet for the women who had a hankering for public speaking. Undoubtedly the opportunity it offered along this line was to many women one of its chief appeals. This partly explains the niggardliness of even large and wealthy organizations shown in their payment of speakers, the sort of thing of which Charlotte Perkins Gilman, who had a living to earn, complained.[10] So many women were eager for a place on these programs that the professional lecturer through competition fared badly. Although much of this amateur speech-making lacked originality, skill, and interest, in the long run it proved more useful to the women by encouraging them to speak in public and teaching them how to do it than did their passive listening at an earlier period to itinerant orators.

Women's clubs multiplied rapidly, each reflecting local or group interest that gave the organizations great diversity. In spite of this, it was possible for them toward the end of the century to organize the General Federation of Women's Clubs, which in 1901 was granted a charter by Congress. Nine years later it represented directly or by alliance a membership of nearly one million women, and by 1911 it had a state-wide organization in every state in the Union. Although as early as 1869 Mrs. Croly of the Sorosis Club had tried to direct its activities toward reforms in education, hygiene, and the like, it was not until 1890 that there was any considerable drift toward a more practical grappling with matters of social interest. From that time the literary emphasis lessened and in 1904, under the presidency of Mrs. Decker, the General Federation of Women's Clubs became predominantly an organization for social service.

As was to be expected, this movement from the beginning met

with criticism both from men and from women. A charge commonly made was that the women were busy with matters of little importance while neglecting household and family responsibilities. It would have been strange indeed if no women had been attracted to the organizations through lack of interest in housekeeping or from feelings of domestic frustration. Naturally there were then as now women who were eager to find excuse for not doing what they did not want to do, but it was the spirit of prejudice against woman's advance that found in such motives the appeal of women's clubs. Such indictments were not only unjust to what was generally true of the women members but blind to the cravings that developing women felt for other and different sorts of outlets than those provided by the home and the church. The fault-finders were oblivious to the value the occasional club meetings had in stimulating and giving morale to women who otherwise would have felt shackled by the conventions of a housekeeping régime that had not yet responded to the enlarging and changing social life of the American woman.

A different and perhaps more serious attack was made upon the Woman's Club Movement. It was held that these organizations tended toward unrest, radical attitudes, and an emphasis of feminine ambition that was destructive of marriage and family compatibility. For example, some of these critics held the clubs responsible for the increase in divorces and the decline of the sense of the sacredness of marriage. It was true that divorces multiplied during the period when the women's clubs were rapidly spreading. The two movements were indirectly related, since both of them were coming from the increasing self-expression of women and the breaking of the social repression that had been keeping them in so great a measure unconscious even of their own needs. So broad-minded a man as Grover Cleveland in an article in *The Ladies' Home Journal,* in 1905, wrote disparagingly of women's clubs, although tempering his criticism by recognition of the value of those organized for charitable, religious, or intellectual improvement. Hugo Münsterberg, however, the German psychologist that Harvard had brought to this country, had a better appreciation of what was behind the popularity of these clubs when he said that in the United States, in contrast with his own country, the interest of the women in culture was greater than that of the men.

The Woman's Club vogue was at least a protest on the part of women who were beginning to have leisure against the narrow life of men who, saturated with the competitive spirit so characteristic of American male activities, had allowed themselves to be possessed by business, by politics, or by their professions. Just as previously the southern aristocracy had protected itself against one of the most characteristic but hectic features of American civilization, so the newly awakened woman in the North and West for a second time sought satisfaction outside the successes of the acquisitive, conventional ambitions.

During the period another organization came forth to serve women who were outside the range of the Woman's Club Movement. This was the Patrons of Husbandry, commonly known as the Grange. Because it was an organization made up of both men and women and one whose chief activities were only indirectly related to woman's welfare, it is easy to underestimate the significance in the Woman's Movement of this, the first secret order that admitted women as well as men. Women living in small villages and the open country were in great measure detached from the changes affecting woman's status which flourished best in the larger communities, and, as a result, in spite of the strong democratic feeling characteristic of rural people, the farming population even in the West was backward in the practical opportunities outside the family that offered women the means of self-expression.

This was not due to any ingrained opposition but to poverty of social institutions. If the conditions of rural women in other respects had been left unchanged, the latter would eventually have been a considerable drag, holding back the progress of their sisters in political, professional, and industrial progress in urban territory. The Grange became an ideal organization for the meeting of the needs of these wives of farmers who, although separated from the transitional experiences of urban life, were not insensitive to the influences producing them. The fact that the Grange was not a feminine movement, but one open to both sexes, proved in the rural setting an advantage. It brought women new interests, expanded their horizons, added to their prestige, gave them training in public affairs including speaking, and made them conscious of social obligations, yet without marking them off from their husbands and brothers. It brought a new outlook just as did the Woman's Club, but one that could be shared by man and woman because as a result of the family type of farming their interests were closer knit, the division of labor less sharp than was true of the urban women who felt the need to promote their interests and culture by organizations made up exclusively of their own sex.

The Grange had come into being through the insight and pluck of Oliver Kelley. He was a New Englander who had gone into the South to study agricultural conditions there at the request of President Andrew Johnson, who in 1866 had authorized the Commissioner of Agriculture to send some person in his Bureau to gather statistical and other information regarding the situation of farmers in the South. Kelley had the background necessary to understand what he found to be true of multitudes of farmers in the southern states. He was familiar with agricultural problems that had existed prior to the Civil War. Aside from the difficulties that could be charged up to that conflict he discerned the agricultural evils that came from a blind following of farming customs handed on from generation to generation and from an inertia even more costly in its effects. Pondering these ills, he came to feel that there was need of founding some secret order among farmers that would bring to them values somewhat similar to those provided by the Masonic Order in the larger communities.

Fortunately Kelley, upon his return to Boston from his investigation, talked his ideas over with his niece, Miss Terry Hall.

She pled that women be included in his proposed organization as full members. Kelley accepted this suggestion, fortunately, for in the long run no feature of the Grange was to prove more socially useful. In 1867 Kelley was able to enlist the interest of some of his associates; and one fruit grower and six government clerks, all but one having been born on farms, brought into being the Patrons of Husbandry. For some years its progress was so feeble that it barely lived, but by 1873 it had become nation-wide. By that time it had entered all but four states and there were thirty-two state organizations besides the National Grange. That year the control of the national organization came fully into the hands of farmers. Meantime the number of local Granges multiplied more than four-fold, the greatest growth occurring in the Middle West.

It is not difficult to see why, once this order was started, it spread so rapidly. Experiences of the Civil War had been a ferment in rural sections just as they had been in the industrial centers. The farmers were beginning to be rebellious of their lack of leisure and social prestige. They were growing conscious of the little contribution science was making to their means of livelihood. Even the land-grant colleges, made possible by the Morrill Act in Lincoln's administration, were not serving the farmers as they felt such institutions should. Funds that they had a right to expect would be used to develop agricultural instruction were in many instances largely deflected to the conventional classical training.

The farmers themselves felt exploited, especially by railroads and middlemen, and were generally restless, reacting from grievances due to social and economic discrimination. What was true of the men was even more true of the women, since they had little outlet aside from family routine and an ordinarily narrow church life. The men entered the Order primarily that they might have a place to gather and discuss their interests and the possibility through coöperation and other forms of organization of protecting their vocational interests. It was, on the other hand, the social and intellectual opportunities of the Grange that appealed most to the women, and in the end these proved the greatest assets of the organization as it revived from the decline that came from the collapse of its coöperative and business activities in 1875 and achieved its present stability.

One of the most fruitful features of Kelley's plan for the organization had been the creation of an official known as the Lecturer, whose business it was to provide, aside from the ritual read at each meeting, the program of the session. This offered just what was needed as an antidote for the monotony of the farmer's life and as an incentive to make conscious the social desires and cultural needs of the men and women engaged in practical agriculture. As a result there came to the rural folk the means of satisfying the same sort of cravings for a deeper and wider human experience that were back of the Woman's Club Movement. It proved most fortunate that this medium of self-expression was also tied to the economic interests of both the men and the women.

No social order in American life more effectively met the specific needs of a great population than did the Grange, and its effect upon the growth of woman's status was all the greater because it operated so naturally without sex consciousness. To realize the value of what it brought, we must through imagination reconstruct the farmer's life of the past as it existed without rural mail delivery, telephone, good roads, the automobile, the radio, or even any effective agricultural press. There were a few farm journals but their influence was meager compared to what resulted through the activities of the Grange. Even the political power of the farming people was to a great extent unimportant because of lack of organization. The life of the farmer's wife was even more narrow and monotonous, with still less of leisure and of the stimulus of easy contact with others than was her husband's.

In addition to these general features that contributed to woman's advance, there were innovations distinctive to the organization. Some of the officers had to be women who were given a prominent part in the ritual service. On the other hand, all the other positions were open to women as well as to men. It was a custom also for the Master of the Grange, the highest local official, when he went to the state meetings, and for the State Master when he attended the national meetings, to have his wife accompany him. Most frequently also the Lecturer, who had a strategic place as a maker of the program for each session, was a woman.

The Grange's greatest advantage to women came from the fact that the functions of the order for the most part took a family form. This led to women taking part in the discussions and bringing out in the open their sentiments and reactions, and it also influenced the topics chosen and even more the features of the program that were, if in only an elemental way, often expressions of the literary, artistic, and reform interests of women.

The ritual, which now reads florid and artificial, had a meaning then, a sincerity because of contrast with the drabness of everyday experience. The debates and discussions also introduced both men and women to experiences that were new. They gained self-confidence in their ability to think and their power to bring out their ideas. The questions that were put up for debate were generally practical, encouraging the speakers to scrutinize their own experiences, and theoretical, leading the participants to consider matters outside their personal contacts. Local matters were not neglected. This meant that education in some aspect often appeared on the program. The influence of the Order was exerted toward getting better teachers, better textbooks, and particularly toward increasing instruction in agriculture and improving the quality of that already offered. This led the Grange membership toward interest in the state college and the university as well as in the local school system. An example of this was the resolution adopted by the North Carolina State Grange in 1876 asking for instruction in subjects "necessary to the intelligent regulation and management of the farm and the household."[11]

In 1874 the National Grange stated in its declaration of purposes, "We especially advocate for our agricultural and industrial colleges that practical agriculture, domestic science, and all the arts which adorn the home be taught in their courses of study." [12] This latter affirmation reveals the influence of women and in its stress of home economics and household arts is far in advance of the general thinking of the educators of the period.

The effort that the national organization and its local branches made to encourage reading had a double value for women. It brought to many an intellectual opening greatly appreciated. Some of the strongest local Granges even possessed libraries of their own. Frequently local organizations subscribed to several leading agricultural papers which had wide reading among the members. The agricultural periodicals, realizing their opportunity, established departments devoted to Grange interests. In practice the forum was the chief incentive to what was in its time a predecessor of our present adult education. Those who took part, and naturally they were chiefly men and women who had discovered a gift in this type of expression, were encouraged to use both books and papers as sources of the material they needed in their arguments.

Other Grange customs tended to lessen isolation and monotony. Several Granges would meet together for picnics and festivals. There was also a great amount of visitation of masters, lecturers, and state officers who went from one local organization to another, and gathering of local members at state meetings and of state officials at the national conferences. Generally when the husbands went their wives went with them. On a national scale the Order was democratic, unified, and educated, and free from either masculine or feminine dominance. This sex impartiality explains perhaps the unwillingness of the Order to commit itself nationally to woman suffrage. Effort was made to get it to declare for votes for women in 1876, but it failed. There were local organizations that did come out for woman suffrage. The conservative general sentiment was content with giving the women of the Order the same privileges as men, and this policy undoubtedly did more to advance the idea of woman suffrage in rural communities than ever would have been accomplished merely by resolutions.

The anti-slavery movement had awakened some women to their zest and gift for agitation. Once that question was closed, they sought other fields for the expression of their recently discovered talent. Those who were fundamentally captives to the love of crusading turned to woman suffrage for their outlet, while those who were chiefly philanthropic in spirit joined in the assault that was being made on intemperance and other social ills. The second group made such headway in their attacks upon poverty, vice, ignorance, and exploitation that they could rejoice and renew their courage from definite victories gathered during the period. These agitations were not restricted to women, but they furnished leaders and in greater proportion supporters of the various movements that were directed toward improving the conditions of the poor, advancing public health, abolishing the sweat shop, regulating child labor, and especially decreasing one of the most obvious faults of American civilization, intemperance.

The evil of intemperance was not something new, and the attempt to curb it had been going on practically from the beginning of American civilization. In the fifties headway had been made by state prohibitory laws. As early as 1847 Iowa, as a consequence of New England influence, through local option laws drove out the saloons from every county but one. In 1846 Maine passed the State Prohibition Law which through the efforts of Neal Dow became in 1851 an effective statute forbidding the manufacturing or the selling of intoxicants except for medicinal purposes. Other states followed the lead of Maine and passed similar legislation. Kansas in 1859 enacted a law which reflected feminine interest, since it forbade the sale of liquor to persons known to be drunkards or, at the objection of their wives, to married men.

The Civil War gave a setback to this legislative strategy against intemperance. A great many soldiers, young in years, had been initiated during the conflict to the drink habit. The Federal Government also had indirectly encouraged drinking by a system of taxation that made the liquor industry a source of considerable revenue. This blunted the offensive against the use of intoxicants.

Immigration, stimulated by the War and its outcome, also took a turn in hampering laws against intemperance. The Germans, who largely settled in the Middle West, wanted their beer and could not understand the attitude of those who thought it a moral matter. In the East the Irish and the Italians, who naturally congregated in the large cities, were accustomed to a free use of alcohol and demanded the saloon. Capital investments in the liquor business grew enormously, and those interested took care to protect their means of income. As a result much corruption commonly expressed itself in federal as well as local politics.

The stronger the power of the saloon grew, the more determined was the attack made on it, coming chiefly from Protestant Evangelical churches and groups of women. John B. Gough, who could give testimony to the evils of drink from his own personal experience, was the most popular agitator. During the War the prohibition movement had so lost ground that only Massachusetts and Maine were left with restrictive legislation, and in 1868 the Bay State deserted the cause. The legal assault on the saloon became for the most part attempts to close it by local option. This naturally encouraged agitation to stir sentiment in the towns and smaller cities by public meetings. More important, however, was the coming of women's organizations definitely committed to the elimination of the evil of intemperance.

In 1873, at the suggestion of Dr. Dio Lewis, a reformer from Boston, women in certain communities in New York State and Ohio attempted by a praying crusade to close the saloons. The news swept the country that groups of women were singing hymns at the entrance of saloons and even entering the buildings and holding prayers at the bar.

The idea was imitated in many places with varying results. In Zanesville, Ohio, for example, the praying women had the city council stop the sale of intoxicants, while in Chicago they succeeded in having the saloons closed on Sunday. Out of this came a call issued by the church women of Chautauqua, New York, for a national convention, and in 1874 interested women met at Cleveland, Ohio and organized the Woman's Christian Temperance Union. Five years later Frances E. Willard became its head, and from that time it was an organization of great national influence. Her father before her had been committed to the temperance movement. She was a teacher of English at Northwestern University when she first became active in the agitation, and in 1874 she was elected president of the Chicago organization.

Frances E. Willard remained the head of the Woman's Christian Temperance Union until her death in 1898, and under her direction it flourished greatly. Considered by many people the most perfectly organized body of women in the world, it carried on an elaborate program.[13] It brought about temperance instruction in the public schools, and, by getting a quarterly lesson on temperance included in the International Sunday School Lesson Series and by organizing Loyal Temperance Legions, it deeply influenced children. It furthered its program also by constant pressure on political bodies for legislation and regulations aimed against the evils of intoxicants. Many of its leaders were sympathetic toward the Woman's Rights Movement and in general it gave impetus to that cause.

Leaders in the agitation for woman suffrage were nearly always also committed to temperance reform. For example, Elizabeth Cady Stanton even went so far at one time as to suggest a resolution that no woman should remain the wife of a drunkard. Even temperance leaders were shocked at this audacious suggestion. It is interesting to note that in 1931 thirty-eight states and the territories of Alaska and Hawaii made chronic intoxication a ground for absolute divorce.[14] Frances Willard carried her organization into fifty-eight countries and brought into being the World's Woman's Christian Temperance Union.

Another social evil attracted the organized opposition of women, prostitution. This vice had become a generally accepted but not a frankly admitted feature of the cities and large towns of the United States. In the census of 1880, 185 cities confessed to having houses of ill fame, 94 claimed to be largely free of these establishments, while 215 other cities gave no information regarding the matter. As a rule the legislators were reluctant to give legal sanction in any way to prostitution. At times suggestions were made, usually with medical or police motives, that the business be licensed and regulated. This almost always met with violent opposition from the clergy and from women's organizations. For example, in 1871 a law was passed providing for the legal regulation of prostitution in New York State by the legislature. It was given a pocket veto and did not become law.

Four years later the New York legislative committee on crime made a report favoring the licensing scheme and a bill was introduced to incorporate this recommendation in law. This was defeated, in part due to the attack made by the Women's Social Educational Society of New York.[15] New Orleans was one of the cities that did institute the continental plan of segregation and police regulation. Segregation was put in operation as the result of legislation passed in 1897 and was continued until abolished by commands from the War Department at the time of America's entering World War I. This city had previously (from 1857 to 1859) attempted the license scheme, but the enacting laws for this program were declared unconstitutional by the Supreme Court of Louisiana.

In many cities there was practical recognition and regulation of the vice through a policy of intermittent arrests and fines of those engaged in the business, carried out for the purpose of gathering revenue and controlling conditions rather than abolishing commercialized vice. Prostitution in Chicago during the World's Fair of the nineties was without question one of the attractions that grew up alongside of the exposition. Houses of ill fame became the Mecca for prostitutes throughout the nation as with increased staffs they took care of the greater volume of business resulting from the Fair.[16]

The Woman's Movement, reflecting the advancing status of women, struck at prostitution from several angles. It warred against industrial exploitation and encouraged the economic independence of women, repudiated the double standard, and fought at every opportunity any legislative attempt to recognize the business while joining every assault directed against the vice. Little propaganda was necessary to crystallize the strong sentiment against prostitution existing among American women. Most of them, however, had no inclination to grapple with it at close quarters. Prostitution became in both the temperance and the woman suffrage agitations an indictment of masculine social control. This method of attack stirred feeling but at the same time permitted the vice to remain an abstraction. It was not until the expression "white slavery" was thrown from the mind of a drug-crazed prostitute in Chicago, capturing headlines of newspapers everywhere, that woman's revolt took concrete form on a national scale.

It leads to grave misunderstanding of woman's social progress in the United States to attempt to trace her changing status by activities and movements exclusively feminine. The greater part of her progress came from the openings she found through alliance with men. This was particularly true of her entrance into public affairs. Just as she joined with men at first in attacks on slavery and intemperance, so she proved herself in many reforms at first as an ally and very quickly as a promoter of enterprises directed and maintained by members of her own sex. This development from alliance to possession is very clear in the Settlement Movement. Nothing in the nineteenth century is more characteristic of college idealism in the field of philanthropy and reform than the Social Settlement. It was the best gift of the educated group in England and the United States to the program of social justice. No one can follow through its beginning in Whitechapel, London without realizing that from the start it was greatly influenced by two women, Octavia Hill and the wife of its promoter, Mrs. Barnett.

A few social-minded Americans quickly became interested in the new type of service, and in 1886 Stanton Coit went to live at Toynbee Hall and a year later with his friend, Charles B. Stover, opened his home on the lower East Side of New York. From this came the Neighborhood Guild, founded in 1887, the first social settlement in this country. It was during the next summer that Jane Addams visited Toynbee Hall while on her second trip to Europe. The following year, with her friend Ellen Gates Starr, she started the second American settlement, Hull House, undoubtedly the most influential and famous of them all. What she found at Toynbee Hall fitted in with an idea that had been growing from childhood, the novel conviction that living among the poor would not only be useful but more interesting than living with the rich.

Gradually her thought had matured and she had come to see that it would be an advantage to young women seriously concerned with problems of social welfare to live among the people they wished to help. If such residence could be maintained in the spirit of the good neighbor, the presence of the settlement group would be very helpful to the poor and needy people roundabout but without the risk of patronage on the one side and resentment on the other so liable in philanthropic undertakings.

The work at Hull House became familiar to the men and women enlisted in social service throughout the land, but to the college women particularly it became their proudest expression of philanthropic effort. The head of Hull House soon became not only a leading American woman but one of the best known Americans, without reference to sex. She personified perhaps more than any other woman of her time the new attitudes toward social evils that prominent women were beginning to feel.

Jane Addams was fortunate in the character of the group that gathered about her and the practical and often dramatic results she obtained in her efforts to improve the condition of the poor. An example of the way she worked was her gaining the appointment of garbage inspector of the Nineteenth Ward because the Hull House Women's Club, after studying the high death rate, had come to feel that one of the greatest needs was the cleaning up of dirty alleys and the proper removal of refuse. Such philanthropy had a directness that caught the imagination of people everywhere.

The same willingness to grapple at close quarters with social ills appeared in the work of her associates. Florence Kelley's assault on the sweat shops and her organization of the Consumers' League illustrate the spirit of reform that came forth not only from the workers at Hull House but from all the settlements. No woman in her time contributed more than Jane Addams to the forces that were moving artificial social restrictions to one side that women might go forward to a greater social status. Men like Robert A. Woods of the Andover House, Boston, later the South End House, and Graham Taylor of the Chicago Commons contributed wisdom and energy to the Settlement Movement, but undoubtedly it was such women as Jane Addams at Hull House, Chicago, Mary E. McDowell of the University of Chicago Settlement, and Lillian D. Wald of the House on Henry Street in New York, that became in the mind of the public representatives of the settlement ideal. The effect of such careers in changing social sentiment as it affected the careers of women in the United States it is impossible in these days to weigh justly. Undoubtedly they did more to remove the barriers that restricted woman's evolution than any specific agitation. The settlement group, however, were active supporters as a class of every aggressive effort to promote woman's rights.

As was to be expected, the alliance of such practical social statesmanship with suffrage ambition appeared ominous in its possibilities to many of the professional politicians. This fear, which thus far the political expression of women reveals as groundless, added to the reluctance of these men to give women the right to vote. Woman suffrage was feared as something that would disrupt party management and constantly attempt to turn the business of politics into crusading for reforms.

In the religious field there were two activities that offered outlet to woman's increasing self-expression. One was the missionary enterprises, with both home and foreign programs. The Protestant churches in the United States had been zealous in their effort to gain converts from the time of the great awakening of the eighteenth century and there was much rivalry between the denominations in the work both in the home and the foreign field. From the beginning women had been staunch supporters of the various missionary organizations. During the nineteenth century their participation grew in importance. When the Student Volunteer Movement came in 1888, it attracted women, chiefly graduates of seminaries and colleges, just as it did men. From the beginning of her educational career Mary Lyon had felt that one of her responsibilities was the training of young women for missionary service. This was a notable feature of Mount Holyoke. The college came to have a reputation for the number of high-quality graduates who became missionaries or wives of pastors.

The greater meaning of the opportunity the missionary movement brought women is to be found in the local organizations that provided for many of them training in public speaking, in presiding at public gatherings, and in the carrying on of the details of organization. The management of the older aspects of church life, the business responsibilities particularly, were generally regarded as masculine prerogatives, but there was no feeling that women were encroaching as they interested themselves in missionary activities.

There was another movement which even more clearly showed that there was a ferment working in woman's religious experience just as in the political and social side of woman's life. The Young Women's Christian Association can be safely dated as originating in Boston in 1866. There were earlier societies in England and in New York, but it happens that they had a different name.

How definitely this departure was related to the social trends appears in the object of the Boston Association as stated in its constitution, "the temporal, moral and religious welfare of young women who are dependent on their own exertions for support."[17]

The number of young women who had come from villages and country places to the cities had become, as the church leaders began to realize, a problem. The kind of help they needed was something new because it meant serving young women who were outside their normal family life. The motive of the Young Women's Christian Association was chiefly religious, but the thirty ladies who met with Mrs. Henry F. Durant to launch the enterprise understood the situation of young women in business and in industry well enough to see from the start that there must be consideration of their temporal as well as their moral and spiritual needs.

Society after society sprang up in the large cities of the North and Middlewest. In 1875 we find twenty-eight organizations and thirteen of them reported that they had to maintain boarding houses in order to meet their responsibilities to the young women. Some of the other enterprises carried on, as reported at this meeting, throw light on the distinctiveness of the organization. We are not surprised to find ten holding Bible classes or twenty-one having prayer meetings, but it does sound modern to learn that fifteen were helping young women to find employment, ten were creating libraries, seven were maintaining sewing schools, five were holding classes in secular branches including history, writing, and bookkeeping, while seven were furnishing entertainments of different sorts for their young women. Two had restaurants and eight were equipped so that they could offer temporary lodgings.[18]

The boarding home that had been introduced as a necessity soon in response to the needs of the women came to be a major feature of the organization. Even this undertaking felt the force of prejudice, however unconscious, from a civilization of masculine dominance. The Young Men's Christian Association had been introduced into the United States from England before the Civil War. It of course had not only a longer history but a much more substantial support than that given the women's organization. In 1876 one of the Young Women's Christian Associations in its report argues as follows:

> If it be important for the Young Men's Christian Association to have good buildings, and bright pleasant rooms to attract the young men of our land within the influence of religion and Christian morality, it is equally important that our own Associations should have equally pleasant and convenient buildings, where they can offer to the toiling young women of our cities the attractions of social relaxation—books, music, etc.—and throw around them the protecting and refining influences of a Christian Home.[19]

There was certainly need of both organizations, but the distinctness with which they separated their functions reveals how far the promoters of both organizations were from understanding that the men and the women shared a common problem and that the worst feature of their plight was an artificial sex isolation at the time when wholesome preparedness for living needed natural companionship. Here is a picture of conditions in Boston at the time, summarized from investigations made by Mrs. Lucretia Boyd, the city missionary who had taken part in organizing the first association.

> Its records revealed a deplorable state of things in regard to the working girls of Boston. She found the majority in attic rooms of lodging houses, with the lower stories occupied chiefly by young men, many boarding themselves, and struggling with poverty, loneliness and isolation; neglected in sickness, helpless when out of work, and subject to chance acquaintances from among the lower strata of society. They seldom found their way into social circles, but few proved to be regular churchgoers, and only an occasional one in the Sunday school.[20]

One of the effects of the Civil War was to draw to self-expression the talent for philanthropic organization of which some well-endowed women had been unconscious. Louise L. Schuyler turned the experience that she had gathered as an executive in the United States Sanitary Commission, a forerunner of the Red Cross, to the organization of the New York State Charities Aid Association. An associate in war work, Josephine Shaw Lowell, went with her into the new venture. Mrs. Lowell later became a member of the State Board of Charities and in the nineties took a prominent part in the National Consumers' League.

One of the associates of Miss Schuyler was Grace Hoadley Dodge, the daughter of a New York merchant, who at her father's suggestion had enlisted in the Charities' Movement in order to gain experience. Her father had become impressed with Mrs. Schulyer from his knowledge of her work during the War. Miss Dodge later became a leader in several social organizations, including the Young Women's Christian Association, serving as president of the National Board of the Young Women's Christian Association, and in 1903 having much to do with the forming of the New York City Travelers' Aid Society, a form of public service which was rapidly developed in the leading travel centers of the United States.

The decade of the seventies is notable for the number of social service organizations that came into being. Merely to catalogue the most important of these is impressive. The following national organizations have been listed by Mary E. Richmond as having started in this period: the American Prison Association, the Association of Instructors of the Blind, the Public Health Association, the National Conference of Charities and Correction, the American Purity Alliance, the National Woman's Christian Temperance Union, the American Academy of Medicine, the American Association for the Study of the Feeble-Minded, and the International Young Men's Christian Association.[21] The Young Women's Christian Association and the American Social Science Association, which was the forerunner of the National

POLITICAL AND SOCIAL ADVANCE 275

Conference of Charities and Correction, now the National Conference of Social Work, had started in the sixties.

Many influences were behind this social awakening. There was the undercurrent of social progress in Europe, particularly in England, the increasing recognition of the evils connected with the rapid development of industry, the attitudes and experiences resulting from the Civil War, and an increasing participation in public affairs on the part of women. The development of the Charity Organization Movement in the United States illustrates the working together of all these influences. In 1873, in the winter of the great depression, Charles Gordon Ames, pastor of a Unitarian church in Germantown, Philadelphia, launched the first society for organizing charity in the United States. He was familiar with European undertakings, including the Elberfeld system in Germany, the work of Thomas Chalmers at Glasgow, Scotland, and that of Octavia Hill in London.

This society inaugurated the system of volunteer visitation which soon became one of the most distinctive features of American philanthropy and one that provided a practical opportunity for the interest of many women. In 1877 in Buffalo, New York, was launched the first of these societies on a city-wide basis. It also was influenced by European experience and was started largely through the efforts of Rev. S. H. Gurteen, an English clergyman who had been formerly connected with the Charity Organization Society of London.

One of the first women who became prominent in this movement was Fanny B. Ames, the wife of Rev. Charles G. Ames, who at Springfield and Philadelphia also had pioneered in charity organizations and is looked upon by some as the originator of the charity organization work in the United States.[22] Mrs. Ames later became one of the founders of the Children's Aid Society of Pennsylvania. While living in that state she also was the chief advocate of the removal of children from its almshouses. One of the women pioneers in this field of practical charities was Mary

E. Richmond who early in the year of 1891 became an important staff member of the Charity Organization Society of Baltimore. She left her position as bookkeeper and general office assistant of a family hotel for a temporary appointment at $50.00 a month. Her social statesmanship in the subsequent development of American charities justifies the statement that has been made that her professional life represents in epitome the history of the movement and the development of its technique.[23]

Another field of social service that enlisted the sympathies of women was the relief of suffering through war and great disasters due to floods, earthquakes, fires, famines, and the like. This philanthropy had a European origin, but it was Clara Barton, whose executive ability was proved in hospital service during the Civil War, who first came in contact with the activities of the Red Cross during the Franco-Prussian War. She wrote about it in 1878, and her report of its activities interested President Garfield. As a consequence the United States committed itself to the Red Cross treaty. In 1881, when the American National Society was organized at Washington, Clara Barton became its first president. Some of the great disasters for which she directed relief were the Charleston earthquake in 1886, the Johnstown flood in 1889, the Armenian massacre in 1896, and the Galveston tornado and flood of 1900. In 1898, when the Maine was blown up at Havana, she was in Cuba in charge of a cargo of supplies for the reconcentrados, and remaining there she organized the hospital service of the Spanish-American War.

The idea of prevention of war also engaged the attention of women and during the period made headway. One of its most famous advocates was Julia Ward Howe. She had been stunned by the collapse of France in the Franco-Prussian War and had come to believe that all the issues and controversies could have been settled without conflict. Her thinking led her to ask the question that she had never considered before; "Why do not the mothers of mankind interfere in these matters, to prevent the

POLITICAL AND SOCIAL ADVANCE

waste of that human life of which they alone bear and know the cost?"[24] The result of her pondering over this was an appeal that she issued to the women of all countries which included an invitation that they coöperate in a meeting to be held in London to promote universal peace. For two years she carried on correspondence and then in 1872 went to London to promote the Woman's Peace Congress. The meeting which she finally held was somewhat discouraging to her because, although it had a good attendance, it revealed that the woman suffrage movement was the chief interest of women prominent in social agitation.

An earlier interest in peace in the United States had been dissolved through influences of the Civil War. The American Peace Society, for example, had acquiesced in the conflict on the basis that there was a rebellion against the Union which loyal citizens were duty bound to suppress. In protest against this attitude, the Universal Peace Union started in Boston in 1866, and in the same year another peace society was formed by the American Friends in Baltimore. As the century drew to its close, the interest of women in peace increased both here and in Europe. The first Women's Peace League was established in 1895. The idea of arbitration had made headway, and it was this that the women chiefly put forward as a means of eliminating war. By the end of the century there were as many as forty branches of the Universal Peace Union in the United States, and although both men and women enlisted in the cause, the latter predominated.

During the last third of the nineteenth century there was an enormous development of inventions and a rapid progress in discoveries, and both these advances either directly or indirectly affected the life of woman. On the whole she was more profoundly influenced than the man, because many of the inventions brought her vocational openings that did much to establish her economic independence. For the most part the inventions and discoveries had their beginnings in an earlier period. A great many achieved a degree of practicality in the fifties and the sixties. It was, however, in the period of our study that many of these inventions achieved an effectiveness and a distribution that gave them a tremendous social significance.

One of the first inventions that is likely to come to mind when one thinks about the changes taking place in this period is the sewing machine. This invention had been developing over a long period, but we naturally date its success from the patent issued to Elias Howe in 1846. A different type of machine was patented by Singer in 1851 and another by Wilson in 1852. This invention directly entered the life of women, since from the beginning of historic records we find women confronted with the drudgery of sewing. How quickly sewing machines spread appears from the following summary of machines made by the leading companies from 1853 to 1876: [25]

TABLE IV

Manufacturer	1853	1859	1867	1871	1873	1876
Wheeler & Wilson Manufacturing Co.	799	21,306	38,055	128,526	119,190	108,997
The Singer Manufacturing Co.	810	10,953	43,053	181,260	232,444	262,316
Grover and Baker Sewing Machine Co.	657	10,280	32,999	50,838	36,179	......
Howe Sewing Machine Co.	...	.....	11,053	134,010	90,000	109,294
Wilcox & Gibbs Sewing Machine Co.	...	.....	14,152	30,127	15,881	12,758
Domestic Sewing Machine Co.	...	.....	.....	10,397	40,114	23,587

The typewriter is another mechanical device that had a considerable history before it was ready for office use about 1873. It is not too much to say that this brought woman a new profession. Another line of influences based upon the rapidly accumulating discoveries that affected the life of women was in the field of bacteriology. A practical application of the newly attained knowledge considerably influenced the food habits. If at first the invention of canning added to the work of the household, in the end this process through its commercial development was to become one of the chief means of lessening the burdens of housekeeping. It also was to offer women in greater proportion than men a means of livelihood as wage earners outside the home.

Although the American diet during the period was still excessively heavy, progress was made and gradually commerce took over the responsibilities that previously had been carried chiefly by women. The development of refrigeration and the packing industries added to the available foodstuff while at the same time lessening the routine that had been followed by the housewife. Bacteriology brought changes in home practices and in association with the competitive developments of the plumbing industry reconstructed household sanitation in ways that made for the comfort and the greater physical security of the American family. The textile industry also responded to the competition of constant improvements in machinery and in the processes of manufacturing. More and more the average family depended upon clothing made outside the home. This development, as we have seen, to a considerable extent offered employment to women, although the male immigrant encroached upon what had once been exclusively a woman's job.

One of the inventions that directly entered the home and lightened the labor of women was the improvement in gas lighting, especially the Welsbach lamp for which a patent was granted in the United States in 1890. Not only did the use of manufactured gas spread until it became commonplace as a means of illumination in the homes of people living in the cities and larger towns, but the production and use of natural gas also increased. In 1888 this had reached the point where its value for the year was over twenty-two millions of dollars. The electric light was beginning to rival gas illumination and was soon to show itself so superior as to become a commonplace in the home. The invention of the filament lamp by Thomas Edison, for which he received a patent in 1880, marked the beginning of modern electric illumination in the house. Woman's labor had been considerably lightened and family experience enriched by the refinement and wide use of kerosene, but even though this brought improved light, it was a burden and was rapidly pushed aside as electricity developed. Steam radiation, improved cooking ranges, and oil stoves were other aids that shortened the routine of the housekeeper. In the seventies artificial ice was beginning to be commercially produced. Its development in New Orleans in 1871 affected those who had been bringing to the city from the North the natural product.

Although the hoop skirt began to lessen in circumference in 1866, woman's dress was still dominated by an unthinking, arbitrary fashion and remained a considerable handicap, not only limiting the activities of woman but also antagonizing her health. There were critics who insisted that the Woman's Rights Movement should include release from the dictates of fashion. Here and there innovations appeared that were pointing the way toward a freer, more wholesome apparel for women. The Oneida Community had taken an advanced position and had heroically adapted woman's clothing to her more natural way of working.

Dio Lewis, who was prominent in the Woman's Rights Movement, insisted that the conventional dress of the women of the period was a decided impediment to health and one of the chief reasons for the delicacy that was assumed to be true of the American woman. His doctrine had effect and led to reform in the type of garments approved at private schools. The influence of the earlier example and preaching of Amelia Bloomer against woman's enslavement to skirts appeared in the gymnasiums of some of the colleges where classes were held with women dressed according to adaptations of her idea.

The bustle was in vogue in this period and also the atrocious posture of the "Grecian bend." The trend, however, was unmistakably toward a more sensible dress for women and there was intimation of the approaching freedom which in the next century was to permit women to enjoy sports in clothing as comfortable and as well-adapted to life in the open as that of men.

The woman suffrage movement made headway during the years

from the Civil to the World War. This was not merely because of its aggressive leadership but rather, as it is easy now to see, chiefly on account of the momentum it gathered from the going forward of woman's status along all lines. The woman suffrage movement can be traced as an independent development, but it can never be rightly understood unless it is related to the changing circumstances of the social life of the American woman.

The first convention called in the demand for woman's rights was held at Seneca Falls, New York, July 19, 1848, and was organized by women who had returned from attending the anti-slavery convention in London.[26] It is now difficult to realize the courage it took to issue the following invitation, the onslaught it evoked, or the significance of the fact that there had come a time when leading women were determined to move more rapidly toward equality with men.

Seneca Falls Convention

Woman's Rights Convention.—A Convention to discuss the social, civil, and religious condition and rights of woman, will be held in the Wesleyan Chapel, at Seneca Falls, N. Y., on Wednesday and Thursday, the 19th and 20th of July, current; commencing at 10 o'clock A. M. During the first day the meeting will be exclusively for women, who are earnestly invited to attend. The public generally are invited to be present on the second day, when Lucretia Mott, of Philadelphia, and other ladies and gentlemen, will address the convention.[27]

Although the hostility to this audacious, unfeminine declaration was widespread and especially strong in churches, it was not until later, after the Civil War, that the opponents of the movement began to take it seriously. At that time the spear point of the Woman's Rights Movement was the agitation for woman suffrage. The first serious contest that appeared in the history of the Movement was the New York convention of 1867. A discussion of the claims of women for the right of suffrage was forced upon the gathering, resulting in the first genuine debate of the idea. Woman suffrage was voted down by a vote of sixty-three to twenty-four, but not until the fundamental issue had been brought into the open. In asking for suffrage, advocates insisted that they were seeking not a special privilege but a removal of an artificial handicap. They were human beings, citizens needing opportunity to guard their interests through the power of suffrage, as men could. Other arguments were advanced, but this forced forward the logic that eventually justified equal suffrage.

The first break with tradition came when women were granted the right to vote in school elections. Colorado in 1876 made this a right embedded in its Constitution. Other states followed this attempt to compromise the issue. As a step forward this limited suffrage was welcomed, but instead of satisfying the women's demands, as many politicians had hoped and expected, it rather gave them encouragement to ask for more. Once Wyoming came forward with a constitution granting full suffrage to women on the same basis as men, political expediency, as it was determined by professional party leaders, could only obstruct the ongoing of the suffrage movement and this strategy as it was carried out merely increased the zeal and ingenuity of the suffrage leaders.

In comparison with the pace of most social readjustments, the woman suffrage movement advanced with great rapidity, gaining one minor victory after another. The pressure for a nationally established equal suffrage program became not only continuous but ever-increasing. Likewise, the opposition grew less and less, and naturally the attitude of party leaders, both in state and nation, reflected this progress on two fronts—more confident resolution on the one side and a dissolving of opposition on the other. This well organized and skillfully directed agitation surely helped to bring to women in America the right to vote, but the convincing influences that overcame the indifference of many women and the hostility of more men came forth from the mass of social changes that were working together to lift at every point the status of woman.

It was an exceedingly gifted group of women that rallied about the woman suffrage cause. Elizabeth Cady Stanton and Susan B. Anthony in an extraordinary fellowship were the chief strategists and the ablest advocates. Margaret Fuller was perhaps the foremost partisan among the intellectual aristocrats. None of the women were more fiery and uncompromising than Lucy Stone. She brought, by gaining a husband, Henry Blackwell, a male ally that proved unwavering in his loyalty to the Movement.

One of the members of the famous Beecher family entered the crusade. Isabella Beecher Hooker called the first woman suffrage convention in Connecticut and had a prominent part in the organizing of the Connecticut Woman Suffrage Association. She insisted that women already had the right to franchise as citizens of the nation and in 1871, at her own expense, brought about a national convention at Washington "for the purpose of calling the attention of Congress to the fact that women were already citizens of the United States under the Constitution, interpreted by the Declaration of Independence, and only needed recognition, by that body, to become voters."[28] Procuring many signatures of women who agreed with her, she was invited personally to present her argument before the Committee on the Judiciary of the United States Senate. It is interesting, as an illustration of the intense passion that gathered about this controversy, that this presentation before the Committee led some of her opponents to charge her with shamelessness, even with promiscuity.[29] In 1888 she joined the group of women leaders in the movement at the first International Convention of Women held at Washington, where she read the first printed argument dealing with the constitutional rights of American women.[30]

None of the woman suffrage leaders had such a spectacular career or created such furor as Victoria Claflin Woodhull. With her sister Tennessee Claflin, she had, through her editorship of the Woodhull and Claflin's Weekly, become one of the best known, although not one of the most admired, women of the United States. Until she became socially subdued in her later years in England, her coming into any enterprise was sure to mean publicity, tumult, and clashing. So it was when she enlisted in the Woman's Movement. In 1872 Miss Anthony, then in the West lecturing, was startled to read in an issue of the Woodhull and Claflin's Weekly that a group of undesignated citizens, in response to the invitation of the National Woman Suffrage Association, were planning to hold a convention in New York on May ninth and tenth for the purpose of forming a new political party, adopting a platform, and nominating candidates for the presidency and vice presidency of the United States.

When the National Association came together on those dates at its annual meeting, Mrs. Woodhull attempted to steal control. Miss Anthony, who had taken Mrs. Stanton's place as president, had to adjourn the first evening meeting as a consequence of Mrs. Woodhull's interruption. The meeting came to an end but it was necessary to turn out the lights to stop the latter's tirade. The next day the Equal Rights Party was formed, and after a fiery speech, Victoria C. Woodhull was nominated for the presidency of the United States, thus achieving the distinction of being the first woman to stand for this high office. This honor, such as it was, was all that came out of the Equal Rights Party. The new organization dissolved as rapidly as it had been formed, while its candidate found herself thoroughly occupied as she tried to protect herself from the legal storm that burst upon her at this period of her career.

Her memorial, however, that she had previously defended upon invitation of the Judiciary Committee of the House of Representatives at their meeting in January, 1871, remained as a logical and forceful expression of the Woman's Rights Movement. Her address at that time was well made and the response it received at least bore tribute to the physical attractiveness of the speaker. In spite of her entanglements with free love and an unsavory past, her argument penetrated to the heart of the issue that the women were forcing upon the country as she said:

Men trust women in the market, in the shop, on the highway and railroad, and in all other public places and assemblies, but when they propose to carry a slip of paper with a name upon it to the polls, they fear them. Nevertheless, as citizens, women have the right to vote; they are part and parcel of that great element in which the sovereign power of the land had birth; and it is by usurpation only that men debar them from this right. The American nation, in its march onward and upward, can not publicly choke the intellectual and political activity of half its citizens by narrow statutes. The will of the entire people is the true basis of republican government, and a free expression of that will by the public vote of all citizens, without distinctions of race, color, occupation, or sex, is the only means by which that will can be ascertained.[31]

Mrs. Woodhull's activities for votes for women brought protest from many members of the National Suffrage Association. Eventually this forced from Mrs. Stanton the following public statement:

"In regard to the gossip about Mrs. Woodhull, I have one answer to give all my gentlemen friends: When the men who make laws for us in Washington can stand forth and declare themselves pure and unspotted from all the sins mentioned in the Decalogue, then we will demand that every woman who makes a constitutional argument on our platform shall be as chaste as Diana. If our good men will only trouble themselves as much about the virtue of their own sex as they do about ours, if they will make one moral code for both men and women, we shall have a nobler type of manhood and womanhood."[32]

Privately in a letter to Lucretia Mott she explained her attitude as follows:

I have thought much of Mrs. Woodhull and of all the gossip about her past, and have come to the conclusion that it is great impertinence in any of us to pry into her private affairs. To me there is sacredness in individual experience which it seems like profanation to search into or expose. This woman stands before us today as an able speaker and writer. Her face, manners and conversation all indicate the triumph of the moral, intellectual and spiritual. The processes and localities of her education are little to us, but the result should be everything.[33]

The fight for woman suffrage was carried on by two nation-wide organizations. The older was the National American Woman Suffrage Association, which concentrated upon the effort to get Federal legislation. The other was the American Woman Suffrage Association, which centered its energies upon getting favorable action in the States. One was led by Elizabeth Cady Stanton and Susan B. Anthony and the other by Lucy Stone. They tried to divide the field and to interfere with the efforts of each other as little as possible. In time it became clear that this separation led to occasional conflict, and through the effort of the younger members of these two organizations they were in 1890 united, becoming the National-American Woman Suffrage Association, with the following object:

> The object of this Association shall be to secure protection in their right to vote to the women citizens of the United States by appropriate national and State legislation.[34]

Leaders in this movement were not merely struggling against social tradition, inertia, and the fears of vested interest as represented by men in the liquor traffic, professional politicians, and exploiters of women and children workers in industry. There was also a well organized counterattack carried on by the Association Opposed to Suffrage for Women as the principal opponent. The protest of women against having the burden of suffrage forced upon their sex always proved a convenient argument in the hands of men who were for political or business reasons against suffrage. They made again and again the plausible promise that when all the women really wanted the vote it would be given them but that it could not be forced down the throats of women who were so strongly opposed to it. The indifference of many women and the hostility of many prominent women to votes for women may not have been the greatest influence in the legislative defeats of suffrage, but they were the most frequent explanations put forward by the practical politician for his negative vote.

CHAPTER IX

WOMAN'S INDUSTRIAL AND EDUCATIONAL ADVANCE

From the Civil War until the turn of the century the energy of the nation was chiefly directed toward the rapid expansion of industry in the Northeast and the Middle West. The War had greatly stimulated manufacturing and trade. Although this artificial incentive passed when hostilities came to an end, there were other influences that continued prosperity. The policy of a high protective tariff, the growth of population, crop failures in Europe that encouraged the exporting of wheat, corn, and cattle, the English demand for cotton, the construction of railways, including the trans-continental line, the increase in the mining of iron, copper, silver, and gold, and the development of the making of steel not only brought good times but began to change fundamentally the complexion of American culture.

The nation was being rapidly urbanized and industrialized, and as a consequence significant advances in woman's status appeared through her economic opportunities. The nation, however, did not enjoy an unbroken prosperity, for over-expansion and speculation, along with the reduction of tariff duties in 1872, brought a business and industrial panic the following year. Again, in 1884, there was a financial panic.

The spread of industry into the Middle West was most impressive. This movement of manufacturing showed up forcefully in the census of 1870. This indicated that while there had been an increase in manufacturing establishments of eighty per cent for the nation as a whole, the number had more than doubled in Indiana, had increased threefold in Illinois, and had more than trebled in Missouri. This invasion of industry into what had formerly been agricultural territory indicated how rapidly the United States was changing from a predominantly agricultural civilization.[1]

The little influence that the South contributed in the changing life of woman during the period must have larger explanation than the indifference and aloofness of leading women in the South. Their separation from the contemporary problems of concern to women would have come about from conditions in the South, even though there had been no tendency to withdraw from the agitations that in the North and West reflected the changing circumstances of woman's life.

The Civil War left the South in a situation exactly opposite that which favored the industrial expansion of the North. The Confederate states, once the conflict ceased, found themselves prostrated. The wreckage of the War appeared everywhere. Villages were ruined; plantations were bankrupt; railroads destroyed; cotton, their only wealth, had been burned, confiscated or spoiled for the market by exposure to the weather. Not only had southern people invested heavily in Confederate bonds, now worthless, but in addition their wealth represented by slaves had been swept away by emancipation, and they were left without means of carrying on the work of the plantations in the only way they knew. There had to be an immediate transference from production by slaves to an agriculture based on free labor. The transformation was as difficult for the colored people as for the white. The freedmen tended to drift from the rural sections to the cities. They were left without the discipline of plantation control, and they had not as yet learned the self-mastery which the new conditions demanded of them.

The planters, finding themselves bankrupt, attempted to raise cotton on borrowed funds and with the use of wage labor. For the most part their efforts failed and the drift was toward the leasing of land on shares with agreements of varying conditions. Thus by necessity was ushered in a productive scheme that long has been one of the greatest of the economic burdens carried by the South.

Whatever the disposition of southern women, however strong their reluctance to link themselves with the ambitions or the crusades of the female reformers and agitators in the industrial territory, there were still stronger reasons for their separation from the woman's movement in the other sections of the country. Fate demanded of them that they keep their attention upon the need of doing their part in the efforts of recovery from the almost complete collapse of their former economic régime. Even had they been sympathetic toward the trends in woman's life elsewhere, they would have been pushed aside from the main turn of feminine activity by the events that had assigned them the task of helping their men to rebuild a broken civilization.

We cannot realize the crisis they faced unless we remember that added to the poverty, shock and demoralization of the moment was the loss in man power. At least a third of the adults of the male white population had either died in battle or returned home unfitted to work or contribute to family support. The realities were too pressing to encourage interest in discussions that, if thought about at all, seemed in comparison with the problems with which southern women were wrestling curious, insignificant, even impracticable. Finally, even though conditions had been perfectly normal, southern women would have been led away from attention to northern and western trends by their rural economy and even more by their need of dealing with one of the most difficult of all social problems—the adjustment of two different races suddenly thrown out of cultural equilibrium.

Along one line of manufacturing certain sections of the South were introduced to modern industrialism. In spite of many advantages, such as abundant water power, nearness to raw material, ample labor supply, and the like, cotton manufacturers did not get much start in the southern states until the decade between 1870 and 1880. During that period South Carolina cotton mills doubled their productive capacity, and the growth of the industry in North Carolina and Georgia was nearly as great. At the end of the decade the southern mills were producing about one-fourth as much cotton textiles as were coming from New England. This development was, of course, made possible for the most part by northern capital. Similar investments on a smaller scale were also made in the Southeast in exploiting the coal and iron resources and the phosphate deposits in Florida, South Carolina, and Tennessee that were used in the making of fertilizer, the development of the citrous fruit business in Florida, and the growing of rice in Louisiana and Texas. Important and prophetic as these undertakings were, their influence was not great enough to change the rural setting of the South.

One of the most important results of the war boom in the North was the growth in size of factories and work shops as a result of the stimulus of the conflict. This encouraged the labor unions. The workers had no other means of self-defense than organization and collective bargaining. This tendency toward the unionizing of labor appeared even before the end of the War. The Brotherhood of Locomotive Engineers, one of the strongest of American labor organizations, was formed in 1863. By 1866 there were thirty to forty national trade unions. One of their demands was protective legislation for women and children in industry.

The Noble Order of the Knights of Labor, the most influential of all from 1886 when it had more than a million members until its entrance in politics in 1896 led to its decline, started in Philadelphia in 1869 through the effort of garment cutters to bring all wage earners, whatever their occupation, race, sex, religion, or nationality, into one organization. As the Knights of Labor began to decline, the American Federation of Labor, a confederation of various trade unions, became dominant. Its strategy avoided political alliances and concentrated upon advancing the status of the wage earner by increasing his security and by lifting the standard of living.

The trade unions as a class had in the past a less sympathetic program in their attitude toward women wage workers than did the

Knights of Labor. Their policies regarding the female worker fell into three types. The power of the organization was used in the effort to keep women out of its occupations. This program is illustrated by the history of organizations of printers. As early as 1832 the Typographical Society of Philadelphia, for example, learning that there was a movement to employ women in the industry protested so forcefully that the employer in question felt called upon to write a letter to be spread upon the minutes of the society denying that he had ever intended to employ women.[2] As late as 1899 the president of the National Typographical Union admitted, as a witness before the Industrial Commission, that although women were freely employed in Boston by master printers, care was taken to keep them on straight composition, as much as possible to make automata of them and not to permit them to reach high standards as printers.[3]

Another reaction of the labor organizations of men toward women workers had been to recognize their possible competition and to encourage their alliance for motives of self-protection. This appeared, for example, in the cigar making trade. The president of the Cigar Makers' International Union in 1881 encouraged the bringing of women into the Union, because, so long as they were unorganized, there was risk that they become the means of reducing the employment of men and their wages. This led to the attempt to maintain the same wages for women as for men, but it is obvious that the individual male worker often looked upon the woman employee as a dangerous competitor rather than as a co-worker.[4]

A third policy was to ignore the female worker and merely to keep her from sharing the advantages provided the members of the men's unions. Sometimes as a result not only did women organize themselves separately but they acted independently of men and even more aggressively. An example of this is found in the strike of the Fall River weavers in 1875. The preceding year the men weavers had met without the women and had accepted a reduction in wages, whereupon the women came together by themselves and voted to strike in only three mills so that some women could work and help support those who were forced to be idle. They made this decision not knowing what the men, who had already committed themselves to an opposite policy, would do. The men's committee determined to support the action of the women and thus brought about the general strike of 1875.

There were several strikes in the boot and shoe industry of Massachusetts in 1872, and one of them reveals again an aggressive attitude on the part of women workers. It came about from the attempt of the employers to lessen the pay of the best workers and increase that on the lowest wage scale in order to bring about more uniform prices. When the women protested, the employers decided among themselves to force every woman worker to agree to give two weeks' notice before stopping work or to pay a fine of five dollars. Immediately nine hundred women workers assembled and voted not to sign the agreement.

The resolutions they passed are notable because they reveal an independence and courage in contrast with the docile acquiescence forced upon the great mass of women workers at the time, especially those earning an existence in the sweating industries. These Lynn women were successful in their opposition. This is what they voted to spread on their records.

> We, the Workingwomen, in convention assembled, do accept the following resolutions, as an earnest expression of our sentiments;
>
> Whereas, we have long been sensible of the need of protecting our rights and privileges, as free-born women, and are determined to defend them and our interests as workingwomen, to the fullest extent of our ability; therefore, be it
>
> *Resolved,* That we, the workingwomen of Lynn, known as Upper Fitters and Finishers of Boots and Shoes, do enter a most solemn protest against any reduction of wages, on any pretext whatever; and that we will not submit to any rules binding us that do not equally affect our employers.
>
> *Resolved,* That we feel grateful to the shoemakers of Lynn

for their interest and determination to stand by us in our time of need.

Resolved, That we, the free women of Lynn, will submit to no rules or set of rules that tend to degrade and enslave us.

Resolved, That we will accept no terms whatever, either with regard to a reduction of prices, notices to quit, or forfeiture of wages. That while we utterly ignore the spirit of selfishness and illiberality which prompted the late action of our would-be oppressors, we will not hesitate to resist, in a proper manner, the unjust encroachments upon our rights.

Resolved, That a copy of these resolutions be given to each one of the committee, to be by them presented to each girl in every shop, and her signature thereon obtained, that she will adhere to the terms of the resolutions; and should any one of the employees of the shop be reduced in her wages, or ill treated, we will desist from our work until she has obtained her rights.

Resolved, That a copy of the above be inserted in the Lynn papers, and a large surplus number be provided for distribution among the girls.[5]

Undoubtedly to a considerable extent the employment of women in industry along with that of children tended to keep down the wages of men. In manufacturing especially employment was offered on a family basis, and survival was possible merely because all members of the household old enough to work were employed. This had been customary from the beginning of textile manufacturing in the United States. Abbot has given us a contract written in 1815 for a worker in a Lancaster, Massachusetts, mill. It is interesting because it provides for the wages to go to the head of the family and also because it shows the difference between the wages paid men and those paid women.

Dennis Rier of Newbury Port has this day engaged to come with his family to work in our factory on the following conditions. He is to be here about the twentieth of next month and is to have the following wages per week:

Himself	$5.00
His son, Robert Rier, 10 years of age	0.83
Daughter Mary, 12 years of age	1.25
Son William, 13 years of age	1.50
Son Michael, 16 years of age	2.00
	$10.58
His sister, Abigail Smith	$2.33
Her daughter, Sally, 8 years of age	0.75
Son Samuel, 13 years of age	1.50
	$4.58 [6]

The wages paid women and children no longer went to the head of the family, but the discrimination against female labor was maintained throughout the period covered by this chapter, as indeed it largely is at present. This lower scale of wages for women workers was influenced greatly by the fact that many women were not entirely dependent upon what they earned. Many of them sought employment in order to enjoy small luxuries or to lift the family standards of living higher than was possible if only the man of the house worked. The effect was to bring down the earnings of those entirely dependent upon their own efforts.

Individual trade unions differed in their attitude toward women workers, but although they emphasized masculine interests even when they had both men and women members, it would be difficult to prove that the policy of these organizations had been a discrimination against women, as was natural in certain trades when women first began to push their way into an occupation and were relatively few in number. Then the male workers attempted to discourage the increase of feminine laborers and were reluctant to organize them, since this would mean that they were put in a position to be more effective rivals of the men.

In 1819 and in 1835 we find tailors striking in the effort to prevent the entrance of women into their trade. The same hostility appeared in the early period of American manufacturing among the makers of shoes, among cotton mill employees, and in other trades. This program failed as a barrier to the increasing employment of women and when this was recognized most trades changed their policy, realizing that the male worker was certain to suffer more from the competition of the unorganized than of the organized woman employee.

As one would expect, in practice the union's interest in women wage workers in any locality was influenced by the prevailing social status of women and the acceptance of their position in the industry. This often appeared not so much in discrimination against women in the union as in lack of interest in bringing them in or in considering their special needs. The trade union merely reflected the general social thinking as it had to do with women, ranging from strong masculine emphasis to a near-equality of the sexes. These differences of sentiment, as they showed themselves in the history of American trade unions, were influenced by class experience as well as by sectional attitude.

Henry, writing in 1927, states that the United Brotherhood of Carpenters and Joiners, the Journeyman Barbers' International Union, and the International Molders' Union, in spite of the fact that women were engaged in various phases of these several trades and because of their lack of organization were lowering wages, nevertheless refused to permit women to become members of their trades.[7] Even when women were freely admitted, their influence in unions made up of both sexes was less than that of the men, not only because of their generally relatively smaller numbers but also because, just as was true in other fields, men were reluctant to vote women into positions of authority. This was not necessarily discrimination from hostility toward feminine workers but merely the outcoming of the general social attitude toward women which showed itself in politics, in education, in medicine, in the churches, and everywhere where men and women were engaged in similar pursuits.

It would be a mistake, however, to regard the inferiority position of women in the trades as merely due to this tendency toward masculine dominance in organization and in policy. There were conditions, due to the disposition and circumstances of women themselves, that seemed to have a greater significance. Women were less committed to the union ideals because as individuals they were not finally committed to employment itself. Like the single male workers, they looked forward to marriage, but with the difference that the realization of their hopes might mean the abandonment of their wage-earning.

It was true that numbers of them preferred to compromise home life and to continue after marriage their out-of-the-home work. The majority had a different preference, and, in any case, the woman who married faced a handicap unshared by the man who married. This fundamental difference between the industrial status of the male and female worker appeared in every aspect of the woman's industrial career. The employer recognized it as did the male fellow worker, and most of all the woman herself frequently regarded her working as something temporary and in all her attitudes reflected this feeling.

As a result, it was more difficult to unionize the women than the men. In addition, the experiences of girlhood did not give the woman training for organization nor the understanding of the need of solidarity of action that came to the boy as a product of his everyday life. The significance of woman's lesser rôle in the history of American labor unions must be found not in these facts of relative importance but rather in the meaning her situation had as evidence of general social inferiority, biological handicap, and ineffective educational preparation for life.

The employer rarely wished to encourage the forming of strong trade unions in his business. As a rule, he found his women workers more docile than men, more willing to avoid antagonizing him by joining an organization. In times of strikes he was sometimes able to use women to break the power of the men. He could be more free in changing their wage scale or moving them from one position to another when they were unorganized and not allied with the men. This proved a great advantage to him in times of industrial crisis or when for some reason a program of readjustment had to be carried through in his business.

The situation of American women as wage workers could not be explained as a consequence of their having so recently entered industry. As has already been brought out in an earlier chapter, the woman worker appeared in American manufacturing at its very beginning. The discrimination against woman as wage earner was evidence in a particular field of her activities of the fundamental problem of the relation of the sexes that modern life had reopened and was then in the process of bringing again to a temporary settlement. As is always true in moments of social transition, the social structure, as it had to do with the relationship of the sexes, had been disturbed and to a considerable measure broken up and was reforming just as chemical crystals dissolve and reshape themselves. The industrial experiences of woman had a battle significance in her larger social campaign.

There can be no doubt about woman's inferiority in industry during the period of our study. We can best gather the facts by turning to the authoritative, detailed investigation reported in the Federal Census of Manufacturers issued during the fifth year of the new century. It tells us that of the one million female factory workers sixteen years of age or more, 18.2 per cent received under four dollars a week, 49.4 per cent less than six dollars, and 77.6 per cent less than eight dollars. Only 8.3 per cent of the workers earned more than ten dollars a week. This wage scale was obtained from the payroll of the employers themselves during the busiest week of the season. There were differences between sections of the country, and the record in the South was the lowest. In southern factories about three-fourths of the women received less than six dollars a week and more than nine-tenths less than eight dollars. The Far West had the highest wage scale, while the North Atlantic states came second.[8]

The large proportion of young girls in industry influenced the position of the woman wage earner. Nearly one-third of the women workers reported in the 1910 census were under twenty-one years of age as compared with one-sixth of the men. In almost all of the industries investigated for the Federal report on the conditions of woman and child wage earners there appeared a predominance among the women of workers under twenty-five, ranging from two-thirds to three-fourths of the total number of women. In all these industries there was a large number of women who fell in the age period of sixteen and seventeen.[9] This lowered the wages and lessened the stability and industrial reputation of women workers. The younger group of women wage earners tended to regard their occupation as a temporary expediency while their more serious ambitions turned toward the winning of a mate. Their lack of experience and their large turnover, in part through the leaving of the work by many who became married, led both their employers and their male fellow workers to think of them as industrial birds of passage. Those among them who had family responsibilities or were entered upon a life career suffered from the willingness of the other women to accept low wages, long hours, and unsanitary conditions because they regarded themselves as transient members of industry.

The penalty of the feebleness that came from their lack of organization appears most in the sweating industries. This exploitation received increasing attention and opposition from social-minded leaders during the period. It was chiefly women and children that suffered from this low standard type of employment. Although there was no necessary connection between the contract system in the clothing industries and the existence of the sweat shops, the letting out of work encouraged this, the lowest means of livelihood, with the exception of prostitution, offered women. Sweating trades flourished by providing employment on the piece work basis and chiefly in tenements in the large cities. Half of these shops were rooms in the tenement occupied as living quarters by the contractor and his family. There was great crowding in badly ventilated, dark and dreary, ill-adapted shops. Sometimes these were located in basements.

The hours of labor varied with the season, being stretched during rush periods at both the beginning and the end of the work day. The shops in New York in the nineties varied from sixty hours a week for inside shops to eighty-four hours outside. There was, however, always a possibility of overtime and even, in addition to this, the taking home of work that had to be finished before the opening of the shop the next day.

The wages varied greatly but were low. For example, the cloak and sack makers of inside shops of Boston, chiefly women and girls, are said, according to the report of the Massachusetts Bureau of Labor for 1884, to have had to work hard to earn the average of $6.00 a week throughout the year. In Baltimore, in 1884 and 1885, women cloak makers are reported to have earned from $3.50 to $5.00 a week.[10] Even entire families, working fourteen hours a day in New York City, could earn only $12.00 to $15.00 a week.[11]

This sweat shop method of production was not made necessary as a means of providing inexpensive clothing. It was rather that the cheapness of the labor retarded the use of machinery and the most efficient methods of production in the clothing industry. The low wages and unhygienic conditions of work led to the need of charity, particularly in the form of medical care, when ill health came as a result of the unwholesome régime and conditions. The purchaser even of expensive garments often came into possession of clothing that had been made under conditions of filth and disease. The competition of the tenement form of clothing manufacturing, with its exploiting wages and hours, hampered the advance of working standards in the better managed and equipped factories.

Agitation and legislation directed against the evils of the sweating system in the clothing industry had beneficial influences, but the natural trend of the industry toward factory production did most to lessen this exploiting of women and children. Industry rapidly developed away from domestic to factory methods during

INDUSTRIAL AND EDUCATIONAL ADVANCE

the decade from 1890 to 1900. The concentration of industry in large establishments favored union organization which in turn lifted the standards of employment and struck against the evil of child labor. One of the consequences of this was the spread of the industry outside the large cities as a result of the attempt of some manufacturers to escape the regulations and standards imposed by the international union.[12]

These shops were known as fugitive or runaway establishments. They hampered the advance of women in the clothing industries but they did not, as a rule, revive as menacing conditions of employment as had characterized the sweating industries in the major cities during the earlier period. On the whole, in the latter part of the nineteenth century there was a marked trend toward industrial concentration in clothing manufacturing in accord with the general tendency of industry toward combination and centralization.

There were prominent men and women who, narrowly reacting against the difficulties and the menaces of woman's entrance into industry, feared and condemned her leaving the home for the factory, the office, and the store. This opposition appears constantly in the sociological literature of the period. There was much coming from the experiences of women gainfully employed to encourage this reaction. Not only was the going into the lower levels of industry opposed as a departure from the proper business of the woman, but also the ambitions of the trained, gifted woman who sought to break into commerce or the professions were likewise deplored. These writers failed to see the evils of the alternative. Exploited as woman was along every line in comparison with the male worker, the opportunity of wage earning outside the home was nevertheless an advantage. Often stern necessity denied any choice. The widow, the wife of an invalid husband, the one who found her family could not be supported upon the earnings of her mate alone, was driven out of the home into the mill or factory, whatever may have been her preferences.

The woman who was not coerced by the grocer and the landlord also had her motives for going out of the home to work. The scant attention she received from her critics reveals how little thought was given to the exploitations of woman that appeared in orthodox form throughout her status as mother, wife, and housekeeper. It was easy to see the stress, the over-fatigue, the inadequate income, the insecurity, and the unsanitary conditions faced by workers who were massed together in some manufacturing or commercial enterprise. The bringing together of many women advertised their disadvantages and enlisted the interest of the philanthropist and the reformer. Overwork in the family, the burden of too many children, the constant anxiety of expenses that always kept ahead of income, the continuous feeling of frustration, often heightened by the sense of obligations that could not be fulfilled, were little reacted against because these evils appeared in scattered form within the privacy of individual homes.

The position of the housewife seemed to a multitude of women harder, leading to a more precarious existence for the family, than the exploitations and limitations that she met, once she went out to earn her living as a member of some vocational group. The men and women who urged her to remain at home contrasted what they knew was facing her in industry with a non-existing idealized family experience, the sort of life with which they were personally familiar. The significance of woman's entrance into industry, which proceeded in spite of the effort of its critics to restrain the feminine trend, can be found only when this movement is related to the other facts of woman's social situation at the time.

There was no way by which women could increase their independence and lessen masculine dominance other than by accepting a program that affected marriage, motherhood, and family traditions. Economic independence was the most effective method of advancing social status. There is, of course, for no person in the modern world an absolute independence in economic relations. The working men were only relatively free. Their wives, however, were doubly dependent. They had to accept all the hazards of their husband's position and in addition they were dependent upon the habits, the dispositions, and the injustices of their mate. If the family income went largely through the weakness or viciousness of the husband into the till of the saloon keeper, to the enrichment of the promoter of gambling, or was merely foolishly thrown away, what could the woman do? If her life was one of drudgery, overwork, constant worry, for whatever reason, what way of escape was there for her?

Legislation made no attempt to regulate the standards of domestic life. The law entered the home only when overt crime occurred. The woman in a multitude of cases was merely a drudge, a sex partner, frequently less respected in the privacy of the home than the better type of prostitute by her clients, or a bearer of children, crushed by the repeated pregnancies dreaded both by herself and her husband.

It was the penalties of a social inferiority that produced the family burdens and the home atmosphere in contrast with which gainful employment in industry seemed, and was, to many American women a way of escape from a more hopeless type of existence. These women may not have been forced into working for wages by pressure of possible starvation, but they were impelled nevertheless by economic or personal hardships. Urging them to return to their homes was futile, either because it was impossible or in their own thinking seemed undesirable.

This situation must not be interpreted as something only to be found upon the lower economic levels. The form of the pressure changed and women belonging to the middle and wealthy classes did not seek vocations from stark necessity, but the same motives operated upon them as upon their less fortunate sisters. In a different way they too felt a dependence, a frustrating definition of their proper rôle which antagonized their normal cravings as human beings. Thus they were ushered into the still persistent and vexing problems of the career-desiring, ambitious woman.

On these higher levels the ambitions or personal needs of

women were as likely to prevent marriage or parenthood as to draw the woman who married away from the conventional life of wife or mother. All women who went outside the domestic sphere and labored, or who achieved in the out-of-the-family world, helped to improve the status of women in general not only by lessening economic dependence upon the man but also by lifting the standards of domestic experience. The great distance which had existed between the male and female in their economic status was lessened. The nearer woman came to man's situation as a worker, the greater was her prestige. It is impossible to judge whether those who flooded into industry or the smaller number of women who broke through barriers into professions did the more to open up opportunities for their sex and dissolve coercive traditions.

There can be no doubt, however, where the greater prestige appeared. In accordance with the social law that the influence of society spreads downward, the career of the few women who got into professions did most to challenge the conventions that reflected woman's long-time economic dependence on man. On the other hand, the inroads of women into the trades forced men for their own self-protection to recognize the interests and the rights of the woman as a fellow human being. In the end it would seem as if this more massive reaction brought most disturbance in the relationship of the two sexes, forcing a new social attitude. In addition to this direct influence, woman by increasing her economic activities encouraged other trends, particularly those in education that were enlarging her rôle.

The inclination to see the flow of social culture in a narrow, consistent stream tends toward understatement of the minor, less striking, contrasting trends. Looking back upon the conditions women encountered as they went into the industries of this period, it is easy to see the exploitations, the menacing influences of the occupations open to women. To picture justly the full sweep of woman's experience in industry, it is necessary to remember that she was drawn by incentives in a multitude of cases rather than forced by abject economic need to go out of the home for wages. The village girl, the dependent adolescent, the young woman who, although in comfortable circumstances, wanted to have additional spending money for luxuries, or preferred gainful employment to isolation or to dependency or to doing without much desired pleasures, sought work. It was most especially those women who flirted with industry and business who felt these enticements toward work outside the home.

The enlarging of woman's vocational opportunities, through changes in industry, lifted her prestige both before and after marriage. It was not merely that there were greater employment possibilities, there was also a more general acceptance of the idea of women working out of the home. There were, as has already been noticed, a considerable number of women both North and South even in the colonial days who supported themselves in some business or trade. Even though these women were socially acceptable in their communities, their careers were regarded as something exceptional as compared with the usual practices of women. It was otherwise when machine industry got started. From the first there was a place for women in the factories and on the level where economic pressure was severe the working woman, both married and unmarried, became a convention.

Later when Lowell, Waltham, Fall River, and other industrial centers attracted young women of the lower middle class from farming communities, this attitude toward the working of women spread upward and began to influence the sentiment of the entire middle class. It made the entrance of ambitious women into the professions easier and encouraged leading women to demand for their sex full economic and political equality. The idea of woman's economic independence met with opposition, as it still does, but reinforced as it was by the attitude of men and women filled with western tradition, the gainful employment of women became increasingly conventional.

The added prestige that this brought woman as it affected her life before marriage appeared chiefly in the freedom it gave her.

Marriage began to lose the appeal it had had because it provided a means of economic support when woman through it exchanged dependence upon her parents for a self-chosen, more self-respecting dependence upon her husband. This economic advantage marriage had to surrender as women found means to support themselves independently in industries and in businesses. Immediately some women turned away from the desire to marry, who under different circumstances would have felt the need of a matrimonial career. Others were more exacting and more cautious in their mating.

A selective process accompanied the increasing opportunities of women in industry. Without doubt this operated in many cases to influence men in mating with women inferior to those they would have married had there been no open gate into industry. Some superior women were so demanding during courtship that they remained unmarried. Since this selective influence still persists, it is well to see it in its long-time consequences. It means from this viewpoint that the prestige of woman and her realization of her needs lessens her willingness to accept marriage as an expediency when it does not promise fulfillment of her life's craving. This is more than a liability in the mating of the men of any generation; it is an educational force continuously operating to mature the attitude of men in their relations with women.

Although this is a force that cannot be measured and that usually remains unconscious, it influences the American male to some degree in every class and tends on the whole to emphasize the human rather than the feminine characteristics of the American woman. Its significance can be realized only when we imagine what would happen if the woman of today suddenly were driven back to an economic dependence upon the male, either as a member of her father's family or as a wife. Nothing would so quickly change the complexion of her career in America. This tells us how much woman's economic independence has contributed and is still giving to her advance toward equality with man.

Agitation for woman's rights, even had there been incentive, would have availed little to extend woman's opportunity had there not been working for her advantage an ever-increasing economic independence. Of course, the tradition of a long dependence upon man for economic support, and therefore an inevitable inferiority as compared with him, hampered the woman in industry and encouraged her exploitation. Nevertheless, economic independence was her only way of escape. Those who regard woman's approach to equality with man along all lines as a biological catastrophe should seek the closing of economic opportunity to women, for only through dependence can she be driven back to her one-time status.

The new prestige that woman attained through her vocational expansion also influenced her career in marriage. The general trend here is unmistakable, but in individual families there was and is great variation, ranging from an old-fashioned subserviency with a full support of the docile, even parasitic woman by the man, to a most modern attempt at equal partnership struggled for by both the woman and the man. Domestic experience moved toward a relationship of persons of the same order. The woman instead of catering to the man, seeing things as they appeared in a masculine setting, injected more freely her own motives, expressing her own sentiments and stressing her standards. This, however, becomes an exaggeration if the change is made anything more than one in degree.

Since from the beginning the American woman began to advance her status through the new environment's breaking with European traditions, the freer she had been in earning a livelihood before her marriage the more easily could she turn, if she chose, to self-support out of the home, and most naturally in the family setting appeared expressions of her greater freedom. One of these that at last in our time has become considerable was her attitude toward the coming of children. Under masculine dominance childbearing is an automatic consequence of marriage. There is at least no substantial public opinion that leads either men or women to regard this matter as something that should be decided by women much more than men. It is otherwise as woman gains prestige through greater economic self-sufficiency.

Woman's progress, in large measure a derivative of economic changes, brought forth during the period in both England and the United States evidences of a changing feeling about her rights as a potential childbearer. Agitation for birth control, to use a modern broad generalization for the demand for contraceptives, was not always related to the increasing economic independence of women, but that was its basic root. As early as 1822 in England, Francis Place, who of all men was most sensitive to the industrial situation, began to popularize and encourage the notion of contraceptive practices. His appeal was made largely to factory workers on a basis of self-interest. In one of his contraceptive handbills put forth in 1823 we read:

. . . To those who constitute the great mass of the community, whose daily bread is alone procured by daily labour, a large family is almost always the cause of ruin, both of parents and children; reducing the parents to cheerless, hopeless and irremediable poverty; depriving the children of those physical, moral, and mental helps which are necessary to enable them to live in comfort, and turning them out at an early age to prey upon the world, or to become the world's prey.[13]

Place and his disciples stimulated interest in the United States where Robert Dale Owen, through his *Moral Physiology*, published in 1830, and Dr. Charles Knowlton, through *The Fruits of Philosophy*, published two years later, pioneered. It was in 1872 that John Humphrey Noyes of the Oneida Community brought out his chief tract, *Male Continence*, but as early as 1848 he had announced his opposition to involuntary procreation.[14]

Although a movement toward conventional birth control was greatly supported in the early days of the agitation in the United States by men who came to the discussion with convictions gathered from medical practice, the greatest influence in spreading the idea was the loosening of the social restraints that muffled woman's impulses for self-expression. What she gained in opportunities for self-support not only weakened the barrier imposed by conventions expressive of masculine experience but brought to self-consciousness and strength the latent disposition to make motherhood a voluntary decision. In addition the pre-marriage life frequently established habits or desires that lessened the inclination of women to have children. Especially was this true in the career area where the awakening of ambitions led the woman to attempt both marriage and her profession and, as a result, the limitation or the avoidance of chiildbearing. Even so, woman's interest in this particular form of self-decision did not keep pace with her pressure toward what she considered her educational, legal, political, and even industrial rights. Her self-seeking was curbed by the teachings of orthodox religion, the strength of family tradition, and for a considerable group by isolation that left her ignorant of the birth control movement.

Even if the industrial development of women had gone hand in hand with an acceptance of birth control, as it did not, the birth rate would not have clearly reflected the changed viewpoint of women. Not only was there the counteraction of immigrant women possessed by contrary traditions, but also even the general use of the birth control practices of the time could not have affected reproduction greatly, because the science of contraceptives was in its pioneering stage. Now, when a great multitude of women have accepted the idea of contraception and the methods of birth control have been greatly improved, we are in a position to recognize the results of a movement that got its start before the Civil War and was greatly stimulated by the influences that appeared in woman's life in the later growth of modern industrialism.

The preachment against the outgoing of women from their homes into the professions was more aggressive than that directed against women entering industry. The ambitious woman who sought a career in the masculine sense by entering law, medicine, or the ministry was indicted on two counts. Her critics insisted that it was not good for her to attempt the educational career that efficient preparation for such professions required and that she was by endowment unfitted for such vocations.

This controversy against the undertaking of college and particularly professional requirements for a degree was perhaps sharper in the 'fifties and 'sixties than in the 'seventies. The Civil War shook severely the ideas that had been so widely held regarding the inherent weakness of the female human organism. Her war experience had taught the woman and also the man to question the assumption that had so long influenced social practices.

Moreover the greater freedom of woman helped her by making possible a more hygienic way of life. Previously fashion and tradition had discouraged active, healthful practices for many women until the fainting of the frail, clinging type of female had come to seem a sex trait, almost a social propriety. To be sure, never was this the vogue among the great majority of women, especially those active in the conquest of the great West, but the tradition of the woman's biologic inferiority lingered chiefly in the social class that dominated fashion through its prestige.

The woman who sought to enter teaching had never met with the opposition encountered by her sister who attempted to get into some other well-established profession. It was only when the woman began to demand the same preparation for teaching and to move up to the college level that she met with antagonism. Those who sought to protect her from her own zeal argued against her undertaking so strenuous a study as the college degree required and engaging in so exacting a life work as she coveted. Such arguments were the more forceful when they attempted to keep women out of law, medicine, and the ministry. There were writers and publicists who insisted that women were not capable of carrying on in the masculine professions, but greater and more impressive opposition came from those who granted that she could do what men did but only at the expense of her health, her fertility, her happiness as a normal female.

Those who feared that the entrance of woman into industry and into the professions would hurt her health, turn her aside from her proper biological purpose, and disturb her socially, had reasons for this attitude that do not exist at present. There were abnormal circumstances that brought liabilities of temporary type, due to the conditions under which women worked in industry and the newness of their efforts in business and in the professions.

The women who went into the factories, particularly those exploited in the sweat shops, were subjected in ways no longer true in the United States to influences that were detrimental to physical and mental health. The hours of labor were excessive, opportunities for periods of rest or relaxation were absent through the long day, or insufficient. The physical environment was often unsanitary, unhygienic, and its psychic suggestions a source of constant strain. In addition frequently there was great monotony and little opportunity for relief from the too-great speed of the machines which required continuous concentration, and when the day was over the woman worker, drained of energy, turned heavy footsteps toward lodgings that were usually depressing, in a noisy, over-crowded, dismal neighborhood. As compared with the present, there was little recreation of wholesome character within the means of multitudes of women wage earners in factories and shops. Mill owners rarely had the interest in the living conditions of their workers that had been true when Lowell, Waltham, and similar industrial communities were attracting the interest of humanitarians both in this country and from Europe.

The Settlement Movement, conceived in the slums of Whitechapel, London, began in favored cities in this country to meet the challenge of the most depressing and least resourceful sections of the larger cities. In the smaller industrial towns little was offered along recreational lines except the meager, restricted offerings of churches and religious organizations and the license of the saloon. The latter was indeed in some measure a social club for the men. Custom made it a menace to the woman who turned to it to satisfy cravings for something in contrast with the dreariness of her daytime experience. Its only offering was alcohol or an association with men that because of its unconventional character quickly became, particularly for those who were young, a real menace.

The woman who was married and who had children often went from the grind of a job to a home of poverty, perhaps to work that had to be added to what had already been done, however tired she might feel. So dismal a picture, fortunately, cannot justly be made from the experience of all women who for one reason or another were gainfully employed outside the home. There were favored establishments and small industries in villages where conditions were much brighter and more wholesome. On the other hand, the most kindly disposed factory owner felt the competition of rival enterprises that were carried on without any regard for the welfare of the workers.

The larger the concern, the more difficult it was to maintain any personal relationship between the employer and employee. Then, also, there was even greater difficulty on the part of the mill management in influencing community standards and resources because of absentee ownership and control. The superintendent or agent at the head, even when he had personal contact with and knowledge of the workers, frequently had little freedom to improve either their conditions during labor or their life in the community after the work of the day was over.

The woman who went into business on a high level or into a profession also met difficulties that gave to those arguing against her ambitions a force that would not now be true. She not only became a competitor of men, but received from many of them hostility, ridicule, suspicion, in a persistent attack that made her undertaking an artificial strain. How strong was this feeling toward women who stepped out of the ordinary routine appears in such examples as that of the woman editor whose own reporters conspired to delay their news so that competitors could have a scoop. Such sabotage, a violation of the strongest principles of newspaper ethics, shows how deep was masculine protest against the women that broke conventions to enter unfeminine occupations. The following, whether true or unfounded hearsay, was

INDUSTRIAL AND EDUCATIONAL ADVANCE

certainly in accord with the temper of masculine authority toward women who pursued study out of their proper field.

I have been informed that on one occasion the authorities of the Royal Astronomical Society had a discussion as to whether they should award their gold medal to Miss Caroline Herschel for her discovery of five comets. It was understood that it would undoubtedly have been given had the discoverer been a man. But they came to a determination akin to that of the Royal Geographical Sociey—not to recognize or reward services to science when rendered by a woman, and the medal was withheld.[15]

The intellectual broadside against the breaking out of women through untraditional undertakings was directed chiefly against her demands for higher education, especially for training in preparation for professions. This was fortunate, because at no point was convention less ready to withstand the pressure of woman's changing status. The arguments that were advanced by those seeking to block the advance of women along these lines were those that had been so long employed to challenge every aggression of the woman's movement from the days of Mary Wollstonecraft.

Feminine ambitions were the abandonment of divine decree registered in the physiological structure of the woman. They led toward the hardening of feminine character, the loss of sex appeal, the throwing away of the instinctive satisfactions of motherhood, the surrender of domestic companionableness for the deceptions and disillusionments that followed the attempt to imitate men. The penalties of such ambitions were race suicide, physical and nervous ill health, loss of marriage opportunity, and social disorganization. The women who chose to break into higher education destroyed their charm, selfishly rebelled against the obligations and sacrifices that belonged to women and without which there could not be a civilization safe for either men or women. If the woman went to a coeducational college she ran the risk of losing the qualities that were the necessary stimuli for mating. If she went to the segregated institutions, she aborted the normal sex growth and encouraged a morbid outlook upon life and lost during her formative years the educational value of association with admiring men.

Women who refused to be discouraged in their quest for greater knowledge and better training frequently found through personal experience that many of these assertions were not idle prophecies. These women were looked upon as peculiar; they were isolated from men and subjected to the unnecessary but none the less troublesome strain that came from hostilities, obstructions, and injustices. It is easy now to forget how restrictive and how firm were the conventions that defined the proprieties of the American woman. Even at Oberlin, where extraordinary advancement had taken place, it was as late as 1870 considered improper for a woman to address a mixed audience.[16]

The taboos that attempted to regulate the life of women were considered necessary protections rather than restrictions. Even such a warrior as was Catherine Beecher for the better education for women accepted the fundamental assumption of woman's inherent weakness as compared with man. She said: "Heaven has appointed to one sex the superior, and to the other the subordinate station, and this without reference to the character or conduct of either." [17]

The force of contemporary attacks on the movement to give women higher education, as we gather them from the discussions of the time, has so departed that it is a task of the imagination to realize how convincing they seemed to a great majority of the thoughtful readers of the period. Only, however, against such a background can one realize the struggle there had to be to break through even at its weakest place the conventional code that blocked the social advance of American women.

The following are fairly representative of the onslaughts that appeared in books and periodicals.

> . . . For our part we are convinced that too much has been done already in forcing girls through courses of hard study, and that any further steps in that direction will necessitate

hospitals and asylums alongside of Colleges for women. The training provided for girls in our common schools even, largely incapacitates them for the duties and the joys of their natural future, and that without raising either their character or their intelligence materially above what these would have been with a simpler training; if indeed moral and mental health are not decidedly lowered by the physical depression induced by hard study. And in our great schools of learning, the admission of women, to any great extent, must simply mean a virtual abdication of their best functions by a considerable class of women; and that without reason, either in any service to be rendered by it, or in any happiness to be found in it, but through a mistake full of unreason and fruitful of sorrow.

It already appears to an alarming extent, that this is the tendency, although by far the greater portion of these sad fruits of error will be reaped chiefly after some years by the next generation. We have always found that inquiries, directed particularly to this point, revealed a terrible skeleton in the Colleges which receive women, or which attempt to give girls the severe training to which boys are subjected.[18]

Writing in the Congregationalist in 1871, the Rev. John Todd, D. D., asked questions familiar to the opponents of woman's advance into higher education.

If ladies enter our colleges and compete in the long course, with the other sex, they must do it by sacrificing the female accomplishments—the piano, cultivated singing, and attractive dress. Why must they? Simply because they can't compete with the young men without using all their time and exhausting all their strength.

Is it certain that the delicate, nervous, physical organization of woman is such—(I admit all you ask as to her quickness of mind, and fine mental attributes,) that she can endure the physical strain requisite for a regular, old-fashioned, college course? I am informed that in institutions where the experiment has been tried, of 100 young men who are fitted for college, sixty-six go through the course. Out of 100 females, *only six* go through the course. Exceptions there may be but as a general thing, can the female constitution bear the long strain?

Are we prepared to change the whole organic plan of our colleges—introducing the accomplishments which are as natural to woman as her breath, which accomplishments the Bible recognizes—"that our daughters may be polished after the similitude of a palace"—shaping the course of study so that she will not sink under the strain—(for an army *must* grade its march to the feeblest battalion)—having women on the Board of Trustees and in the Faculty—for it must come to that—throwing aside the experience of ages in the hope that our new experiment is to advance human improvement? [19]

The influential *Edinburgh Review* writes with more friendly caution, pointing out the difficulties ahead of the women seeking professional training that many of them could have testified from personal experience were no fictions of the imagination.

... Thus success in a profession—nay, the mere initiatory possibility of success—requires from a woman not equality with man, but an amount of intellectual and moral superiority over him, which can only be found in the rarest and most isolated cases. To him the prospect of marriage is the strongest incentive to industry and exertion. To her it is simple ruin, so far as her work is concerned. If then she has the magnanimity and self-devotion to cut herself off from all that is popularly considered happiness in life—from all that youth most dreams of, and the heart most cares for—she is free to enter into and pursue, and very likely will succeed in a profession, which men, with all solaces of love and help of companionship, pursue by her side at not half the cost. Perhaps even then, after she has made this sacrifice, she will find that she is the pot of earth making her way among their pots of iron; and that their superior physical powers and bolder temperament will carry them beyond her, notwithstanding the superior devotion she has shown and the price she has paid. But this is the best we can promise her when all is done—to (perhaps) succeed as well, at the cost of everything, as her competitors who go into it with the commonest of motives and at no cost at all.[20]

The report comes down to us of a social science convention held May 14, 1878, at which the higher education of woman was featured on the program and brought forth a discussion which helps us to relive a controversy that now seems distant and sterile. Thomas W. Higginson, who had already chosen to champion woman's struggle for intellectual equality, after attacking the prejudices which he considered the barriers against woman's ongoing, announced his optimistic forecast of a progress toward higher education for women that would even break through the Harvard wall of tradition.

... All the problems of education seem to present themselves in the same way at Harvard for boys, at Vassar for girls, at Michigan and at Cornell for the two united. The logic of events is sweeping with irresistible power to the union of the sexes for higher education. West of the Alleghenies, as even its opponents admit, public sentiment is irresistible in its favor, and east of the Alleghenies the tendencies are all one way. The tide is sweeping in—the smaller New England colleges are swept away, and if the others do not follow, the promised Boston University with its vast endowments will soon make it unimportant whether they follow or not.[21]

In the spirit of compromise, Professor Agassiz suggested that although he admitted the necessity of granting women in any enlightened community all the privileges, political and educational, which any man has a right to claim, the best policy at the moment was to trust to time while using opportunities to advance woman's cause, in so far as this could be done without attempting to run far ahead of social sentiment. His strategy was illustrated by the fact that:

... when he was appointed professor at Harvard, as soon as he could without opposition, he opened the door of his lecture-room to women, and when the museum—which is independent in almost every feature of the government at Harvard—was founded, he secured admission then legally to all teachers, whether male or female. At this moment, said the Professor, the number of assistants of both sexes belonging to the museum is about equal; the number of hearers in my lecture-room is, I think, of the same character. I do not know but the ladies are more numerous than the gentlemen. There has never been any complaint made of the topics I have treated before them. I have treated every significant question relating to the state of nature there as I think it ought to be treated. I am now delivering a course of lectures upon reproduction to the same mixed audience.[22]

With characteristic straightforwardness, President Eliot insisted that coeducation was on the wane in the West and that male and female minds are not alike and should not be treated the same educationally. He then committed himself to the thinking of those who believed there were biological risks in woman's attempt to invade the territory that belonged to man on account of his superior nervous and physical endowment.

... if a leader in education wants to know the probable effect upon the physique of women of certain changes which are contemplated in the methods of her education; and any one not a specialist in such a matter will naturally go to doctors and physiologists for an answer to these questions. He wished to say that all the competent and eminent men whom he had consulted upon this question, including the distinguished anatomist and physiologist who had addressed them, testified that they did not consider that women could bear the stress that is put upon men. He had never heard any difference of opinion on this point among men competent by special experience to speak on it. He had heard female physicians bear testimony in corroboration of Dr. Clarke's evidence.

INDUSTRIAL AND EDUCATIONAL ADVANCE

On these two grounds of Western experience and *a priori* education, he shrunk from taking his part of the responsibility of introducing the education of women in Harvard College. It is very different to be in a position where one must act and take responsibility, and to be in a position where one has only to maintain honest convictions without responsibility. As far as the argument from the rising tide is concerned, he had only to say that if the tide rose high enough it would rise over Harvard.[23]

Words, even though they came forth from well-entrenched prejudices, were found unavailing as women continued to push forward. Indeed it was fortunate for the strategy of the Woman's Rights Movement that intellectual opposition was centered about this particular controversy. The current toward greater opportunity along educational lines was flowing from too extensive a watershed to be held back. It was bound to prove a great advantage to other aggressions that so great an effort was made to block the equality trend where there was least hope of successful opposition.

The development of the education of girls, first on the elementary level and then on the secondary, had reached the point where the coming of the college opportunity was the logical, the inevitable outcome of what already had happened. Thirty-nine years before the establishment of schools in any other colony, Franciscan missionaries of the Roman Catholic church opened in Florida, in 1594, the first formal education in the eastern territory of what is now the United States, and from the beginning girls were admitted to these schools, although the subjects offered them were adapted to their needs.[24] Thus it appears that the Spanish peoples settling North America had a more liberal and modern attitude toward the training of girls than was true in the early period of the English colonies.

In spite of the handicaps of this early discrimination against girls, educational facilities for them constantly increased. The education for girls had after the Civil War reached the secondary level with a momentum that could not be discouraged. The female seminary was the first product of this extension of the training of girls beyond the elementary grades. From 1775 to 1870, approximately a century, it took shape as a well-defined unit of American education and prospered. It not only created the need of still higher education, it to some extent became a substitute for it, and there were seminaries that, except in name, functioned as colleges. Indeed at first the two terms were used synonymously even of institutions for men.

The spread of elementary education, its increasing recognition as a necessary activity of a democratic state, not only carried forward girls as well as boys who demanded secondary training but also furnished attractive opportunities for women in teaching. Their entrance into this profession, already increasing, was naturally greatly stimulated by conditions during the Civil War. It soon became necessary to provide training for these women who desired to teach, and this task at first fell to the female seminary.

There were also missionary motives expressed through the founding and the growth of female seminaries. The Congregational, the Presbyterian, the Episcopalian, and the Roman Catholic leaders were especially educational-minded as they tried to establish their faith in the great frontier. As a consequence, those interested in the welfare of the girl responding to missionary zeal turned to the female seminary as a moral and religious influence as well as the means of bringing education in the narrow sense to the girl.

Catherine Beecher, who had in 1833 removed from Hartford where she had been in charge of a seminary, expressed this typically in a letter to the friend whom she was trying to interest in the effort to establish a female seminary in the pioneering but rapidly growing city of Cincinnati. Speaking of the mission of the seminary she was hoping to start, she wrote:

> I see no other way in which our country can so surely be saved from the inroads of vice, infidelity and error. Let the

leading females of this country become refined, well educated and active, and the salt is scattered through the land to purify and save.[25]

Although religious interests were stressed in all the seminaries during the first quarter of the nineteenth century, perhaps in none did they so permeate an institution as at Mount Holyoke under the guidance of Mary Lyon. How far this enthusiasm went, but not without a tinge of morbidity, appears in the protest of Emily Dickinson who refused to fast in preparation for the Christmas season at the suggestion of the zealous principal and who, as a consequence, severed her connection with the institution.[26]

After 1870, in accord with the democratic trend appearing in public school education, the high school rapidly developed and in time came to have even more girl than boy pupils. The monopoly of the female seminary was broken and its functions passed on to several different types of institutions. The normal school came into being as a means of training teachers for the elementary and secondary public schools. Some seminaries, of which Mount Holyoke is an example, eventually matured into colleges. Other seminaries became private schools, catering to the parents of wealthy children and offering training that extended into the program of the orthodox college.

The establishing of colleges for women on seminary foundations went on for about fifty years, beginning at least as early as 1825 and achieving clear expression when Mary Sharp College, previously known as the Tennessee and Alabama Female Institute, offered its graduates an A. B. degree based on a course comparable in content and quality with that granted by colleges for men. Later Elmira and Vassar assumed the responsibilities of college training for women. The West had already brought its contribution to woman's advanced instruction by its even more radical departure from academic tradition—coeducation.

Coeducation in the high schools had been a natural growth from the general practice of teaching boys and girls together in elementary classes. Many of the seminaries were, especially in the West, coeducational from the beginning. In the eighteenth century, when few schools on the secondary level had been developed exclusively for girls, some academies took in both sexes. The most important of these in New England was Leicester, incorporated in 1784, and Westwood Academy, in 1793.[27] As a rule, the eastern development of the seminaries and academies accepted the idea of sex separation, but although New England largely contributed to the founding of settlements in the Midwest, the educational trend there, reflecting the more modern attitude toward women characteristic of the section, favored coeducational institutions.[28]

After the Civil War the popularity of the female seminary or academy began to decline. By 1872, it appears from reports from twenty-nine states to the Bureau of Education that 175, or about half, of these institutions giving higher education were designating themselves colleges. Even though this often meant nothing more than the choice of a title, it revealed how strongly sentiment was moving toward a higher type of education for women. The decline of the female seminary was more rapid in the North than in the South after the War, a trend which again reflected the social status of woman. In the West the advanced training for women chiefly came about from permitting them to enter institutions that previously had been monopolized by men, while in the Northeast we have the establishment of new institutions seeking to train women by themselves but with the same scholarly standards as the older colleges provided for men.

It was not surprising that these institutions challenging the prevailing notions about the undesirability of advanced education for women at first aped the male colleges and universities. They were founded not only to meet a definite demand but also in the spirit of a crusade. They were institutions that felt their mission and thought themselves destined to break a pathway for greater intellectual justice for women. In 1834 Daniel Chandler, whose father had been an enthusiastic advocate of better educational

INDUSTRIAL AND EDUCATIONAL ADVANCE

facilities for women, made an address at the University of Georgia, advocating the giving of the same educational opportunities to women as to men and pointing out that of the sixty-one colleges then to be found in the United States "not one is dedicated to the cause of female education." [29] Two years later the legislature voted a charter for the Georgia Female College, to be located at Macon.

The first attempt in the North to provide an institution of genuine college grade for women came from the interest of a group of clergymen and laymen who first discussed the project in 1851. The next year the Auburn Female University was chartered. The undertaking met with discouragement through failure to gather the funds needed, and, receiving an offer of help from Elmira in 1855, it changed its location and became known as Elmira Female College. Its first degrees were given in 1859. In 1857 Ingham Collegiate Institute, at Leroy, New York, became Ingham University, open only to women, and gave degrees based upon a regular four-year course. Because it enjoyed an endowment greater than that of any other college for women at the time, Vassar, chartered in the first month of 1861, celebrated a new era. It started operation in the last year of the War. It was the ambition of its founder to establish for women the same type of college as had developed for men. "It is my hope," he declared, "to be the instrument, in the hands of Providence, of founding and perpetuating an institution which shall accomplish for young women what our colleges are accomplishing for young men." [30] Wells College, changed in 1870 from a seminary, was another pioneer. Five years later came Smith College and Wellesley.

The requirements and the courses studied at both of these "modern" institutions for the satisfying of the ambitions of the new type of women were influenced by the curricula of colleges for men, the one by Amherst and the other by Harvard. Soon followed Bryn Mawr, chartered in 1888, which took the most advanced position of them all, Mount Holyoke, which graduated from its seminary status the same year, and Goucher five years later.

Women had at last reached the point where those in the front rank were determined to disprove the fundamental inequality of the sexes that had so long been socially supported. The question was not what they needed in training for life but rather what they could demonstrate regarding their capacity, their nervous and physical preparedness for the highest expressions of intellectual life. They were more determined in their purpose to disprove inherent deficiencies of the intellect than were those accepting the coeducational opportunities in the open West, because they were more conscious of the clashing of two antagonistic definitions of women, sharply brought into contrast by the great inroads of women into industry, the aggressiveness of those who had absorbed masculine ambitions and were asking as rights, opportunity to study at colleges and at universities, freedom to enter professions on equal footing with men, and even, with the greatest audacity imaginable, laws permitting them to vote and to hold public office.

The opponents, both men and women, of this attempt to open up higher educational privileges to women were neither silenced nor convinced by the trends so apparent, but if they could have read the social horoscope, they would have known that their resistance was destined to prove futile.

CHAPTER X

THE AMERICAN WOMAN IN THE TWENTIETH CENTURY

From the beginning of the twentieth century to World War I there were four marked trends in woman's life, all of them continuations of movements previously begun. There were changes in domestic and social habits as a result of the influences of science, inventions, discoveries, and, mostly as a consequence of these, a reshaping of the conventions. Secondly, there was a greater invasion of women workers into industry and the professions and a breaking down of opposition to this on the part of both men and women. Third, remarkable progress was made in women's organizations. This included the springing up of many new societies, the consolidation of many that were similar in purpose, thus adding to their effectiveness, and a great increase of membership in the older organizations.

Women's organizations were advancing on four fronts. They were attempting to increase the rights of women, to provide opportunities for the expression of their rapidly multiplying interests, particularly along cultural lines, to obtain through a united front protection and advancement in the industries and professions, and to further religious, ethical, philanthropic, and social reform programs.

The fourth trend, the most subtle, but also the most distinctive and significant, was the change in feeling, a new outlook on life, an unprecedented recognition of value that more than anything else measured the distance women had traveled toward social equality with men.

Merely to list some of the organizations that sprang up toward the end of the century and the beginning of the new, illustrating the variety of interests of women, is impressive. In 1903 came the National Woman's Trade Union League of America. This organization shows the sense of self-interest that had developed among the women in industry. It was supported not only by the wage earners but by their allies, women who enjoyed education, leisure, and wealth. Its purpose was the following:

> To assist in the organization of women wage earners into trade unions and thereby to help them secure conditions necessary for healthful and efficient work and to obtain a just return for such work.[1]

The first national organization of women in the profession of medicine was formed in 1904—the Women's Homeopathic Fraternity. In 1908 came the American Home Economics Association. In the preceding decade there were organized several patriotic societies. The National Society of the Daughters of the American Revolution started in 1890 as a protest against the policy of the Sons of the American Revolution in excluding women from membership. A year later, because of dissension in the organization, the Daughters of the Revolution was formed. The Colonial Dames of America in 1891, the U. S. Daughters of 1812 in 1892, and the United Daughters of the Confederacy in 1894 were representative of this new interest. The Parliament of Religions held during the World's Fair in 1893, strongly supported by women, had many by-products. One was the permanent organization of the Jewish Women's Congress which had met in connection with the religious forum. This resulted in the National Council of Jewish Women.

Another result was the stimulation of the peace movement among women. Miss Sarah Farmer, whose father's inventive genius had so largely contributed to the electrical success of the Fair, was a leader in this. She also took a prominent part in the considerable growth, due to the influence of the Parliament meetings at this time, of the Bahai doctrine, a brotherhood of peace based upon religious motives and tolerance. The National Consumers' League was organized in 1899, the National Congress of Mothers in 1897, the National Association of Colored Women in 1896, the Council of Women for Home Missions in 1908, the Junior League in 1901, bringing together young women of wealth for the support of philanthropic and civic activities, and the Women's Peace Party in 1914. The American Association of University Women, appearing in 1881, the National Pan Hellenic Association in 1891, and the National Association of Deans of Women in 1909 revealed the strength of the college group of women.

Another evidence of woman's enlarging interest shows up in the proceedings of the annual meetings of such an organization as the General Federation of Women's Clubs. Such topics as the improvement and enrichment of education, anti-child-labor laws, pure food legislation, attacks on the white slave traffic, prove the range of the discussions at these sessions.

In addition to the self-expression provided by their own organizations, women increased their participation and influence in many societies made up of both sexes. This fact grew more and more an effective argument for giving women the same suffrage rights as men. It became increasingly inconsistent with what was actually happening in the field of practical philanthropy, civics, and industry to withhold from women the right to vote. The arbitrariness of the prevailing political policy was enforcing the reasonableness of the further advancement of women, breaking down the opposition of men and women who were against woman suffrage, and adding incentives to the women who were crusading for full political rights. Although hostility to the pushing forward of woman's status was on the retreat, it challenged the trend stubbornly and vociferously. The pages of the *Ladies' Home Journal,* a magazine having great circulation and influence, attest to this continuing opposition. Here are samples of this sentiment.

As I have said before, I regard Woman's rights, women and the leaders in the new school of female progress as the worst enemies of the female sex.[2]

I am persuaded that there are Woman's Clubs whose objects and intents are not only harmful, but harmful in a way that directly menaces the integrity of our homes.[3]

World War I greatly accelerated the social trends of concern to women. It quickened the woman's rights movement in all its phases. It tore down barriers against women's entrance into important industries and gave convincing demonstration of the unsuspected adaptability and efficiency of women in occupations that had been largely closed to them by social conventions, the prejudices of masculine-dominated labor unions, and the bias of employers. On the surface, the most clearly along industrial, professional, and political lines, World War I proved a great advantage to American women. For them, as for the men, its value came from its eruptive influences. It broke through the crust of tradition, thus allowing new ideas, the seeds of social change, to come to life. It also brought special stimulation by disturbing the prevailing routine and artificially multiplying the willingness to experiment, the conflict, the unrest, that are unavoidable at times of rapid revamping of the relation of the sexes.

The adventuring and the freedom of women, as a consequence of the War, tended to increase instability within the domestic sphere in its widest meaning. The adoption of a freer sex code by a portion of women swept by sentiment coming from the War especially added to the confusion. The military mortalities, although less significant here than in the warring countries of Europe, had results that struck against sex equilibrium. Of American men who entered the army from Continental United States, leaving out Alaska and the Canal Zone, 118,279 died during World War I. This necessarily affected the balance of the sexes. The dysgenic effect of the War was another result that, as will be true of World War II, for a long time antagonized domestic welfare, especially as it had to do with the marriage possibilities and careers of the superior group of women. Nearly 237,000 American young men were rejected for military service on account of defects, a considerable proportion of which were hereditary. Of the total number of defectives exposed by examination, eighty-three per cent were sent back home where in the natural course of things, particularly in the War situation and its aftermath, many of them married and became parents.

From the opposite quarter came a different sort of dysgenic influence. The enlistment of men whose achievement gave presumption of superior endowments was greater than that representing the population as a whole. This appears in the following table:

TABLE V [4]

Group	Number in Group	Per Cent Enlisted
Continental United States	15,639,178	11.67 ± .005
Doctor of Philosophy or of Science	636	17.14 ± 1.01
Master of Arts or of Science	2,278	17.95 ± .54
Graduates with distinction	2,969	22.06 ± .51
Bachelor of Law or Doctor of Juridical Science	3,234	25.57 ± .52
Graduates without distinction	7,243	28.88 ± .36
Doctor of Medicine or of Public Health	1,183	39.31 ± .96

It is estimated that the death rate of Harvard men was forty-one per cent higher than that of the soldiers of the United States taken as a whole.[5] Thus from this angle World War I complicated the lives of women influenced by its results. Some it sentenced to the single life. Others married but on a lower mating level than would otherwise have occurred. Some were led away from marriage by their war-time experience and still others were repelled from marriage by a dearth in their social contacts of the type of men that could attract them.

The effect of the War on the vocational opportunities of women is most apparent and easily lends itself to statistical statement. The conflict forced an immediate tremendous expansion of industry and an unparalleled readjustment. The stable manufacturing processes had to be carried on in a way to pour out ever-increasing quantities of supplies, and in addition there was a vast range of productive and distributing activities that were directly created by needs developed by the War itself. These latter included chemicals and ammunition and the shipping required to get to France the military supplies that became more and more decisive in the contest between German submarines and the allied blockade.

Some idea of the great quantity of supplies demanded appears in the following official statement of the War Department: "in the American ordnance catalogue of supplies during the recent war [World War I] there were over a hundred thousand separate and distinct items."[6] Great factories found themselves called upon to furnish, for the successful prosecution of the War, vast supplies of materials and arms necessary which they had never manufactured in peace time. This enlargement and reshaping of mass production not only offered new opportunities for women as wage earners but also made their employment imperative.

The longer the War continued and the more soldiers were transported to Europe, the greater grew the demand for women's labor. This was true in every occupation that made definite contribution to the carrying on of the War. A few illustrations of the increase of women workers in certain industries give a picture of what was happening. One hundred and eleven plants making explosives were reported as employing only seventy-three women in the 1914 census, while after the second draft twenty-five plants had nearly 12,000 women workers.[7] Factories manufacturing airplanes and airplane parts numbered sixteen in 1914 and had one woman among 211 wage earners. In contrast with this at the height of the War, after the second draft, we find forty plants having 6,118 women in a total of 26,470 wage earners. One firm producing hand grenades reports that nineteen out of every twenty workers were women. In a factory making gas masks, 8,500 out of 12,000 employees were women. The number of women per thousand of employed persons in the major industries in 1916, after the first draft, compared with what was true after the second draft, shows the effect of the war. This is the record:

TABLE VI [8]

Industry	\multicolumn{3}{c}{Women Number per 1,000 employed}
	1916	After first draft	After second draft
Iron and steel and their products	65	108	157
Metal and metal products other than iron and steel	152	167	206
Lumber and its remanufactures	31	45	114
Leather and its finished products	252	286	316
Chemicals and allied products	35	69	131
Automobiles, including bodies and parts	47	59	175
Electrical machinery, apparatus, and supplies	114	62	233
Instruments, scientific and professional	74	219	237
Other industries	144	182	237

The demand for woman's labor created by the War was reinforced by two other conditions. The great influenza epidemic of 1918 created a shortage of workers of both sexes. The decrease in immigration also cut off a supply of labor that from colonial days onward had been attracted by the opportunities offered on this side of the Atlantic for personal advancement. However important the part women played in the productive activities of the nation during the War period, the essential thing that came from their increased employment, so far as their status was concerned, was the further breaking down of barriers that arbitrarily had restricted the occupations of women. They proved themselves efficient along lines that industrial conventions would have kept foreign to them, had it not been for the necessity of their labor as a result of war conditions.

They could not hold all the ground they had taken, once the men came back from France. Against them were previous industrial habits, prejudices of employers and male workers, and in many cases the promises of reëmployment made to the men at the time they enlisted. Undoubtedly, some women were carrying on in businesses and in factories less adequately than the men of experience whom they had replaced. The opposite also was true. Nevertheless, even though a part of this progress of women in industry represented a temporary expediency, there came from it increased tolerance of the woman worker in industry and a much greater appreciation of her adaptability and efficiency. This change of mind came to women as to men who, had it not been for the demonstration during the War period, would have continued strong in prejudice against any further going out of the home by women to enter gainful occupations.

The experiment of opening to women opportunities in skilled work in iron, steel, and other metal industries, had consequences more lasting than the specialized activities called forth by the War. The type of labor demanded was similar to that required in peace time in many types of manufacturing such as the making of automobile parts, optical material and instruments, airplanes, and the like. In other words, women were introduced to new craft processes and in these fields proved their ability to carry on. As a result, when the production of war materials in the metal industries came to an end, the newly opened gates were not entirely closed to women. A portion of them maintained their footing in peace industry in lines of work where precision and attentiveness were prerequisites of skill and man's superior muscular strength of no consequence.

Women would have held a greater portion of this territory which they invaded under war pressure had it not been for a considerable feeling against their employment on the part of their fellow male workers. The unions of these industries were strongly organized, and although women were not often formally declared ineligible to membership, sentiment was against their becoming members, and on occasion this opposition took positive form. Many of these organizations required a long apprenticeship under conditions that frequently excluded the possibility of women starting the trade. Union laborers were willing to accept the employment of women in their trades as a substitution for male workers during the War period when they were not sympathetic toward their permanent employment. An example of this handicap of women, due to union policy, appears in the fact that in 1918 we find about 400,000 members of the machinists' union, only about 12,500 of whom were women.[9]

During the War emergency some firms had provided special training for women as a substitute for apprenticeship, but with the coming of peace there was no longer need of such activities and they were discontinued. In spite of the natural reaction to the flowing in of women in the metal trades with the ending of the War, we find from the reports of 562 firms that after the second draft 37,683 women of the 68,717 that had been substituted for men in various industries were employed in the metal trades.[10]

The demand for quantity production in all industries affected by the War made the greater employment of women in industry a necessity. Women responded to their new opportunities with varying motives. Some were forced to work in order to make up loss of family income as the result of son, husband, or father having enlisted. Some, especially married women, were attracted by the appeal of patriotism or the novelty of new undertakings. Other women merely returned to occupations which they had previously followed but had left because of marriage or parenthood. In industries situated in small towns and villages there developed a local patriotism to support the manufacturers who urged the coöperation of women that they might be able to fulfill their war orders. Some women went to work because they had left their homes to follow their husbands who had been assigned to some cantonment or war undertaking. Sometimes an advertising campaign was carried on in the larger cities in order to gather in enough women workers. There was a growth also in the number of part-time women workers.

The need of workers and the competition between employers for their services tended to lift wages for women as it did for men. It is easy now to see the effect of this upon women through the fear of men in charge of industries in which there had been many women workers before the War that women were having their heads turned and would be dissatisfied with normal conditions at the coming of peace. Trade journals also reflected this feeling. An example is an article in the *Textile World Journal,* the spirit of which appears in the following sentence: "Women have been able to do such good work in new occupations that they will likely remain 'on the job' even after normal conditions as to labor supply have been restored." [11]

This expansion of opportunity for women in industry caused by the War added itself to the other influences coming from the conflict that were making women more self-confident and freer from artificial limitations. A similar result appeared in the college group through the experiences of those who entered actively into such war work as nursing, ambulance driving, recreational organization, public speaking, and the like. Barriers to which women had been so long accustomed that they took them as a matter of course were pushed aside by the force of circumstances, and opportunity, new adventure, and social tolerance gave many women a chance to prove their worth in unexpected activities, thereby gaining a self-realization which was largely thrust upon them and a self-expression that they had not consciously sought. Naturally their line of advance went farther ahead than could be maintained once the War came to an end.

The reaction that came with peace became in turn a surprise and many found themselves driven from work that they were doing efficiently merely because men were protected by better organization and by a masculine social code. Individual women felt the injustice of being thrown out of occupations in order to make place for returning soldiers. Many of the latter thought themselves even more unjustly treated when they were not given back their former jobs because women taken on as substitutes had become permanent employees. A consequence of this industrial disturbance was a heightening of the feeling of self-interest on the part of many groups of men and of many groups of women. The final effect of women's experience on industry because of war needs was toward increasing their economic independence and their desires for greater equality with men.

The largest reduction in the demand for women laborers after the coming of peace was in the iron, steel, and chemical industries. This was true of male workers also. In the textile industries, although there was a greater proportionate decline in the employment offered women as compared with men, the demand of employers for women workers was more than twice that for men. Another fact that brings out what was happening to a vast number of women was the increased demand and supply of labor in domestic and personal service. Although the increase here was relatively greater in the case of men than of women, the actual number of men employed was small in comparison with the group of women that shifted from industrial occupations to their former type of employment.[12]

In April, 1930, according to the census reports, there were 10,752,116 American women who could be classified as gainfully employed. This represented an advance of 25.8 per cent in the ten year period. During the same time the increase of all females ten years of age and over was 20.6 per cent.[13] In order to get clear how strongly women were entrenched in work for wages and salaries outside the home, these statistics must be put beside an increase in gainfully employed women during the preceding ten years of 2,202,605, a net gain of less than half a million, or but six per cent. Perhaps the best way to illustrate trends in women's work outside the family is to list the proportion of men employed per hundred women in the ten main occupational groups. This is done by the following table:

TABLE VII [14]

MEN PER 100 WOMEN IN EACH OF 10 MAJOR OCCUPATIONAL GROUPS: 1930, 1920, AND 1910.

Occupational group	Men per 100 women		
	1930	1920	1910
All occupations	354	387	373
Servants and allied occupations	36	35	24
Clerical and kindred pursuits	112	129	214
Factory and laundry employees	271	294	282
Professional pursuits	104	109	128
Agricultural pursuits	1,078	909	599
Saleswomen, "clerks" in stores, etc.	270	232	296
Housekeepers, stewardesses, and practical nurses	9	11	11
Telephone and telegraph operators	28	38	74
Business men and business women	1,384	1,773	2,044
Sewing occupations	69	48	27
All other occupations	2,576	3,183	3,074

Between 1910 and 1930 the number of women who could be classified as in business and the professions more than doubled while saleswomen, clerks in stores, and women engaged in other selling occupations increased 93.3 per cent. It is interesting to find women engaged in operating or managing business concerns increasing from 114,133 in 1910 to 262,950 in 1930, or 130.4 per cent. Women engaged in personal services that can be classified as beauty culture increased in the ten years nearly three and one-half times. There was a marked decrease in women engaged in agriculture, leaving out those who owned and operated their own farms. In this group there was little change. The great decline in agriculture has been explained in part by more careful classification in the census returns. There were fewer women working in the sewing trade. In 1930 there were only thirty-six per cent of the number so engaged in 1910.

New inventions and improvements in existing machinery have profoundly affected the employment of women. The trend has been for new developments to encourage the employment of women. An example of this appears in the cigar making industry.

As machinery has taken the place of hand labor, it has led to an increase in the proportion of women workers. The large-scale, machine-equipped cigar making plants in Ohio are illustrations. Except for a few maintenance men, the employees were women and the manufacturers affirmed that they were preferred because they were faster, neater, and more economical wrappers than were men.[15]

It is, however, in the typewriter and the telephone that we have the clearest picture of the way in which the increased use of mechanical devices led to the opening up of new industrial fields for women. Shorthand and the typewriter brought a multitude of women into office work. The invention of other labor-saving office devices, such as the calculating machine, and the specialization that has come about in large offices have developed new fields of occupation that have been increasingly attractive to women.

Between 1910 and 1920 there was an increase of women workers in clerical occupations of 140 per cent and during the next ten years of forty per cent. In the same periods male workers increased sixty per cent and twenty-one per cent. This probably means that women have somewhat displaced men and even more that the new opportunities that have come have been filled more by women than by men. Indeed, a study of the clerical field made in 1927 revealed that in the minds of office managers typing, stenography, office machine operating, bookkeeping machine operating, filing, and secretarial work were thought of as "women's trades."[16] On a higher level we have private secretaries, public stenographers, accountants, court reporters, and the like, that constitute an aristocratic invasion by women of the field of office and managerial occupations.

The telephone has led to a great army of women employees. Feminine qualities, whatever the explanation of their origin, appear always to have favored the employment of women in this field. The introduction of the automatic telephone has lessened the employment of women, and since 1920 there has been a disproportionate rise in the employment of men.[17] Since women were so largely employed at the switchboard, the installation of a mechanical device to do their work automatically affected them as workers more than men, who were chiefly employed in other lines of the industry. Undoubtedly these same feminine qualities that gave women a psychological advantage as competitors with men in telephone operation also helped them in clerical work, particularly in typing and stenography. Feminine qualities must not be thought of as synonymous with sex differences. They are composite, as clearly and as certainly environmental in origin as products of heredity.

It is most misleading to consider the increasing employment of women outside the home during the period as merely indicative of changed attitudes toward the family or of desires for economic independence. As a matter of fact, in a great number of cases there was no choice. Economic pressure was so severe that the woman could do nothing else but go out and try to add to the inadequate income of the male supporter of the family or assume the full responsibility of maintaining a family on account of the death of the husband or his divorce or disappearance.

A great many unmarried women also had no choice. Parents or other relatives were dependent in part, and in some cases fully, upon a daughter's or sister's earnings. Studies that have been made suggest that daughters are in such cases more loyal to family obligations than are sons. This working for the family is of course nothing new but merely an expression in out-of-the-home employment of what in earlier times was carried out in the house or on the farm or through a combination of domestic and agricultural labor.

There is another motive which leads to women's employment outside the family that explains the presence of a great multitude of women in industry, business, and even in the professions. The male supporter of the family in many instances cannot provide adequate income or at least not enough to maintain the standard of living that husband and wife think necessary. This is frequently true in the early years of marriage. Were it not possible for the woman after the wedding to continue in some sort of out-of-the-home employment, the marriage would be delayed for economic reasons. This not only explains the gainful employment of a large group of women but also brings to the surface a complex problem that has great domestic and social significance.

The fact that these women temporarily do go out to work for wages, but with the intention as soon as possible of abandoning their occupation in order to give full time to the home, affects the industrial status of women, their wages, and in cases not a few the wages of their husbands. This program assumes the possibility of delaying parenthood and this in turn demands an effective, available knowledge of birth control. This disposition to look upon employment as mere temporary expediency discourages the organization of employed women as a means of economic group protection and as a consequence encourages their exploitation and adds to the tendency already strong to continue a double standard of wages established not on an efficiency but on a sex basis.

A proportion of these women from choice or from necessity continue their employment outside the home even though they persist in looking forward eventually to leaving it for the career of wife or mother. There are a great many women workers who seek wages to lift their standard of living or to provide luxuries during the courtship period as they seek to find their mate. This group tends to obscure the significance in industry of those other women who are heads of households or persons who support from their earnings dependents and are therefore as committed to employment outside the home as are men. They carry the same burden as the male bread earner but with added handicaps because of their sex. Industry and business are apt to group them with the other type of women rather than with men who like themselves expect to continue in gainful employment.

The necessity of some women going out to earn a living in industry and businesses standardized to masculine interests, the disposition of other women to seek employment as a mere stop-gap experience, the opportunity both groups provide for exploitation, and women's lack of organization, work together to make their employment outside the family a major social and economic problem. The growth of humanitarianism in the field of industry and the prevailing notion of woman's frailty, in no small measure the result of conditions due to prevailing conventions of dress that restricted outdoor life and the like, naturally led to agitation for protective laws to safeguard women as potential mothers and as members of the weaker sex. During the period a great part of the energy of the Woman's Movement turned to agitation for labor legislation to improve the conditions of woman's work and strengthen her economic security and to lessen the evils of child labor.

Since it was obvious that women were being discriminated against, it was inevitable that women leaders and their men allies interested in the welfare of the working woman turn to state and national authority for legal protection against the exploiting of women. Far-sighted employers, unlike the opposite type, finding themselves helpless to safeguard their women workers because of economic competition, welcomed legislation that would standardize the conditions of an entire industry. There were, however, impediments of a legal nature that retarded the development of this legislation, and implications that were bound to appear eventually and alienate from such a program for dealing with the industrial problems a considerable group of women who preferred to wipe away all discriminations against woman rather than protect her in her weakness.

Even those who now sympathize with this second group must realize the naturalness of the first approach and its seasonable advantages. Such an attack was encouraged also by the tendency of American people to look to the law to cope with difficulties that often are too deep to be reached by legislative enactments unless these are enforced by changes in the thinking and social habits of a great part of the population.

Women as they went into industry were indeed the weaker sex and liable to greater exploitation than the men. The sweating industries in their earlier period, when great numbers of women were employed at inadequate wages and under unsanitary conditions, became an object lesson of the risks associated with women's entrance into gainful employment. This was but one example of the unwholesome working conditions and insufficient earnings forced upon women because of their inferiority status in industry.

Public-minded men and women who thought through the consequences of this predicament of women as wage earners recognized the menace this was not only to the women as individuals but in the long run to the vitality of the nation, and in increasing numbers and with greater aggressiveness they sought legal protection for the women workers. These efforts at reform were directed along two lines, the regulation of woman's employment and in certain occupations its prohibition. The first program concentrated on shortening the working day, making night work illegal, improving hygienic conditions, and requiring opportunities for relaxation and the establishing of minimum wages. In the belief that women could not safely carry on in certain vocations, laws were advocated to make their employment in such industries illegal.

The task that confronted those interested in protective legislation for women was formidable and their progress painfully slow, requiring an enormous expenditure of energy in social education, in advocating definite bills before state legislatures and the Federal congress, in defending laws passed, when their constitutionality was attacked in the courts, and in demanding adequate and honest enforcement of the laws enacted by responsible officials.

Those who were advancing this program could not expect any considerable amount of active support from the beneficiaries. Many working women were indifferent to their industrial status because they regarded their employment as a short-time expediency, and others dared not endanger their jobs by any protest. Many working men took little interest in these agitations for bettering the conditions of women in industry because they were prejudiced against the presence of women and wished to do nothing to attract more women to employment that would increase their competition with men. In addition to the inertia to be expected under the circumstances the advocates of legislative reforms encountered opposition from persons whose interests were or were interpreted to be affected adversely by the specific laws proposed in the effort to safeguard women workers.

The first attempt to regulate by law the length of the working day appeared in an act passed by the legislature of New Hampshire as early as 1847. This made the standard working day ten hours, although there was a provision which in practice emasculated the statute, that the period of actual labor could be more when agreed to by both parties. This, of course, had no special application to women, and it was not until 1887 that a maximum ten-hour day and sixty-hour week working period was made the legal standard exclusively for women.

Florence Kelley has dated the effort to reform women's working conditions by enactments of law as beginning in 1876. The history of the agitation divides into two epochs, the first when the attention of the reformers was chiefly devoted to the getting of laws passed and the second when they were establishing the constitutionality of the legislation. Increasing bitterness was felt by the advocates of the regulating and prohibiting laws for the welfare of women when the fate of these enactments was decided not by their advantage or drawback to women but by the opinion of the majority of the courts as to their legal status, a judgment that was interpreted as often merely reflecting the economic attitudes of the judges themselves. Actually the judiciary itself was thrown into the dilemma inevitable in a government based upon a written constitution in a period of rapid transition. On the one hand not only was the letter but sometimes the spirit of the basic law challenged by the new enactments. On the other hand was the pressure of change from an unprecedented situation, creating manifest evils that needed correction, and demanding legislation in the effort to conserve human welfare.

It was not, however, enough to pass laws. A reconstruction had to take place in legal thinking. Undoubtedly, as is always true in human experience, the individual dispositions and backgrounds of the judges at times influenced their decisions, but nevertheless it was also logic rather than personal feeling that in many instances led to decisions of unconstitutionality. Whatever the motivation, the definite verdicts of the courts throwing out laws that had been finally passed through the great effort of the reformers led to the emotional indictment of judges as lacking in humanitarian outlook, in sensitiveness to human progress, and even as being prejudiced toward vested interests.

However discouraging the adverse decisions were to the promoters of legislation designed to protect the interests of women in industry, the legal trend was unmistakable and, taking into account the historic background and strength of the obstructing traditions, now seems relatively rapid. By 1931 there were only four states without some sort of law regulating the hours of work for women. Ten states had limited this work period to a day of eight-hours. Nineteen states and the District of Columbia had passed statutes requiring breaks in the period of women's employment. Thirteen states made it necessary that a period of time ranging from thirty minutes to an hour be provided for meals.

Twelve states and the District of Columbia limited the hours the woman could be permitted to work, usually five or six, before having an opportunity to rest or eat. Sixteen states made the night work of women in certain occupations or industries unlawful. At that time there were only twenty-two states and the District of Columbia that had no legislation regarding the conditions under which women could work in industries considered especially hazardous or prohibiting their employment under any conditions. Six states made unlawful the employment of women for certain periods preceding and following childbirth. Mississippi appears at the time to have been the only state that did not require by law some seating accommodation for women workers.[18] At the close of 1935 we find mandatory minimum wage laws in sixteen states. Three additional states had passed laws that were not carried out through lack of appropriation. In all of these states but one the laws are applicable to women and to minors of both sexes. In Minnesota the law was held constitutional only as it applied to minors. In South Dakota the act covered only girls and women. In seven states all occupations are included, but in practice Wisconsin was the only one of them that regulated the rates of domestic workers, and no state attempted to set a minimum for women in agriculture. Because of a decision adverse to the attempt to fix a minimum wage on the basis of the cost of living,[19] the minimum wage laws had been framed on the principle of a fair return for the services rendered.

It had been supposed that the principle of the earlier legislation had been decided as within the Constitution by the evenly divided decision of the United States Supreme Court handed down in 1917. Upon an appeal, however, to the highest court against the decision of the Court of Appeals, the District of Columbia law establishing a minimum wage on the basis of living costs was declared unconstitutional in so far as it applied to adult women. This explains the reshaping of the legislation so that the minimum basic wage was defined as a fair return for the services rendered.[20]

This adverse decision of 1923 has given the minimum wage movement in the United States a precarious legal status. Massachusetts, for example, in the effort to protect its law, has created no penalty other than publicity for wage scales below the minimum. In some states the law has been secured by the support of employers in the absence of any legal test of constitutionality. This type of legislation represents the most definite attempt to distinguish women's interests in industry and to give them on a sex basis special protection. The history of the passage of the first minimum wage law in Massachusetts in 1912 reveals the wide support the legislation received from women's organizations. Investigations carried on by the Federal Bureau of Labor had awakened a great many public-spirited citizens to the unfortunate situation of a multitude of women and child laborers. Labor unions, representing both men and women, committed themselves to the demand for minimum wage legislation.

A bill was introduced in the legislature and passed without significant opposition, creating a commission to study the wages of women and minors and to report on the advisability of establishing a minimum wage board. A commission of five was appointed, headed by Henry Le Favour, president of Simmons College,[21] and its findings and recommendations were sent to the legislature in 1912. The suggestion of one of the members of the commission that the law be made non-mandatory, that is, that it be enforced only by pressure of public opinion, was incorporated in the law passed in 1912 largely through the influence of those who were not in sympathy with the legislation and against the preference of the majority of its promoters. Experience seems to have proved that this provision has not destroyed the effectiveness of the legislation. There has been, however, a constant bombarding of the law. Up to 1928 it had been twice tested before the courts as to its constitutionality and twice sustained. Four different attempts have been made to get the legislature to repeal it.[22]

As a rule legislation for the protection of women in industry has received the support of male labor unions. This has been given on humanitarian grounds, but it is obvious that the motives of self-interest also have determined their attitude. They have favored legislation in the attempt to protect their own position while lessening competition from poorly paid women. Frequently laws have been pushed in the belief that the gain made by women would open up opportunity for similar advance on the part of male workers. Legislation has also been encouraged by male organizations with the avowed purpose of safeguarding the welfare of women when the effect of the legislation has been to shut out women from industries where their competition was feared. Examples of this sort of legislation are the law passed in 1899 in New York prohibiting women from operating or using machines for buffing and polishing and the laws of Massachusetts and New York of 1912 and 1913 regulating the work of women in core rooms.[23]

As the various laws aimed to protect women in industry from exploitation and to safeguard their interests went forward, successfully surmounting one legal hurdle after another, the essential principle of such laws began to be challenged by a group of women who grew more and more convinced that these attempts to improve the working conditions of women were certain to prove in the long run a handicap. They felt that all the laws creating a special class on the basis of sex were cementing in the legal system a recognition of the inferiority of women and thereby creating restrictions and limitations that could only hamper women whose weakness in industry fundamentally came from a social status that denied them the rights of men.

To these women the proper strategy for advancing the welfare of woman as a class was to seek to establish their full legal and political equality with men, and in their opinion the great body of legislation that had been passed as a special protection for the sex evaded the real issue and obstructed the progress of women toward the goal that alone could bring them social justice. About this point of view the National Woman's Party rallied. Their insistence that the practical effect of most of the legislation that had aimed at the improvement of women's conditions was to create a sex liability in the economic field, thus weakening the position of women in industry and building up an artificial advantage for men, made imperative an investigation of the practical effect of the laws that were being enacted to help women in industry.

The controversy soon appeared to be fundamental, affecting both the strategy and the tactics of the Woman's Movement. Recognizing the significance of this challenge of what had become the established routine for advancing woman's welfare, the Woman's Bureau of the Department of Labor appointed a committee of specialists to investigate the practical consequences of labor legislation affecting the employment of women.

In any attempt to appraise the evidence of the advantage or disadvantage of this legislation as it pertains to women, certain distinctions must be kept in mind. There is a difference between passing laws to regulate labor conditions of women in a definite industry and passing laws that, although they refer to both sexes alike, chiefly or perhaps exclusively affect women because the latter predominate in a certain branch of industry or even in the entire industry. There is also a difference between the direct, specific consequences of such legislation and what may be termed its suggestive cumulative tendencies.

Although the first is by no means a simple matter, investigation with reference to it can approximate statistical measurement. The second is much more subtle. It represents the liability of the laws as they tend to build up the idea of woman's weakness and inequality and to foster among employers the feeling of preference for the male worker as a freer, more mature type of worker. This suggestion which encourages prejudice may not prevent the hiring of women because they may be economically indispensable or at least more desirable than men but tends nevertheless toward giving women an inferior status, the basic cause of the exploitation that the protective legislation has attempted to correct.

The report of the commission investigating the effect of this protective labor legislation for women upon their industrial opportunities may be briefly summarized as follows: It is difficult to measure the effect of the prohibitory laws as they affect women in industry. Since women are employed in many of these occupations in states where they are free to work there does appear to be some loss of opportunity for employment. The regulatory laws act as a rule to establish proper standards and do not handicap women. In slight degree the opposite is true, where the regulations have been applied to specific occupations not entirely akin to the industrial work for which the laws were drawn. Laws against night work for women as a rule merely express the policy of employers not to hire women but in some instances have lessened their opportunities for work. When these prohibitions have been applied to professional or semiprofessional women they have been a definite handicap.

The commission states that the more serious influences that hamper women are independent of laws attempting to regulate the hours or the conditions of working women. Labor supply, its cost, the nature of the manufacturing processes, and the general psychology of the times appear to be the more important influences that limit women in industry.[24] In regard to the last of these the question naturally arises as to how far this special legislation for the protection of women is an expression of this psychology, basically the notion of woman's inferiority, and whether in any degree such protective legislation perpetuates and encourages such an idea.

This difference in policy brings to the surface the fundamental issue whether it is better for the American woman to have special legal protection, which assumes her inferior position because of her disabilities, or whether all legislation of this type regarding industry should be made applicable to both sexes even though in practice it may chiefly concern women. The latter program also raises the question whether legislation of this kind affecting both sexes should enforce standards representing man's or woman's status in industry. Any attempt to think this through brings one face to face with the final problem whether there is a biological difference between men and women, as expressed in industry, that demands that women be given special consideration.

The depression starting in 1929 brought to the nearly eleven million gainfully employed women the same problems of insecurity and loss of jobs that it put upon working men. Although unfortunately not the first depression in our history, it is unique in so far as American women are concerned, because it came when the Woman's Rights Movement was at full tide. So much had been made of the opportunity of the woman of ability, skill, and ambition in business and the professions that her subsequent loss of position or decrease in salary came as a shock, she had become so certain of her security.

Never before had so many women with this outlook and self-assurance suffered because of industrial prostration. Their background, their training, and their previous feeling of independence forbade their being passive victims. They were accustomed to self-expression and, unlike most employed women in earlier depressions, refused to be silent sufferers. Those who had been complacent, feeling that woman's only serious obstruction was her still persisting inequality with men, were thrown into uncertainty and forced to re-think the problems of woman's progress.[25] Their predicament could not be conceived of as merely feminine. They were fellow-sufferers with men and their experience led them to scrutinize the economic situation without reference to sex. This was not true of many individuals who found themselves eliminated from employment because when there was a shrinkage of business men were preferred.

On the whole, however, the depression appears to have struck men harder than women. At least from a study made in 1931 it seems as if the percentage of unemployment of women was much less than that of men. This investigation found 26.2 per cent of men unemployed as compared with 18.9 per cent of women.[26] A survey of conditions in South Bend, Indiana, from August 1, 1931 to July 31, 1932, again shows that women gainfully employed were more fortunate than men. More than three-fourths of all the women had obtained some employment during the year as compared with not quite three-fifths of the men and women workers taken together.[27]

The composition of these women workers shows most of them employed in manufacturing, the next largest part in domestic and personal service, somewhat less in clerical service, and a much smaller number in stores. Undoubtedly the women who had pushed farthest forward in the new openings found by them, where competition with trained men was keenest, suffered most and it was chiefly in this group that we find the leadership of the Woman's Movement of the period.

The depression not only brought them face to face with a decrease of income or loss of position, it also revived prejudices and struck at the status women had already achieved. Men became vociferous in their demands that since there were too few jobs for all women go back to their families and give males the right of way.[28] Particularly was there insistence that the married woman surrender her position, and in many fields this sentiment began to discriminate against the married woman without regard to whether she was the main support of a family or the source of necessary supplementary income. One consequence of this was to discourage the marriage of young people who dared not enter matrimony when it would become a hazard to the joint earnings without which they could not establish a home of their own.

This blocking of what had become for many the only entrance into marriage led in a proportion of cases to a repudiation of the conventional sex code. This reaction, which is always liable to occur when the roadway to marriage is obstructed, was stimulated, rationalized, and popularized by new knowledge gathered by recent science as to the physiological and nervous significance of mature sex adjustment. The widespread knowledge of birth control practices, by removing fear of pregnancy, led a part of the young men and women who were denied marriage to accept a substitute for what they preferred or at least what under ordinary circumstances most of them would have sought.

In addition to these consequences of the depression peculiar to the new conditions of women, we have also the widespread family disturbance through unemployment, loss of savings, reduced income, lower standards of living, that always had burdened women as mothers and as wives in times of economic disturbance and insecurity. The chief reactions to their experiences are found within the family routine. Husbands and wives grew apart or in other families grew closer together as a result of their ordeal. A great proportion, however, registered the bewilderment that comes from having familiar moorings cut and feeling adrift. This recoil from the unexpected necessity of reshaping family finances was less pointed among the women who had been economically self-sustaining in business and the professions, but it was massive and deep.

The struggle for the right of suffrage came to an end during World War I. Throughout the period the advance of this cause, although intermittent, went forward and the trend forecast the eventual surrender of the opposition. The crisis came in 1912. That was the year when the new Progressive party made its appearance in the national campaign. This party was committed to woman suffrage, and the effect that it had in breaking Republican ranks and electing Woodrow Wilson tended toward strengthening the movement for suffrage. Since the Constitution of the United States left to the states the right to regulate the manner of election of presidential electors, the leaders in woman suffrage in Illinois in 1913 brought to the legislature a bill giving women the right to vote in municipal and presidential suffrage, meaning the right to vote for any state officer not especially named by the State Constitution as one to be elected by male voters.

Bitter and strong hostility against the bill developed, but the progressive members of the legislature held the balance of power over all law-making. Finally, after every effort had failed to keep the bill from coming up for decision, it was permitted to come to a vote, and after five hours' debate was passed in the Senate. The record was twenty-nine ayes and fifteen nays; and in the House, eighty-three ayes and fifty-eight nays.[29] The effect of the passage of this bill was immediate and tremendous on political sentiment. Up to this time no great state with a large number of electoral votes had been committed to suffrage. Now there were twenty-nine electoral votes coming from a suffrage state that had to be reckoned with in the building of political strategy. It is said that at the first Illinois election after the passage of this law, 250,000 women in Chicago alone voted.

The women voting in this municipal election in Illinois, their first suffrage test, revealed a decided trend toward local option in the effort to curb intemperance, and this led the liquor interests of the state to test the constitutionality of the Suffrage Bill. This attack added to the suffrage cause a considerable number of persons who were chiefly concerned with the evils of intemperance and committed to its solution through prohibition. In 1914 the entire bill, and not merely its municipal features which had been made a point of contest by saloon interests, came before the Supreme Court of the state and was upheld. Immediately the opponents strove to repeal the bill but the support behind it was too substantial, and it became clear that this gain of suffrage by the women of the state would remain as a factor with which party strategists would have to reckon.

This same year Montana and Nevada granted women the right

to vote. These victories were cumulative. The suffrage cause was helped even more by the advantage of winning the legal battle in a clear testing of the constitutionality of the right of women to vote in presidential elections.

The passage of the Illinois law was the turning point in woman's struggle for suffrage in the United States. At the time this fact was obscured by the defeat suffered in other states. By 1918 fifteen states had granted women the suffrage, but of these only New York and Michigan were east of the Mississippi. None of these victories had come easily. One reason for the bitter, well-organized, powerful opposition was the connection in the public mind between prohibition and the equal suffrage movement. It seems an exaggeration to assert that had it not been for this alliance women would have been given the right to vote two generations earlier.[30] This statement minimizes the social inertia and the social prejudices that were the more fundamental barrier against the political advance of women. It is doubtful also whether, had it not been for the success of the prohibition movement, equal suffrage would have been delayed another generation.[31] Certainly many men and women sincerely against woman suffrage found in the general support of prohibition by suffrage leaders an illustration of their chief reason for their position. They felt that women, lacking in experience and being more easily swayed emotionally, would attempt to over-use the power of law to bring about immediate reforms.

Again and again men of influence like ex-President Taft,[32] utterly free from ulterior motives, registered their fear that if given the vote women would, because of their lack of experience and their emotional tendencies, use their newly-given political power to pass legislation that would make existing evils worse than ever. Writing in 1922, the leading sociologist of the time, Franklin H. Giddings, expressed his belief that the immediate effects of the influence of women as a class on public life would be harmful. He, too, indicted them for lack of experience and an emotionalism which tied them to an instinctive life from which their aggressive leaders vainly attempted to wean them.[33]

It is true that the liquor interests fought, tooth and nail, every attempt to advance woman suffrage, from motives of profit. Many men and women, however, who were on their side were as opposed to what the saloon stood for as the most ardent prohibitionist. They penetrated deeper into the meaning of the evils of intemperance and considered the program of prohibition supported by the vast majority of woman suffrage leaders a demonstration of the dangers of feminine influence in politics.

Without question women in greater proportion than men were responsible for the amendment to the Constitution that later established prohibition. The repeal of this is proof that the majority of American citizens finally decided that this most spectacular evidence of women's political impulse was disappointing and contrary to public policy. This repudiation of national prohibition only shows the naturalness and the strength of the opposition to suffrage that came from conservative people who distrusted a proposed policy which was regarded as a characteristic disclosure of feminine traits. Wholesome in the family, these qualities of woman were looked upon as dangerous outside the home, particularly in the realm of practical politics.

The evidence is clear now that if prohibition did not successfully solve the evil of intoxicants, it is just as certain that its repeal has done no better. It is, therefore, illogical to use the history of the Eighteenth Amendment as proof that the opponents of woman suffrage did correctly forecast the social hazards of the emotionalism, which they believed inborn in women. Women turned to the policy of prohibition in the characteristic American manner of those who have a fetish confidence in the power of law. At most the women can be charged with inexperience in the task of shifting strong, long-continued social habits.

There can be no question whether the women that made up the lobby maintained by the suffrage organization at Washington were competent realists. No group of persons interested in federal legislation ever studied Congress more thoroughly or came to understand better the tactics of political pressure. From the beginning the leaders of the movement had looked forward to a federal amendment enfranchising all women. They had devoted themselves to state campaigns from expediency, with their eyes always turned toward federal legislation. They were quick to sense the opportunity provided by World War I to push forward their demands for equal suffrage.

When the Wilson administration took office in March, 1913, the suffrage leaders at once brought forward their constitutional amendment providing for equal suffrage throughout the nation. This was taken up in the Senate in March, 1914, and rejected by a vote of thirty-five to thirty-four, the rest of the senators not voting. A two-thirds vote was necessary. The previous month a delegation had tried to enlist the interest of President Wilson. His position was that he could not commit himself since his party's platform upon which he had been elected had not endorsed woman suffrage.

Entrance of the United States into World War I and the services of women in connection with it gave great momentum to the suffrage movement. The amendment giving women the right to vote in the national election was passed by the House of Representatives in January, 1918. It failed in the Senate in the fall of 1918 and in the spring of 1919, through lack of a two-thirds majority. When the new Congress assembled, after President Wilson appeared before it and recommended the passage of the Federal Suffrage Amendment, the House readopted it by a larger majority than before, and on June 4, 1919, it was finally accepted by the Senate. By the end of the year twenty-two states had ratified and on August 18, 1920, Tennessee, by its approval of the Amendment, completed the thirty-six states required to make it law. The Nineteenth Amendment had been added to the Constitution about half a century after the passage of the Fifteenth Amendment which had been submitted in 1869.

In the twentieth century education specifically directed toward preparing women for their family responsibilities came to a mature expression. The program emphasized three distinct features: the economic housekeeping interest, child care and child-training activities, and the problems and practices of the husband-wife relationship. Their development historically as a definite instruction and technique were in the order of domestic science, parenthood education, and preparation for marriage. Instruction came from many sources. The first achieved the firmest foothold in the educational routine, the second more largely resulted from organizations carrying on adult education, and the third depended for the most part upon promotion carried on by interested individuals, as is still true, although increasingly it has found a place in the program of organizations. One of the first of these was the American Social Hygiene Association.

Looking backward, it is possible to find early in the preceding century evidences of educational thought that led toward formal domestic training in school and college. In 1814, for example, Emma Willard, as she planned for a female seminary in Troy, New York, included domestic education. She stated that housewifery might be greatly improved by being taught not only in practice but in theory.[34] She was unable to carry out her idea but she did emphasize the principles and habits looking toward efficiency in housekeeping through her management of dormitory life in her institution. Mary Lyon in 1837 also expressed an interest in training for domestic experience, although she felt that the actual instruction should be given in the home.

In 1840 Catherine Beecher made domestic education an important part of her effort to further educational reform. In that year her treatise on domestic economy for the use of young ladies at home and at school was published. It became a popular book, went through many editions, and attracted some attention among educators. This book has been declared the first textbook in home economics. It was based upon her belief that the proper education of man decides the welfare of an individual but when a woman is educated the interests of a whole family are secured.

These and other early glimpses of an approaching domestic science education indicate a foreseeing of changes taking place in the life of women that were bound to bring to maturity specific instruction for the vocation of homemaking chosen by most women. Science and invention were increasingly bringing information and improvement of technique applicable to the home, and these needed to be distributed through education. Increasing leisure and advancement along other lines of social experience meant that the standards in the home needed to be lifted and drudgery lessened. The rapid development of commercial productions that competed with family activities and more and more replaced them was changing the function of the housewife, making her less a work woman and more a manager.

The application of science to problems connected with child nurture, at first concentrating upon the physical care of the infant, grew not only as a special interest of preventive medicine, but as a new insight due to the recognition by more and more mothers of the significance of childhood experience in its social and psychic consequences. This better appreciation of the meaning of child life followed rapidly after the new understanding of the importance of the early physical career of the infant and child. The lifting of the standard of living, the increase of leisure, communication and cultural distribution provided the conditions necessary for a more efficient and science-regarding treatment of children. Undoubtedly the falling birth rate stressed the value of the child.

The third effort to conserve domestic interests by education followed the others. It was favored by the freer expression of domestic incompatibility, the increase in divorces, and the glimpses that science gave, leading toward realization of the physical and psychic importance of human sex adjustment. It was hindered, as indeed is still true, by the break that such a point of view made with the taboo attitude which so long had dominated. Its earliest expressions were outside the academic routine. The freer life of youth, their independence, the temporary anonymity provided by the automobile, the growth of serious literature in the science and ethics of sex, especially the Freudian hypothesis, the looser control of children by parents, the leisure and the pleasure trends, the spread of irresponsible ideas concerning sex that went on outside the family, the school, and the college had created and made more and more apparent the need of education for life including training for the family and for marriage.

The increase of women in industry and their entrance into the professions had never misled most of the leaders in the Woman's Rights Movement into forgetting that most women would find their careers within the home. Conviction grew in the minds of those who began to feel the force of the problems of women committed to domestic life that the home for such women must be more than a division of labor. Homekeeping was beginning to be a specialization in the same sense that this was true of a profession. The fact that it could be carried on by tradition as a routine did not mean that this program was either efficient or safe but merely that the non-competitive character of the household made it easier for women to fall behind the advance made possible by modern science, thus making family life an obstruction of social progress.

One of the women of the period who saw this clearly and expressed it with great force was Charlotte Perkins Gilman, regarded by many students of the period as the most thoughtful interpreter of the domestic needs of women. Her book *Women and Economics* became dynamic in its influence on the thinking of both the men and the women who were concerned with the problems of the family. It first charted the course that needed to be taken to provide preparation for family experience. In many respects the most significant book of special interest to women in its generation, it pled for the use of modern resources in household occupations, a reconstruction of the feminine ideal in order that women might be genuine partners to men, a refinement of sex that their fellowship might be on a higher plane than that of passion, and a maturing of the impulses of motherhood through the insight of science. The spirit of the book is expressed in this prophecy:

> The home would cease to be to us a workshop or a museum, and would become far more the personal expression of its occupants—the place of peace and rest, of love and privacy—than it can be in its present condition of arrested industrial develop-

ment. And woman will fill her place in those industries with far better results than are now provided by her ceaseless struggles, her conscientious devotion, her pathetic ignorance and inefficiency.[35]

Another pioneer pushing forward the modern concept of housewifery and motherhood was Anna Garlin Spencer, who appeared on the stage later when considerable instruction in preparation for household responsibilities was already in process. Her contribution came from the more adequate objectives she advocated in educational programs that were attempting to equip women resourcefully for their household responsibilities.

Mrs. Spencer was an ordained clergywoman who had become professor of sociology and social ethics at Meadeville Theological Seminary in 1913. That same year she brought out *Woman's Share in Social Culture,* which struck at the deficiency in woman's life through her failure to participate in just proportion in the advances of modern civilization.

Home economics as a field of instruction was gaining in both the high school and the college curricula. Conditions were ready for the next step in the development of science in preparation for the domestic career, and this was made when Mrs. Spencer started in the summer session at Teachers College, Columbia University, in 1919 a series of lectures on social problems of the family, which she was to continue for twelve years.

The next development came through offering a full-credit course of instruction at college level designed to prepare for family experience in all its aspects. This the author inaugurated at Boston University in 1922. This type of instruction was so in accord with the needs not only of women but of men that it developed rapidly throughout the country in both the Home Economics Departments and the Sociology Departments of colleges and universities. Now it is not only one of the standard courses of the college curriculum and one of the most popular, but even in a somewhat different form is spreading through the American high schools.

Any choice of a beginning of instruction for motherhood seems arbitrary because from the colonial period down we have evidence of at least spasmodic interest in parent education. The best way to distinguish this earlier attention from what is now an important part of our adult education program is to date the modern type of instruction from the time when the science of child-care rather than ethical and religious ideas was made its foundation. Even with this approach, the birth-moment in time and place cannot be safely placed. It is clear, however, that the motive and the material for the training of parents commenced to gain momentum from the time when G. Stanley Hall began his contribution to the field of child study at Clark University and from the period of Dr. L. Emmett Holt's book for mothers, *The Care and Feeding of Children,* which won widespread popularity.

Both of these influences appeared in the late part of the nineteenth century. The first more quickly influenced school practices and ideals. Nevertheless it began the building of an abundant literature out of which has come, as it has continued to develop, the material that gives substance to the present-day instruction of parenthood. This pioneering work at Clark University leaned toward the emotional and intellectual significance of childhood. Dr. Holt's contribution came out of the pioneering stage in preventive medicine. It tackled the problems of the physical care of the infant and young child, particularly that of feeding. The book not only represented the best thinking of medical science at the time but was so presented as to give mothers the practical help and confidence they needed in newer ways of dealing with the child, without which the great majority of them could not have been led to a better routine of child care.

The extraordinary spread of the idea of training for parenthood along the lines of both physical and psychic interests in childhood was so great during the first third of the twentieth century that it is evident that a multitude of women was conscious of the need of something better than the traditional background that had for so long dominated in parent-child relationships. Undoubtedly there is nothing in the period more revealing of its fundamental change in the woman's outlook upon life than this interest in child welfare. One of the evidences of this was the slight recognition, chiefly regarding the physical care of children, that appeared in the syllabus of home economics adopted by the American Home Economics Association in 1913.

The next year came the persuasive book by Dorothy Canfield Fisher, *Mothers and Children*. With the appearance of Norsworthy and Whitley's *Psychology of Childhood* in 1918, courses in child psychology began to be offered in a few universities. In 1917, through the insight and leadership of Bird T. Baldwin, who had studied with G. Stanley Hall, the Child Welfare Research Station was established at the University of Iowa. Another important departure was the starting of the nursery school at the Iowa State College of Agriculture and Mechanic Arts.

An additional expression of the new interest came through the organization of what is now the Child Study Association of America. This impetus, sponsored by the forerunner of the present organization, first appeared in 1888 as a single group of women and reflected the influence of Felix Adler, who also fathered the Ethical Culture School, one of the first attempts to give the child a new type of education in accord with the developing of the science of childhood.

The nursery school movement as it developed in the United States chiefly resulted from interest in the science of the child. Only incidentally was it an effort to relieve the mother from a portion of her responsibility for the training of the preschool child. From 1931 to 1932 there were 203 nursery schools, according to reports made to the Federal Office of Education. The new knowledge being gathered on the growth needs of the child not only influenced the practices of mothers but the demands they made upon the schools. The chief product of the latter trend was the progressive school idea which, breaking from the traditional routine of the public school system, found such a wide and varied outlet through private institutions that in 1919 there was founded through the effort of Stanwood Cobb, one of the pioneers of this movement, the Progressive

Education Association. These modern-spirited schools not only provided superior opportunity for children of favored families but also became a decided influence in leading to a measure of reform in the more conventional public school routine.

An original and increasingly productive means of preparing parents for their tasks and of supplementing their efforts to train the child through the application of the new knowledge of the science of human behavior appeared in the mental hygiene movement. This development started at least as early as 1896 through the work of the psychological clinic of Professor Lightner Witmer at the University of Pennsylvania. In 1909 we find William Healy directing a line of service in his study of the youthful offender at the Chicago Juvenile Psychopathic Institute. This innovation was made possible by the insight and support of Mrs. William F. Dummer of Chicago.

The work of Dr. Healy was broadened by his undertaking later a similar function under the auspices of the Judge Baker Foundation of Boston. The National Committee for Mental Hygiene, which came into being to carry out more effectively the mental hygiene program started by Clifford Beers, soon turned toward preventive work in the field of juvenile delinquency. From this effort, demonstrated by clinic organizations in several of the larger cities, came the Child Guidance Clinic. This organization not only provided help for parents in trouble but soon contributed greatly to the knowledge of the child and his needs and to the scientific literature which, accumulating from many different interests, was revealing both the necessity and the means of training mothers and fathers to meet in a modern way their parental obligations.

The wife's side of the woman's career in the home has received the latest expression so far as definite, systematic instruction is concerned, but as an interest receiving intermittent attention it also goes far back. This came chiefly through books dealing with some phase of the maternal relationship and appealing to laity readers. One of these discussions which perhaps can be reckoned in its point of view as the first of the development that took place was

Moral Physiology by Robert Dale Owen, published in 1830. This brief book, chiefly emphasizing contraception, had a wide reading. Seventy-five thousand copies were sold in the author's lifetime.

In 1832 a second discussion of the same type appeared, entitled *Fruits of Philosophy,* by Dr. Charles Knowlton. Each of these, although primarily interested in birth control, recognized the significance of sex adjustment in marriage. George H. Naphey's book, *The Physical Life of Woman: Advice to the Maiden, Wife, and Mother,* published in its fifth edition in 1875, seems now amazingly modern in its attitude and insight. A series of books that quickened the interest of the scientist in problems of sex was Havelock Ellis's *Studies in the Psychology of Sex* which were brought out by an American publisher beginning in 1897.

During the first third of the twentieth century a great variety of popular books attempting to interpret the art of love and to help men and women achieve marital happiness were published, and many of them had a large circulation. The great need and the very conscious desire for help on the part of both women and men provided not only a ready market for useful, serious, sincere discussions but also for exploitation. The difficulties created by the Comstock law and decisions of federal courts hampered writers and publishers from bringing forth the kind of material that would be most useful.

The franker social conventions became in dealing with the marital aspects of marriage, the more certain it appeared that there was need of specific instruction in preparation for marriage. The clergy came to realize the evils of this neglect of a much-needed instruction from their experiences as pastors, and in the twentieth century some among them began to advocate sex education and marriage preparation. The development of psychiatry, and particularly the contribution of Sigmund Freud and its popularization, greatly stimulated interest in problems of sex and made thoughtful people more conscious of the difficulties men and women of the modern world were having in their sexual careers both before and after marriage.

In the academic field the development of instruction in preparation for marriage was slowest of all. As a definite, factual, detailed study of equal rank with other subjects in the college curricula, it is very recent. Its inclusion in the college program has nearly always come from the demand of the students and until recently of men rather than women. Preceding this instruction, however, for a long time some attention, varying both in amount and in value, has been given certain aspects of courtship and marriage through instruction offered college students by physical education, social hygiene, and ethics departments.

The first course which attempted to prepare students on the college level to meet successfully the problems of marriage experience by means of specific credit-giving instruction was offered at the University of North Carolina in 1925. Although this came about at the request of the male members of the senior class, it is interesting to find that the incentive that led the students to petition for it came from a series of lectures given at Chapel Hill by Chloe Owings, at that time representing the American Social Hygiene Association. More than sixty years had passed before Herbert Spencer's plea that those directing education recognize that a program of preparation for life should include definite instruction for marriage had finally found recognition in a university curriculum.

Early in the twentieth century the interests of women began to get specific attention in undertakings authorized by federal and state governments to protect and promote the welfare of children and the home and especially of employed women. In 1907 Federal Congress appropriated three hundred thousand dollars that the Secretary of Commerce and Labor might investigate and report upon the industrial, social, moral, educational, and physical condition of the woman and child wage earner in the United States. When in 1911 this study was finished, its findings filled nineteen volumes. The report made a profound impression on the social thinking of the nation and led to the creation of the woman's division in the Department of Labor for the purpose of safeguarding the interests of women in industry.

In 1918 the Woman's Bureau began to function. Under Julia C. Lathrop the work of the Children's Bureau, which had started in 1912, had through its usefulness demonstrated the need of a similar organization to investigate the conditions of woman's labor in industry and to improve them. In spite of opposition, and with the backing of leading women's organizations, the Woman's Bureau was placed upon a permanent basis in 1920.

There was in the period a decided interest, which rapidly grew and expanded, in the problems of mothers attempting to care for dependent children, of maternal and infant mortality, and of illegitimacy. Laws providing for the subsidizing of mothers without adequate income, who were otherwise competent to care for their family, spread through the states, starting in a local district in Missouri in 1911. Massachusetts in 1913 passed a law establishing aid for mothers. The following shows the spirit of this legislation:

> Section 2. In every town the Overseers of the Public Welfare shall aid all such mothers, *if they are fit to bring up their children*. The aid furnished shall be sufficient *to enable them to bring up their children properly in their own homes*.[36]

A federal law, known as the Sheppard-Towner Act, passed by the Sixty-Seventh Congress in 1921 and approved by the President, sought to promote the welfare and hygiene of maternity and infancy. An appropriation of $1,240,000 for a five year period was authorized. Administration of this service was assigned to the Children's Bureau. At the time that this bill was introduced, the progress that was being made in the hygiene of maternity and infancy was chiefly in urban areas. The act not only extended this undertaking into the rural areas but did much to impress social workers and leaders of public opinion with the importance of the problems involved.

The taboos that had prevented a rational attack on illegitimacy, or what more generously was becoming increasingly known as unmarried motherhood, were dissolving under the influence of a more mature understanding of the problem and new trends showed both in public attitude and in the law leading toward a more just policy than that which had been enforced by tradition. This movement was influenced and strengthened by the interest of the Children's Bureau. Here again the greatest support of the reform came from women and from women's organizations.

The second decade of the twentieth century is notable in the number of beginnings that we find of movements which later became significant in the changing status of woman. One of these which is still highly controversial but commonly recognized as of the greatest importance was popularly known as birth control. It was in 1912 that Margaret Sanger, from her experience as a nurse, was driven to the conclusion that the only effective way of tackling the problems of poverty, ill health, and incompatibility that were rooted in excessive or too rapid births was to popularize a knowledge of contraception. Her efforts soon brought her in collision with the Comstock law passed in 1873. The struggle to legalize the contraceptive method of birth control was the most revolutionary of the happenings of concern to the American woman. The medical profession was as a whole indifferent or hostile. This also was true of the clergy and the churches. Birth control was too controversial a question to win the support of most of the leading women's organizations.

Women who from personal experience knew best the need of contraceptive knowledge were for the most part inarticulate. There were, however, trends in American life that were working on the side of the birth control agitation. Although the birth control movement still divides both men and women of social outlook into supporters and opponents, at the present time in the United States there are over five hundred birth control clinics [37] or medical centers giving contraceptive information, and a large number of private practitioners.

A different type of reform that also influenced marital conditions centered in the work of the American Social Hygiene Association, an organization which had started to lessen the menace of the venereal diseases. In the beginning this was promoted chiefly to deal with problems created by men, but its legislative and educational program has contributed greatly to the welfare of women and of children.

CHAPTER XI

THE AMERICAN WOMAN AND HER CHANGING STATUS

MODERN civilization everywhere has changed the life of woman. In the United States it has also changed her status. This is so obvious that only those untouched by the swift stream of modern culture or insensitive to its effects are unknowing of what has happened and what is still in process. Nothing is more distinctive in American civilization, more revealing of its temper, or more disturbing in its consequences. By forces chiefly of social origin woman has been moved toward a near-equality with man. Unless influences antagonistic to the long-continued trend appear and dominate—and at present they are not in evidence—the social momentum will carry American women still nearer to equality with men if not to a full cultural parity.

Even if during prehistoric or early historic periods the relation of the sexes has been similar to what now exists in our country, concerning which there is at present considerable controversy, the American situation is nevertheless unique. The conditions of modern life are so different, it is necessary to interpret the present status of woman as original, experimental, and possibly probationary. Moreover it can neither exist in its present form nor proceed further, as one would expect, without changing not only social experience in all its aspects but likewise the social disposition, the motivations, and the emotional reactions of woman herself.

Not only has there been a shifting of the foundations of our social institutions, but as their premises of masculine superiority are removed there must be still more, as well as a redirecting and qualifying of their functions. Most significant of all, there has been and must continue to be a reshaping of woman herself as she more consistently, habitually, and in some degree more consciously adapts herself to the new order. Nothing in social experience can be so revolutionary, indeed, nothing brought forth by American life has already had such far-flung, radical results. It is useless to say that what woman wants she will have, leaving the decision as to her future career to her innate cravings. She has no greater knowledge than man of her inmost uncoerced desires. She is in equal ignorance with him as to the consequences of the present trends that so concern her. Her wishes are concrete and particular responses to her circumstances and are essentially the outflowing of social currents more powerful than her own feeling. The motives that impel her are specific, temporary, and in great measure derivatives of mass suggestion.

There has been and there can be no plebiscite of women's motives or needs. Woman like man has to meet modern life as a pressing, untried, uncharted opportunity. In America she has been wrenched from the security of the old order as she has gained more than her sisters in ways that make for self-determination. Her passage from the old to the new has not been sudden, although, taking into account the rate with which society ordinarily changes, it has been rapid. In such reconstruction of the fundamentals of human experience strain is inevitable. It cannot be avoided by man and with greater meaning it is unescapable by woman. At present it appears in problems of concern to women in government, religion, ethics, education, and industry, and most important of all shows itself, in many cases as a disruptive force, in the family, in marriage, and in parenthood.

The present moment in the American woman's social status is highly transitional. Any description of what is now true can be realistic and interpretative only as it attempts to summarize woman's temporary situation as she stands, the product of the past and a major challenge to the future. It is not enough to catalogue the achievements of the American woman or to locate her present standing in the various lines of her advance. There is something intangible that goes beyond a mere record of the changes in status that have occurred. There is a more subtle but decisive transformation of attitude that may best be called social disposition or social personality. This essentially creates the new woman, and although it is a shift due to circumstances, it has meaning far beyond that of the forces which have brought it into being. It has brought forth the modern career for women who now wrestle with the problems of human existence in a setting altogether new.

The large number of women reported as gainfully employed in the twentieth census made clear how large a stake they had come to have in industry in all its ramifications. There are misgivings on the part of those who fear that the present trend of women into industry is contrary to the interests of men, of women, and of the family. One thing has been made certain and that is the uselessness of trying to interpret the rôle or the interest of women merely from the domestic angle. A major concern, indeed for many of these women their dominant concern, is their industrial status. That the trend has been toward a wider opportunity for women, a greater individual security, is beyond question. This, however, does not mean that women have reached in all fields of competition a parity with men but merely that their distance from the men has been lessened, especially after the outbreak of World War II.

An analysis of the situation of women in business and industry leads to distinctions in motive and circumstances that can be recognized in a fourfold classification. A portion of the women gainfully employed represents the consequences of the economic changes that have lessened the value of the woman's contribution in the one-time paramount productive activities of the home. In the earlier period of agriculture the majority of rural people carried on a family farming existence that made both husband and wife producers. The task of the housewife was more than that of a manager using money income to meet the consumptive needs of the members of her family. She was an active partner with her husband in the support of the family. Indeed even the children had, according to their age and strength, a part in the same enterprise.

Although a great many women in rural sections duplicate this one-time rôle to a considerable extent, there is also a multitude who have become economic dependents in the sense that they cannot add to the family income but must depend entirely upon the earnings of their husbands, although their contribution to family experience is still indispensable. A few are thoroughly parasitic, but this is more rare than people suppose even in families of great wealth. The important thing about the status of the average urban woman is that it reflects the husband's situation. Her security is contingent upon that of the male worker. She presides over a home that has lost many of its former economic functions while at the same time she does not attempt to work outside in gainful employment.

In contrast with this group of women we have those who are economically independent in the same sense as the male worker. They may have only a frail security but nevertheless they work in their own right and have thrust upon them the problems of self-decision and self-maintenance. They carry no family responsibilities, although many of them have in reserve parents whose help they can call upon in times of trouble. A part of this group of women view their situation as something temporary, since they look forward to an eventual marriage with or without orthodox homekeeping. On the other hand, many have no ardent hope of matrimony, either thinking of it as a vague possibility or finding in the marriage career no appeal.

There is still another group of women who are gainfully employed but rather more from necessity than choice. They are in their relationship modern successors of the farm-producing type of woman. They supplement their husband's earnings or those of some other family member. They go out into business or industry as does the mill worker who carries responsibility.

If they are married, there is one difference between them and men. Their occupation is generally less secure. However acceptable they may be to their fellow workers as individuals, they encounter from the unmarried woman and from the married man attitudes that express opposition by both these competitors to the idea of the married woman working. They also often feel the strain that comes from being a wife, a mother, and in some degree a housekeeper, in addition to being a wage earner. However justly the husband and wife try to work out together a program of marriage and home life that will demand no more of the woman than of the man, enough of the prevailing domestic conventions will seep in to make it very difficult for the woman not to carry a heavier load of responsibility than her husband. This proves true in varying degree whether they maintain their own house, rent an apartment, or become roomers and board out.

There is also the question whether—whatever may be expedient in the individual family—this policy does not operate, the larger the numbers of such women workers, to reduce the earnings of men and so increase the need of women's working outside the home. Room must be found in this group of women for those who go out for wages and salaries because of their personal inclination, their ambition, their dislike of housekeeping, their gregarious habits, their wish to enjoy luxuries otherwise impossible, to increase the economic security of the family, or to rationalize their unwillingness to bear children.

There is the final group of women, often forgotten, that seek employment because they are literally heads of families. There is no difference between them and male workers so far as their function is concerned. Being females, they nearly always face a considerable handicap, no matter in what field they seek their means of support. To them status is no academic question but a vital concern. They have placed upon them the same burdens as those carried by the male breadearners, but rarely do they have anything like equal opportunity. This cannot come to them short of achieving a status of full equality with men in the social order, a parity that at least in the field of employment will wipe out all distinctions of sex.

Although there is great variation, even some few exceptions that prove the rule, the one prominent fact common to all women gainfully employed is their inequality with men. This is expressed in four discriminations that operate against women who work.

The first of these is the greater difficulty they have when compared with men in getting into certain professions and occupations, especially positions offering large opportunity. The second is inequality of wages and salaries. In spite of recent, rapid progress there is still a traditional disposition to pay a woman carrying out a given operation or holding a certain responsibility a lesser wage or salary than the man who performs the same service. However this is interpreted, whether with emphasis upon past economic and social history, the transient aspects of employment of women, the inexperience and lack of organization of women workers, or the psychic or physical inferiorities of the female organism as it functions in work as compared with that of the male, there can be no doubt of the practical consequences of the industrial handicap that the modern woman faces. It still remains a social injustice which hampers the employed or professional woman, but the progress already made in this country shows that the trend is toward full parity with man.

The third inequality that she experiences is her obvious difficulty of advancing. As she moves upward in any vocation, her headway becomes increasingly difficult. This is usually an impersonal barrier to her ongoing. It is not in accord with the ordinary scheme of things to advance women over men. Often this means that the superior woman is given a position that permits her to reinforce the less competent man, because to reverse their position would run counter to what is customary and perhaps become itself a handicap in carrying on a competitive business and would require frequent explanation and defense. It would also become disruptive because of the obvious recoil not only of men but also of women from subordination to a woman. This relationship is so unlike what is usual that both sexes feel a loss of self-respect from being placed under a woman.

Women explain their reaction against having one of their own sex in authority by insisting that women, when in such positions, are more difficult, more partial, and more exacting than are men. Generally, however, when the practice has continued for a considerable time in any enterprise and has become an accepted convention, this indictment is rarely heard. Probably pioneering women who push out from obscurity reveal their ambition and aggressiveness in ways that render them unpopular. To a greater degree, however, it seems that what we find in this reluctance to accept the woman as boss or executive is recognition of the lesser prestige of a woman because of her sex in any undertaking usually given to men.

Women's colleges, because of their emphasis upon non-self-seeking services instead of incitement toward acquisitive, materialistic careers, have been held responsible for the poor showing of women in business. It is difficult to believe, however, that there is any great difference between the training that women have received in college and that given to men, so far as it is related to motivation for business careers.[1] In any case, in Mrs. Woodhouse's study of 6,665 graduates of land grant colleges, of 654 in the business world only 162 were found above clerical or minor supervisory situations.[2] Most land grant colleges are coeducational, and it is very doubtful whether there is any genuine difference in the influences in such institutions as they fall upon the women and the men.

The obstruction is more fundamental. It is an indication of an inferior status so usual as to escape notice. We are so accustomed to advancing men from the lowest to the highest levels that to open up any avenue to both sexes alike, with absolutely free competition, is too great a strain upon group feeling and thinking. As woman lifts her status her progress becomes easier. As she increases her successes in spite of difficulties she adds status. Meanwhile one proof of her inequality in the field of economic support is her handicap in advancement.

The fourth inequality we find that affects women is their lesser prestige. This in great measure is a consequence of the fact that men occupy in business, in industry, and in the professions most of the higher positions. Too sweeping a statement can be made concerning this form of masculine superiority, for in some instances the woman is distinguished rather more than less on account of sex. Also there are vocations almost exclusively possessed by women, such as nursing, that do have social standing and as a result the women in them have prestige. The general rule, however, is that the male sex has the advantage of prestige, and when a woman in free competition with men obtains distinction, it is regarded as remarkable and individual. Madame Curie, the chemist, is an example of this common reaction to the woman who becomes famous. It is more significant when one remembers that in many occupations women show skills and capacities that would seem to make them as likely to go forward to eminence as men. Statistical research, like chemistry, seems to offer opportunity for the precision, accuracy, and care of detail that women as technicians in both these fields clearly reveal.

The lesser prestige of women is all the more impressive when one considers that those who compete with men in high places are as a rule highly selected, the most promising of their sex in the chosen field. The discrimination is certainly not one for which men alone are to be held responsible. In the case of the woman doctor we find clear evidence that women are reluctant to recognize the skill of members of their own sex even in specialties of medicine, like gynecology, where the woman doctor would seem to have an advantage.

The prestige processes are still saturated with the spirit of masculine dominance. Indeed, it may be here in the social approval of marriage success as compared with that of the out-of-the-family career that brings distinction that the inequality of woman will be hardest to dislodge. The ideal of the standard or typical woman will continue to be to most men and many women the domestically inclined woman who avoids competition with men and accepts a life-program in sharpest contrast. This reaction makes it harder for the other kind of woman to fulfill her cravings and gain fame.

It may be objected that women have a special advantage in their possible sex appeal and that they often make use of this to advance their interest, thus gaining what they could not obtain from their efficiency, their worth as an employee. Undoubtedly it is true that women have such an asset and that some seek to use it and in a proportion of cases are successful. However intriguing such happenings are to the student of human nature, they play a very minor part in the industrial drama of women. Competitive business has small place for those seeking to capitalize sex. In ambitious women sex appeal sometimes becomes an antidote for the artificial handicaps of social conventions. Rarely does it become in itself a means to success. In industry it is also true that the time when the working girl found favor by permitting her sex to be exploited by her employer or overseer has long passed. Such happenings are now so rare as to have become front-page news.

In any effort to establish the status of women in American industry, two fundamental facts are to be taken into account. The *mores* even yet greatly influence the career of women in every line of out-of-the-family work for wages or salaries by two assumptions firmly embedded in the ongoing tradition. One is the notion of what is proper. This concept has greatly lost its spread as women have widened their opportunity, but it still has a remnant of meaning. The other is the idea of an inherent weakness, at least a source of nervous or physical limitation, that is a product of the female organism. As the status of women advances it has to contend with these two obstructions. They are both modified by class, by section, and by the strength of past tradition at the moment in any particular circle.

At present when we seek to analyze in what ways the inferiority status of woman in industry is revealed, we discover that she has less freedom of choice in her selection of a life occupation than has man. She is also in many cases less able to get the preparation that she needs for the work she wants to do or for the advancement in it that she expects to achieve. She is also troubled by a conflict of responsibility because of her triple interests, at least potentially pressing for recognition—those of mating and wifehood, those of childbearing and motherhood, and the demands of her work as an employed person. Even when these do not clash in actual practice, they are confusing as the woman seeks to prepare herself for life. She may have to surrender one or more that she may fulfill her other desires or adapt herself to unescapable circumstances as she makes an adjustment much less required of men.

It is not always true that her choice decides her responsibility. She sometimes enters marriage, for example, determining not to have children, only to find herself switched by forces that she has failed to control into the obligations of a mother. She sometimes marries with the intention of going on as usual as one gainfully employed only to find that her status is changed, that she is much less secure than she was before she married.

In comparison with men she also has a lesser private life. The conventions, although much more tolerant than they once were, still guard her in a way that is not true of men. This means sometimes that she has to surrender what she would prefer because of its possible risk to her as an employed person or one trying to make headway in a profession. Finally her lower status shows itself in the fact that she earns less, as a rule, than a man doing what she does without greater skill or efficiency. Her status as an employed person has measurably advanced with the evolution of American society, but it has not yet attained parity with that of man.

The political status of woman is similar to her situation in industry in her inability to reach, in anything like the proportion of men, high places in practical political management, government appointments, or elective offices. Her influence on the contrary is far greater in politics than in industry. Although women have failed to take interest in politics to the degree that both the promoters and critics of the woman suffrage movement expected, the potential power of women voters has been so incalculable in the strategic planning of party managers that the practical effect of woman suffrage is something beyond the actual voting strength of women.

It is impossible to know the percentage of women that have voted in national elections since they gained the right of suffrage, as compared with men. We know that there has been a great number of eligible voters who have refused to use the opportunity of the ballot in each national election since 1920, when women first voted. That year the National League of Women Voters started an effort to get more women to vote. The next national election showed a slightly decreased percentage of persons free to vote who had made use of the ballot. Investigations that have been made of the registration of men and women indicate that the interest of women in voting is increasing and, although their record is not so good as that of men, it is proportionately gaining.[8]

This indication of increasing interest on the part of women in their suffrage opportunity is in accord with the observation of many who have had experience in politics. The registration increase is not always to the advantage of women. We also have evidence that sometimes a greater proportion of the men than of the women registered vote. In any case, it would be a great mistake to attempt to estimate the political significance of woman suffrage from the proportion of women who vote as compared with the proportion of men.

Without doubt the possibility of voting has had a decided effect in bringing the American woman closer to the American man. Suffrage has encouraged legislation of advantage or designed to be of advantage to women. It has quickened the trend toward greater legal equality. It has forced party managers to recognize reform movements that have been especially attractive to women. It is questionable whether the great majority of women have become politically minded to any large extent, but at least in most cases they have an added satisfaction from their possession of suffrage rights.

Thus far it seems as if the greatest benefit that has come from woman suffrage was the reënforcement this has given to the lobbying activities of women interested in various lines of legislation. They have brought in great degree to public affairs a new point of view with different emphasis than that of men. They have been especially concerned with matters affecting child welfare, marriage, and divorce, laws tending to remove discrimination against women, with education, public health, consumers' rights and needs, working conditions of women in industry, peace, temperance, social and mental hygiene, and various phases of social security.

The anti-slavery agitation, temperance, the reform movement, the fight for woman suffrage, and similar activities trained women as effective lobbyists, and their influence has been felt by Congress, by state legislatures, and by executives, both national and state. Since the practical politician has never been sure of the party allegiance of women to the degree that he has reckoned on the loyalty of men, and since he has always feared a possible uprising of women voters evoked by a woman's block, through the defeat of some proposed legislation, he has been forced, contrary to his preferences, to clear the way for definite reforms.

Such organizations as the General Federation of Women's Clubs, the National League of Women Voters, the American Association of University Women, the American Federation of Teachers, the National Association of Business and Professional Women's Clubs, the National Consumers' League, the National Woman's Party, have had influence because of the fact that there was behind them a group of voters who in any election might hold the balance of power. This possibility has given them political recognition that would never have come without woman suffrage. A great quantity of legislation has been advanced by the coöperative efforts of various women's organizations carried through by the Woman's Joint Congressional Committee.

Although women are disproportionately few in the higher positions of politics and government, they are not without representation. Recent presidential campaigns have given the best evidence of the seriousness with which party managers considered the votes of women. Women were recognized through organizations, radio appeals, literature, and their appearance on the platform. A few women have found entrance into places of political eminence as governors of states, judges of courts, members of Congress, both the House and the Senate. One of the innovations of the administration of President Franklin D. Roosevelt was the giving of a cabinet appointment for the first time to a woman, one who had had a long experience in the field of industrial reform.

Although a great proportion of the women who do vote merely duplicate their husband's political thinking, woman suffrage has operated to lift their status, remove their disabilities, widen their outlook, and give them incentives for a more socialized, mature program of life.

The greater participation of women in politics has raised the fundamental issue that divides those interested in advancing the industrial and social welfare of women, on account of their differing strategy, into two distinct groups. One seeks to protect women by special legislation and the other, best represented by the National Woman's Party, regards laws distinguishing women from men as liabilities that work in the long run for the advantage of the latter. Their program would eliminate these, to them, artificial handicaps in the competition of women with men and in their place enact protective legislation that would apply equally to men and to women.

In order to get rid of what they interpret as discriminations against women, both in the statutes and in the common law, they advocate an equal rights amendment to the Constitution to read as follows: "Men and women shall have equal rights throughout the United States and every place subject to its jurisdiction. Congress shall have power to enforce this article by appropriate legislation." They are not opposed to protective labor legislation but insist that it should be based upon the nature of the work and not upon the sex of the worker.

They hold that it is hopeless to expect women to receive equal pay for equal work if they are restricted on account of their sex by special legislation, even though it is passed in the name of woman's welfare. They are opposed to laws prohibiting night work for adult women, and are also against minimum wage legislation that applies only to women. On the other hand, labor leaders have generally been hostile to the idea of laws fixing minimum wages that do not distinguish between women and men, believing that such legislation will tend to bring the wage of men down to that of women. The National Woman's Party assumes that such laws applying to both sexes would help bring women's wages to the level of men's.

Although the two groups of women, those favoring special legislation to protect women's interests and those advocating equal legislation to guarantee their rights, both seek to advance woman's status, their opposite programs bring out clearly the fundamental question now confronting the American woman. The decision of the United States Supreme Court in a test of the New York State minimum wage law for women rendered June 1, 1936, by a five-four majority establishes the point of view of the National Woman's Party in these words:

> While men are left free to fix their wages by agreement with employers, it would be fanciful to suppose that the regulation of women's wages would be useful to prevent or lessen the evils listed in the first section of the Act.
>
> Men in need of work are as likely as women to accept the low wages offered by unscrupulous employers. Men in greater numbers than women support themselves and dependents and because of need will work for whatever wages they can get and that without regard to the value of the service and even though the pay is less than minima prescribed in accordance with this Act.
>
> It is plain that, under the circumstances such as those portrayed in the "factual background" prescribing of minimum wages for women alone would unreasonably restrain them in competition with men and tend arbitrarily to deprive them of employment and a fair chance to find work.[4] *

In the realm of intellect the status of woman in this country has advanced closest to that of man. Educationally she still occasionally meets with artificial restrictions and more commonly with handicaps born of social custom and prejudice. Significant as these are,

* Later, however, by a five to four decision, the Supreme Court upheld the constitutionality of the Washington State minimum law for women.

they are contrary to the general trend which unmistakably leads away from sex distinctions or sex differences in the programs and achievements of the secondary schools, colleges, universities, and even the professional schools.

Recently a distinguished president of one of the oldest women's colleges, when given an honorary degree, was cited as a leader in "a vital experiment in education, the training of the college woman of today." If interpreted as a statement of the insecurity of the American woman in college and university, this runs contrary to fact. In no other field of competition with men is her position so well established. If emphasis is placed upon the second part of this assertion, it brings out the challenging questions that arise from the firm footing woman has gained in the educational world. There are issues involved profoundly important, due not to the differences of capacity between the human male and female but to the fact that in the great majority of cases at present men and women differ in their social function.

The success of woman in her educational career at every plane where she can be compared with man only makes more apparent the significance of the questions that arise. They are more searching than in any other aspect of her life because it is here that she at last faces parity with man and its consequences.

If in this field the literary activity of women be marked off by itself, the American woman can be said to have come closer still to an absolute equality with man. Any judgment that appraises the literary worth by itself of any undertaking becomes indifferent to the question of sex. In the realm of authorship, where her intellect has freest play, woman rarely meets with any disparity. The poem, the story, the novel, the autobiography, even the book of science, is given neither discrimination nor advantage on account of the sex of the author. The significance of this lies in these two facts. It is in this field that woman longest has enjoyed freedom to compete with man, and it is in the life of the intellect that we find the most distinguishing qualities of the human organism. The American woman has reached her greatest equality with men in the activities that function on the highest level of human evolution. As an illustration of this we find that in a list of the thirty best sellers in fiction from 1901 to 1936, as reported in the New York Times Book Review for December 20, 1936, sixteen are by women. These are the titles:

"To Have and to Hold," Mary Johnston.
"Rebecca of Sunnybrook Farm," Kate Douglas Wiggin.
"The House of Mirth," Edith Wharton.
"The Lady of the Decoration," Fannie Macaulay.
"Freckles," Gene Stratton Porter.
"Pollyanna," Eleanor H. Porter.
"Mrs. Wiggs of the Cabbage Patch," Alice Hegan Rice.
"The Man in Lower 10," Mary Roberts Rinehart.
"The Brimming Cup," Dorothy Canfield.
"Gentlemen Prefer Blondes," Anita Loos.
"Vein of Iron," Ellen Glasgow.
"Death Comes for the Archbishop," Willa Cather.
"So Big," Edna Ferber.
"Years of Grace," Margaret Ayer Barnes.
"The Good Earth," Pearl Buck.
"Gone With the Wind," Margaret Mitchell.

Women gained their firm footing in literature in the seventies. The world-wide popularity of *Uncle Tom's Cabin*, written by Harriet Beecher Stowe in 1852, contributed to this. Since this was the first book of fiction written by an American woman that became an international best seller, it is interesting that in 1936 the most rapidly selling book, *Gone With the Wind*, was also written by a woman and deals with the Civil War that Mrs. Stowe's book did so much to provoke. The contrast between these two literary successes measures the distance the present woman artists have traveled in the field of literature from the standard set by *Uncle Tom's Cabin*. The first novel bubbled forth from subjective feeling and was a flight of pure fancy with no regard to the actualities of southern experience, of which the author had no personal knowledge. Against its emotional exaggeration it is striking to put the craftsmanship of *Gone With the Wind* with its historic accuracy, its realism, and its constraint of partisanship. Nevertheless, Mrs. Stowe put an end to any thought that women must accept a minor rôle in the literary world.

Once *Uncle Tom's Cabin* was out, eight power presses, running night and day, could not keep up with the demand. Three hundred thousand copies were sold during the first year in the United States and a half million in Great Britain and her colonies. Even among some southern readers it met at first with approval. One friend that soon was to be proved a wretched prophet wrote Mrs. Stowe: "Your book is going to be the great pacificator; it will unite North and South." [5] In spite of literary flaws recognized by some critics from the beginning, the book achieved a translation into twenty-seven languages and dialects and a sale that made it for a time the book not of the month but of the world.

There were, however, more substantial influences at work to open up the literary career for women than the marvelous sales of the most history-making book of the period. The Civil War must be added to the forces that stimulated women toward writing. Most effective of all was the increasing opportunity given women in the field of education. This not only helped prepare writers but added greatly to their clientele.

Although it is not safe at any time to state the beginning of woman's entrance into literature on an equality basis with man, distinction must be given Margaret Fuller D'Ossoli. Gifted with an intellect of the first rank, the meaning of her career can best be emphasized by the fact that her biography was written by such eminent persons as James Freeman Clarke, William Henry Channing, Ralph Waldo Emerson, Julia Ward Howe, and Thomas Wentworth Higginson. During most of her public life she was unmarried and we know her as Margaret Fuller.

Many-sided, endowed with a brilliant mind crowded with ideas, it is not strange that in her time she won a fame that has made some designate her the "female Emerson," but in her reasoned attack upon a masculine civilization that denied women their rights, she more resembled Mary Wollstonecraft. Even this comparison is unfair if in any way it suggests that she duplicated any other thinking, for she made her own intellectual pathway. She was even more a pioneer in breaking a way for women's literary genius than was Mrs. Stowe, for her career ended when she was lost in a shipwreck off the shores of Long Island two years before *Uncle Tom's Cabin* was published.

The outburst that came from women's self-expression in the field of literature is suggested by the fact that in the decade beginning in 1870 in the *Atlantic Monthly,* leading literary magazine of the time, apart from 108 poems by the five best-known American poets—Longfellow, Whittier, Holmes, Lowell, and Aldrich, 450 poems appeared, of which 201 were written by women.[6] Another way to realize the awakening of women who felt the literary impulse is to catalogue those who in the seventies and eighties came to prominence. Here are some of the widely read women who produced mostly during these two decades: Elizabeth Stuart Phelps Ward, Harriet Prescott Spofford, Rose Terry Cook, Helen Hunt Jackson, Sarah Orne Jewett, Louisa M. Alcott, and Rose Hawthorne Lathrop. Mary E. Wilkins Freeman and Alice Brown won their spurs later. It is interesting to find not only that many of these writers had felt the glow of New England's great day in literature but also that some of them were the second generation of those who had shared in New England's greatest achievement.

It was not only, however, in that section that women were beginning to gain reputations as writers. This list of books and their authors suggests what was happening: [7]

1868. *Little Women,* Louisa M. Alcott (1832–1888).
1868. *The Gates Ajar,* Elizabeth Stuart Phelps (1844–1911).
1870. *Verses,* Helen Hunt Jackson (1831–1885).
1872. *Poems,* Celia Thaxter (1836–1894).
1875. *After the Ball and Other Poems,* Nora Perry (1841–1896).
1877. *Deephaven,* Sarah Orne Jewett (1849–1909).

1878. *The China Hunter's Club,* Annie Trumbull Slosson (1838-1926).
1875. *A Woman in Armor,* Mary Hartwell Catherwood (1847-1902).
1877. *That Lass o' Lowrie's,* Frances Hodgson Burnett (1849-1924).
1883. *The Led Horse Claim,* Mary H. Foote (1847-1938).
1884. *In the Tennessee Mountains,* Mary Noailles Murfree (1850-1922).
1884. *A New Year's Masque,* Edith M. Thomas (1854-   ).
1886. *The Old Garden and Other Verses,* Margaretta Wade Deland (1857-   ).
1886. *Monsieur Motte,* Grace King (1852-1932).
1887. *Knitters in the Sun,* Alice French (1850-1934).

Emily Dickinson rightly should appear as the greatest of them all, but her extraordinary gift found only fragmentary expression in the bursting forth of the very essence of word music. With a genius that flamed in glimpses like the glow of the quick-passing firefly, she had to wait until the twentieth century for any considerable appreciation.

The status changes of the American woman that are most spectacular and perhaps most disturbing can best be catalogued under the term "recognition of individuality." This brings together various forms of self-expression originating in a keener sense of personal right, both in woman's single life and in her marriage experience. These tendencies are for the most part unconscious products of social circumstances and therefore more subtle but not less strong. They lead to contention between persons representing the traditions of the past and the drifts of the present, often indefinite and unrecognized in the most intimate of relationships. The nearer women draw toward equal opportunity with men along these lines of self-life, the clearer it becomes how uncompromising with past conditions, standards, and conventions the social evolution of women must be when carried to its goal. Freedom in dress shows the progress already made. Changes in sex attitudes show up the social reconstruction now in process. Questions of expediency with reference to the woman's right to her name when married reveal the inexorable sweep of present trends.

We have already noticed the beginnings of the effort to change woman's dress so as to make it easier for her to enjoy an active life. By the end of the fifties, except in women's gymnasiums, interest in dress reform had died out, even Mrs. Bloomer herself eventually surrendering to convention. As late as 1893 we find the customary apparel of women so little changed that in that year Dr. Robert L. Dickinson, pleading for simple and practical methods of dress reform, illustrated the dress of the day as consisting of twelve different articles, with seventeen layers at the waist.[8] In his article this far-seeing physician recommended a dress of four garments.

It was not through the effort of a few reformers, far in advance of the thinking of their time, that a more suitable manner of dress was to come to women but from the vogue of the bicycle. The popularity of bicycling which followed the introduction of the low-wheel type of machine opened up to women a sport that required a more sensible dress. This innovation was but the beginning of a trend which was rapidly enforced by women breaking into all sorts of outdoor activities. As the dress changed so did the ideas of modesty. Only by an examination of the fashions dominant in the various periods throughout our history can one have any realization of what a radical departure from the past woman's present dress is.

The change has been doubly important. Undoubtedly a great part of the ill health of which we hear so much in the experience of American women from colonial days until early in the present century was a product of the restrictive, burdensome garments demanded by the prevailing fashions. In addition, because of such dress, women were denied opportunity to engage with the freedom given men in all out-of-the-home undertakings, unless they discarded, as much of the time they just had to do, a part of the restrictive clothing imposed by convention. Always there was a subtle influence affecting the behavior of women, born of fashion, which made it improper for even the young girl to live as naturally and actively as the boy. In the opinion of many, women now have gone farther in sensible dress than have men with the one exception of their shoes. The high heel which came into vogue with the silk stocking and short skirt led to regression at this one point, and its popularity among employed women in many occupations—for example, clerking in the department store—handicaps the woman in comparison with the man.

Woman's gain in status in the field of sex is possibly the most impressive in popular thinking of all her changed circumstances. In this movement also the Oneida Community pioneered. Noyes, its founder, insisted that his new covenant should revolutionize the love experience as well as religion. The art of love to him was not only a spiritual achievement but one that required the mutual contribution and satisfaction of man and woman. This was a far more radical attack on conventional thinking than was his marriage scheme upon the matrimonial code. This part of his program had no more effect upon popular sentiment than his group marriage notion had upon the institution of matrimony.

It was not until the twentieth century that women's reaction to sex and their frank recognition of its meaning in their life came close to the masculine attitude. Freud had much to do with the great change that took place in the feeling of women toward sex. The Freudian theory of psychoanalysis, with its emphasis upon sex, popularized the idea that both women and men had sex endowments that significantly affected the emotional life. Later this recognition of the personality significance of sex was reënforced by discoveries in the field of endocrinology and the new knowledge of the chemical contributions made to the body life of the individual by the sexual organs.

A third influence came from the increasing attention of science to the normal sex life. Such sexology as had developed in the nineteenth century was chiefly concerned with abnormal experience, the pathology of human sex. World War I was a crystallizing crisis that brought quickly to expression the franker recognition of woman's sex life that was in process of growth. Associated with this was another trend toward constantly enlarging the freedom of women and placing upon them greater self-responsibility.

Although the history of American morals in its main outline follows from the colonial days along the cultural march of occidental civilization, we do have almost from the beginning, as a result of pioneering and later western conditions of life, a distinguishing freedom of women. This varies according to class and section and comes soonest to its American maturity in the Middle West. Stephen A. Douglas reports an incident that at least shows how accustomed the pioneering woman was to taking care of herself. One night he had to put up in a cabin with only one room. The young seventeen-year-old daughter of his host refused to recognize his hints that he wished a chance to get ready to retire, until finally in order to get to sleep he proceeded to undress. When he was ready for bed she said, "Mr. Douglas, you *have* got a mighty small chance of legs there." In relating this incident Douglas declared that it was merely illustrative of pioneering habit, that there was no one in Illinois more modest than this same girl.[9]

The western idea of self-protection rather than the notion expressed in the conventions of the chaperon has become characteristic of the social code of the American woman. Once this trait became allied with the recognition of the significance of woman's sex life, the confusion of our present situation followed, the product of a transition from a code of masculine sex dominance to one attempting to establish the sex integrity of the woman as an individual as well as that of the man.

The effect of this has been greatest in marriage and has given a new meaning to the term "sex incompatibility." To be sure, the earlier convention that discounted the sex needs and desires of the woman represented in great measure a concealment rather than a description of the actual marital experience of women. It did, however, establish masculine superiority, and although just how this operated in normal domestic relationships is little better known by us than the domesticity of neolithic peoples, since taboo blocked its entrance into history, it seems a fair inference from the facts we have that for a great number of American women marital life was a sacrifice rather than a satisfaction.

The awakening of the modern woman to the significance of her sexual life in varying degrees of realization and her greater frankness in facing the problems this involves are radically changing the character of marriage adjustment. Women, increasingly subordinating economic or other ulterior motives for marrying, demand from the experience a fulfillment of personality which more and more includes satisfactory sexual relationships. The consequence has been a reversal of the former program. The husband not only has to recognize the sex interest of the wife but also has to contribute to the matrimonial felicity with a skill and understanding rendered difficult by traditions of male self-assertion. The masculine prerogative in marital relationships has been in the past both socially and legally firmly established. Its justification has carried an interpretation of woman that modern science is increasingly proving false.

So great a shifting of emphasis under any circumstances would be disturbing but it is at present all the more so because at the same time divorce is growing easier and meeting with less recoil. Thus the sexual relationships of husband and wife frequently become symbolic of more severe tension as along other lines feminine aggressiveness collides with assumptions of masculine dominance.

The tendency toward recognizing the sex integrity of the woman has not only drawn woman and man closer to equality in this sphere of experience but for the most part has led woman to assume man's attitude rather than man to assume woman's. This was inevitable because the former code gave man in the sex life self-expression and the woman self-sacrifice. The passive rôle was surrendered with the advance toward a stressing of sexual mutuality.

This readjustment also has led to disturbing consequences. World War I, the rise in the standards of living, the length of professional training, especially in the middle class, the depression, the revival and popularizing of radical theories of sex conduct, along with the development of birth control, and World War II have aggravated the disorganization that must always accompany fundamental transition of social experience and outlook.

Although the majority of women who have felt the full force of new conditions have looked to marriage for sex fulfillment, a minority have chosen a premarriage sex alliance as an anticipation of the matrimonial union expected later or have turned to sexual relationships, promiscuous or concentrated, as a substitute for marriage.[10] These variations must not be interpreted as similar to the irregularities that have always accompanied the standard sex code. They represent a non-acceptance of the conventions, the feeling of self-right in the realm of sex that is, as a considerable disposition, new in our social history. Especially is this true in middle class attitudes where the most significant changes in woman's sex conduct have occurred.

There are those close to the behavior of youth who believe that there has been of late a conservative reaction chiefly from young women's recognizing through personal experience that they have been exploited by men who have selfishly taken advantage of the opportunities provided by the freer code, and from experiences of unwanted pregnancies that have shown that there was greater confidence in popular methods of birth control than the facts have justified. However true this opinion may be, it is clear that woman's advance toward sex equality with man is certain to put unprecedented responsibility upon her and at least temporarily to add to the ever-present strain the modern young woman meets in her precourtship, courtship, and engagement associations.

A third issue that has to do with the woman's status as an independent person raises the question of her name after marriage. For a portion of American women this is a closed subject. Having gained before marriage a distinction or having for some reason need of keeping their maiden name, they do not in their public career after marriage change their name to that of their husband. The loss that would follow if they did is so obvious that their decision, unlike that of Lucy Stone when she first challenged custom at this point, is generally approved. On the other hand, unless there is some special interest at stake, social convention still expects the wife to give up her former designation and accept her husband's. Clearly this was a logical procedure when even in law her status as a wife was a reflection from his. It is not, however, in harmony with the trend leading toward woman's equality with man.

Even those women who seem to have no personal motive for holding to their premarriage designation do experience a shrinkage of identity as they make the transference. To some extent they are cut off from their earlier career and are lost to acquaintances who fail to record or remember the new name given at marriage. Any man who doubts this needs only to imagine what it would mean for him to lay aside at marriage the name given him at birth and henceforth to be known as a title stressing the fact that he is his wife's husband.

The position of the Lucy Stone League is consistent with the full recognition of the rights belonging to woman as an independent personality, whether single or married. The influences of the present custom are, however, so subtle and the freedom of the professional or distinguished woman to keep her former name if she chooses is so well established, that there is little interest even among women in insisting upon a universal break with social tradition. It is likely nevertheless that the tendency will be toward an increase in the number of women who after marriage keep their maiden name.

If objection is made that this is undesirable because it will make easier illicit relationships, the answer will be that this method of maintaining morals cannot under conditions of modern life have great significance. The more serious problem arises when one asks what will happen in the case of children being born. There are several possibilities. The woman may, as is so often true, keep two names, the children and herself in social contacts taking that of the husband. It may eventually happen that the child will be given either the father's or the mother's name as at birth seems desirable. It is conceivable that the child may be given a new name, but so long as our present form of family life prevails this appears improbable. A combination of both wife's and husband's names offers no solution after the second generation, it soon becomes so long and awkward.

There is certainly need of distinguishing men by title as married or single if the present vogue of Miss and Mrs. with reference to women shall prevail. In the days when social custom was standardized to masculine dominance, it was natural for the man to wish to know at presentation whether the woman was single or married. The more nearly the *mores* travel toward social equality of the sexes, the stronger will grow the argument that what has been expedient for the man is in like manner an advantage under modern conditions for the woman.

Another marked trend in our time, so clear that it has become one of the most common topics of public controversy, is toward deliberate parenthood.[11] This has been made possible by improvement in the technique of contraception and the widespread distribution of knowledge of this and other methods of birth control.[12] No happening in social experience could potentially have more volcanic influence. The desire of men and women to control the reproductive processes is not original with our generation. The ability to accomplish this with any degree of precision is a new achievement. Since it is true that motherhood as such is not an organic urge [13] but has come to humans as to all higher animals as a by-product of sexual intercourse, the power to separate these two experiences, long allied in the sex career of the woman, is disturbing to the social order at the point where marriage has had its most ancient and strongest support.

Parenthood has been the chief training school for human nature and also has furnished society with social habits and reactions that have contributed most to its security. With accidental, unchosen parenthood tied up with one of the strong human passions, not only has human survival been guaranteed but under favorable conditions growth of population also. Now increasingly the question whether to become or not to become a mother is a free choice for married women.

Whatever the personal, the domestic, and the social hazards of this, birth control provides another means of establishing the integrity of the woman as a self-determining personality. It becomes possible for her to share with the man sex experiences that carry no risk of consequences outside the act itself. At least this is theoretically true.[14] In practice there still remains a risk of unwanted parenthood on account of possible failure in the contraceptive technique. There are powerful personal motives as well as pressure from social traditions and conventions almost certain to continue that impel women to become mothers. There is, therefore, no evidence that even perfect contraceptive birth control knowledge, universally distributed, would mean race suicide. The woman, however, through her choice of motherhood has become co-equal with man in experiences where previously a biological burden was forced upon her, even when she wished with all her will not to be a mother.

Knowing how large and important a part women now have in the religious life of the United States, it seems at first strange that they have not in this particular field attained full equality with man. Our reaction of surprise at this is in itself proof of the progress that has been made. Women have become so free that we are led to forget the strength of theological definitions of her nature that once hampered her and of the religious and ecclesiastical traditions that limited her self-expression in religious experience. She is nearly free from the theological dogma that separated her from man and inflicted upon her inferiority. She has made less headway in breaking through ecclesiastical barriers and attaining full professional opportunity in religious leadership. So many women have escaped from the one-time prejudice that it no longer is considered unseemly to have women speak in public in the churches even when they are denied ordination as full-fledged members of the clergy. From the start, as in so many other ways, the Quakers in the United States gave women an equality recognition in religion that, viewed from its historic background, now seems extraordinary. In spite of the strength of religious convention, from the days of Anne Hutchinson onward individual women have rebelled against their inferior status and found a place for themselves in religious leadership.

It is easy to discount the influence of woman on the religious life of America, since it was far greater than the recognition that her sex received officially in ecclesiastical organizations. In 1774 Ann Lee with her followers established the Shakers. In 1766 Mrs. Barbara Heck, in the effort to counteract irreligious conditions, induced Philip Embury to preach against gamblers and other sinners, and thus started in this country the Methodist denomination. This denomination, the Baptist, and the Disciples of Christ, all three adapted to conditions on the frontier, necessarily in accord with western spirit stressed the sex equality that was inherently embedded in their faith. Indeed, it would be contrary to what happened to describe any of the national church organizations as consistently holding to notions of masculine dominance. In spite of teaching which stressed the prerogatives of the male, especially in domestic life, woman contributed greatly to the progress of the churches and her rights and needs were given recognition. For example, women played a large rôle in the development in this country of the Roman Catholic Church. It was likewise in the history of the Episcopal Church. These two were ecclesiastically the most conservative in regard to woman's participation in public religious service.

The most original development that took place in American religion occurred in the nineteenth century through the leadership of a woman, Mary Baker Eddy. This came not from a cleavage in theological interpretation within an existing group of religious believers, as was so common during the eighteenth and nineteenth centuries, but from a revolutionary change of emphasis in religious outlook. Although it had its historic root, an example of which was its attenuated kinship with the philosophic system of Bishop

Berkeley, the doctrine was new and aside from its specific preachment had implications that explained William James's statement that it was the most thorough-going of all the optimistic attempts to deal with the problem of evil.[15] Naturally from its origin it has gone farther than any other American religion in wiping out distinctions of sex in either church organization or spiritual teaching.

Unless there is a reversal of tendencies that have been showing themselves from the beginning of American religious history, the trend toward woman's full equality with man will continue, supported as it is by the fact that women constitute so large a part of church membership. It is easy now to see the exasperation that led Elizabeth Cady Stanton to issue her commentary on the scriptures which became known as "The Woman's Bible." In her effort to advance woman's rights she found herself constantly meeting obstructions that grew out of theological interpretations and the commitment of the churches to masculine dominance.

Her book brought such widespread protest that it seemed to some likely seriously to retard woman suffrage, and at the National-American Convention of 1896 an issue was made of this publication and finally, after considerable debate, with a vote of fifty-three to forty-one the following resolution was adopted: "This association is non-sectarian, being composed of persons of all shades of religious opinion, and has no official connection with the so-called 'Woman's Bible' or any theological publication."[16] By general consent and in the spirit of the time passages of the Bible that were once used to enforce the inferiority of women now receive little attention and are seldom used in any effort to block woman's advance toward equality with man. They were used by opponents of woman suffrage but have been largely ignored following the failure of this opposition to the political emancipation of women.

Changes in the legal status of women have accompanied her social progress along other lines. If at times the removal of the disabilities placed upon the married woman by common law has appeared slow, the advance perhaps has been all the more certain because it has come so gradually. After the American Revolution the English colonists took over as their basic law the judicial principles that they had inherited from the motherland. The most important feature of this common law as it had to do with women was the distinction in status between the unmarried and the married woman. The first was in most respects at least theoretically entitled in law to all the civil rights and privileges accorded men. In practice, because of her inability through lack of physical force or other handicaps, she was unable to assert her rightful claim. She had the right to own property, to make contracts, and to act as administrator and to assume financial obligation with almost the same freedom as men.

It was otherwise with married women. By her marriage contract the wife lost her legal personality during her wifehood. This became the possession of her husband and except under certain conditions she ceased to have separate existence before the law. As a consequence, the husband could make no contract with his wife, since that would be the same as making a contract with himself, nor could he give her property for a similar reason. The wife lost control of her real property and even the title of her personal property with the exception of her paraphernalia—wearing apparel, ornaments, and such. The personal property which she had acquired prior to marriage, as well as that which she received subsequently during her wifehood, or coverture as it was called, became absolutely her husband's and was as much his as if he had himself acquired it. On his death it went to his personal representatives even when his wife survived him.[17]

Although the wife's real estate did not become the property of the husband while she lived, he had so large a control over it that it was practically his until his death, if there were children, or at the wife's death if there were none. Without the wife's consent he could lease or sell his interest in it. The general principle behind this definition of the husband-wife relationship was that marriage established a family and the man was its head. This rested upon Christian teaching and ecclesiastical doctrine. One of the earliest statements of the married woman's status appears in the oldest volume of American law reports referring to a case decided in 1786 and reads as follows: "The general policy of the law with regard to marriage makes the wife one with her husband, and disables her separately or without him to make any contract, or do any legal act to bind his interest or her own." [18]

In contrast with this English concept of marriage it is interesting to find the French code of Louisiana tying up with the Roman law which had defined the matron's position in the family as that of an independent individual in spite of certain legal limitations.[19]

The movement to enlarge the legal status of woman and to soften her liabilities as a wife appears early in colonial days and reveals an underlying pressure toward the notion of mutuality which is now well-entrenched in our contemporary domestic law. The tendency of the colonial courts was toward an emphasis of the reciprocal rights and duties of the husband and the wife. This appeared along three lines in the attitudes of the courts. They maintained the right of both husband and wife to enjoy the companionship of the other spouse, enjoining cohabitation upon couples whom indifference had separated and ordering wife-deserters to return. They forced negligent husbands to support their wives and children and in the South actions were frequently brought for alimony independent of suits for judicial separation. The married woman was also protected against abuse, cruelty, and improper conduct on the part of the husband.[20]

The courts also moved toward an enlarging of the proprietary capacity of the married woman, giving her greater contractual and tortious rights and liabilities.[21] The fact that colonial women carried on businesses and estates for themselves and also in behalf of their husbands in their absence struck at the theory of the union of the husband and wife in marriage as a legal personality represented in the person of the husband. We even find in New England grants of land to wives who had husbands living. As a rule, women who were actually heads of families were given their share of planting land.[22]

Husbands who were forced to be away from their businesses or farms, as is illustrated by the cases of John Adams and Benjamin Franklin, frequently placed the management in the hands of their wives and gave them power of attorney. The legality of antenuptial contracts between the man and the woman was upheld. As early as 1673 we have the General Court of Connecticut authorizing the taking of a part of the estate of Thomas Fairchild to satisfy his pre-nuptial obligations to his wife.[23] In 1762 we find the Governor and Council of Massachusetts making a similar decision. In spite of the fact that according to common law conveyances between husband and wife were disallowed, we find in the seventeenth century the American colonies recognizing post-nuptial contracts. These usually had to do with settlements made in view of separation.[24] These few illustrations show that almost from the beginning of the colonial settlement the environmental situation tempered the harshness of the married woman's status of the English common law and gradually changed its definition.

The pioneering conditions west of the Alleghenies struck even more aggressively at the notion of the wife's submergence in her husband. The sentiment of the pioneer was intolerant of decisions that reflected European or eastern attitudes.[25] This disposition appears, for example, in the more liberal attitude of the legislatures than of the courts toward the granting of divorces to women. The former were more influenced by general feeling than were the judges who through training turned toward precedent.[26]

The atmosphere of pioneering life encouraged the notion of independence and equality. The legal fiction of the married woman transferring her personality to that of the husband was so contrary to the actual practices that decisions and statutory laws moved rapidly away from the definition of woman's inequality that had been passed to our courts by English tradition. The pressure toward the removal of legal incapacities and discriminations concerning women has been nationwide, although most forceful in the West where European traditions were weakest and in the Northeast where the industrial development revealed the injustices of woman's law-imposed disabilities.

The changing status of woman in law, just as is true in other fields of her social reconstruction, has brought forth confusion and new problems of justice. The first is illustrated by the division of opinion as to what should be the legal adjustment of husband and wife with regard to individual income. One group would separate husband and wife from any property entanglement except through their own contract. This program appears in the thinking of those who propose legislation and litigation that establish the wife's right to regard her personal earnings as her own separate property.

The other group seeks as the wise solution a coöperative fellowship in which husband and wife share alike in joint income. The difficulty that the new situation brings is also illustrated by the problems that arise as soon as the equality of rights of the two sexes is established in any specific way by statute. For example, laws that have taken away former powers and prerogatives of the husband have sometimes failed to lighten the burdens that have been placed upon husbands because of their one-time authorities or advantages.[27] The liberalizing movement in legislation as it affects the married woman tends to give her equality with her husband, with unmarried women, with men, while removing the disabilities of coverture.[28]

Along with the trend toward establishing the equality of the woman, married or single, with man has gone also the effort to give her as a mother special protection. In practice the woman, when she has become a criminal, has also received preferred treatment. It is so contrary to American sentiment in criminal prosecution to carry out even-handed justice without reference to sex that the woman criminal nearly always has an advantage over the man.

The sweep of American culture has brought woman to a near-equality with man in almost every aspect of her social career. This has been one of the most characteristic and important results of the evolution of the American people. Although it brings a long-continued effort near fulfillment, it is not a solution of all the problems born of the difference between the man and the woman.

In no sense can even full equality become the end of the cultural process and bring to final settlement the yearnings and the strivings that have been a part of woman's advancing status. Instead, although some problems may now be labeled *finis,* filed away in historic records, others as perplexing, as pressing, as compelling, although on a higher plane, take their place.

There are three parties concerned as adjustments to the new order are attempted: woman, man, and biologic nature. The third has such commanding authority that if it decides against present trends, society, to survive, must find its way back, driven by pain-pressure, to the more ancient ways of man-woman relationships.

In the new order woman not only has a more active part but must with greater self-consciousness and more searching of soul share responsibility for American social life. She has never been a spectator nor an inactive partner, but at last she contributes to the ongoing of our civilization with the same sense of self-determination that possesses man.

CHAPTER XII

NEAR EQUALITY WITH MEN

THE economic aftermath of the World War of 1914-1918, although felt first in Europe, lingered longest in the United States. Before this country had made full recovery ominous warnings began to appear of a second and more terrible global conflict. In spite of the disturbing results of the depression as they affected women chiefly through unemployment, postponement of marriage, and domestic strain, there was no serious retrogression in the social trend toward woman's greater opportunity and advance in status. Indeed, on the contrary, some of the legislation, particularly of Federal origin, which provided financial relief and security through governmental grants and enterprises contributed to the movement that had been bringing women nearer equality with men.

Meanwhile, beginning with 1900 when for the first time the significance of the ovary as an organ of internal secretion was clearly demonstrated,[1] an important new insight as to the distinction between male and female rapidly developed through discoveries in the field of endocrinology. Belief in the magical effect on the body of certain organs was very ancient. Preliterate peoples for example commonly felt assured that the individual could add to his power by eating organs obtained from animals through the hunt, or enemies killed in battle, that were supposed to have special value. For example, apparently from prehistoric times sex-gland material has been regarded as a source of erotic strength. In 1889 Brown Sequard, a famous French student, finding himself with diminishing virility, injected into his body testicular extracts and reported the results of his experiments. Although this is regarded as the birthday of endocrinology it was not until the beginning of the present century that enough progress was made in understanding the workings of the internal secretions to impress students of medical science. The significance of what we now know as the endocrine organs has become one of the greatest advances in the understanding of the working of the body as well as of the origin of many diseases concerning which in the past there was little factual knowledge.

Out of this advance in medical science is coming a new understanding of the differences in body structure and the physical career of the man and the woman. These discoveries could not put an end to the controversies that for so long a time had clouded the discussion of the issues pushed forward by the changing social life of women in the modern world, but it did withdraw some of the problems from speculation and dogmatism and throw upon them light gathered from experimental science.

The ground was cleared so that we now know the source of the physical distinction of male and female, its complexity and its variability. The substance that originates and controls the mechanism that normally leads to the development of the male or female body is endocrine in character, a product of the gonads, the sex glands which in the male are known as the testes, in the female as ovaries. In addition to the two different body forms, we also have to recognize the difference between sex and reproduction. Even though they are allied they are not synonymous and it is therefore no longer possible to interpret the woman and her physiological characteristics as entirely related to her function as a reproducing organism. Science now knows that there is not that sharp separation between maleness and femaleness that has been so long commonly assumed but instead there is in each individual a blending of both traits, and the proportion not only decides the sex to which the individual belongs but also the quantity of masculinity or femininity organically possessed.[2] This finding of science reënforces what sociology has long stressed, that much that seems to distinguish the man from the woman is cultural in origin and more to be explained by tradition expressed in folkways and *mores* than by influences coming from the physiological differences of the male and female.[3] The fact that both man and woman are composite in sexual characteristics and not marked off from members of the opposite sex with the exactness once regarded true increases all the more the significance of the causal influences of social origin that encourage the development of conventional traits which have been wrongly supposed to be the physical and psychic expression of the masculine or feminine personality.

When Charles Eliot, President of Harvard, set himself so rigorously against coeducation, being trained as a chemist, he spoke in the spirit of science. Had those working in his specialty uncovered at that time the significance of the endocrine basis and the dualistic composition of every man and woman, he would have shown greater caution in his opposition, knowing that experimental science forbade the grouping of human species into two rigid divisions as if there were absolute distinction rather than, as we now know, gradations in each individual of the male and female characteristics.

One of the questions that always arises in any discussion of the woman's rôle in industry or a professional career has been the significance of menstruation as a possible handicap in any competition with men. Strange as it may seem, it is only recently, due to the development of endocrinology, that we have had any considerable understanding of the menstrual functioning of the reproductive female. Now that we know the origin of the causation that operates, a much more complex physiological process than ever was suspected in the past, we are better able not only to judge the meaning of the monthly cycle but also to deal with the menstrual discomfort or pain which previously was considered a necessary accompaniment of the period. If at present it is too much to say that science can entirely eliminate any handicap an individual woman may have in the carrying on of her activities during the monthly flow, it is true that there is less tendency among physicians to regard discomfort or pain as normal and an increasing power to lessen or remove such disability when it occurs. Menstruation may be for some women a genuine handicap but it is certainly not true of all women and there is every reason to suppose that progress in endocrinology will be able increasingly to take away from most women any periodic impediment in their work or career due to menstruation.

There is no longer any scientific support of the easy-going generalizations, usually in accord with the prejudices and predispositions of the speaker or writer, that for so many centuries have been made regarding the inherent characteristics of men and women. It is no longer possible to consider the sexual endowment as fixed as soon as the anatomy of the body conforms to the male or female pattern or to regard the causal influences of the endocrines as merely local in their effect. Hormones enter the blood stream and therefore reach the cells of the brain.[4] The individual personality, a superstructure resting on a hormone basis, can no longer be interpreted as an expression of instinctive activities which can be catalogued as masculine or feminine. The possibilities of a woman's social career therefore must be found in the world of experience where she can be judged by her accomplishments rather than in arguments based upon anatomical predestination.

The woman has a more complex reproductive function than the man, but whether this through its social consequences limits her in her career as a human being living in the modern world is a question of fact, to be decided only as she is relieved of any cultural handicap placed upon her by the prevailing culture. In recent years there has been great momentum along another line of progress in medical science of concern to women. This new insight, which is by no means limited to the discoveries in the field of endocrinology, has been gained through better understanding of the problems of human reproduction. It is particularly in the causes and treatment of infertility, the body changes during pregnancy and the care of the mother, the delivery of the child, the safeguarding of infancy where the results of our greater knowledge and improved techniques are most impressive. Not only has there been great improvement in the skilled care of the physician, there has also been success in distributing information and in popularizing knowledge of the modern standards of maternal and infant care. Many individuals and organizations deserve recognition for their part in promoting the program that has decreased the deaths for both mothers and babies. The National Maternal and Child Health Council, formerly The National Council for Mothers and Babies, has been one of the most useful of the various organizations that have contributed constructively to the leadership in this field where preventive medicine has made such spectacular strides. In spite of recent progress there still remains a considerable waste of life appearing in the needless deaths of mothers and babies. It is estimated that in 1941 there were seventy-two thousand preventable deaths connected with pregnancy and childbirth.[5] The problem is chiefly that of prenatal and natal care.[6]

Although many men, especially doctors, have had an important part in it, progress in caring for the pregnant woman and protection of the infant and child is one evidence of the influence of women. A masculine culture in which women have small place as social individuals, being subservient to the interests of men, is largely indifferent to the hazards of motherhood. As recently as our own colonial period we find a prevailing complacency regarding the high maternal death rate. Without the advances of science the attempt of women's organizations and leaders to conserve motherhood would have proved discouraging but there can be no doubt that the concern of women, their increasing participation in public affairs, has done much to stimulate interest in this particular field of preventive medicine.

Nature's decision concerning the reproduction on the higher animal level which relieved the male from the ordeal of bringing offspring into the world was doubtless good strategy from the viewpoint of evolution. This accomplishment, however, carried some disadvantages. No one can doubt that, had pregnancy been a possible experience of the male as well as the female, the social attitude toward childbearing would earlier have disclosed an aggressive effort, such as has appeared in recent centuries, to lessen the suffering and the dangers of childbirth. It is doubtful whether under such circumstances the horrible doctrine that a woman through her pain and childbirth erased her major share of responsibility for introducing sin into the world would ever have developed to retard the advance of obstetrics.

It was in 1847 that James Y. Simpson, Professor of Obstetrics at the University of Glasgow, incurred the wrath of Scottish theologians by first using chloroform to lessen the pangs of childbirth. Fortunately for him, Queen Victoria in 1850 accepted chloroform at the birth of Prince Leopold, who survived, and then she frankly acknowledged the difference between her two kinds of experiences. Previously she had delivered six times without the aid of anesthesia and therefore could give convincing testimony as to the advantage of the new method.

The welfare of the child, especially the female child, also does not become a major interest unless women contribute to cultural attitudes. It is interesting to note that the nineteenth century, which is said to have been the century of the child, was the period when the Woman's Movement gathered great momentum and the masculine dominated culture began to respond to the pressure of feminine influences.

Social changes that affect women are still in transition. The general trend has been unmistakably toward greater recognition of woman as an individual and the opening up for her of new opportunities. This movement in our present culture, still dominated by masculine traditions, can be exaggerated just as the earlier recognition of women and provisions for their self-expression can be minimized. There has not occurred in this country a complete reversal of one type of culture by the other, nor has the line of social change been consistently forward. An evidence, and a consequence, of this situation is the persisting discussion of the social problems of women. No one could deny that many of the difficulties of social adjustment in the life career of the woman remain a special topic of controversy in a way not true of man's interests. Questions of women's needs and obligations, criticisms of the attitudes of men toward women, and women's interpretation of handicaps and attempted solutions appear constantly not only as themes for novels but also as an outburst of the author's personal feeling in many books and articles dealing with American social life. This literature is strikingly different from that associated with the controversy over woman suffrage. That tremendous departure from the one-time axiom of political thinking has been thoroughly accepted and rarely, at least in this country, is the wisdom of the change ever challenged.

The trend now taken by the "woman's question" stresses the psychiatric and the sociological viewpoints. Although it has become more difficult than ever to distinguish the inherent traits of the woman as compared with those of the man, aside from the physiological body differences associated with two opposite rôles in reproduction, much is made of feminine characteristics that make more difficult the woman's career in the modern world. For example, one school of Freudian thought takes as a cornerstone of its system the female child's lack of the more noticeable genital structure of the male. Thus we have the castration complex, frequently with little recognition of the fact that the girl's feeling of deficiency becomes a symbol of the numerous limitations of social origins with which she gets acquainted in her early years. In spite of a very great change which is lessening her social disadvantages, the girl does not escape suggestion, rules of conduct, ideals and other coercive influences that make her less free than the boy. This social discrimination is revealed in the common assumption that the mother who has brought forth a male child has reason for special gratification. Thus, before the girl even enters life, she is socially discriminated against and it would be a miracle if in the early days of childhood consciousness she never coveted the freer and therefore more attractive rôle of the boy.

Pressure of the social code which distinguishes between the boy and the girl is so constant and so familiar that it attracts less attention than from its significance might be expected. College regulations for example assume the necessity of treating the woman differently from the man. In 1942 we find Antioch College, brave as always, taking the unconventional departure from the customary routine and abolishing freshman rules for women and replacing them with rules that are the same for both men and women. Concerning this change the editor of the college paper at Antioch wrote: "The common situation of rules for women and none for men, while accurately mirroring the condition of society in general, does little for the men and in the long run little for society either." [7]

Disappointment has frequently been expressed that the coming of woman suffrage did not bring the political reforms the leaders of the movement had prophesied. Since the new influx of voters was drawn into the existing political system, the influence of women did not show itself as distinctly as had been expected. It certainly would have been undesirable to have had a woman's party standing by itself and attempting to divide the voting population on a sex basis. The alternative meant incorporating women in the existing political system. This necessarily limited their influence but, although there was not the spectacular progress that the enthusiastic suffrage leaders had promised, it is contrary to fact not to recognize that woman suffrage elevated political standards and, what is much more important, brought up the status of women. The changes that occurred were cumulative, and perhaps nowhere is it more noticeable than in the higher education of women. It is startling to find as an illustration of this trend the offering at Syracuse University in 1942 for the first time in the history of higher education in America a course dealing exclusively with the social and economic activities of women. The title of the new course, offered in the Department of Sociology by Dr. M. Eunice Hilton, Dean of Women, was The Status and Responsibilities of Women in the Social Order. In explaining the purpose of the course, Dr. Hilton said that little attention has been given to the special interests of women and that it was hoped through this course to do a real service for women and to fill in the large area of material regarding women missing in current courses dealing with social, political, economic, legal, and educational data of the past and present.[8]

It is certain that unless women had been moving forward in their social status they would never have been given the economic justice which came with the recommendation of the National War Labor Board Panel in the General Motors Case that the same wage rate be established for women and men when doing the same work. The justice of this principle of equal pay for women's work was given recognition in their wage negotiation both by the A. F. of L. and the C. I. O. in unions in major aircraft plants.[9] In Michigan the legal requirement that women who do the same work as men shall receive the same pay was upheld in the courts with the consequence that back wages were ordered, restoring to women who had been paid less per hour than men what they had lost merely from being females.[10] A similar law compelling manufacturers to give equal pay for equal work, effective July 1, 1944 was passed by the State of Illinois. This law requires that where six or more persons are employed, men and women must receive equal wages for equal work with allowances for individual experience, skills, and other differentials.[11]

A great war breaks through social tradition as a disk-harrow breaks through hard ground. The Revolutionary War, the Civil War, and the First World War disturbed social convention and permitted a marked advance in the status of women. This, as has already been brought out, was especially true in the First World War. Its successor, the Global War, has had a much greater effect because it brought about such far-reaching volcanic results in every aspect of American life and also on account of the previous advance that women had effected which made it easier for public opinion to accept what otherwise would have seemed radical and unfeminine departures. The earlier experiences of England, Germany, and Russia prepared the American people for a war program that gave women a more active part than ever before had been possible.

As soon as America declared war it was recognized both by military and civilian leadership that there would be need of enlisting women, not for active service in the field but in occupations that would relieve soldiers and sailors, marines and coast guardsmen from routine assignments and thus permit them to serve on the field of battle. The first women's organization authorized by Congress was the Woman's Army Auxiliary Corps, commonly designated as the WAACS. It was made possible by a bill signed on May 15, 1942. The following day the Secretary of War, Henry L. Stimson, appointed Mrs. Oveta Culp Hobby its director. Recruiting started at once and on July 20 there were 440 candidates for officer positions in the new organization at the training center at Fort Des Moines, Iowa. Later by Federal law this organization became a part of the regular Army and was then known as the Woman's Army Corps.

This enlistment of women as a means of hastening the victory met with general approval and soon provision was made for similar organizations in the Navy, Women Appointed for Voluntary Emergency Service or the WAVES, Women's Reserve in the United States Coast Guard or the SPARS, and finally the Woman's Marine Corps. Each of these groups was given a distinctive uniform and organized on a military basis. There were also many other organizations not part of the armed forces that assumed various other responsibilities, some of which, like the Red Cross, had been carried on in the First World War. One which would not have been thought of earlier as a proper service for women was the Women's Auxiliary Ferrying Squad, popularly known as the WAFS.

The most important contribution of American women during the Second World War came through their employment in war industry. This was a repetition of what happened in the first war with Germany, but during the global contest the employment of

NEAR EQUALITY WITH MEN

women both in quantity and in the number of occupations entered was unprecedented. For example, for the first time in 141 years in the history of the New York Navy Yard at Brooklyn women were hired as apprentice mechanics to take over the jobs of men who left shops in the yard. Half the 6,000 women who had been tested by September 1942, had been qualified for the Navy Yard jobs. It was expected at that time that 6,000 would be at work by the end of the year.[12]

From every sort of industry there was demand for women workers in war production. Likewise pressure for more women trained in science, business, and the professions was placed upon the schools and colleges. Changes were made in the curriculum of many of the higher institutions of learning. As an example of this we find Ohio State University offering a nine months' course in the engineering aspects of industry open only to women and offered primarily to those whose previous college work had not been along lines directly related to the war effort. Also shorter cram courses were provided at night for women employed during the day.[13]

The advertisements on page 412 taken from the Sunday issue of one of our metropolitan newspapers [14] illustrate the eagerness with which various corporations sought women workers.

In 1940 the employed women totalled 11,138,178 or 24.7% of all employed persons. It was estimated early in 1943 that by the close of the year there would be 18,000,000 women at work or 34% of all employed persons.[15] Throughout the War there was in almost every type of work a general shifting from manpower to womanpower as men were drafted and their places were taken by women. Experience demonstrated that women could be trained to use tool equipment and carry on occupations that had previously been exclusively men's. An illustration of this was the estimation that by the close of 1943, 75% of the total employees in small arms manufacture were likely to be women, and as many as 40% in cannon manufacture.[16]

The influx of women into nearly every kind of industrial occupation was a national necessity. No country can fight success-

GIRLS! WOMEN!

No Grease—No Grime
in this simple war job!

NO EXPERIENCE NECESSARY

Hundreds of men and women began work in July at Chance Vought Aircraft

where you are offered

—$47 per week after 4 months (55-hour week).
—$33 per week from the start (54-hour week).
—after 2 weeks to $37.
—increases on merit.
—congenial fellow-workers... clean, safe working conditions.
—rooms located by the company.
—living conditions similar to those in New York.
—careful training and supervision.
—interesting, vital war work with a good future.

CHANCE VOUGHT AIRCRAFT
STRATFORD, CONN.

Must be over 18 years old with at least two years' high school. Persons in war work or essential activity not considered without statement of availability.

For interview with company representatives
MON. & TUES. 10 A. M. TO 5 P. M.
Apply only at
UNITED STATES EMPLOYMENT SERVICE
of the War Manpower Commission
79–87 Madison Ave.
28TH ST.   N. Y. C.
NO PLACEMENT FEES

OPPORTUNITY
FOR WOMEN
OVER 45

Full-time inside work transferring messages in operating rooms, also occasional specialized clerical work—all vital to the war effort—no experience necessary—clean, pleasant surroundings—beginners average upward from $20 weekly, or $90 monthly—free physical examination and proof of age required, also evening work but at bonus pay.

INTERVIEWS DAILY 9:30 A. M.–4 P. M.
ON SATURDAYS TO 1 P. M.

WESTERN UNION
ROOM 400   60 HUDSON ST.

A short walk from all subways
NEAR CHAMBERS STREET

Persons in war or essential work not accepted without availability statement

NEAR EQUALITY WITH MEN

fully a modern war if it depends upon manpower alone. It would be a mistake, however, to regard the new opportunities brought by war as nothing more than a temporary acceptance of women as substitutes for men. Germany and Japan also shifted much of their labor in industry from men to women, but in those countries this did not lead to the lifting of the status of women as was true in our country. The reason for this difference is found in the social position of women in the opposite cultures. Here women were already advancing and were prepared to take advantage of the new situation and through their war work obtain greater economic and social recognition as they moved toward greater equality with men, while in the other countries the inferiority of women was so thoroughly cemented in a different way of life that the war merely increased the burden placed upon women without giving them greater security or prestige. The Woman's Bureau was quick to appreciate the strategic openings as well as the new responsibilities this greater industrial dependence upon women brought. Thus an experienced leadership was prepared not only to help in the training and the placing of women but also to stress principles such as equal pay for equal work.

In America there were well-trained professional women who found the doors opening to them in an unprecedented way. Women doctors, dentists, chemists, personnel directors, lawyers, pharmacists, found themselves suddenly in great demand and largely free from the handicap that previously had hampered their professional careers. For a time the law made it impossible to induct women doctors into the Army and Navy although a few of them were given appointments based upon contracts. This discrimination was removed by an act of Congress but there was slow response to the legal provision for the commissioning of qualified women doctors. Probably this was due chiefly to the fact that these women were already committed to the responsibilities of private practice as they helped meet the scarcity of doctors in many American communities.[17]

The rapid growth of communities busy with war production

not only disturbed families who moved from one locality to another but this shifting of population also created problems of housing and feeding, especially for the single woman. Washington, as a result of the tremendous expansion of governmental activities, a trend markedly apparent before the war but accelerated by it, became the star example of the problems of transportation, housing, and feeding that created greater difficulty for the incoming women than for the men.

The aircraft industry, particularly in southern California, is in many ways the most striking evidence of the response of women to a new industrial opportunity. In February 1942 there were 500 women on the production lines, in June there were 18,000 carrying on a wide variety of occupations. It was estimated that the number required by the end of 1942 would be 75,000. Possibly the most surprising result coming from the employment of women was the discovery that they could quickly be taught a new precision work in the manufacturing of delicate instruments in highly skilled operations that previously had been exclusively carried on by men.

Every important enterprise connected with the war brought its problems. The larger employment of women in industry was no exception. Soon absenteeism on the part of women was charged against them by many employers. An investigation disclosed that there was a slight difference between women and men in this staying away from the job. The reasons for this, however, gave no basis for indicting women as less serious in their commitments than men. It was rather that they were subjected to many more liabilities. The major cause of involuntary absence was sickness. The record of women was not quite so good as that of men. They appeared to be more susceptible to fatigue. Most of the deliberate absenteeism on the part of women, where it became a serious problem for the employer, was explained by the greater number of responsibilities of the women who entered war work. Many wives and mothers carried on an apparently necessary part of housekeeping while at the same time spending as many hours at their factory as men. The rationing of food, for example, created great difficulties for many women. They had to purchase food for their families, and at a time when stores were crowded. Frequently they felt that they had to stay away from work because only so could they get articles necessary for their family since after the end of the factory day they found the stores closed. Then the plants themselves had not been prepared to take in women and changes had to be made by the management in order to provide the comfort and relaxation which they needed in order that they might get on with their jobs.

"In a recent survey of 183 war plants, Bureau agents found that 123 gave 30 minutes for lunch, not paid for in the worker's wages. A total of ⅕ of the plants paid for lunch periods, ranging from 15 to 30 minutes. Of 177 plants reporting on facilities, about 60 per cent had cafeterias or mobile canteens serving hot food of some kind. The findings reflected a wide variety of conditions—some meeting fully Woman's Bureau standards. But these statistics don't tell the whole story. Here's what the Bureau also discovered:

"Thousands of war workers have no hot food during working hours.

"Thousands of war workers must eat lunch in 15 minutes.

"Thousands of workers eat in the open, exposed to all weather variations.

"Thousands of workers eat in unsanitary rest rooms.

"And the results? Lately people have been calling it absenteeism. Personnel offices call it anemia, indigestion, nervous debility and work lag. You can see it in the girl at an ordnance plant who doesn't even attempt to eat in her 15-minute dinner hour—she catnaps on a bench in the hall.

"Conditions such as these have a number of causes. The primary one is an inadequate supply of food at places of work. Secondly, workers cannot always bring food with them from home—many live in boarding houses, others have too many home duties to spare the time for preparation of lunches or do not want to take rationed items from the family group. Thirdly, peacetime service facilities simply cannot cope with the huge increase on top of labor shortages and rationing. The rapid conversion of the production set-up to a war economy has brought in its wake dislocations in essential civilian establishments that cannot be easily overcome." [18]

This influx of women was naturally unwelcome to some employers. H. Oliver West of Boeing Aircraft, according to the press, was one of them. The critics complained that the women flirted, were finicky, and had no flair for mechanics. This indictment brought from Donald W. Douglas, President of Douglas Aircraft, a statement that women have brought the same sense of responsibility and resourcefulness to strange and complicated jobs of aircraft building that for generations has gone into the efficiency of American homes. Robert E. Gross, President of Lockheed Aircraft, in his reply said in part: "Women workers are replacing the men as they leave, with great competency. There is no reason as far as I can see why they should not be able to take over 100% of the work if necessary." The industrial magician, Henry J. Kaiser of the Oregon Shipbuilding Company, asserted that the hiring of 270 women welders since May 1942 was merely the beginning of a policy to use women in work which in times past had been thought too strenuous for them. Even from Reno came testimony that the placing of women in the gambling establishments of that city was proving most satisfactory. The War Manpower Commission was petitioned for permission to raise the salary ceiling of these women workers to $15 per day.[19] By November 1942 the Office of War Information, U. S. Department of Labor, was able to report that women were replacing and supplementing men in many war industry jobs without change or interruption in factory processes and that there was no real distinction in war industry as to what constituted a man's or a woman's job. It was not uncommon for a job to be performed by women during the day while men took over on the night shift in a continuous production schedule. Women were also doing work formerly done entirely by men with no substantial change made in the content or physical characteristics of the job. It was not uncommon also for men and women to work together, as, for example, when riveting aircraft machines.

One of the greatest innovations was that of the Pennsylvania Railroad in hiring women conductors on some of their suburban trains out of New York. This change, although it attracted attention for a few days, worked out well. Earlier, women had begun to take over the work of the men in street transportation, both electric power cars and buses.

Although women entering war industry proved their ability to do almost anything men have been doing, it was found that they had a higher percentage of labor turnover than men. There were many reasons for this; chiefly difficulties resulting from the household or mother responsibilities of the women. Many who had children entered war work, and many more attempted to carry on a home to which previously they had given their major attention. A large proportion of these women went into industry or one of the women's organizations associated with the armed forces from patriotic motives and in many instances they found that they had been overzealous. As a result each announcement of an important victory by the United Nations was followed by the dropping out of women workers from essential war industries and especially from volunteer services. The Red Cross and Civilian Defense Volunteer Office, for example, found that every Allied success gave a signal for some of their volunteer women workers to go home. The reasons for these desertions boil down to three: money problems, fatigue, and what has been called the "peace panic." [20] Some of these women, mothers of small children, had volunteered believing that they could carry on with the aid of a maid. Soon the maid was drawn into some sort of war industry and with the rising cost of living the mother found no means of maintaining her household. The consequence was that she resigned, especially if the war situation began to improve. Others had to give up volunteer work because they had taken over a regular factory job. They soon found that they did not have the energy to carry on both commitments. Another group had been drawn into volunteer service because it seemed a stark necessity but as soon as things began to go better they felt free to drop out.[21]

There can be no question of the seriousness of the problem many of these women faced. Evidence of this appears in the rise of delinquency both in England and in the United States. In some of the families where both the father and the mother were working, and had children too old to be in a nursery and yet not mature enough to be safe without parental control, their boys and girls drifted into various forms of reckless conduct. Unlike what happened during the First World War, delinquency found its greatest increase in the younger adolescent and especially the teen-age girl. This was most evident in communities near army camps, as a result of the breakdown of family life and the disorganizing influence of war conditions. The seriousness of this problem was quickly recognized by leading women all over the nation who immediately interested themselves in various sorts of constructive programs. Even if these efforts did not eliminate this war-time delinquency they kept it from increasing to a still greater social menace.

In no period of American life did there develop among conscientious and thoughtful women such interest in the family and its problems as during the years following the First World War. The guide for study and research prepared by Harriet Ahlers Houdlette of the American Association of University Women, entitled *The American Family in a Changing Society*, is representative of this concern. As a consequence there was greater preparedness among the women active in social leadership for the strain put upon the family by the second world conflict than otherwise would have been true. This was fortunate because the stress which the family had to meet in the Global War was as much greater than the earlier ordeal as the survival struggle itself.

The social problems created by the war could never have reached the proportions they did if there had been from the beginning greater recognition of the need of having more women in positions that influenced state and national policies. Minnie L. Maffett, President of the National Federation of Business and Professional Women's Clubs, addressing the Board Meeting at Lake

George, New York, July 8, 1943, forcefully brought out the government's failure to make full use of women's insight, thus disclosing that in political planning, especially, masculine dominance persisted to such an extent as to discriminate against the potential usefulness of women even during our period of greatest crisis. Dr. Maffett summed up the situation as follows:

"But in one respect, let us remember well that our nation has failed signally in regard to its womanpower in that women are not yet permitted in any way to help direct the policies of this government. It is of paramount importance that they do so, for women are among those responsible not only to our own country and to our fighting men, but to the generations to come, for shaping the pattern of actual and future conditions. A rather careful study of this situation convinces me that we have made little, if any, progress toward assuming this responsibility for helping to shape the conduct of national affairs. I am not sure that an easy and correct diagnosis as to why this is true can be made.

"It is easy, however, to dismiss the question by answering that the higher powers, whoever they be and how they ever got that way, evidently think that the judgment of the women of the nation is not yet ripe for such recognition and that they are still unqualified mentally, emotionally, or by experience to take part in the national counsels.

"But—facts, if they are considered, prove otherwise. Convincing evidence during the past year and a half especially shows that women can do their part side by side with men—and with no favors asked and no quarter given.

"But, again, in spite of this much good showing and much convincing evidence as to ability, loyalty, and efficiency, they have not been trained by experience to help administer public affairs to any appreciable extent. This may come yet but I assure you that, if it does, it will not be through wishful hoping but by more aggressive action in public affairs than we have shown to date.

"We have given much lip service and have done much whistling in the dark to keep up our courage but we still have elected few women to important public posts, only a handful to Congress and just one to our august Senate, none have even been on the Supreme Court bench, no large city system of schools has a woman Superintendent, and, I think I am entirely correct in saying, no State University, though supported by public funds, has ever had a woman President.

"Last year at the Denver Board Meeting, it was my privilege to report to you on the almost complete absence of women in policy-making posts in our national government. Again, I will refer to the roster taken from the latest pamphlet issued by the government as evidence that women have made only the slightest advance during the past year in securing a voice in shaping the affairs of this nation—either in the capitol or in the regions and areas of the country. In the various war emergency agencies, the places of importance held by women at this time are far from impressive—as evidenced by the fact that:

"In the National War Production Board—among the 146 ranking officials—only one is a woman. This is a microscopic gain. Of the 209 regional officers throughout the country, only two are women.

"Office of Price Administration: among the 69 officials in Washington, there is still but one woman. In the regional offices, there is only one woman listed among the 64 members.

"Office of War Information: in which has been incorporated the offices of Facts and Figures reported on last year—among the 23 top ranking officers, there is one woman who serves as Chief of the Bureau of Public Inquiries. Last year, all the top ranking officers in the Office of Facts and Figures were men.

"Office of Civilian Defense: among the highest officials, there is still no woman.

"National War Labor Board: of the 45 top ranking officials, there is likewise no woman. From the troubles of this particular Board in recent weeks, they may, after all, be a bit lucky.

"Office of Defense Transportation: among the top ranking officials of the 40 leading divisions and regions, there is no woman.

"Office of the Coordinator of Inter-American Affairs: of the 17 high ranking officials, there is no woman.

"Office of Defense Health and Welfare: among the 11 top ranking officials, there is no woman; of the 5 committees in this office, four are headed by men as Chairmen while one is headed by a woman.

"Board of Economic Warfare: of the 11 top ranking officials, there is no woman.

"National Housing Agency: among the 12 top ranking officials, there is no woman.

"Federal Housing Administration: among the 2 top ranking officials, there is one woman.

"War Manpower Commission: of the 11 top ranking officials, there is one woman, Frances Perkins, Secretary of Labor.

"We must point with pride, however, to the fact that there is a Woman's Advisory Committee to the War Manpower Commission, under the direction of our own First Vice-President, Margaret A. Hickey. She has the honor of sitting on the National Management-Labor Policy Committee of the War Manpower Commission, true, *but* she has *no vote*. She has a fine group of women on her committee, and it is to be hoped that they make their presence felt. Regionally, the War Manpower Commission has appointed at least one woman as Regional Director." [22]

Perhaps even more important was the speaker's realization that with the end of the war this failure to give women the representation they deserve in the policy-making functions of government would prove a greater handicap to our social security than in the war period.[23]

"I solemnly charge that the war is being slowed down here in America by the failure of the government to use women's brains and training in their specialized fields, which include all problems related to food, welfare, rehabilitation, housing, clothing, rationing, and foreign and domestic policies that concern the world to which women are willing to give their best thought and effort. They must be used now, too, in planning for post war economic, social, and political development at home and abroad. We have a momentous job ahead and we must act now if we are to make an effective contribution in solving these problems." [24]

It became clear to an increasing number of women that the status of women as determined by legislation could not safely continue on the basis of apparent expediency but should be determined once and for all by the constitutional assertion of the full equality before the law of women and men. This reversal of the former legislative program designed to protect women's interests naturally met with considerable opposition from leading women, especially those who had been prominent in earlier years in advocating various reforms to shelter women from exploitation. The need, however, of this right-about-face bore testimony to the advance women have finally made, in part because they had been given these legal defenses at a time when they were either politically impotent or unable through lack of experience, especially in self-protecting organizations, to defend themselves against discrimination and exploitation. This protective legislation which had developed in the United States served well as a temporary scaffolding when women were so legally and socially limited that they were unable to defend their own interests but increasingly it was becoming a social anachronism, a structure out of accord with the progress toward the equality of the sexes that had already taken place in this country. It is not difficult to understand the reluctance with which some of the women who had had a conspicuous rôle in bringing about special legislation designed to strengthen the defense of women in industry recoiled from the new order consistent with and made desirable by the advance in woman's status that was already an accomplished fact. It is never easy to remove reforms brought about through struggle and sacrifice but the forward-going of woman's welfare could not be anchored even in the benevolence of the early years of this century. The interests of women had already matured beyond the need for a legislative guardianship. An increasing number of men and even more women realized that the best possible protection of the rights of women and their welfare could be found only in their full legal equality with men.

Evidence of this increasing realization, especially among those sensitive to the recent changes in the conditions that affect women, appeared in the conviction that the establishment of equal rights for men and women by constitutional amendment was the natural and inevitable outcome of the evolution of American culture. This belief was stimulated by the consequences of the Second World War. An illustration of this adjustment to woman's changing circumstances was the indorsement of the legal rights amendment by the Board of Directors of the General Federation of Women's Clubs, July 1, 1943. The Honorable Winifred C. Stanley, Representative at Large from New York State, well expressed the feeling of an increasing number of women that the American principle of democracy at stake in the world conflict was inconsistent with any legal recognition of the social or political inequality of men and women.

"The Equal Rights Amendment has my hearty endorsement. In this time of national and world crisis, American women are making a record of loyalty and service. In the American home, in defense industries, in business, in the professions, in voluntary war services of all kinds, and in the Nurses' Corps, the Waacs, the Waves, the Spars, the Women's Auxiliary Marine Corps, they are performing magnificent work to maintain our constitutional form of Government. Like Madame Chiang Kai-shek and other brave women of the allied nations our women stand ready to defend this country to the limit of their capacity. We are coming to realize more and more deeply as the war continues that we must strive for equal rights for everyone if our civilization is to continue." [25]

The Second World War was fundamentally an absolute collision of opposing cultures. This was understood not only by the people of the United Nations but also by those in authority on the other side. The irreconcilable differences covered a vast territory of human interests. At no point was the clashing of the two philosophies of life more apparent than in the unlike conceptions of the proper function and social status of woman. The German point of view repudiated the progress woman had made even in central Europe in expanding her opportunity as an individual and reassigned her to the rôle of the traditional female in which physical sex, reproduction, and family tasks became the limit of her usefulness. This interpretation of woman was even more restrictive in Japan. There the conventions that controlled the life of woman had advanced almost not at all,[26] even though the Japanese had abstracted considerably from western culture. If we compare the status of women in the United States, Canada, Australia, and New Zealand with that existing in Japan, we see in most intense contrast the significance of one of the basic contributions of the American evolution of society. We with our closest allies in cultural sympathy are committed to the latest and most thoroughly modern attempt to determine the relationship of the two sexes. In essence it is an endeavor to recognize the mutual rights of men and women as individuals; each sex achieving the greatest personal fulfillment and contributing most to the general welfare. Nothing in our American way of life is more characteristic or more revealing of the trends of the social evolution of the American people than this lessening of the one-time masculine dominance of culture. Whatever consequences this departure from European and Asiatic traditions may bring with the passage of time, it is clearly a goal toward which we in this country have been moving from the birth of our nation. It is an achievement of both men and women working together but it can be secured only by the latter as they make good use of their unprecedented opportunity.

FOOTNOTES

CHAPTER I

THE CULTURAL BACKGROUND OF THE AMERICAN WOMAN

[1] R. Briffault, *The Mothers*, Vol. III, p. 360.
[2] *The Catholic Encyclopaedia*, Vol. I, p. 771.
[3] *The Jewish Encyclopaedia*, Vol. V, p. 224.
[4] J. Hastings, *A Dictionary of the Bible*, Vol. I, p. 768 (Philo Judaeus, *Quod Omnis Probus Liber*).
[5] Josephus, *De Bello Judaico*, Vol. II, Books 8 and 13.
[6] J. Hastings, *op. cit.*, (Eusebius, *Praeparatio Evangelica*).
[7] *The Jewish Encyclopaedia*, Vol. V, p. 228.
[8] J. Hastings, *op. cit.*, p. 771.
[9] *The Jewish Encyclopaedia*, Vol. V, p. 232.
[10] J. Hastings, *op. cit.*, p. 771.
[11] R. Briffault, *op. cit.*, p. 349.
[12] W. W. Fowler, *The Religious Experience of the Roman People*, p. 466.
[13] St. Jerome, *The Nicene and Post-Nicene Fathers*, Vol. VI, p. 25.
[14] *Galatians*, 2: 20.
[15] F. C. Porter, *The Mind of Christ in Paul*, p. 219.
[16] R. Briffault, *op. cit.*, p. 372.
[17] A. Harnack, *The Mission and Expansion of Christianity in the First Three Centuries*, Vol. I, p. 216.
[18] I *Timothy*, 2: 9.
[19] A. Harnack, *op. cit.*, Vol. II, p. 64.
[20] *Galatians*, 3: 28.
[21] *Philippians*, 4: 3.
[22] A. Harnack, *op. cit.*, Vol. II, p. 67.
[23] *Romans*, 16: 1–2.
[24] See I *Timothy*, Ch. 5.
[25] A. Harnack, *op. cit.*, Vol. II, p. 71.
[26] For a stronger statement see S. D. Schmalhausen and V. F. Calverton, *Woman's Coming of Age* (A Symposium), p. 52.
[27] E. Gibbon, *The Decline and Fall of the Roman Empire*, Vol. I, p. 414.
[28] St. Jerome, *op. cit.*, Vol. VI, p. 31.

[29] *Ibid.*, p. 75.
[30] *Ibid.*, p. 71.
[31] *Ibid.*, p. 260.
[32] *Ibid.*, p. 29.
[33] W. Goodsell, *A History of Marriage and the Family*, p. 170.
[34] *The Writings of Clement of Alexandria*, Vol. II, p. 193.
[35] *Ibid.*, p. 196.
[36] *Ibid.* p. 197.
[37] *The Writings of Cyprian*, Vol. I, pp. 348–349.
[38] *Ibid.*, p. 346.
[39] *Ibid.*, p. 346–347.
[40] W. E. H. Lecky, *History of European Morals*, Vol. II, p. 122.
[41] See *Encyclopaedia of the Social Sciences*, Vol. XII, p. 554; also, Paul LaCroix, *History of Prostitution*, Vol. II, especially Ch. VI.
[42] L. Eckenstein, *Woman Under Monasticism*, p. 152.
[43] G. G. Coulton, *Five Centuries of Religion*, Ch. 28.
[44] *The Encyclopaedia of the Social Sciences*, Vol. III, p. 284.
[45] G. B. Fisher, *History of the Christian Church*, pp. 62 and 101.
[46] *The Encyclopaedia of the Social Sciences*, Vol. III, p. 284.
[47] M. B. Messer, *The Family in the Making*, p. 167.
[48] W. Goodsell, *op. cit.*, p. 227.
[49] *Ibid.*, p. 226.
[50] Buckstaff, F. G. "Married Women's Property in Anglo-Saxon and Anglo-Norman Law," *Annals of the American Academy of Political and Social Science*, 4, 1893–1894, p. 261.
[51] *Ibid.*, p. 262.
[52] *Ibid.*, pp. 256–257.
[53] C. A. and M. R. Beard, *The Rise of American Civilization*, p. 25.
[54] *Ibid.*, p. 26.
[55] *Ibid.*, p. 26.
[56] L. B. Wright, *Middle-Class Culture in Elizabethan England*, p. 202.
[57] *Ibid.*, pp. 506–507.
[58] *Ibid.*, p. 507.

CHAPTER II

THE COLONIAL WOMAN

[1] M. Fordham, *A Short History of English Rural Life*, p. 75.
[2] ———, *The Rebuilding of Rural England*, p. 7.
[3] C. M. Andrews, *The Colonial Period of American History*, p. 57.
[4] *Ibid.*, p. 54.

FOOTNOTES

[5] P. A. Bruce, *Economic History of Virginia in the Seventeenth Century*, Vol. II, p. 51.
[6] *Ibid.*, Vol. I, p. 583.
[7] *Ibid.*
[8] *Ibid.*, p. 608.
[9] *Ibid.*, p. 615.
[10] *Ibid.*, Vol. II, p. 15.
[11] *Ibid.*, p. 112.
[12] *Ibid.*, p. 34.
[13] *Ibid.*, p. 35.
[14] *Ibid.*, p. 37.
[15] C. A. and M. R. Beard, *The Rise of American Civilization*, p. 44.
[16] C. M. Andrews, *op. cit.*, p. 134.
[17] M. A. Beard, *America Through Woman's Eyes*, p. 13.
[18] P. A. Bruce, *op. cit.*, Vol. I, p. 215.
[19] W. B. Weeden, *Economic and Social History of New England 1620–1789*, Vol. II, pp. 867 and 868.
[20] S. Van Rensselaer, *History of the City of New York in the Seventeenth Century*, Vol. I, p. 480.
[21] A. W. Calhoun, *A Social History of the American Family*, Vol. I, p. 169.
[22] W. H. Kilpatrick, *The Dutch Schools of New Netherlands and Colonial New York*, p. 217.
[23] *Ibid.*, p. 201.
[24] T. Woody, *A History of Women's Education in the United States*, Vol. I, pp. 211–212.
[25] A. W. Calhoun, *op. cit.*, p. 204.
[26] T. Woody, *op. cit.*, p. 178.
[27] A. W. Calhoun, *op. cit.*, p. 205.
[28] *Ibid.*, p. 206.
[29] *Ibid.*, p. 223.
[30] M. S. Benson, *Women in Eighteenth Century America*, p. 31.
[31] W. H. Payne (ed.), *Rousseau's Emile*, pp. 260 and 263.
[32] M. S. Benson, *op. cit.*, pp. 24–27.
[33] J. C. Spruill ms., Women's Life and Work in the Southern Colonies, Ch. XIV, "Tavern Hostesses and Planters."
[34] E. A. Dexter, *Colonial Women of Affairs*, p. 115.
[35] *Ibid.*, p. 20.
[36] J. C. Spruill, *op. cit.*, Ch. XIII, "Shopkeepers and Artisans."
[37] T. J. Woofter, Jr., *Black Yeomanry*, p. 111.
[38] *Mass. Colonial Records*, Vol. II, p. 203 (Taken from E. A. Dexter, *op. cit.*, p. 79.
[39] A. W. Calhoun, *op. cit.*, p. 72.
[40] E. A. Dexter, *op. cit.*, p. 89.
[41] *Ibid.*, p. 126.
[42] See E. Crawley, *The Mystic Rose*.
[43] See H. Van de Velde, *Sex Hostility in Marriage*.

CHAPTER III

THE FRONTIER WOMAN

[1] E. D. Branch, *Westward*, p. 282.
[2] F. J. Turner, *The United States 1830–1850*, pp. 13 and 15.
[3] T. Speed, *The Wilderness Road*, p. 7.
[4] C. A. and M. R. Beard, *The Rise of American Civilization*, Vol. I, p. 535.
[5] *Ibid.*, p. 527.
[6] J. G. Leyburn, *Frontier Folkways*, p. 215.
[7] R. Pound, *The Spirit of the Common Law*, pp. 116–117.
[8] F. J. Turner, *The Frontier in American History*, p. 354.
[9] D. Crockett, *The Autobiography of David Crockett*, pp. 49–50.
[10] *Ibid.*, pp. 51–52.
[11] *Ibid.*, p. 69.
[12] E. C. Stanton, S. B. Anthony, and M. J. Gage, *The History of Woman Suffrage*, Vol. I, p. 290.
[13] T. Speed, *op. cit.*, p. 44.
[14] E. D. Branch, *op. cit.*, p. 288.

CHAPTER IV

THE WOMAN OF THE NORTH FROM THE REVOLUTION TO THE CIVIL WAR

[1] Letter of Abigail Adams, July 31, 1777.
[2] *Ibid.*, December 23, 1782.
[3] Capt. Marryat, *A Diary in America*, Vol. I, p. 11.
[4] *Eighth Census of the United States in 1860*, p. 593.
[5] *Ibid.*, p. xviii (Introduction).
[6] *Ibid.*
[7] *Ibid.*, p. xxxiii (Introduction).
[8] *Compendium of the Seventh Census of the United States, 1850*, p. 101.
[9] *Report on Manufactures. In American State Papers, Finance*, II (Gallatin), p. 427.
[10] T. Dwight, *Travels; in New-England and New-York*: Vol. IV, p. 352.
[11] *Ibid.*, p. 359.
[12] R. M. Tryon, *Household Manufactures in the United States 1640–1860*, p. 272.
[13] E. Abbott, *Women in Industry*, pp. 46–47.
[14] *A Century of Population Growth in the United States 1790–1900*, p. 93.
[15] H. U. Faulkner, *American Economic History*, pp. 275 and 278.

FOOTNOTES

[16] E. Abbott, *Women in Industry*, p. 38.
[17] A Survey of Sandwich, New Hampshire, directed by the author.
[18] *Compendium of the Seventh Census of the United States, 1850*, p. 49.
[19] T. Woody, *A History of Women's Education in the United States*, Vol. II, p. 9.
[20] *American Notes*, p. 66.
[21] N. Ware, *The Industrial Worker 1840–1860*, p. 96.
[22] *The Atlantic Monthly*, Vol. XLVIII, p. 610.
[23] *Fifth Annual Report of Massachusetts State Board of Education*, p. 98.
[24] W. L. Chenery, *Industry and Human Welfare*, p. 20.
[25] *Massachusetts Senate Document No. 21*, 1868, p. 23.
[26] W. L. Chenery, *op. cit.*, p. 39.
[27] R. T. Ely, *The Labor Movement in America*, p. 49.
[28] E. Abbott, *op. cit.*, pp. 363–364.
[29] W. L. Chenery, *op. cit.*, pp. 70–71.
[30] A. Henry, *Women and the Labor Movement*, p. 42.
[31] H. Martineau, *Society in America*, Vol. III, p. 118.
[32] *Ibid.*, pp. 131–132.
[33] C. Lyell, *A Second Visit to the United States of North America*, Vol. I, p. 122.
[34] Capt. Marryat, *op. cit.*, p. 52.

CHAPTER V

THE WOMAN OF THE SOUTH FROM THE REVOLUTION TO THE CIVIL WAR

[1] T. J. Woofter, *Black Yeomanry*, p. 21.
[2] See *American Notes*, pp. 131–133, and *Western Travel*, Vol. II, Ch. III.
[3] Sir H. H. Johnston, *The Negro in the New World*, p. 380.
[4] J. S. Buckingham, *The Slave States of America*, Vol. I, pp. 188–189.
[5] See T. N. Page, *Social Life in Old Virginia before the War*; H. W. Odum, *An American Epoch*; E. Ripley, *Social Life in Old New Orleans*; and T. C. De Leon, *Belles, Beaux and Brains of the 60's.*
[6] J. K. Paulding, *Letters from the South written during an Excursion in the Summer of 1816.*
[7] J. S. Buckingham, *op. cit.*, pp. 199–200.
[8] W. M. Polk, Vol. I, p. 202. Permission granted by Longmans, Green & Company, publishers.
[9] J. S. Buckingham, *op. cit.*, p. 123.
[10] See E. Hawkridge's *Indian Gods and Kings.*
[11] January 24, 1853.
[12] H. W. Odum, *op. cit.*, pp. 47–48. Permission granted.
[13] A. W. Calhoun, *Social History of the American Family*, Vol II, p. 313.
[14] T. C. De Leon, *op. cit.*, p. 21.

[15] G. Hunt, *Life in America One Hundred Years Ago*, p. 77.

[16] E. R. Groves and W. F. Ogburn, *American Marriage and Family Relationships*, p. 234.

[17] *Ibid.*

[18] Quoted in A. W. Calhoun's *Social History of the American Family*, Vol. II, p. 25.

[19] F. B. Simkins & J. W. Patton, *The Women of the Confederacy*, Ch. I.

CHAPTER VI

THE WOMAN OF THE MIDDLE WEST AND THE GREAT PLAINS

[1] F. J. Turner, *The Frontier in American History*, p. 129.

[2] W. P. Webb, *The Great Plains*, p. 24.

[3] L. F. Ward, *Pure Sociology*, Ch. XX.

[4] D. L. Leonard, *The Story of Oberlin*, p. 165.

[5] J. H. Fairchild, *Oberlin: The Colony and the College, 1833–1883*, p. 176.

[6] F. J. Turner, *op. cit.*, p. 193.

[7] E. C. Stanton, S. B. Anthony, and M. J. Gage, *History of Woman Suffrage*, Vol. III, p. 730.

[8] G. R. Hebard, "How Woman Suffrage Came to Wyoming." (A paper loaned through the courtesy of Miss Alice Lyman, State Librarian of Wyoming.)

[9] *Ibid.*

[10] *Ibid.*

[11] W. P. Webb, *op. cit.*, p. 506.

[12] R. E. Riegel, *America Moves West*, p. 398.

[13] G. F. Milton, *The Eve of Conflict*, p. 38.

[14] B. M. H. Shambaugh, *Amana That Was and Amana That Is*, p. 53.

[15] *Ibid.*

[16] *Ibid.*, p. 66.

[17] *Ibid.*, p. 121.

[18] *Ibid.*

[19] E. C. Stanton, S. B. Anthony, and M. J. Gage, *op. cit.*, Vol. I, p. 293.

[20] *Ibid.*, pp. 294–295.

[21] *Ibid.*, p. 292.

[22] S. P. Morrison, "Some Sidelights of Fifty Years Ago." (A paper loaned through the courtesy of Miss Estelle Wolf, Reference Librarian, Indiana University Library, Bloomington, Indiana.)

[23] See D. C. Peattie, *Green Laurels*, Ch. XI.

[24] G. M. Stephenson, *A History of American Immigration*, Ch. III, "The Scandinavians," and Ch. IV, "The Germans."

[25] R. E. Riegel, *op. cit.*, pp. 195–196.

[26] A. H. Shaw, *The Story of a Pioneer*, pp. 25 and 26. Permission granted by Harper & Brothers, publishers.

FOOTNOTES

CHAPTER VII

WOMAN, NORTH AND SOUTH, DURING AND AFTER THE CIVIL WAR

[1] J. B. Jones, *A Rebel War Clerk's Diary*, Vol. II, pp. 432–433.
[2] W. M. Polk, *Life of Leonidas Polk*, Vol. I, p. 202.
[3] S. D. Smedes, *A Southern Planter*, pp. 108–109.
[4] See N. B. Lewis, *Raleigh News and Observer*, May 3, 1925.
[5] F. W. Dawson, *Our Women in the War*, p. 10.
[6] Mrs. R. A. Pryor, *Reminiscences of Peace and War*, p. 171.
[7] F. A. Beers, *Memories*, p. 81.
[8] M. M. Davis, *Clinics, Hospitals, and Health Centers*, pp. 4–5.
[9] English Merchant, *Two Months in the Confederate States*, pp. 176 and 278.
[10] F. W. Dawson, *op. cit.*, pp. 12–13.
[11] *Ibid.*, p. 13.
[12] *Ibid.*, p. 17.
[13] Mrs. R. A. Pryor, *op. cit.*, p. 327.
[14] R. W. Winston, *Robert E. Lee*, p. 371.
[15] ———, *A Garland for Ashes: An Aspiration for the South* (Address before North Carolina Bar Association, June 28, 1934), p. 12.
[16] M. P. Branch, *Memories of A Southern Woman*, p. 44.
[17] Pp. 193 and 195.
[18] M. L. Avary, *A Virginia Girl in the Civil War*, p. 364.
[19] A Lady of Virginia, *Diary of A Southern Refugee During the War*, p. 360.
[20] W. E. H. Lecky, *Democracy and Liberty*, pp. 1–98.
[21] *The Autobiography of Charles Francis Adams*, pp. 83–88. (Published by Houghton, Mifflin Company for M. H. S. in 1916.)
[22] H. J. Eckenrode, *Rutherford B. Hayes, Statesman of Reunion*, p. 239.
[23] E. F. Andrews, *The War-Time Journal of A Georgia Girl 1864–1865*, p. 364.
[24] H. A. Bruce, *Woman in the Making of America*, p. 190.
[25] K. C. Hurd-Mead, *Medical Women of America*, p. 32, and T. Woody, *A History of Women's Education in the United States*, Vol. II, p. 74.
[26] E. A. Hurn, *Wisconsin Women in the War*, p. 111.
[27] *Ibid.*, p. 109.
[28] L. P. Brockett and Mrs. M. C. Vaughan, *Woman's Work in the Civil War*, p. 121.
[29] E. D. Fite, *Social and Industrial Conditions in the North During the Civil War*, p. 289.
[30] F. D. Watson, *The Charity Organization Movement in the United States*, p. 174.
[31] *Recent Social Trends in the United States*, Vol. II, Ch. XXIV, "Public Welfare Activities" by H. W. Odum, p. 1225.
[32] T. Woody, *op. cit.*, p. 351.

[33] K. C. Hurd-Mead, *op. cit.*, p. 66.
[34] E. D. Fite, *op. cit.*, p. 9.
[35] A. W. Calhoun, *A Social History of the American Family from Colonial Times to the Present*, Vol. II, p. 357.
[36] E. A. Hurn, *op. cit.*, pp. 80–81.
[37] E. D. Fite, *op. cit.*, p. 187.
[38] See *New York Sun*, June 12, and September 21, 1864.
[39] E. D. Fite, *op. cit.*, pp. 246–247.
[40] E. D. Fite, *op. cit.*, p. 245.
[41] *Ibid.*
[42] J. C. Croly, *History of Woman's Club Movement*, p. 54.
[43] A. W. Calhoun, *op. cit.*, p. 364.
[44] *A Decade of Progress in Eugenics* (Scientific Papers of the Third International Congress of Eugenics held at American Museum of Natural History, New York, August 21–23, 1932), "Is War Dysgenic?" by H. R. Hunt, pp. 244–248.
[45] R. L. Dabney, *Defence of Virginia and the South*, pp. 286–287.

CHAPTER VIII

WOMAN'S POLITICAL AND SOCIAL ADVANCE

[1] K. Coman, *The Industrial History of the United States*, p. 369.
[2] G. M. Stephenson, *A History of American Immigration 1820–1924*, p. 156.
[3] A. W. Calhoun, *A Social History of the American Family*, Vol. III, p. 217.
[4] *Representatives Report* No. 47, Sixty-First Congress, p. 12.
[5] B. and M. Van Vorst, *The Woman Who Toils*, p. 128.
[6] L. Levine, *The Women's Garment Workers*, p. 23.
[7] T. Woody, *A History of Women's Education in the United States*, Vol. II, p. 458.
[8] L. E. Richards and M. H. Elliott, *Julia Ward Howe*, Vol. I, p. 283.
[9] J. W. Howe, *Reminiscences, 1819–1899*, p. 281.
[10] C. P. Gilman, *The Living of Charlotte Perkins Gilman* (an Autobiography), pp. 312–314.
[11] S. J. Buck, *The Granger Movement*, p. 290.
[12] *National Grange Proceedings*, Vol. VII (1874), p. 58.
[13] S. B. Anthony and I. H. Harper, *The History of Woman Suffrage*, Vol. IV, p. 1046.
[14] C. G. Vernier, *American Family Laws*, Vol. II, Section 70, p. 48.
[15] H. B. Woolston, *Prostitution in the United States*, p. 27.
[16] See W. G. Stead, *If Christ Came to Chicago*.
[17] M. S. Sims, *The Natural History of A Social Institution–The Y.W.C.A.*, p. 6.
[18] *Ibid.*, p. 7.
[19] *Ibid.*, p. 15.
[20] *Ibid.*, pp. 9–10.
[21] M. E. Richmond, *The Interrelation of Social Movements* (a paper given at the National Conference of Charities and Correction in 1910), p. 2.

FOOTNOTES

[22] F. D. Watson, *The Charity Organization Movement in the United States*, p. 176.
[23] *Encyclopaedia of the Social Sciences*, Vol. 13, p. 382.
[24] J. W. Howe, *op. cit.*, p. 328.
[25] E. W. Byrn, *The Progress of Invention in the Nineteenth Century*, p. 188.
[26] E. C. Stanton, S. B. Anthony, and M. J. Gage, *The History of Woman Suffrage*, Vol. I, p. 67.
[27] *Ibid.*
[28] L. B. Stowe, *Saints, Sinners and Beechers*, p. 348.
[29] *Ibid.*, p. 349.
[30] *Ibid.*, p. 350.
[31] S. B. Anthony and I. H. Harper, *op. cit.*, Vol. II, p. 446.
[32] See A. Graham, *Ladies in Revolt*, p. 184.
[33] See *Ibid.*, p. 184.
[34] C. C. Catt and N. R. Shuler, *Woman Suffrage and Politics*, p. 268.

CHAPTER IX

WOMAN'S INDUSTRIAL AND EDUCATIONAL ADVANCE

[1] A. Nevins, *The Emergence of Modern America 1865-1878*, p. 46.
[2] E. Stewart, "Early Organizations of Printers," *Bulletin of the U. S. Bureau of Labor*, Vol. XI, p. 884.
[3] *Reports of the Industrial Commission*, Vol. VII, p. 277 (Testimony of Mr. Samuel B. Donnelly).
[4] E. Abbott, *Women in Industry*, pp. 206-208.
[5] *Ibid.*, pp. 171-172.
[6] *Ibid.*, pp. 268-269.
[7] A. Henry, *Women and the Labor Movement*, p. 99.
[8] E. J. Hutchinson, *Women's Wages*, p. 15. (Taken from Columbia University Studies in History, Economics and Public Law.)
[9] *Ibid.*, p. 51.
[10] L. Levine, *The Women's Garment Workers*, pp. 21-22.
[11] *Ibid.*, p. 22.
[12] *Ibid.*, p. 386.
[13] N. E. Himes, *Medical History of Contraception*, p. 214.
[14] *Ibid.*, p. 270.
[15] L. E. Becker, *Contemporary Review*, March, 1869.
[16] A. W. Calhoun, *A Social History of the American Family*, Vol. III, p. 92.
[17] L. Markun, *Mrs. Grundy*, p. 525.
[18] From the *College Courant*, September, 1872. (See J. Orton (ed.), *The Liberal Education of Women*.)
[19] J. Todd, *Congregationalist*, August 31, 1871.
[20] From the *Edinburgh Review*, October, 1869.

[21] "Higher Education of Woman." A paper read before the Social Science Convention, May 14, 1873. (In the series *Woman Suffrage Tracts*, No. 9. Boston, Woman's Journal Office, 1873.)
[22] J. Orton (ed.), *The Liberal Education of Women*, pp. 318–319.
[23] *Ibid.*, p. 322.
[24] Sister M. M. Bowler, *A History of Catholic Colleges for Women in the United States of America*, p. 8.
[25] L. B. Stowe, *Saints, Sinners and Beechers*, p. 118.
[26] J. Pollitt, *Emily Dickinson*, p. 47.
[27] T. Woody, *A History of Women's Education in the United States*, Vol. I, p. 341.
[28] *Ibid.*, p. 371.
[29] *Ibid.*, Vol. II, p. 140.
[30] M. Vassar on the Founding of Vassar College, quoted in *Harper's New Monthly Magazine* (1875–1876), LII, pp. 549–550.

CHAPTER X

THE AMERICAN WOMAN IN THE TWENTIETH CENTURY

[1] S. P. Breckinridge, *Women in the Twentieth Century*, p. 27.
[2] Cardinal Gibbons. (January, 1902.)
[3] Grover Cleveland. (May, 1905.)
[4] H. R. Hunt, "Is War Dysgenic?" *A Decade of Progress in Eugenics*, p. 246.
[5] *Ibid.*, p. 248.
[6] *The New Position of Women in American Industry* (Women's Bureau Bulletin No. 12), p. 13.
[7] *Ibid.*, p. 17.
[8] *Ibid.*, p. 89.
[9] *Ibid.*, p. 33.
[10] *Ibid.*, p. 94.
[11] G. D. Crain, Jr., "Increasing Competition for Female Labor," *Textile World Journal* (July 21, 1917), p. 84.
[12] *The New Position of Women in American Industry*, op. cit., p. 91.
[13] M. V. Dempsey, *The Occupational Progress of Women, 1910 to 1930* (Women's Bureau Bulletin No. 104), p. 1.
[14] *Ibid.*, p. 53.
[15] *Variations in Employment Trends of Women and Men* (Women's Bureau Bulletin No. 73), p. 50.
[16] F. G. Nichols, *A New Conception of Office Practice*, Harvard Bulletins in Education No. 12 (Cambridge University Press, 1927), pp. 49 and 79.
[17] *Variations in Employment Trends of Women and Men*, op. cit., p. 50.
[18] F. T. Smith, *Chronological Development of Labor Legislation for Women in the United States* (Woman's Bureau Bulletin No. 66–II), pp. 165 and 173.

FOOTNOTES 435

[19] *Adkins v. Children's Hospital*, 261 U. S. 525.
[20] M. E. Pidgeon, *Summary of State Hour Laws for Women and Minimum-Wage Rates* (Women's Bureau Bulletin No. 137), p. 3.
[21] F. P. Smith, *History of Labor Legislation for Women in Three States* (Women's Bureau Bulletin No. 66), p. 58.
[22] *Ibid.*, p. 61.
[23] *Ibid.*, p. 2.
[24] *Ibid.*, p. 61.
[25] L. Pruette (ed.), *Women Workers Through the Depression*, p. 2.
[26] *Employment Fluctuations and Unemployment of Women* (Women's Bureau Bulletin No. 113).
[27] H. A. Byrne, *The Effects of the Depression on Wage Earners' Families* (Women's Bureau Bulletin No. 108), p. 17.
[28] D. Thompson, "Women in the Modern World," *Child Study* (November, 1936), pp. 35–38 and 60.
[29] C. C. Catt and N. R. Shuler, *Woman Suffrage and Politics*, p. 191.
[30] *Ibid.*, p. 279.
[31] *Ibid.*
[32] *Ibid.*
[33] F. H. Giddings, *Studies in the Theory of Human Society*, pp. 186–189.
[34] *Women in the Modern World, The Annals*, Vol. CXLIII (May, 1929), p. 361.
[35] C. P. Stetson (Gilman) *Women and Economics*, p. 247.
[36] R. W. Kelso, *Poverty*, p. 281.
[37] *1942 Directory of Planned Parenthood Services* (Planned Parenthood Federation of America, Inc., New York, N. Y.

CHAPTER XI

THE AMERICAN WOMAN AND HER CHANGING STATUS

[1] H. H. Adler, "The Manufacturing Industries," *College Women and the Social Sciences* (Essays by Herbert Elmer Mills and his former students), p. 220.
[2] C. G. Woodhouse and R. Schiffman, *After College—What?* p. 20.
[3] S. P. Breckinridge, *Women in the Twentieth Century*, pp. 240–253.
[4] Morehead v. New York ex rel Tipaldo (1936) 80 L. Ed. 921; 56 S. C. 918.
[5] L. B. Stowe, *Saints, Sinners and Beechers*, p. 185.
[6] F. L. Pattee, *A History of American Literature Since 1870*, p. 335.
[7] *Ibid.*, pp. 220–221.
[8] R. L. Dickinson and L. Beam, *The Single Woman*, p. 11.
[9] G. F. Milton, *The Eve of Conflict*, p. 22.
[10] F. Kirchwey (ed.), *Our Changing Morality* (A Symposium); V. F. Calverton, *The Bankruptcy of Marriage;* K. B. Davis, *Factors in the Sex Life of Twenty-Two Hundred Women;* G. V. Hamilton, *A Research in Marriage;* E. R. Groves, *The Marriage Crisis;* J. K. Folsom, *The Family*, Ch. XIII; Ira S. Wile (ed.), *The Sex Life of the Unmarried Adult;* J. Tenenbaum, *The Riddle of Woman*, pp. 159–160;

M. Hirschfeld, *The Sexual History of the World War*, pp. 29–30; V. F. Calverton and S. D. Schmalhausen (eds.), *Sex in Civilization*, "The Sexual Revolution" by Schmalhausen, pp. 349–436.

[11] D. Russell, *The Right to be Happy*, pp. 166–201; G. V. Hamilton, *op. cit.*, Ch. VI; E. Charles, *The Twilight of Parenthood*, pp. 161–190; G. H. Groves and R. A. Ross, *The Married Woman*, Ch. VII.

[12] V. F. Calverton and S. D. Schmalhausen, *op. cit.*, "The Civilizing Force of Birth Control" by M. Sanger, pp. 525–537.

[13] J. Tenenbaum, *op. cit.*, p. 27.

[14] M. E. Harding, *The Way of All Women*, p. 180.

[15] W. James, *The Varieties of Religious Experience*, pp. 106–107.

[16] S. B. Anthony and I. H. Harper, *The History of Woman Suffrage*, Vol. IV, p. 263.

[17] J. W. Madden, *Handbook of the Law of Persons and Domestic Relations*, p. 83.

[18] E. Peck, *The Law of Persons and of Domestic Relations*, pp. 216–217.

[19] H. S. Daggett, "The Civil-Law Concept of the Wife's Position in the Family," *Oregon Law Review*, Vol. XV, No. 4 (June, 1936), p. 293.

[20] R. B. Morris, *Studies in the History of American Law*, p. 127.

[21] *Ibid.*, p. 128.

[22] *Ibid.*, p. 131.

[23] *Ibid.*, p. 136.

[24] *Ibid.*, p. 139.

[25] R. Pound, *The Spirit of the Common Law*, p. 118.

[26] Gallaher, R. A., *Legal and Political Status of Women in Iowa*, p. 21.

[27] C. G. Vernier, *American Family Laws*, Vol. III, p. 4.

[28] *Ibid.*, p. 24.

CHAPTER XII

NEAR EQUALITY WITH MEN

[1] Corner, George W., *The Hormones in Human Reproduction*, p. 79.

[2] Hoskins, R. G., *Endocrinology*, p. 196.

[3] Mead, Margaret, *Sex and Temperament in Three Primitive Societies*.

[4] Crile, George, *Intelligence, Power and Personality*, p. 155.

[5] *Journal of the American Association of University Women*, March, 1941, p. 161.

[6] *Proceedings of the First American Congress on Obstetrics and Gynecology*, p. 572.

[7] *Journal of the American Association of University Women*, pp. 109–110, Vol. 31, No. 2.

[8] *New York Times*, June 4, 1942.

[9] *Equal Pay for Women in War Industries*, United States Department of Labor, Woman's Bureau, Bulletin No. 196, 1942.

FOOTNOTES

[10] General Motors Corporation v Read et al (1940), 294 Mich. 558; 293 N. W. 751.

[11] *New York Herald Tribune*, July 24, 1943.

[12] *New York Herald Tribune*, September 15, 1942.

[13] *New York Times*, June 14, 1942.

[14] *New York Herald Tribune*, Sunday, August 22, 1943.

[15] *Labor Information Bulletin*, February, 1943.

[16] Anderson, Margaret K. *Employment of Women in the Manufacturing of Cannons and Small Arms in 1942*, United States Department of Labor, Woman's Bureau, Bulletin Nos. 192–193.

[17] *New York Herald Tribune*, July 20, 1943.

[18] Office of War Information, United States Department of Labor, Woman's Bureau, Advance Release for Sunday Papers, June 13, 1943.

[19] *Durham (North Carolina) Herald-Sun*, Section 2, p. 2, July 18, 1943.

[20] *New York Times*, Sunday, August 22, 1943.

[21] *Ibid.*

[22] Maffett, Minnie L., President, National Federation of Business and Professional Clubs, address given at the Board Meeting, Lake George, New York, July 8, 1943. Quoted by permission.

[23] *Ibid.*

[24] *Ibid.*

[25] Stanley, Winifred C., Statement in *Equal Rights*, March, 1943.

[26] Ishimoto, Shidzue, *Facing Two Ways;* Mishima, Sumie Seo, *My Narrow Isle.*

INDEX

Abbess
  a professional woman, 28
  power of, 28
Aborigines, sex relations with, 113
Absenteeism, 414
Accountants, 337
Adams, Abigail, 60, 106-108
Adams, John, 106
Addams, Jane, 252, 269, 270
Addison, 55
Adjustment to new order, 400
Adler, Felix, 360
Advertisements, 411
Advertising in newspapers, 66
A.F. of L., 409
Agassiz, Professor, 317
Agitator vs. moralist, 202
Agriculture, English, 39
Alcott, Louisa M., 384
Allegheny Mountains, 52, 167
  culture west of, 75, 110
Allegiance, oath of, 50
Allies, female political, 109
Amana society, 191
  Lord's will concerning, 192
America
  opportunity in, 40
  permanent settlers of, 9-10
American
  civilization transported from Old World, 6
  conflict, 202
  culture, 246
  diet, 279
  education, 320
  life, trends in, 72-73
  planter vs. English squire, 144
  poets, 384
  religious history, 394
  sentiment toward aristocracy, 154
  slums, 250
  thinking, 151

American, *continued*
  towns, 62
  wilderness, 75
  woman migrant, 186
  women
    amalgamation of, 248
    background of, 8
    cultural background of, 5
    economic aggressiveness of, 130
    evolution of, 228
    increased opportunities of, 59
    social status of first, 7
    way of life, 424
American Academy of Medicine, 274
American Association
  for the Study of the Feeble-Minded, 274
  of University Women, 327, 378, 418
American family in a changing society, 418
American Federation of
  Labor, 291
  Teachers, 378
American Friends in Baltimore, 277
American Home Economics Association, 326, 360
American Labor Movement, 131
American Mercury, The, 68
American Notes by Charles Dickens, 124
American Peace Society, 277
American Prison Association, 274
American Purity Alliance, 274
American Revolution, the, 53, 56, 395-396
American Social Hygiene Association, 355, 363, 365
American Social Science Association, 236, 274
American Woman Suffrage Association, 286
Americans in Texas, 179
Ames, Charles Gordon, 275

INDEX

Ames, Fanny B., 275
Amherst College, 323
Anarchy, social, 224
Anatomical predestination, 404
Andrews, Eliza Frances, 223
A New Home, Who Will Follow, 198
Ante-nuptial contracts, 398
Anthony, Susan B., 182, 241, 244, 283, 286
Anti-child-labor laws, 327
Antietam, battle of, 234
Antioch College, 408
Anti-slavery
  agitation, 227, 378
  movement, 264
Appalachian Mountains, 53
  breaking through the, 74
Architecture in the Northeast, 118
Aristocracy
  American sentiment toward, 154
  benevolence of, 147
  feudal-spirited, 203
  intellectual, 174
  of the Puritan Colony, 47
  prestige-emphasis of, 210
  southern, 153, 203
  traditions of, 154
  wreckage of, 204
Aristocrat, misunderstood, 205
Aristocratic *mores*, 172
Aristocrats, intellectual, 283
Art of love, 362, 387
Asceticism
  defined, 11
  influencing woman, 26
  origin of, 11
  St. Paul and, 13
  trend toward, 191
Ascetics, female, 18
Association of Instructors of the Blind, 274
Association Opposed to Suffrage for Women, 286
Astell, Mary, 56
Atlantic Monthly, 384
Atlantic Seaboard, 48
Auburn Female University, 323
Australia, 424
Autocratic culture, 83

Bacteriology, 279
Bahai doctrine, 326
Baldwin, Bird T., 360
Baptist denomination, 394
Baptists, persecution of, 70
Barnett, Mrs., 269
Barriers broken by war, 241
Barton, Clara, 234, 237, 276
"Battle Hymn of the Republic," 255
Battle of Bull Run, 211
Beecher, Catherine, 175, 314, 320, 355
Beers, Clifford, 361
Believers during Middle Ages, 19
Berkeley, Bishop, 395
"Best sellers" by women, 381-382
Bethel, Missouri, 191
Bible in the South, 158
Bible, Woman's, 395
Bicycling, dress for, 386
Biologic nature, 400
Biological responsibilities of childbearing, 92
Birth control, 164, 339, 350, 390, 393
  agitation, 308
  clinics, 365
  legalizing of, 365
Birth rate
  in early marriage, 163
  lowered, 242-243
Bishop Hill, Illinois, 190
Black
  death, 39
  magic, 71
Black Sea, 169
Blackwell, Elizabeth, 238
Blackwell, Emily, 237
Blockade of English fleet, 138
Bloomer, Amelia, 280, 386
Boarding houses, 133
  mill-owned, 124
Body structure, differences, 402
Books
  by women, 384-385
  on housekeeping, 57
  on marriage, 58
Boone, Daniel, 81
Boston Association's objective, 272
Boston Radical Club, 256
Boston working girls, 273
Boyd, Belle, 219
Boyd, Lucretia, 273
Bozarth, Mrs., 99
Bradstreet, Mrs. Simon, 69
Bright, William A., 181-182

INDEX

Brotherhood of Locomotive Engineers, 291
Brown, Alice, 384
Bryn Mawr, 323
Buckingham's description of the slave's life, 148-149
Bull Run, Battle of, 211
Buras, Anne, 43
Bureau of Education reports, 322
Business Women of the Reformation, 34
Bustle vogue, 280

Calvin, 33
  at Geneva, 46
Calvinistic Scotch-Irish, 77-78
Campbell, Governor John A., 183
Canada, 424
Capital debt for roadbuilding, etc., 171
Capitol City society life, 253
Care and Feeding of Children, The, 359
Career vs. housekeeping, 371
Carolina settlers, 53
Carson, Kit, 178
Cary, Alice, 255
Cass, Lewis, 188
Castration, 22, 407
Catholics, Celtic Irish, 52
Catt, Carrie Chapman, 400
Census of 1870, 288
Chalmers, Thomas, 275
Chandler, Daniel, 322
Channing, William Henry, 383
Chaperonage of young people, 103
Charitable organizations, 236-237
Charities' Movement, the, 274
Charities, organized, 236-237
Charity Organization Movement, 275
Charity Organization Society of
  Baltimore, 276
  London, 275
Charity schools, 50
Charles I, 46
Charles II, 41
Charleston earthquake, 276
Chiang Kai-shek, Madame, 423
Chicago Commons, 270
Chicago Juvenile Psychopathic Institute, 361
Child
  preschool, 360
  study, 359
  welfare, 360

Childbearing, 307
  biological responsibilities of, 92
Childbirth, 164
  dangers of, 406
Child-care, 359
Child Guidance Clinic, 361
Child Health Council, 405
Child Study Association of America, 360
Child Welfare Research Station, 360
Children
  illegitimate, 42
  in factories, 120
  mill-workers, 128
  strikers, 130
Children's Aid Society of Pennsylvania, 275
Children's Bureau, 364
Chivalry
  compensation through, 209-210
  in the Middle Ages, 32
  southern, 209
Christian dogma, 10
Christianity
  an incentive, 18-19
  liabilities of, 11
  Roman highways and, 9
  woman's part in, 17-18
Church
  doctrines, 10
  Fathers, 12
Church of the Brethren, 51
Cigar Makers' International Union, 292
Cigar-making plants, 337
Cincinnati female seminary, 320-321
C.I.O., 409
Civil War, 382, 409
  loyalty of Negroes during, 150
  nurses, 213
  outcome of, 151
  social pressure before, 156
  South's condition after, 289
  vs. World War, 223
  women affected by, 205
Claflin, Tennessee, 283
Claflin, Victoria, 283
Claflin's Weekly, 283
Clark, routes charted by, 178
Clark University, 359
Clarke, James Freeman, 383
Class
  differences in the South, 153-154
  distinctions, 83

INDEX

Class, *continued*
  restrictions of Old World, 173
Clement of Alexandria, 22-23
Clerical occupations, 241, 337
Cleveland, Grover, 257
Clothing industry, 50
Clubs, development of, 254
Coastal towns, 76
Cobb, Stanwood, 360
Coeducation, 318, 403
  at Oberlin, 176
  beginning of, 175
  college, 321
  high school, 321-322
  of Quakers, 177
  western, 176-177
Coeducational seminaries, 322
Coit, Stanton, 269
College idealism, 268
Colleges
  for women, 321
  land-grant, 260, 373
Colonial
  settlements, 74
  settlers, 8
  taverns, 62
  woman, 54
  women in trade, 66
Colonial Dames of America, 326
Colonies, education in the, 48-49
Colonization movement, 39
Commissary Department, plundering of, 223
Commissioner of
  Agriculture, 259
  Immigration, 242
Committee on Interstate and Foreign Commerce, 249
Communities
  coastline vs. frontier, 76
  seaboard, 54
Community of True Inspiration, 191
Compensation through chivalry, 209-210
Competition
  free, 78
  manufacturing, 250
Competitive business, 375
Confederacy, breaking up of, 223
Confederate
  bonds, 289
  cause, 220

Confederate, *continued*
  states, 289
Congregational leaders, 320
Congress of Parents and Teachers, 299
Connecticut Woman Suffrage Association, 283
Constitution, the
  implications of, 108
  of the United States, 350
Consumers' League, 270
Continental United States, 328
Contraception, 362, 365
Contraceptive technique, 392
Contraceptives, pioneering stage of, 309
Contracts, nuptial, 398
Conventions, challenge of, 304
Cook, Rose Terry, 384
Coordinator of Inter-American Affairs, 421
Cotton, 138-139
  mills in the South, 290-291
Council of Massachusetts, 398
Council of Women for Home Missions, 327
Court
  functions of, 88
  of Appeals, 344
  reporters, 337
Courtship
  art of, 161
  code, 103
  demands of working women, 306
  vs. marriage, 210-211
Credit, public, 172
Creek Indians, 97
Crockett, David, 95-98
Croly, Mrs., 255-256
Cromwell
  followers, 70
  tyranny of, 41
Crusaders, women, 264
Cultural
  break of colonies and motherland, 105
  differences of westerners, 167
  groups, 44
  integration, 248
  reconstruction, 75
  shift, 400
Cultural background of
  American women, 5
  colonial settlers, 8

INDEX

Culture
  autocratic, 83
  blending in the West, 168
  dilution, 247
  levels in the South, 164
  midwestern, 81
  New World vs. Old World, 228
  southern, 204
  west of the Alleghenies, 75
  western, 86
Curie, Madame, 374
Cyprion's
  condemnation of public baths, 24-25
  exaltation of virgins, 23-24

Daughters of the Revolution, 326
Deaconesses, 18
Death, black, 39
Debates, Lincoln-Douglas, 167
Debts, war, 236
Decker, Mrs., 256
Declaration of Independence, 108, 147, 283
Defense Health and Welfare, 421
DeFoe, Daniel, 55
De Leon's description of family connections, 162
Delinquency, 418
Democracy
  educational, 92
  practical, 174
  western, 174
Democratic trend favoring women, 84
Department of the Treasury, 242
Depression, 401
  family strain during, 350
  loss of jobs during, 348
  of 1873, 275
  periods, 248
  postponement of marriage during, 349-350
  unemployment during, 349
Deserters, wartime, 223
Determinism, economic, 169
Diary-keeping by women, 69
Dickens, Charles, 124, 126, 133, 142, 255
Dickinson, Emily, 321, 385
Dickinson, Robert L., 386
Diet, American, 279
Digges, Elizabeth, 63-64

Dike's report on immigrants, 249
Disciples of Christ, 394
District of Columbia wage law, 344
Divorce, 356, 389, 398
  grounds for, 266
  increased, 257
  interest in, 37
  legislation in Indiana, 192
Dix, Dorothea, 232, 237, 238
  leadership of, 233
Doctors, women, 241
Dodge, Grace Hoadley, 274
Dogmatists, 202
Domestic
  incompatibility, 356
  life standards, 303
  science education, 355
Dommett, John, 68
D'Ossoli, Margaret Fuller, 383
Double
  code of sex, 209
  standard, 244
Douglas, Donald W., 416
Douglas, Stephen A., 139, 188, 388
Dow, Neal, 264
Dress
  change in women's, 386
  recommended by Dr. Dickinson, 386
  restrictive, 386-387
Dubre, Hannah, 65
Dummer, Mrs. William F., 361
Dunkers, the, 51
Durant, Mrs. Henry F., 272
Dutch period, termination of, 48
Dwight, Timothy, 77, 86, 115
Dyes, home-made, 217

East Side of New York, 269
Eastern
  authority, suspicion of, 87
  institutions of higher learning, 92
  markets, 170
  traditions subordinating women, 13
Ecclesiastical traditions, 393
Economic
  determinism, 169
  exploitation, 251
  pressure on
    colonization movement, 39
    women, 338-339
  Warfare, 421

INDEX

Economy, Pennsylvania, 190
Eddy, Mary Baker, 394
Edinburgh Review, 316
Edison, Thomas, 279
Education
  adult, 355
  democratic trend in, 321
  early interest in, 91
  elementary, 320
  for girls, 50, 314-320
  for women, 175
    onslaughts on, 314-317
    opponents of, 324
  higher, 91
  in the colonies, 48-49
  midwestern, 91, 172
  New England, 91
  popular, 67-68
  problems of, 317
  public school, 321
  twentieth-century, 354-355
Educational
  democracy, 92
  opportunities of mill workers, 126
Eighteenth Amendment, 353
Elberfeld charity system, 275
Electric vs. gas illumination, 279
Eliot, President, 318, 403
Elizabeth, Queen, 35
Ellis, Havelock, 362
Elmira, coeducation at, 321
Elmira Female College, 323
Emancipation of slaves, 224
Embury, Philip, 394
Emerson, Ralph Waldo, 383
Émile, Rousseau's, 56
Emotional immaturity, 87
Emotions affecting the organism, 200
Employer vs. employee, 312
Endocrine, 402
Endocrinology, 200, 387, 401-404
England
  break with, 106
  discontent in, 40
  industrial revolution in, 119
  "Merrie," 40
  the Reformation in, 34
English
  agriculture, 39
  common law, 398
  culture, 75
  fleet, blockade of, 138

English, *continued*
  lodgings, 134
  mores, 48
  Puritanism, 36
  Quakers, 190
  settlements, 55
    in America, 39
Englishman's description of southern life, 152
Epidemics on the frontier, 199
Episcopal Church, the, 394
Episcopalian leaders, 320
Equal rights, 78
  amendment, 379
  party, 284
Equality
  American theory of, 147
  of the sexes, 210
Erie Canal, 171
Essenes, the, 11-12
Ethical Culture School, 360
European
  books on women, 58
  environment a factor in New World culture, 9-10
  immigration, 246
  markets, 203
  recognition of the South, 222
  society in transition, 26-27
  stock Americanized, 75
  traditions, 83, 307
Europeans, herding of, 250
Eve's responsibility for sin, 72
Evolution, social, 151

Factories
  children in, 120
  wartime, 216
  women employed in, 120, 123-124
Factory
  hours, 128-129
  population, mobility of, 127
  system
    evolution of, 119
    in Middle Atlantic States, 127
Fairchild, Thomas, 398
Fall River
  industries, 121
  strike, 292
Family
  altar, 158

INDEX

Family, *continued*
  aristocratic, 89
  courses, 358
  culture of the West, 197
  men, 85
  system, southern, 155
  variations, 307
Family life
  disorganization of, 242
  in the South, 158-159
  western, 75
Faneuil, Peter, 66
Far West, the
  appeal of, 200
  people of, 185
Farmer, Sarah, 326
Federal
  Congress, 363
  Government, 171
  Government's taxation of liquor, 265
  loans for Erie Canal, etc., 171
  troops, 221
Federal Bureau of Labor, 344
Federal Census of Manufacturers, 298
Federal Housing Administration, 421
Federal Office of Education, 360
Female
  deficiencies, 92
  political allies, 109
  rôle, idealization of, 157
  seminaries
    decline of, 322
    missionary motives expressed through, 320
Femaleness, 402
Females, excess of, 122-123
Feminine
  aggressiveness, 389
  pattern, southern, 151
  protest, 8
  qualities in business, 338
Ferry-keepers, women, 63
Feudal disabilities of women, 31
Feudalism
  breaking up of, 35, 39
  its effect on women, 30
Fiction best sellers, 381-382
Fifteenth Amendment, 354
Filament lamp, 279
First woman medical student, 237
First World War, 409-410, 418
Fisher, Dorothy Canfield, 360

Fisherman, left by westward movement, 74
"Flesh," definition of, 17
Flirtation, 160
Floods, 276
Folkways, 403
Forest, Mrs., 43
Fort Mimms, 97
Fourteenth Amendment, 244
Franciscan Missionaries, 319
Franco-Prussian War, 276
Franklin, Benjamin, 50, 58
Franklin, Mrs. Benjamin, 60
Free labor, 289
Freeman, Mary E. Wilkins, 384
Fremont, John, 178
French
  code of Louisiana, 397
  resistance, 54
Freud, Sigmund, 362
Freudian
  hypothesis, 356
  theory of psychoanalysis, 387
  thought, 407
Frontier
  communication, 79
  conquest in the South, 54
  contrasted with the colonies, 82
  democratic attitude on the, 83
  dress, 100
  epidemics, 199
  household equipment, 100
  illness on the, 198
  interpretation of, 86
  land, 116
  last, 184, 200
  life, independence of, 103
  New England, 76-77
  political power of, 77
  radicals of the, 196
  religious life, 89
  settlers, unity of, 78
  trades, 74
  Trans-Appalachian, 83
  westward movement of, 167
  wives, ordeal of, 197
  women
    responsibilities of, 79
    self-made, 90
Frontiersmen
  the last, 185
  types of, 94

Fruits of Philosophy, 362
Fuller, Margaret, 283, 384
Fur-trader, aggressiveness of, 75
Fur-traders' contact with Indians, 75
Fur-trading in the Middle West, 74

Gallatin describes household textiles, 114
Galveston tornado, 276
Garfield, President, 276
Gas lighting, 279
General Court of Connecticut, 398
General Federation of Women's Clubs, 256, 327, 378, 423
General Motors, 409
Gentlemen, southern, 210
Georgia Female College, 323
Georgia settlers, 54
Germ plasm, superior, 243
German
 culture in the West, 173
 migrants, 172
 point of view, 424
 schools, 50
Germans
 educational ambitions of, 173
 individualism of, 77
 in Pennsylvania, 50
 political unrest of, 196
 westward migration of, 77
Germany, 413
Gibbons' writings regarding marriage, 20
Giddings, Franklin H., 352
Gilman, Charlotte Perkins, 256, 357
Girls
 education of, 50, 254
 higher education of, 177
 southern, 161
Glanvill, 31
Glanvill's interpretation of woman's legal status, 30
God's anointed, 202
Gold, discovery of, 179
Gone With the Wind, 382
Gough, John B., 265
Government, constitution for a new, 147
Governor of Massachusetts, 398
Grandmothers, young, 162
Grange, the, 258-263
Grant, Zilpah P., 175

Great Britain
 claim of, 179
 opposition to policy of, 53
Great Lakes, the, 170
Great Plains, the, 170
 a barricade, 187-188
 hazards of, 170-171
 repellent to women, 186
 women of, 185-186
"Grecian bend" posture, 280
Gretna Green, Greensboro a, 161
Gross, Robert E., 416
Gurteen, Rev. S. H., 275
Gynecology, 374

Haec-Vir, 36
Hale, Edward Everett, 255
Hall, G. Stanley, 359, 360
Hamilton, a political leader, 119
Harmonists, the, 190
Harnack's remarks about women, 17-18
Harvard, 323
 admission of women to, 318
 men, war death rate of, 329
Hayes, Rutherford B., 225, 227
Haywood, Eliza, 56
Heale, William, 36
Healy, William, 361
Heck, Barbara, 394
Henry, 296
Herschel, Caroline, 313
Hickey, Margaret E., 421
Higginson, Thomas W., 317, 383
High heels, 387
Highlanders vs. Lowlanders, 54
Hill, Octavia, 269, 275
Hilton, Dr. Eunice, 408
History
 American religious, 395
 from the masculine viewpoint, 105
Hitchcock, Enos, 58
Hobby, Mrs. Oveta Culp, 410
Holiness and sex conflict, 17
Holt, Emmett L., 359
Holy Mother, 18, 19
Home
 -made dyes, 217
 manufacturing, 121
 wartime industries, 215-218
Home Economics Departments, 358
Homekeeping, a profession, 357

INDEX

Hooker, Isabella Beecher, 283
Hooker, Thomas, 45, 76
Hoop skirts, 280
Hormones, 404
Hospital
    life at Ringgold, Virginia, 213-215
    service in Spanish-American War, 276
Hospitals
    a soldier's description of, 233-234
    United States, 215
Hostess, White House, 109
Houdlette, Harriet Ahlers, 418
House of Representatives, 354
House on Henry Street, 270
Household improvements, 117
Housekeeping
    books on, 57
    vs. career, 371
Housewife
    position of, 302
    responsibilities of, 116-117, 369
Howe, Elias, 278
Howe, Julia Ward, 255, 256, 276, 383
Huguenots, hostility toward, 53
Hull House, 252, 269
Hull House Women's Club, 270
Human
    behavior, 361
    evolution, 381
Humanitarianism, 340
Humanity on the march, 110
Hunter, the
    life of, 94
    pioneering, 93
Husband-wife relationship, 396-397
Husbands, pioneering, 59-60
Hutchinson, Anne, 58-59, 253, 394
Huterian brethren, the, 190

Ice, artificial, 280
Idealistic groups in the West, 190
Illegitimacy, 364
Illegitimate children, 42
Illicit relationships, 391
Illinois
    labor law, 252
    State Board of Labor, 252
    suffrage bill, 351
Illness on the frontier, 198
Imitation, woman's progress through, 247

Immigrant
    factory workers, 135-136, 247-248
    peasants, 247
    prostitutes, 249
Immigrants
    early vs. later, 249
    influx of, 242
    in the New World, 37
    marital relations of, 249
    pioneering, 74
Immigration
    advance of, 188
    and class unsettlement, 153
    European, 246
    influence of, 246
    intemperance hampered by, 265
    legislation encouraging, 242
    problems of, 248
    records, 248
    sentiment toward, 248
Immigration Society in London, 44
Incomes, joint, 399
Incompatibility, 356
    sex, 388
Independence, Declaration of, 108, 147
Indian
    conflicts, 99
    Creek, 97
    Holy Men, 11
    hostility, 54, 78
    women, marriage with, 113
Indiana legislation
    divorce, 192
    marriage, 192
Indiana Woman's Rights Society, 194
Indians
    a menace, 59
    dangers from, 84
    fear of, 43
    truce with, 97
Indigo, cultivation of, 64
Individualism, 89, 160
    in the West, 173
    of frontiersmen, 85
Individuality, recognition of, 385
Industrial
    centers attracting women, 305
    changes influencing women, 119
    Commission, 292
    competition of women, 249
    humanitarianism, 340
    legislation, 340

Industrial, *continued*
  pioneers, 128
  prostration, 348
  Revolution in England, 119
Industries, home and war, 215
Industry
  expansion of, 288
  in agricultural area, 289
  long hours of, 128
  northern vs. southern, 144
  woman's inferiority in, 298
Inequality of women, 43
Infant care, 405
Infant mortality, 364
Inferiority of women challenged, 61
Infertility, 404
Infidelity, monogamic marriage and, 29
Ingham Collegiate Institute, 323
Ingham University, 323
Intellectual aristocracy, 174
Intemperance, 264, 351
Internal secretion, 401
International Convention of Women, 283
International union regulations, 301
International Young Men's Christian Association, 274
Intoxication, 266
Invention
  hampering women, 246
  of machines, 138
Inventions
  affecting women, 336-337
  development of, 277
  influencing women, 277
Iowa State College of Agriculture and Mechanic Arts, 360
Irish immigrants, 240
Isolation in the West, 190
Italians in sweat shops, 250

Jackson, Helen Hunt, 384
James II, 41
James, William, 395
Janson, Eric, 190
Japan, 413, 424
Jay-hawkers, 223
Jerome, literature produced by, 18
Jerome's writings on
  marriage, 20
  virginity, 21-22

Jesus
  ascetic trend during life of, 13
  birth of, 91
Jewett, Sarah Orne, 384
Jewish
  immigrants, 250
  teaching of asceticism, 11
  women, 91
  workers, 250
Jewish Women's Congress, 326
Jews
  a separate people, 19
  ascetic trend of, 13
Joan of Arcs, southern, 219
John the Baptist's teachings, 12
Johnson, President Andrew, 259
Johnstown flood, 276
Journalists, women, 68
Journeyman Barbers' International Union, 296
Judge Baker Foundation, 361
Judiciary Committee of the House of Representatives, 284
Junior League, 327

Kaiser, Henry J., 416
Kansas, slavery agitation in, 189
Kansas-Nebraska bill, 188
Kelley, Mrs. Florence, 252, 270, 342
Kelley, Oliver, 259
Kentucky
  an inviting frontier, 78
  and Ohio occupation, 167
  pioneers, isolation of, 79
  population growth of, 80
  quest of, 81
  rapid growth of, 78, 180
Kerosene, 280
Kidnapping, 41
King Charles I, 46
King Charles II, 41
King James II, 41
King Philip's War, 68
Kirkland, Caroline Matilda, 198
Knight, Madam, 68
Knights of Labor, 292
Knowlton, Charles, 308, 362
Knox, John, 33

Labor
  division between sexes, 155
  leaders, 379

INDEX

Labor, *continued*
  legislation, 346, 347
  -saving office devices, 337
  unions, 291
Ladies' Home Journal, The, 257, 327
Ladies' Sanitary Commission, 237
Lancaster mill contract, 294-295
Lancastrian plan of education, 254
Land grant colleges, 373
Larcom, Lucy, 126, 127, 134-135
Lathrop, Julia C., 364
Lathrop, Rose Hawthorne, 384
Latin schools, 68
Latter Day Saints, the, 189
Law, lynch, 87
Lawlessness, 87
Lawrence industries, 122
Lecturer, the, 261
Lee, Ann, 394
Lee, Robert E., 221
Le Favour, Henry, 345
Legal strait-jackets, 87
Legislation
  minimum wage, 344
  prohibiting women workers, 345
  protecting working women, 345
  protective, 291
Leicester, Mass., 120
  coeducation at, 322
Lewis, Dr. Dio, 265
Life of Leonidas Polk, 149
Lincoln, Abraham, 90, 151, 242
Lincoln-Douglas debates, 167
Lincoln's
  administration, 260
  assassination, 227
  call for volunteers, 231
Literary
  careers for women, 383
  equality, 381
Literature
  on women, 37
  woman's entrance into, 383
Livermore, Mary E., 239
Living costs, 240
Lobbying women, 252
Locke, John, 55
Logan's Fort, 99
Love, art of, 362, 387
Lowell industries, 121
Lowell Offering, 126
Lowlanders vs. Highlanders, 54

Lucas, Eliza, 64-65
Lucy Stone League, 391
Luther's attitude toward women, 33
Lyell's description of boarding houses, 134-135
Lynch law, 87
Lynn women workers' resolutions, 293-294
Lyon, Mary, 175, 271, 321, 355

McDowell, Mary E., 270
Machine industry
  development of, 113
  trend of, 121
Machinery improvements, 336-337
Machines
  invention of, 138
  labor-saving, 242
Machinists' union, 333
Madison, Dolly, 109
Maffet, Dr., 419
Maffet, Minnie L., 418
Magic, black, 71
Maine disaster, 276
Male Continence, 308
Male
  immigration, 242
  self-assertion, 389
  vs. female economic status, 304
Maleness, 402
Males
  excess of, 112
  seeking marriage, 113
Man
  self-made, 147
  -woman association, 73, 400
Managerial occupations, 337
Manassas, Battle of, 211
Manchester industries, 121
Man's fear of woman, 71
Manufacturers, prestige of, 143
Manufacturing in the home, 121
Maritagium
  husband's rights in, 32
  of wife, 31
Marital relations, 48
Markets, eastern, 170
Marriage
  a spiritual risk, 192
  an investment, 103
  appeal of, 306
  books on, 58

Marriage, *continued*
  competition, 113
  contract of Robert Dale Owen and wife, 194
  courses, 363
  early, 161-163
  factors preventing, 304
  family connections influencing, 162
  in the Middle Ages, 20
  legislation in Indiana, 192
  Luther's conception of, 32-33
  masculine prerogative of, 389
  mores, 103
  motives, 370
  name-change at, 390-391
  Owen's theory of, 191
  plural, 189
  preparation for, 36-37, 355, 362
  success, 374
  titles, 391-392
  vs. careers, 374
  vs. courtship, 210-211
  western, 75
  with Indian women, 113
Married men favored, 45
Married woman
  contractual rights of, 397
  status of, 396-397
  worker, 349
Marryat, Captain, 111, 135
Martineau, Harriet, 125, 133, 142, 143
Mary cult, the, 20
Mary, mother of Jesus, 19
Mary Sharp College, 321
Maryland religious tolerance, 53
Masculine
  mores, 61
  opposition, 8
  ostentatiousness, 30
  prerogative in marriage, 389
  superiority, 367, 373, 400
Masculine dominance, 108, 253, 307
  in the church, 394
  on the Great Plains, 187
  undermining of, 111
Mason and Dixon line, 188
Masonic Order, 259
Massachusetts' school law, 68
Master of the Grange, 262
Mate, death of, 103
Maternal
  care, 405

Maternal, *continued*
  death rate, 405
  mortality, 364
Mather, Cotton, 52, 58
Mating in wartime, 243
Meadeville Theological Seminary, 358
Medical School of Geneva, 237
Medical student, first woman, 237
Medicine, preventive, 356
Medicine-making, 217
"Melting Pot," 52
Men
  married, 45
  replaced by women, 240
  surplus of, 103
  teachers replaced by women, 240-241
Mennonites, the, 190
Menstrual functioning, 403
Menstruation, 404
Mental hygiene movement, 361
Merrimack corporation, 126-127
Methodist denomination, 394
Metz, Christian, 191
Mexican governors of California, 179
Middle Ages, the
  believers during, 19
  chivalry in, 32
Middle class
  in the South, 204
  southern vs. northern, 205
  vs. aristocracy, 205
  women, 59
Middle States, maturity of, 229
Middle West, the
  attitude toward slavery in, 167-168
  industry in, 288
  women of, 198
Midwestern culture, 81
Midwife supplanted by physician, 67
Military
  adventure, Crockett's thirst for, 98
  mortalities, 328
  rejections, 329
Mill
  boarding houses, 124, 133
  contract with workers, 294-295
  owners
    prestige of, 143
    responsibilities of, 132-133
    socially-minded, 131
  strikers, 130
  workers

INDEX 451

Mill, *continued*
  articles written by, 126
  children of, 127
  educational opportunities offered, 126
  immigrant, 135-136
  living conditions of, 311
  morals of, 131-132
  rules of conduct of, 125
  teachers as, 126
  wages of, 129, 295
Mills
  laissez faire policy of, 127
  long hours in, 128-129
  opportunity of women through, 128
Minimum wage
  board, 345
  laws, 343, 380
  legislation, 344, 379
Missionaries in Oregon, 178
Missionary
  activities, 254
  enterprises, 271
  movement, 271
Mississippi transportation, 170
Mississippi Valley, population growth of, 80, 177
Missouri, population spread across, 188
Mitchell, Margaret, 382
Mob spirit, Scotch-Irish, 87
Modern
  industrialism in the South, 290
  woman, conflict of, 156
Monastery, social value of, 26-27
Monastic ideal, the, 27
Monogamic marriage and infidelity, 29
Monthly cycle, 403
Moody, Helen Wills, 400
Moral
  crusade in Kansas, 188-189
  lapses of early church members, 21
Moral Physiology, 308, 362
Moralist vs. agitator, 202
Morals of mill workers, 132
Moravian denomination, 50-51
Mores, 403
  American, 147
  English, 48
  masculine, 61
  past and present, 8-9
  reflecting frontier life, 84
  southern, 210

Mores, continued
  weakening of, 93-94
Mormon Settlement, 46
Mormons in Utah, 189
Morrill Act, 260
Morris, Esther, 182
Morrison, Sarah Parke, 194
Mother, good, 100
Motherhood
  hazards of, 405
  instruction for, 358
  preparation for, 36-37
  unmarried, 365
  voluntary, 309
Mothers
  of the West, 198
  Pilgrim, 45
  subsidizing of, 364
  wartime suffering of, 211-212
Mothers and Children, 360
Mott, Lucretia, 281, 285
Mount Holyoke, 271, 324
Mount Holyoke Female Seminary, 321
Mount Vernon, 145
Mountains
  Allegheny, 52
  Appalachian, 53
Münsterberg, Hugo, 257

Name-change at marriage, 390-391
Naphey, George H., 362
National-American Convention on Woman Suffrage, 395
National-American Woman Suffrage Association, 286
National Association of Business and Professional Women's Clubs, 378
National Association of Colored Women, 327
National Association of Deans of Women, 327
National Committee for Mental Hygiene, 361
National Conference of Charities and Correction, 236, 274, 275
National Conference of Social Work, 275
National Congress of Mothers, 327
National Consumers' League, 327
National Council of Jewish Women, 326

452 INDEX

National Divorce Reform League, 249
National Federation of Business and Professional Women's Clubs, 418
National Grange, the, 260
   purpose of, 262-263
National Housing Agency, 421
National League of Women Voters, 377, 378
National Management-Labor Policy, 421
National Maternal and Child Health Council, 405
National Pan Hellenic Association, 327
National prohibition, 353
National Society of the Daughters of the American Revolution, 326
National Trade Union, 130
National Typographical Union, 292
National War Labor Board, 409, 420
National War Production Board, 420
National Woman Suffrage Association, 284
National Woman's Christian Temperance Union, 274
National Woman's Party, 346, 379, 380
National Woman's Trade Union League of America, 326
Negro
   advance of, 144
   dependency, 148
   domestic service, 240
   loyalty, 150
   marriages, early, 163
   midwives, 67
   race, progress of, 146
   suffrage, 225
   the southern, 47
   voters, 244
Neighborhood Guild, the, 269
New Bedford industries, 121
New England
   farmers, 114
   frontier, 76-77
   industry, 47
   intellectual women, 58
   living conditions, 115
   maturity of, 229
   Puritanism, 76
   sex ratio of women, 123
   witch craze, 72
New England Women's Club, 255, 256
   Hale's tribute to, 255

New Englanders in the New West, 77
New Hampshire legislation, 342
New Harmony, liberal attitude of, 195
New Netherlands, records of, 48-49
New order, adjustment to, 400
New Orleans, 80
Newspaper advertising, 66
New Testament, The, 12, 17, 18, 26
New World
   culture, 5, 9-10
   immigrants in the, 37
   politics in, 37-38
   vs. Old World, 93
   woman's status in, 6
   women in the, 42-43
New York City Travelers' Aid Society, 274
New York Navy Yard, 411
New York State Charities Aid Association, 274
New York State minimum wage law, 380
New York, women in, 48
New Zealand, 424
Nightingale, Florence, 232
Nineteenth Amendment, 354
   southern attitude toward, 230
   states failing to ratify, 230
Noble Order of the Knights of Labor, 291
Nomadic impulse, 95
Non-believers, 190
North America
   native culture of, 6
   opportunity for women in, 72
North and South
   cleavage of, 140
   tension between, 188
North Carolina State Grange, 262
North vs. South, 151, 201-202
Northeast, the
   architecture in, 118
   farmhouses in, 118
Northern
   atmosphere vs. southern, 143
   vs. southern sentiment, 188
   women
      advance of, 231
      affected by Civil War, 230-231
      leaders, 244
      war services of, 231

INDEX

Noyes, John Humphrey, 196-197, 308, 387
Nun, social prestige of the, 28
Nursery school movement, 360
Nurses
 Civil War, 213
 hardships of, 233-234
 hostility toward, 233
 northern women, 232
 on the battlefield, 234
 wartime, 215
Nursing
 organization of, 238
 professional, 232
 service, organization of, 232
 training school for, 232-233

Oath of allegiance, 50
Oberlin
 coeducation at, 176
 woman's education at, 175-176
Oberlin Community, 175
Obstetrics, women in, 67
Odum's portrayal of southern sex inconsistencies, 159-160
Office
 of Civilian Defense, 420
 of Defense Transportation, 420
 of Price Administration, 420
 of War Information, 416
Office machine operators, 337
Ogburn's findings on early marriages, 163
Ohio
 and Kentucky occupation, 167
 "fever," 77
 fever in, 199
Ohio River, transportation furnished by, 170
Ohio State University, 411
Old Country
 emigrants, 41
 women from the, 41
Old World
 culture in the New World, 7
 mores influencing the New World, 5-6
 restrictions, 173
Oneida Community, the, 196, 280, 308, 387
 sex program of, 197

Oregon
 American outpost, 179
 caravan journey to, 178
 settling of, 178
Organizations
 southern vs. northern, 229
 wartime, 231-232
Oriental
 markets, 179
 woman, 13
Origen, literature produced by, 18
Origen's castration of self, 22
Ovary, 401-402
Overseers
 plantation, 150, 206
 Public Welfare, 364
Owen, Robert, 190, 191
Owen, Robert Dale, 195, 308, 362
Owen's
 contribution to Indiana Legislature, 192-193
 marriage contract with wife, 193-194
 theory of marriage, 191
Owings, Chloe, 363

Pacific Coast, 167
Parent
 -child relationships, 359
 education, 359
Parenthood
 delayed, 339
 deliberate, 392
 education for, 355
 training, 359
 unwanted, 393
Parliament of Religions, 326
Parties, starvation, 219
Pastorius, Francis Daniel, 49
Patriarchal families, 160
Patrons of Husbandry, 258, 260
Paul, the Apostle, 20-21
Peace movement, 326
Peacock, Mrs., 67
Pelham, Mary, 66
Penn, William, 49
Pennsylvania
 advancement of women in, 49
 colonial period in, 52
 Germans in, 50
 Quaker influence in, 48
 Scotch-Irish in, 51-52

INDEX

Pennsylvania Gazette, 65
Pennsylvania Railroad, 416
Pennsylvania State Medical Society, 241
People, differences between, 146-147
Perkins, Frances, 421
Peter's exhortation to continence, 21
Philadelphia County Medical Society, 241
Philadelphia's aid to soldiers, 235
Philanthropy
  practical, 327
  wartime, 235
  women in, 242
Philo, 11-12
Phoebe, a servant of the church, 18
Physical Life of Woman, The, 362
Physicians, women, 237-238
Pietistic movement in Germany, 49
Pilgrim
  leaders, 45
  mothers, 45
Pilgrims
  unity of, 45
  vs. Puritans, 46
Pinckney, Col. Charles, 65
Pioneering
  husbands, 59-60
  individualism, 87
  problems, diversity of, 185
  woman, 388
    handicaps of, 59-60
    life of, 96-97
Pioneers
  children of, 91
  in education for women, 175
  industrial, 128
  self-achievement of, 92
Place, Francis, 308
  contraceptive handbill by, 308
Plantation
  a business concern, 145
  life, 203
  mistresses, 206
    responsibilities of, 207
  overseers, 150, 206
  vs. New England farms, 144
  wives, duty of, 65-66
Planter's wife, 143, 206
  career of, 145
  obligations of, 154, 207
  routine of, 149-150
  Smedes' picture of, 208

Planter's wife, *continued*
  vs. mill owner's wife, 145, 207
Planters
  bankrupt, 289
  philosophy of, 147-148
  prestige of, 143
Pliny's letter to Trajan, 18
Plow, evolution of, 117
Plural marriage, 189
Plymouth
  backed by English merchants, 45
  church members, 45-46
  colony vs. the Puritans, 46
  family life, 45
Political
  changes affecting women, 108
  dominance of Middle West, 178
  equality demanded by women, 244
  inequality of women, 43
  leadership, southern, 203
  maneuverings of women, 253
  oligarchy, 224-225
  refugees, 173
  restrictions of Old World, 173
Politics
  feminine influence in, 353
  New World, 37-38
  planter's interest in, 143
Pollock, Sir Frederick, 31
"Poor whites," 47, 146
Pope Damascus's prose and verse, 20
Popular sovereignty, 188
Population
  cleavage, 247
  diversity of, 164
  growth, 163, 164, 177, 178
  Mississippi Valley, 177
  westward drift of, 74
Populist Party, the, 197
Post
  -nuptial contracts, 398
  -war opportunities for women, 332-334
Prairie land, 170
Pregnancy, 404
Preliterate peoples, 401
Premarriage sex alliance, 390
Prenatal care of women, 164
Prenuptial obligations, 398
Presbyterian leaders, 320
Presbyterians, Scotch-Irish, 52
President, wife of the, 109

INDEX

Presidential suffrage for women, 230
Prestige
  centers, 299
  of southern women leaders, 229-230
  of women, 374
  processes, 374
Preventive medicine, 356
Priesthood, elevation of, 29
Prince Leopold, 406
Private secretaries, 337
Professions
  closed to women, 67
  vs. trade, 67
Progressive
  school movement, 360-361
  trend in woman's status, 184
Progressive Education Association, 361
Progressive Manual, 241
Progressive Party, the, 350
Prohibition
  laws, 264
  legislation, 264-265
  repudiation of, 353
Prohibition Law of Maine, 264
Prostitution, 27, 244, 249, 266, 267, 268
Protective legislation, 291, 422
Protestant churches, 271
Protestant Evangelical attack on saloons, 265
Protestantism, 32, 33-34
Psychoanalysis, 387
Psychological clinic, 361
Psychology of Childhood, 360
Public
  school education, 321
  stenographers, 337
Public Health Association, 274
Pure Food legislation, 327
Puritan
  colony, aristocracy of, 47
  influence in America, 54
  jealousy, 87
Puritanism
  and women, 35
  English, 36
  in New England, 76
Puritans
  Massachusetts, 47
  migration of, 76
  vs. Pilgrims, 46
Putnam, Amelia Earhart, 400

Quaker
  influence in Pennsylvania, 48
  women, 49
Quakers
  coeducation of, 177
  education of, 49
  persecution of, 70
Quakers' recognition of woman, 393-394
Queen Elizabeth, political efficiency of, 35
Queen Victoria, 406

Race mixing, 42
Rapp, George, 190
Rationing of food, 414
Reconstruction, 107, 225
Recreation of mill workers, 126
Red Cross, Civilian Defense Volunteer Office, 417
Red Cross, the, 274, 276
Reflections on Courtship and Marriage, 58
Reformation
  business women of the, 34
  woman's advance during the, 33
Reformists, power-craving, 202
Refrigeration, 279
Refugees, 235
Regiment riots, 223
Relief, distribution of, 236
Religious
  groups, pioneering, 190-191
  life of the frontier, 89
  symbolism, 89
  tolerance in Maryland, 53
Renaissance
  new order of, 39
  women and the, 32
Resettlement of colored slaves, 224
Revolution, the American, 53, 56
Revolutionary War, 66, 105, 409
  women and the, 105
Rice, cultivation of, 138
Richardson, Samuel, 56
Richmond Enquirer, 157
Richmond, Mary E., 274, 276
Ringgold, Virginia, war hospitals, 213-215
Rivalry, woman's escape from, 152
Robinson, Mary Jane, 193
Rôle, husband's vs. wife's, 208-209

INDEX

Roman Catholic Church, 394
  leaders, 320
  reform, 32
  schools, 319
Roman Empire
  breaking down of, 25-26, 29
  social conditions in the, 17
  woman's status in, 31
Roman law, 397
Roosevelt, Eleanor, 400
Roosevelt, Franklin D., 378
Roosevelt, Theodore, 89
Rousseau, 55
Rousseau's theory about women, 56-57
Routes charted by Lewis and Clark, 178
Rowlandson, Mrs. Joseph, 68, 69
Royal Astronomical Society, 313
Royal Geographical Society, 313
Rural women, 258
Rush Medical School, 237
Russian Jews in clothing industry, 250

Salem, North Carolina, 51
Sales competition, 250
Saloons
  legal assault on the, 265
  praying crusade against, 265-266
  Sunday closing of, 266
Sandys, Sir Edwin, 44
San Francisco, women in, 197
Sanger, Margaret, 365
Sanitary Commission, the, 231
Scandinavians, dissatisfaction of, 196
Schools
  charity, 50
  free, 49
  in Massachusetts, 68
  Latin, 68
Schoolteachers, women, 67
Schoolteaching as a profession, 67
Schuyler, Louise L., 274
Scoresby, Rev. William, 125
Scotch-Highlanders in the Carolinas, 53
Scotch-Irish
  family altar, 158
  in Pennsylvania, 51-52
  mob spirit, 87
  prejudice against, 51-52
  Presbyterians, 52
  westward migration of, 77-78

Seaboard communities, 54
Secession
  unity of sentiment after, 164
  women's attitude toward, 211
Second World War, 410, 423
Secret order accepting women, 238
Secretary of Commerce and Labor, 363-364
Self-achievement of pioneers, 92
Self-made
  man, idealization of, 78, 90, 91
  woman, 90
Self-protection of backwoodsmen, 84
Seminaries, 320
  coeducational, 322
  religious interests stressed in, 321
Senatorial distribution, 178
Seneca Falls Convention, 281
Separatists, 45, 190
  westward movement of the, 80-81
Sequard, Brown, 401
Serious Proposal to the Ladies, 56
Servants, white, 42
Settlement group's promotion of woman's rights, 270-271
Settlement Movement, the, 248, 311
Sewall, Samuel, 70
Sewing machine, 278
Sex
  adjustment, 356, 362
  appeal, 374-375
  attitudes, 385
  books, 362
  code
    double, 209
    of women, 328
    repudiation of, 350
  conflict and struggle for holiness, 17
  differences, 155-156
  discrimination, 180
  distinctions, 105, 400
  equality, 210, 394
  equilibrium, 328
  exploitation, 132
  gland, 401
  incompatibility, 388
  program of Oneida Community, 197
  promiscuity, 390
  relations
    of white women and male Negroes, 42
    with aborigines, 113

INDEX

Sex, *continued*
  standards, 159
  suppression, 132
  vs. spiritual progress, 16
  women's reaction to, 387
Sexes
  cleavage between, 92
  comparison of, 251
  fellowship of labor between, 93
  inequality of, 324
Sexology, 387
Sexual mutuality, 389
Shakers, the, 394
Shaw, Anna Howard, 100, 199
Sheeks, Ben, 182-183, 184
Sheppard-Towner Act, 364
Sherman's
  march, 220-221
  military strategy, 222
Shifting of population, 414
Shoe-making, 128
Shorthand, 337
Short skirts, 242, 387
Silk
  cultivation of, 65
  stockings, 387
Simpson, James Y., 406
Sixty-First Congress, 249
Sixty-Seventh Congress, 364
Skirts
  short, 387
  women's enslavement to, 280
Slater, Samuel, 127
Slave
  culture in the Southwest, 167-168
  owner, obligations of, 205
  system, influence of, 148
Slavery
  agitation against, 140
  attack on, 203
  influence of, 143
  laissez faire attitude toward, 139
  passing of, 139
  tension regarding, 188
Slaves
  after the War, 224
  economic security of, 145
  emancipation of, 224
  house vs. field, 148-149
  resettlement of, 224
Slums
  American, 250

Slums, *continued*
  of Whitechapel, 311
Smallpox, 43
Smedes' picture of planter's wife, 208
Smith College, 323
Social
  anarchy, 224
  change welcomed, 185
  discrimination, 407
  equality of frontiersmen, 83
  evolution, 151
  exploitation, 251
  habits, rebuilding of, 93-94
  inequality of women, 43
  inferiority, 303
  pressure
    before Civil War, 156
    on Colonization movement, 39
  progress in Europe, 275
  readjustment, 225-226
  sentiment affecting women, 270
  service organizations, 274
Social Settlement, the, 268-269
Sociological literature, 301
Sociology Departments, 358
Soldiers
  clothing of, 216
  homes for, 235
  hospitality offered to, 235
  suffering of, 213-215
Soldiers'
  aid, 235-236
  return to industry, 335
Soldiers' Aid Society, 231
Some Thoughts Concerning Education,
  55
Sons of the American Revolution, 326
Sorosis Club, 254-255
  activities, 256
  first president of, 255
  purpose of, 255
South, the, 137
  church attendance in, 158
  class differences in, 153-154
  cleavage of North and, 140
  culture in, 137
  destitution of, 236
  economic burdens of, 290
  Europeans' descriptions of, 141
  maturity of, 229
  modern industrialism in, 290-291
  non-slave owners in, 143

INDEX

South, the, *continued*
  Old, 141
  ruin of, 224
  slavery in, 137
  vs. North, 151, 201-202
South Carolina cotton mills, 290-291
South End House, 270
South Pass City, 181
Southeast, the rural, 206
Southern
  aristocracy, 203
  California, 414
  chivalry, 209
  culture
    collapse of, 140
    indictment of, 142
    levels, 164-165
  family
    life, 158-159
    system, 155
  feminine pattern, 151
  gentlemen, 210
  girl, conventions protecting, 161
  leadership, 228
  life described by an Englishman, 152
  middle class, 204
  mills, 291
  mores, 210
  political leadership, 203
  population, diversity of, 164
  sex standards, 159
  society, 151
    stratification of, 153
  vs. western women, 209
  women
    description of, 157-158
    elevation of, 210
    historic background of, 156-157
    indictment of, 146-147
    leaders, 229-230
    losses of, 227
    rôle of, 155
South's
  hope of European recognition, 222
  influence on women, 289
Southwest, slave culture in, 167, 168
Sovereignty, state, 165
Spanish-American War, 276
Spanish peoples' attitude toward education, 319
SPARS, 410
Spectator, the, 55

Spencer, Anna Garlin, 358
Spencer, Herbert, 363
Spinster's career, 103
Spiritual
  discipline, 11
  progress, 16
Spofford, Harriet Prescott, 384
St. Clair, 98-99
St. Helena's Island, 64
St. Paul
  and asceticism, 13
  as a soldier of Christ, 15
  marriage discouraged by, 15-16
St. Paul's
  acknowledgment of women, 18
  influence on women of later generations, 17
  instruction to his churches, 13-14
  letters regarding women, 14
  support of religious equality of sexes, 18
Stanley, Rep. Winifred C., 423
Stanton, Elizabeth Cady, 244, 266, 283, 286, 395
Starr, Ellen Gates, 269
Starvation parties, 219
State
  supremacy, 165
  universities, western, 174
State Board of Massachusetts, 237
State's rights, 165
Statistical measurement, 347
Status of women, 408, 422
Steam radiation, 280
Steele, 55
Stenography, 337
Stevens, the vindictive, 225
Stimson, Henry L., 410
Stoicism, doctrine of, 12
Stone, Lucy, 286, 390
Story of a Pioneer, The, 100
Stover, Charles B., 269
Stowe, Harriet Beecher, 207, 382, 384
Strait-jackets, legal, 87
Strike, Fall River, 292
Strikers
  children, 130
  women, 130
Strikes, industrial, 292
Student Volunteer Movement, 271
Studies in the Psychology of Sex, 362
Suffrage Bill, test of, 351

INDEX

Suffrage
  denial to women, 180
  innovation, 187
  Negro, 225
  women leaders for, 277
Sumner, the neurotic, 225
Superstition, 70-71
Survival, struggle for, 85
Suspicion of inherited wealth, 89
Sweat shops, 129, 250, 251, 252, 300-301, 311
  women agitators against, 251
  working hours in, 300
Sweating industries, 299-301
Swift, 55
Syphilis
  in the South, 163
  Negro birth rate affected by, 163
Syracuse University, 237, 408

Taft, ex-President, 352
Tar-and-feathering, 88
Tariff duties, 288
Tattler, the, 55
Taverns, colonial, 62
Taylor, Graham, 270
Teachers as mill workers, 126
Teachers College, Columbia University, 358
Teachers' salaries, 240-241
Teaching
  affected by war, 240
  as a profession, 126, 320
Technique, contraceptive, 392
Telephone operators, 337
Temperance leaders, 227
Tennessee and Alabama Female Institute, 321
Terre Haute, 99
Tertullian, literature produced by, 18, 20
Tertullian's interpretation of women, 22
Texas, Americans in, 179
Textile industry, 279
Textile World Journal, 334
"The Woman's Bible," 395
Thomas, General George, 165
Tobacco, cultivation of, 138
Todd, Rev. John, 315
Tories, the, 106
Toynbee Hall, 269

Trade
  colonial women in, 66
  unions, 291-292, 295
  vs. a profession, 67
  women in, 297
Traditions
  Asiatic, 424
  European, 424
  freedom from, 91
  irritating, 83
Trans-Appalachian frontier, 83
Transportation
  improved, 116
  western, 168, 172
Travelers' Aid Society, 274
Troy female seminary, 355
Tutors, women, 67
Tuvil, Daniel, 36
Twentieth-century education, 354-355
Tyler, wife of ex-President, 157
Typewriter, the, 278
Typing, a profession for women, 278, 337
Typographical Society of Philadelphia, 292

Uncle Tom's Cabin, 203, 382, 383, 384
Union, the
  forming of, 165
  rebellion against, 277
Unionization of labor, 291
Unions, woman's influence in, 296
United Brotherhood of Carpenters and Joiners, 296
United Company of Philadelphia for Promoting American Manufacturers, 120
United Daughters of the Confederacy, 326
United Nations, 417, 423
United States
  birth of, 105
  first settlers of, 5
  mixed culture in, 52
United States Daughters of 1812, 326
United States Department of Labor, 416
United States Sanitary Commission, 235, 274
United States Supreme Court Decisions, 344, 380
Universal Peace Union, 277
University of Chicago Settlement, 270

INDEX

University of Georgia, 323
University of Iowa, 360
University of North Carolina, 363
University of Pennsylvania, 361
University student, first woman, 194
Unmarried women, 160
Utah women, 189

Vancouver Island, 179
Vane, Governor, 59
Vassar
    coeducation at, 321
    endowment of, 323
Venereal infection, 243-244
Virgin Mary, 19-20
Virginia
    colonizing of, 41
    first families of, 151
    forts, 76
    lack of women in, 44
    woman's work in, 41-42
Virginia Settlement, the, 43-44
Visitation, volunteer, 275
Vocational
    changes in the Northeast, 111
    openings to women, 122
    responsibilities of women, 57-58
Vocations of pioneering women, 61-62
Voluntary motherhood, 309

WAFS, 410
Wage
    inequalities, 372
    investigation, 363
    laws, 343-344
Wages
    men's vs. women's, 380
    mill, 129-130
    sweat shop, 129-130
Wald, Lillian D., 270
Walker, F. A., 163
Walker, Dr. Mary, 237
    army service of, 238
Waltham mills, 125
War
    aftermath of, 144
    bitter memories of, 222-223
    boom, 291
    consequences, 242
    death rate, 329
    debts, 236
    dysgenic effect of, 328-329

War, *continued*
    industries, 215-216
    King Philip's, 68
    northern woman's attitude toward, 166
    of 1812, 120
    of flesh and spirit, 16
    passion of women, 106
    Revolutionary, the, 66, 105
    southern woman's contact with, 220
    woman's advance hindered by, 227-228
    woman's burden in, 106
    women's responses to, 165-166
    wreckage, 289
Ward, Elizabeth Stuart Phelps, 384
Ward, Lester F., 175
War Manpower Commission, 416, 421
War plants, 415
Warfare, women in, 30
Wartime
    deserters, 223
    destruction, 220
    diary, a, 224
    mating, 243
    nurses, 215
    organizations, 231-232, 235
    philanthropy, 235
    vocational opportunities, 329-330
War-Time Journal of A Georgia Girl, The, 223
Washington, George, 145, 253
WAVES, 410
Wealth of the West, 169
Weddings, southern, 162
Wedlock subordinated by the Church, 21
Wellesley College, 323
Wells College, 323
Welsbach lamp, 279
West, H. Oliver, 416
West, the
    a social upstart, 154
    change in, 171
    distrust of, 86
    economic appeal of, 195-196
    freedom offered by, 196
    German culture in, 173
    improved travel in, 171
    individualism in, 173
    mothers of the, 198
    social philosophy of, 151

INDEX

Western
  agriculture, 174
  communication, 171
  communities, 196
  culture, 86
  democracy, 174
  educational facilities, 172
  family life, 75, 197
  transportation, 172
  wealth, 169
Western Reserve University Medical School, 237
Western Sanitary Commission, 235
Westerners, cultural differences of, 167
Westward drift, influence of, 122
Westwood Academy, 322
Wheelwright, brother-in-law of Anne Hutchinson, 58
White
  pine, 170
  servants, 42
  slavery, 41, 268, 327
White House hostess, 109
Whites
  drunken, 97
  "poor," 47, 146
Whitney, Eli, 138, 139
Widow tavern-keepers, 61-62
Widows
  in the church, 18
  remarriage of, 63
Wife
  deserters, 397
  frontiersman's, 79
  hunter's, 94
  personal earnings of, 399
  pioneering farmer's, 94
  plantation owner's, 205
  planter's, 154
    vs. mill owner's, 207
  property rights of, 396
Wife's rôle vs. husband's, 209
Wilderness, the
  incentives for entering, 85-86
  individualism a product of, 82
  richness of, 169
  Road, 99
  women shocked by, 199
Willard, Emma, 175, 355
Willard, Frances E., 266
Wilson, President Woodrow, 230, 250, 354

Winthrop, 45
Witch craze in New England, 72
Witches
  drive against, 71-72
  persecution of, 69-70, 72
Witmer, Lightner, 361
Wives
  ordeal of frontier, 197
  plantation assignments of, 65-66
  slave owners', 146
  wartime suffering of, 211-212
Wollstonecraft, Mary, 55, 56, 57, 313, 383
Woman
  changing status of, 37, 365
  contribution of the southern, 153
  crusaders, 264
  denied ecclesiastical prerogatives, 29
  doctor, 374
  educational career of, 381
  elevation of, 210
  garbage inspector, 270
  good vs. bad, 132-133
  historic background of southern, 156-157
  industrial experiences of, 298
  intellectual status of, 380-381
  in the Middle Ages, 29
  legal status of, 397
  literature concerning, 55
  -man association, 73
  man's fear of, 71
  married vs. unmarried, 396
  medical student, first, 237
  newly awakened, 258
  northern, 47, 105
  pioneering, 74, 388
  political status of, 376
  self-made, 90
  self-reliant, 79
  sexual awakening of, 389
  southern, 47, 137
  subordination of, 372
  superior, 372
  tempter of the flesh, 12
  the silent sex, 6
  university student, first, 194
  vs. male worker, 347
  wage earner, discrimination against, 298
Woman suffrage, 180, 327, 350-351
  advancement of, 282

INDEX

Woman suffrage, *continued*
bill, 181, 182
crusade for, 184
debate on, 281-282
favorable environment for, 184-185
fear of, 271
fight for, 286
granted by Wyoming, 282
increased interest in, 244
leaders, 266
legislation for, 180-181
liquor interests fighting, 353
lobbyists, 353
motives behind, 180-181
movement, 280-281
opponents, 252
political significance of, 377
southern opponents to, 244
victories, 350-352
World War influence on, 354
Woman worker, the
feeling against, 312
incentives of, 304-305
masculine protest against, 312-313
opposition to, 301
prestige of, 305
Woman's
Army Auxiliary Corps, 410
Bible, the, 395
biologic inferiority, 310
burden in wartime, 106
club vogue, 258
dependency, 140
disabilities, 31
dress, 280, 386
education in the Middle West, 177
equality with men, 325
escape from rivalry, 152
inequality, 398
inferiority challenged, 61
law-imposed disabilities, 398
Marine Corps, 410
political equality, 244
progress, 308
recoil from the North, 226
religious experience, 271
sex conduct, 390
social status, fallacy in interpreting, 9
vocational opportunities, 305
weakness, 347
Woman's advancement
during the Reformation, 33

Woman's advancement, *continued*
emotional barrier to, 10
hampered by
St. Paul's teachings, 15
war, 227-228
Woman's and Children's Hospital, 232-233
Woman's Bureau of the Department of Labor, 346, 364
Woman's Central Association of Relief, 231, 237
Woman's Christian Union, 266
Woman's Club Movement, 242, 253
attack upon, 257
community appeal of, 255
experience back of, 261
Woman's Joint Congressional Committee, 378
Woman's life
in the south, 140
trends in, 325
Woman's Movement, the, 168-169, 268, 284, 340, 346
southern sentiment toward, 230
Woman's Party, 379
Woman's Peace Congress, 277
"Woman's question," 407
Woman's rights, 306-307
agitation for, 169, 245
settlement group's promotion of, 270-271
society, first, 194
Woman's Rights Convention, 281
Woman's Rights Movement, 266, 280, 319, 348, 357
accelerated by World War, 328
Woman's rôle
enlarged, 304
in society and politics, 109
in the Episcopal Church, 394
in the Roman Catholic Church, 394
Woman's Share in Social Culture, 358
Woman's status
advance of, 179-180
factors establishing, 7
in the New World, 6
in the West, 174
progressive trend in, 184
Woman's work
expansion of, 61
in the colonies, 41-42

INDEX

Women
  advance of, 111
  advertisers, 66
  aged by war, 218-219
  aging, 164
  antagonistic definition of, 324
  at the Capitol, 109, 253
  authors, 381
  avariciousness of, 247
  background of American, 8
  before and after the Civil War, 219-220
  biological function of, 155-156
  bravery of, 99
  career-desiring, 303
  changing social experience of, 110
  character-testing of, 99-100
  citizens of the United States, 283
  clinical workers, 241, 337
  conflicting responsibilities of, 375
  conventions guarding, 376
  crisis faced by, 290
  criticisms of, 36
  discrimination against, 379
  doctors, 241, 413
    prejudice against, 241
  dualistic attitude toward, 71
  earnings of, 123
  ecclesiastical traditions concerning, 393
  economic independence of, 241, 302
  economic pressure on, 338-339
  education of, 175
  education's effect on, 318
  effect of Civil War on, 205
  eighteenth century literature on, 55-56
  employed in war industries, 215-216
  European books on, 58
  excess of, 112
  exploitation of, 304
  factors determining status of, 205-206
  factory workers, 239-240
  family heads, 371, 397
  favored by democratic trend, 84
  ferry-keepers, 63
  feudal disabilities of, 31
  field workers, 238
  fighters, 98
  first in America, 43
  frontier, 79

Women, *continued*
  gainfully employed, 335-336, 369
  gambling impulse of, 66-67
  handicaps of the pioneering, 59-60
  increased opportunities of, 59
  industrial
    birds of passage, 229
    changes influencing, 119
    competition of, 249
    discontent of, 130-131
    exploitation of, 130-131
  inequality of, 43
  inferiority of, 48, 57, 346, 375
  intellectual, 58
  inventions influencing, 277
  Jewish, 91
  journalists, 68
  laborers, post-war reduction of, 335
  legal status of, 395
  limitations of, 375
  literary expression of, 68
  literature concerning, 37
  lobbying activities of, 378
  lobbyists, 252, 377
    influence of, 378
  magic and, 71
  middle-class, 59
  mill workers replaced by immigrants, 247-248
  mores retarding, 8
  Negroes' attitude toward, 146
  new prestige of, 307
  New York, 48
  northern, 230-231
  of aristocracy in the Southeast, 111
  office jobs held by, 337
  onslaughts on, 314-316
  outdoor activities of, 386
  parasitic, 370
  patriotic immortality of, 105
  peace movement among, 326
  peacetime reaction against, 334-335
  physicians, 237-238
  pioneers in practical charities, 275-276
  poets, 384
  political
    advance of, 352
    changes affecting, 108
    inexperience of, 254
    maneuverings of, 253
  politically eminent, 378

INDEX

Women, *continued*
  politician's fear of, 253
  post-war attitude of, 227
  prenatal care of, 164
  prestige of, 374
  professional, 309-310
    ambition of, 237
    arguments against, 310
    indictment of, 309-310
    protective legislation concerning, 340-343
  public speakers, 256
  punishment of, 42
  Puritanism and, 35
  Quaker, 49
  reform leaders, 251
  religious symbolism of, 89
  repelled by Great Plains, 186
  responsibilities of frontier, 79
  rural, 258
  schooling of, 253
  schoolteachers, 67
  self-responsibility of, 388
  sensitive to social exploitation, 251
  shocked by wilderness, 199
  social
    evolution of, 385
    exploitations of, 72
    sentiment affecting, 270
  socially prominent, 110
  southern vs. western, 209
  South's influence on, 289
  speakers, 314
  special legislation for, 348, 379
  spectacular acts of, 110
  strikers, 130
  students at Harvard, 318
  taboos protecting, 314
  teachers, 126, 240
  technicians, 374
  temporary work of, 339
  tutors, 67
  typing a profession for, 278
  unionization of, 297
  union's interest in, 296
  unmarried, 160
  vocational
    openings for, 122
    responsibilities of, 57-58
  vocations of, 61-62
  voters, 376-377
    fear of, 352

Women, *continued*
  in school elections, 282
  wage laws concerning, 343-344
  war passion of, 106
  wartime
    activities of, 212-213
    employment of, 333-334
    training of, 333-334
  workers' situation analyzed, 369
  working hours of, 343
  writers, 384-385
Women and Economics, 357
Women in
  agriculture, 336
  Capitol City Society, 253
  factories, 120
  higher education, 313
  obstetrics, 67
  poverty, 312
  public affairs, 352
  sewing trade, 336
  teaching, 320
  the Northeast, 118
  the Revolutionary War, 105
  trade, 34-35, 66
  Utah, 189
  war territory, 220
  warfare, 30
Women of the
  Great Plains, 185-186
  Middle West, 118, 167
  North, 47, 105
  Old Country, 41
  Reformation, 33
  South, 47, 137
Women workers, 238-240
  age level of, 299
  married, 371
  resolutions of, 292-294
  wage inequalities of, 372
Women's
  Army Corps, 410
  Bureau, 413, 415
  clubs
    appeal of, 257
    divorce and, 257
    sentiment toward, 327-328
  colleges, 321, 373
  culture, classification of factors influencing, 9
  education, onslaughts on, 314-317
  inferiority, upsetting of, 102

Women's, *continued*
    labor demand, 330-331
    motives, 368
    organizations, 378
        interests of, 253-254
        progress in, 325
        post-war opportunities, 332-334
        resourcefulness, 200
        responses to Civil War, 165
    rights, crusaders for, 241-242
    vocations, 374
    work, trends in, 335-336
    working conditions, 342
Women's Homeopathic Fraternity, 326
Women's Peace League, 277
Women's Peace Party, 327
Woodhouse study of land grant college graduates, 373
Woodhull and Claflin's Weekly, 284
Woodhull, Victoria Claflin, 283, 285
    presidential nominee, 284
Woods, Robert A., 270
Work-day legislation, 342
Working women
    courtship demands of, 306
    in Boston, 273
    laws concerning, 343
World War, 328, 350, 354, 387, 389
    influence on suffrage, 354
    mortalities, 328

World War, *continued*
    vs. Civil War, 223
World War I, 401
World's Fair of 1893, 326
World's Woman's Christian Temperance Union, 266
Wright, Frances, 195
Wright's demand of political equality, 195
Wyoming laws, 183
Wyoming Territorial Legislature, 181
Wyoming's grant of suffrage to women, 282

Yankee rule, 226-227
Young Men's Christian Association, 272-273
Young Women's Christian Association, 271, 274
    Bible classes, 272
    boarding houses, 272
    motive of, 272
    National Board of the, 274
    vs. Young Men's Christian Association, 273

Zakrzewska, Dr. Marie, 233
Zoar, Ohio, 190
Zoarites, the, 190
Zwingli, 33

American Women: Images and Realities
An Arno Press Collection

[Adams, Charles F., editor]. **Correspondence between John Adams and Mercy Warren Relating to Her "History of the American Revolution," July-August, 1807.** With a new appendix of specimen pages from the **"History."** 1878.

[Arling], Emanie Sachs. **"The Terrible Siren": Victoria Woodhull, (1838-1927).** 1928.

Beard, Mary Ritter. **Woman's Work in Municipalities.** 1915.

Blanc, Madame [Marie Therese de Solms]. **The Condition of Woman in the United States.** 1895.

Bradford, Gamaliel. **Wives.** 1925.

Branagan, Thomas. **The Excellency of the Female Character Vindicated.** 1808.

Breckinridge, Sophonisba P. **Women in the Twentieth Century.** 1933.

Campbell, Helen. **Women Wage-Earners.** 1893.

Coolidge, Mary Roberts. **Why Women Are So.** 1912.

Dall, Caroline H. **The College, the Market, and the Court.** 1867.

[D'Arusmont], Frances Wright. **Life, Letters and Lectures: 1834, 1844.** 1972.

Davis, Almond H. **The Female Preacher, or Memoir of Salome Lincoln.** 1843.

Ellington, George. **The Women of New York.** 1869.

Farnham, Eliza W[oodson]. **Life in Prairie Land.** 1846.

Gage, Matilda Joslyn. **Woman, Church and State.** [1900].

Gilman, Charlotte Perkins. **The Living of Charlotte Perkins Gilman.** 1935.

Groves, Ernest R. **The American Woman.** 1944.

Hale, [Sarah J.] **Manners; or, Happy Homes and Good Society All the Year Round.** 1868.

Higginson, Thomas Wentworth. **Women and the Alphabet.** 1900.

Howe, Julia Ward, editor. **Sex and Education.** 1874.

La Follette, Suzanne. **Concerning Women.** 1926.

Leslie, Eliza. **Miss Leslie's Behaviour Book: A Guide and Manual for Ladies.** 1859.

Livermore, Mary A. **My Story of the War.** 1889.

Logan, Mrs. John A. (Mary S.) **The Part Taken By Women in American History.** 1912.

McGuire, Judith W. (A Lady of Virginia). **Diary of a Southern Refugee, During the War.** 1867.

Mann, Herman. **The Female Review: Life of Deborah Sampson.** 1866.

Meyer, Annie Nathan, editor. **Woman's Work in America.** 1891.

Myerson, Abraham. **The Nervous Housewife.** 1927.

Parsons, Elsie Clews. **The Old-Fashioned Woman.** 1913.

Porter, Sarah Harvey. **The Life and Times of Anne Royall.** 1909.

Pruette, Lorine. **Women and Leisure: A Study of Social Waste.** 1924.

Salmon, Lucy Maynard. **Domestic Service.** 1897.

Sanger, William W. **The History of Prostitution.** 1859.

Smith, Julia E. **Abby Smith and Her Cows.** 1877.

Spencer, Anna Garlin. **Woman's Share in Social Culture.** 1913.

Sprague, William Forrest. **Women and the West.** 1940.

Stanton, Elizabeth Cady. **The Woman's Bible** Parts I and II. 1895/1898.

Stewart, Mrs. Eliza Daniel. **Memories of the Crusade.** 1889.

Todd, John. **Woman's Rights.** 1867. [Dodge, Mary A.] (Gail Hamilton, pseud.) **Woman's Wrongs.** 1868.

Van Rensselaer, Mrs. John King. **The Goede Vrouw of Mana-ha-ta.** 1898.

Velazquez, Loreta Janeta. **The Woman in Battle.** 1876.

Vietor, Agnes C., editor. **A Woman's Quest: The Life of Marie E. Zakrzewska, M.D.** 1924.

Woodbury, Helen L. Sumner. **Equal Suffrage.** 1909.

Young, Ann Eliza. **Wife No. 19.** 1875.